MCSE: Windows Server 2003 Active D[...]
Implementation and Maintenance St[...]
Second Edition

Exam 70-294

D0587412

Sybex®
An Imprint of

WILEY

Exam objectives are subject to change at any time without prior notice and at Microsoft's sole discretion. Please visit Microsoft's Learning website (www.microsoft.com/learning).

Sybex®
An Imprint of
WILEY

Win 2003
Active Directory Planning, Implementation, and Maintenance

Study Guide

Second Edition

MCSE:
Windows® Server 2003
Active Directory Planning,
Implementation, and
Maintenance
Study Guide
Second Edition

Robert Shimonski, James Chellis, Anil Desai

Wiley Publishing, Inc.

Acquisitions and Development Editor: Maureen Adams
Technical Editor: Craig Vazquez
Production Editors: Helen Song, Rachel Gunn
Copy Editor: Rebecca Rider
Production Manager: Tim Tate
Vice President & Executive Group Publisher:
  Richard Swadley
Vice President and Executive Publisher:
  Joseph B. Wikert
Vice President and Publisher: Neil Edde
Media Project Supervisor: Shannon Walters
Media Development Specialist: Kit Malone
Media Quality Assurance: Kate Jenkins
Illustrator: Jeffrey Wilson,
  Happenstance Type-O-Rama
Compositor: Craig Woods,
  Happenstance Type-O-Rama
Proofreader: Nancy Riddiough
Indexer: Nancy Guenther
Cover Design: Archer Design
Cover Photograph: Photodisc and Victor Arre
Copyright © 2006 by Wiley Publishing, Inc.,
  Indianapolis, IN
Published by Wiley Publishing, Inc., Indianapolis, IN
Published simultaneously in Canada
First edition copyright © 2003 SYBEX Inc.
ISBN-13: 978-0-7821-4451-2
ISBN-10: 0-7821-4451-9

Sybex®
An Imprint of
WILEY

To Our Valued Readers:

Thank you for looking to Sybex for your Microsoft exam prep needs. The Sybex team is proud of its reputation for providing certification candidates with the practical knowledge and skills needed to succeed in the highly competitive IT marketplace. Just as the Microsoft Training & Certification is committed to establishing measurable standards for certifying individuals who will support Windows systems worldwide, Sybex is committed to providing those individuals with the skills needed to meet those standards.

The authors and editors have worked hard to ensure that the updated edition you hold in your hands is comprehensive, in-depth, and pedagogically sound. We're confident that this book will exceed the demanding standards of the certification marketplace and help you, the Microsoft certification candidate, succeed in your endeavors.

As always, your feedback is important to us. If you believe you've identified an error in the book, please visit the Customer Support section of the Wiley web site. And if you have general comments or suggestions, feel free to drop me a line directly at nedde@wiley.com. At Sybex we're continually striving to meet the needs of individuals preparing for certification exams.

Good luck in pursuit of your Microsoft certification!

Neil Edde
Vice President & Publisher
Wiley Publishing, Inc.

Acknowledgments

This book is the work of a great team. First I'd like to thank my copy editor Rebecca Rider for her excellent job on the editing process. The production editor, Helen Song, was always a pleasure to work with and kept the book moving along and on schedule. Thanks also to technical editor Craig Vazquez for his thorough edit and for keeping me honest.

I would also like to thank Neil Edde, Publisher, and James Chellis who both helped develop and nurtured the MCSA and MCSE series of books since the beginning; and Maureen Adams, Acquisitions and Developmental Editor, for all of her hard work on the initial development of the book and its format and keeping the project on track. I'd also like to thank the proofreader Nancy Riddiough and the indexer Nancy Guenther as this book's success was truly a team effort.

Contents at a Glance

Contents

Table of Exercises

Introduction

Microsoft's Certified Systems Engineer (MCSE) track for Windows Server 2003 is the premier certification for computer industry professionals. Covering the core technologies around which Microsoft's present and future will be built, this program provides powerful credentials for career advancement.

This book has been developed to give you the critical skills and knowledge you need to prepare for one of the core requirements of the Windows Server 2003 track: Planning, Implementing, and Maintaining a Microsoft Windows Server 2003 Active Directory Infrastructure (Exam 70-294).

How Do You Become Certified on Windows Server 2003?

Attaining an MCSE certification has always been a challenge. In the past, students have been able to acquire detailed exam information—even most of the exam questions—from online "brain dumps" and third-party "cram" books or software products. For the new exams, this is simply not the case.

Microsoft has taken strong steps to protect the security and integrity of its certification tracks. Now prospective candidates must complete a course of study that develops detailed knowledge about a wide range of topics. It supplies them with the true skills needed, derived from working with Windows XP, Server 2003, and related software products.

The Windows Server 2003 certification programs are heavily weighted toward hands-on skills and experience. Microsoft has stated that "nearly half of the core required exams' content demands that the candidate have troubleshooting skills acquired through hands-on experience and working knowledge."

Fortunately, if you are willing to dedicate the time and effort to learn Windows XP and Server 2003, you can prepare yourself well for the exams by using the proper tools. By working through this book, you can successfully meet the exam requirements to pass the Planning, Implementing, and Maintaining a Microsoft Windows Server 2003 Active Directory Infrastructure exam.

This book is part of a complete series of MCSA and MCSE Study Guides, published by Sybex Inc., an imprint of Wiley, that together cover the core MCSA and MCSE operating system requirements, as well as the design requirements needed to complete your MCSE track. Please visit the Sybex website at www.sybex.com for complete program and product details.

MCSE Exam Requirements

Candidates for MCSE certification on Windows 2000 or Server 2003 must pass seven exams, including one client operating system exam, three networking operating system exams, one design exam, and two electives. For a more detailed description of the Microsoft certification programs, visit Microsoft's Training and Certification website at www.microsoft.com/learning.

Coverage of Windows Server 2003 R2

In the second edition of this publication, R2 is introduced and covered as it relates to the exam: Planning, Implementing, and Maintaining a Microsoft Windows Server 2003 Active Directory Infrastructure (Exam 70-294). The exam objectives incorporate the newest features of R2 and the exam questions will easily reflect the newest changes in the product. R2 is introduced and covered in greater detail with the first couple of chapters and will be covered throughout.

R2 is nothing more than additions to the core of Windows Server 2003. Within this publication we will cover what is important to know about R2 in reflection to the actual exam. R2 was primarily designed to combine the following elements into one release:

- Windows Server 2003

- Windows Server 2003 Service Pack 1 (SP1)

- Out-of-band updates, now called Feature Packs

When adding SP1 to Windows Server 2003 and then all the latest and greatest Feature Packs, you get Windows Server 2003 R2. The features added to R2 are as follows:

- Active Directory Application Mode (ADAM): ADAM can be used to deploy secure, directory based applications. It is a run-time mode used to deploy directory based applications effectively.

- Automated Deployment Services (ADS): ADS is a set of Microsoft imaging tools designed to help you rapidly deploy Windows Server 2003 remotely on new server's right out of the box.

- Remote Control Add-on for Active Directory Users and Computers: This feature will add on the option to right-click a computer account in the Active Directory Microsoft Management Console (MMC) and choose Remote Control on that computer by opening a Terminal/Remote Desktop connection to that computer.

- Services for NetWare 5.02 SP2: A cumulative set of updates and services that have been offered since the release of Services for Netware 5.01 SP 1.

- Shadow Copy Client: A client update that lets Windows versions earlier than Windows Server 2003 take advantage of the intelligent file storage capabilities of the Shadow Copies of Shared Folders feature.

- Windows Rights Management Services (Windows RMS): An information protection technology that works with RMS-enabled applications to help protect your systems. .

- Windows SharePoint Services: SharePoint is Web based application that allows a group of people to work together and collaborate. Windows Serever 2003 R2 will include Trust-Bridge compatibility for sharing information with partner companies and customers.

- Windows System Resource Manager (WSRM): Provides resource management and enables the allocation of resources among multiple applications based on business priorities.

All of these features and more are added to the text as they are developed into the exam. To stay on top of the latest changes and updates to the exam, please visit the Microsoft Training and Certification portion of their website.

`http://www.microsoft.com/learning/exams/70-294.asp`

For a more detailed description of the Microsoft certification programs, visit Microsoft Learning's website at `www.microsoft.com/learning`.

The Planning, Implementing, and Maintaining a Microsoft Windows Server 2003 Active Directory Infrastructure Exam

The Planning, Implementing, and Maintaining a Microsoft Windows Server 2003 Active Directory Infrastructure exam covers concepts and skills related to Windows Server 2003 Active Directory infrastructure deployment and support. It emphasizes the following elements:

- Planning, Implementing, and Maintaining Forest and Domain Structures

- Planning, Implementing, and Maintaining Organization Unit Structures

- Planning, Implementing, and Maintaining Domain Name System (DNS) Server.

- Planning, Implementing, and Maintaining Group Policy Structures

- Maintaining Users, Groups, and Computers

This exam is quite specific regarding Windows Server 2003 Active Directory requirements and operational settings, and it can be particular about how administrative tasks are performed within the operating system. It also focuses on fundamental concepts of Windows Server 2003's operation. Careful study of this book, along with hands-on experience, will help you prepare for this exam.

Microsoft provides exam objectives to give you a general overview of possible areas of coverage on the Microsoft exams. Keep in mind, however, that exam objectives are subject to change at any time without prior notice and at Microsoft's sole discretion. Please visit Microsoft Learning's website (www.microsoft.com/learning) for the most current listing of exam objectives.

Types of Exam Questions

In an effort to both refine the testing process and protect the quality of its certifications, Microsoft has focused its Windows XP and Server 2003 exams on real experience and hands-on proficiency. There is a greater emphasis on your past working environments and responsibilities and less emphasis on how well you can memorize. In fact, Microsoft says a certification candidate should have at least six months of hands-on experience.

Microsoft will accomplish its goal of protecting the exams' integrity by regularly adding and removing exam questions, limiting the number of questions that any individual sees in a beta exam, and adding new exam elements.

Exam questions may be in a variety of formats: depending on which exam you take, you'll see multiple-choice questions as well as select-and-place and prioritize-a-list questions. Simulations and case study–based formats are included as well. Let's take a look at the types of exam questions and examine the adaptive testing technique so you'll be prepared for all of the possibilities.

With the release of Windows 2000, Microsoft stopped providing a detailed score breakdown. This was mostly because of the various and complex question formats. With the release of the Windows Server 2003 exams, however, Microsoft will once again provide a numerical score, as well as breakdown of how a candidate did in each area of the exam. This is beneficial for candidates who fail an exam, because they will then know what areas they need to focus on when they retake the exam.

For more information on the various exam question types, go to www.microsoft.com/learning.

Multiple-Choice Questions

Multiple-choice questions come in two main forms. One is a straightforward question followed by several possible answers, of which one or more is correct. The other type of multiple-choice question is more complex and based on a specific scenario. The scenario may focus on several areas or objectives.

Select-and-Place Questions

Select-and-place exam questions involve graphical elements that you must manipulate to successfully answer the question. For example, you might see a diagram of a computer network. A typical diagram will show computers and other components next to boxes that contain the text "Place here." The labels for the boxes represent various computer roles on a network, such as a print server and a file server. Based on information given for each computer, you are asked to select each label and place it in the correct box. You need to place *all* of the labels correctly. No credit is given for the question if you correctly label only some of the boxes.

In another select-and-place problem, you might be asked to put a series of steps in order by dragging items from boxes on the left to boxes on the right and placing them in the correct order. One other type requires that you drag an item from the left and place it under an item in a column on the right.

Simulations

Simulations are the kinds of questions that most closely represent actual situations and test the skills you use while working with Microsoft software interfaces. These exam questions include a mock interface on which you are asked to perform certain actions according to a given scenario. The simulated interfaces look nearly identical to what you see in the actual product. Because of the number of possible errors that can be made on simulations, be sure to consider the following recommendations from Microsoft:

- Do not change any simulation settings that don't pertain to the solution directly.

- When related information has not been provided, assume that the default settings are used.

- Make sure that your entries are spelled correctly.

- Close all the simulation application windows after completing the set of tasks in the simulation.

The best way to prepare for simulation questions is to spend time working with the graphical interface of the product on which you will be tested.

We recommend that you study with the WinSim 2003 product, which is included on the CD that accompanies this Study Guide. By completing the exercises in this Study Guide and working with the WinSim 2003 software, you will greatly improve your level of preparation for any simulation questions you might see.

Microsoft will regularly add and remove questions from the exams. This is called *item seeding*. It is part of the effort to make it more difficult for individuals to merely memorize exam questions that were passed along by previous test-takers.

Tips For Taking the Planning, Implementing, and Maintaining a Microsoft Windows Server 2003 Active Directory Infrastructure Exam

Here are some general tips for achieving success on your certification exam:

- Arrive early at the exam center so that you can relax and review your study materials. During this final review, you can look over tables and lists of exam-related information.

- Read the questions carefully. Don't be tempted to jump to an early conclusion. Make sure you know *exactly* what the question is asking.

- On simulations, do not change settings that are not directly related to the question. Also, assume default settings if the question does not specify or imply which settings are used.

- For questions you're not sure about, use a process of elimination to get rid of the obviously incorrect answers first. This improves your odds of selecting the correct answer when you need to make an educated guess.

Exam Registration

You may take the Microsoft exams at any of more than 1000 Authorized Prometric Testing Centers (APTCs) and VUE Testing Centers around the world. For the location of a testing center near you, call Prometric at 800-755-EXAM (755-3926), or call VUE at 888-837-8616. Outside the United States and Canada, contact your local Prometric or VUE registration center.

Find out the number of the exam you want to take, and then register with the Prometric or VUE registration center nearest to you. At this point, you will be asked for advance payment for the exam. The exams are $125 each and you must take them within one year of payment. You can schedule exams up to six weeks in advance or as late as one working day prior to the date of the exam. You can cancel or reschedule your exam if you contact the center at least two working days prior to the exam. Same-day registration is available in some locations, subject to space availability. Where same-day registration is available, you must register a minimum of two hours before test time.

You may also register for your exams online at www.prometric.com or www.vue.com.

When you schedule the exam, you will be provided with instructions regarding appointment and cancellation procedures, ID requirements, and information about the testing center location. In addition, you will receive a registration and payment confirmation letter from Prometric or VUE.

Microsoft requires certification candidates to accept the terms of a Non-Disclosure Agreement before taking certification exams.

What's in the Book?

What makes a Sybex Study Guide the book of choice for over 100,000 MCPs? We took into account not only what you need to know to pass the exam, but what you need to know to take what you've learned and apply it in the real world. Each book contains the following:

Objective-by-objective coverage of the topics you need to know   Each chapter lists the objectives covered in that chapter.

The topics covered in this Study Guide map directly to Microsoft's official exam objectives. Each exam objective is covered completely.

Assessment Test   Directly following this introduction is an Assessment Test that you should take. It is designed to help you determine how much you already know about Windows Server 2003 Active Directory planning, implementation, and maintenance. Each question is tied to a topic discussed in the book. Using the results of the Assessment Test, you can figure out the areas where you need to focus your study. Of course, we do recommend you read the entire book.

Exam Essentials   To highlight what you learn, you'll find a list of Exam Essentials at the end of each chapter. The Exam Essentials section briefly highlights the topics that need your particular attention as you prepare for the exam.

Glossary   Throughout each chapter, you will be introduced to important terms and concepts that you will need to know for the exam. These terms appear in italic within the chapters, and at the end of the book, a detailed Glossary gives definitions for these terms, as well as other general terms you should know.

Review questions, complete with detailed explanations   Each chapter is followed by a set of Review Questions that test what you learned in the chapter. The questions are written with the exam in mind, meaning that they are designed to have the same look and feel as what you'll see on the exam. Question types are the same as question types in the exam, including multiple choice, exhibits, and select-and-place.

Hands-on exercises   In almost every chapter, you'll find exercises designed to give you the important hands-on experience that is critical for your exam preparation. The exercises support the topics of the chapter, and they walk you through the steps necessary to perform a particular function.

Real World Scenarios   Because reading a book isn't enough for you to learn how to apply these topics in your everyday duties, we have provided Real World Scenarios in special sidebars. These explain when and why a particular solution would make sense, in a working environment you'd actually encounter.

Interactive CD   Every Sybex Study Guide comes with a CD complete with additional questions, flashcards for use with your PC or Palm device, a Windows 2003 simulation program, and the book in electronic format. Details are in the following section.

What's on the CD?

CD offers numerous simulations, bonus exams, and flashcards to help you study for the exam. We have also included the complete contents of the Study Guide in electronic form. The CD's resources are described here:

The Sybex E-book for Windows Server 2003 Active Directory Planning, Implementation, and Maintenance   Many people like the convenience of being able to carry their whole Study Guide on a CD. They also like being able to search the text via computer to find specific information quickly and easily. For these reasons, the entire contents of this Study Guide are supplied on the CD, in PDF. We've also included Adobe Acrobat Reader, which provides the interface for the PDF contents as well as the search capabilities.

WinSim 2003   We developed the WinSim 2003 product to allow you to experience the multimedia and interactive operation of working with Windows Server 2003. WinSim 2003 provides video files and hands-on experience with key features of Windows Server 2003. Built around the Study Guide's exercises, WinSim 2003 will help you attain the knowledge and hands-on skills you must have in order to understand Windows Server 2003 (and pass the exam).

The Sybex Test Engine   This is a collection of multiple-choice questions that will help you prepare for your exam. There are four sets of questions:

- Two bonus exams designed to simulate the actual live exam.
- All the questions from the Study Guide, presented in a test engine for your review.
- The Assessment Test.

Sybex MCSE Flashcards for PCs and Handheld Devices   The "flashcard" style of question offers an effective way to quickly and efficiently test your understanding of the fundamental concepts covered in the exam. The Sybex Flashcards set consists of more than 100 questions presented in a special engine developed specifically for this Study Guide series.

Because of the high demand for a product that will run on handheld devices, we have also developed a version of the flashcard questions that you can take with you on your Palm OS PDA (including the PalmPilot and Handspring's Visor).

How Do You Use This Book?

This book provides a solid foundation for the serious effort of preparing for the exam. To best benefit from this book, you may wish to use the following study method:

1. Take the Assessment Test to identify your weak areas.
2. Study each chapter carefully. Do your best to fully understand the information.
3. Complete all the hands-on exercises in the chapter, referring back to the text as necessary so that you understand each step you take. If you don't have access to a lab environment in which you can complete the exercises, install and work with the exercises available in the WinSim 2003 software included with this Study Guide.

> To do the exercises in this book, you must make sure your hardware meets the minimum hardware requirements for Windows Server 2003. See the section "Hardware and Software Requirements" for a list of recommended hardware and software we think you should have in your home lab.

4. Read over the Real World Scenarios to improve your understanding of how to use what you learn in the book.

5. Study the Exam Essentials to make sure you are familiar with the areas you need to focus on.

6. Answer the review questions at the end of each chapter. If you prefer to answer the questions in a timed and graded format, install the Sybex Test Engine from the book's CD and answer the chapter questions there instead of in the book.

7. Take note of the questions you did not understand, and study the corresponding sections of the book again.

8. Go back over the Exam Essentials.

9. Go through the Study Guide's other training resources, which are included on the book's CD. These include WinSim 2003, electronic flashcards, the electronic version of the chapter review questions), and the two bonus exams.

To learn all the material covered in this book, you will need to study regularly and with discipline. Try to set aside the same time every day to study, and select a comfortable and quiet place in which to do it. If you work hard, you will be surprised at how quickly you learn this material. Good luck!

Hardware and Software Requirements

You should verify that your computer meets the minimum requirements for installing Windows Server 2003.

For the exercises in this book, we assume that your computer should have at least a 3GB drive that is configured with the minimum space requirements and partitions for installing Windows Server 2003. Some of the exercises in this book require two Windows Server 2003 computers on the same network. As long as they meet the minimum system requirements for Windows Server 2003 and they can communicate across the network, you should have everything you need to perform the exercises in this book.

Assessment Test

1. Which of the following operations is not supported by Active Directory?

   A. Assigning applications to users

   B. Assigning applications to computers

   C. Publishing applications to users

   D. Publishing applications to computers

2. Which of the following single master operations apply to the entire forest? Choose all that apply.

   A. Schema Master

   B. Domain Naming Master

   C. Relative ID Master

   D. Infrastructure Master

3. Which of the following is *not* a valid Active Directory object?

   A. User

   B. Group

   C. Organizational unit

   D. Computer

   E. None of the above

4. Which of the following pieces of information should you have before you begin the Active Directory Installation Wizard? Choose all that apply.

   A. Active Directory domain name

   B. Administrator password for the local computer

   C. NetBIOS name for the server

   D. DNS configuration information

5. Which of the following is *not* considered a security principal?

   A. Users

   B. Security groups

   C. Distribution groups

   D. Computers

6. Which of the following is a valid role for a Windows Server 2003 computer?

   A. Stand-alone server

   B. Member server

   C. Domain controller

   D. All of the above

7. Trust relationships can be configured as which of the following? Choose all that apply.

    A. One-way and transitive

    B. Two-way and transitive

    C. One-way and nontransitive

    D. Two-way and nontransitive

8. Which of the following should play the *least* significant role in planning an OU structure?

    A. Network infrastructure

    B. Domain organization

    C. Delegation of permissions

    D. Group Policy settings

9. Which of the following file extensions is used primarily for backward compatibility with non-Windows Installer setup programs?

    A. .msi

    B. .mst

    C. .zap

    D. .aas

10. How can the Windows NT 4 file and printer resources be made available from within Active Directory?

    A. A systems administrator can right-click the resource and select Publish.

    B. A systems administrator can create Printer and Shared Folder objects that point to these resources.

    C. The Active Directory Domains and Trusts tool can be used to make resources available.

    D. Only Windows 2000 resources can be accessed from within Active Directory.

11. An Active Directory environment consists of three domains. What is the maximum number of sites that can be created for this environment?

    A. 2

    B. 3

    C. 9

    D. Unlimited

12. Which of the following statements regarding auditing and Active Directory is false?

    A. Auditing prevents users from attempting to guess passwords.

    B. Systems administrators should regularly review audit logs for suspicious activity.

    C. Auditing information can be generated when users view specific information within Active Directory.

    D. Auditing information can be generated when users modify specific information within Active Directory.

13. A systems administrator wants to allow a group of users to add Computer accounts to only a specific organizational unit (OU). What is the easiest way to grant only the required permissions?

   A. Delegate control of a User account.

   B. Delegate control at the domain level.

   C. Delegate control of an OU.

   D. Delegate control of a Computer account.

   E. Create a Group Policy at the OU level.

14. A GPO at the domain level sets a certain option to Disabled, while a GPO at the OU level sets the same option to Enabled. All other settings are left at their default. Which setting will be effective for objects within the OU?

   A. Enabled

   B. Disabled

   C. No effect

   D. None of the above

15. The process by which a higher-level security authority assigns permissions to other administrators is known as which of the following?

   A. Inheritance

   B. Delegation

   C. Assignment

   D. Trust

16. What is the minimum amount of information you need to create a Shared Folder Active Directory object?

   A. The name of the share

   B. The name of the server

   C. The name of the server and the name of the share

   D. The name of the server, the server's IP address, and the name of the share

17. Which of the following is a benefit of using Active Directory? Choose all that apply.

   A. Hierarchical object structure

   B. Fault-tolerant architecture

   C. Ability to configure centralized and distributed administration

   D. Flexible replication

18. Which of the following features of the Domain Name System (DNS) can be used to improve performance? Choose all that apply.

   A. Caching-only servers

   B. DNS forwarding

   C. Secondary servers

   D. Zone delegation

19. Which of the following tools can be used to create Group Policy object (GPO) links to Active Directory? Choose all that apply.

    A. Active Directory Users And Computers

    B. Active Directory Domains And Trusts

    C. Active Directory Sites And Services

    D. Group Policy Editor

20. Which of the following tools can be used to automate the creation and management of User accounts? Choose all that apply.

    A. Active Directory Sites And Services

    B. ADSI

    C. CSVDE

    D. WSH

21. A systems administrator suspects that the amount of RAM in a domain controller is insufficient and that an upgrade is required. Which of the following System Monitor counters would provide the most useful information regarding the upgrade?

    A. Network Segment/% Utilization

    B. Memory/Page faults/sec

    C. Processor/% Utilization

    D. System/Processes

22. Which of the following are considered security principals?

    A. User accounts and groups

    B. User accounts, groups, and OUs

    C. Groups and OUs

    D. Computer accounts and domains

23. Which of the following single master roles does *not* apply to every domain within an Active Directory forest?

    A. PDC Emulator Master

    B. RID Master

    C. Infrastructure Master

    D. Schema Master

24. Which of the following types of server configurations *cannot* be used within a single DNS zone?

    A. A single primary server with no secondary servers

    B. Multiple primary servers

    C. A single primary server with a single secondary server

    D. A single primary server with multiple secondary servers

    E. A single primary server and multiple caching-only servers

25. A GPO at the domain level sets a certain option to Disabled, whereas a GPO at the OU level sets the same option to Enabled. No other GPOs have been created. Which option can a systems administrator use to ensure that the effective policy for objects within the OU is enabled?

   A. Block Policy Inheritance on the OU

   B. Block Policy Inheritance on the site

   C. Set No Override on the OU

   D. Set No Override on the site

26. Which of the following is *not* a type of backup operation that is supported by the Windows Server 2003 Backup utility?

   A. Normal

   B. Daily

   C. Weekly

   D. Differential

27. Which of the following is generally true regarding the domain controllers within a site? Choose all that apply.

   A. They are generally connected by a high-speed network.

   B. They may reside on different subnets.

   C. They are generally connected by reliable connections.

   D. They may be domain controllers for different domains.

28. Which of the following types of servers contain a copy of Active Directory?

   A. Member server

   B. Stand-alone server

   C. Domain controller

   D. Certificate server

29. When running in Windows Server 2003 domain functional level, which of the following Group scope changes *cannot* be performed?

   A. Universal ➢ Global

   B. Domain Local ➢ Universal

   C. Global ➢ Universal

   D. None of the above

30. Which of the following protocols may be used for intrasite replication?

   A. RPC

   B. IP

   C. SMTP

   D. NNTP

Answers to Assessment Test

1. D. Applications cannot be published to computers, but they can be published to users and assigned to computers. See Chapter 9 for more information.

2. A, B. There can be only one Domain Naming Master and one Schema Master per Active Directory forest. The purpose of the Domain Naming Master is to keep track of all the domains within an Active Directory forest. The Schema Master defines the Active Directory schema, which must be consistent across all domains in the forest. The remaining roles apply at the domain level. See Chapter 3 for more information.

3. E. All of the choices are valid types of Active Directory objects, and all can be created and managed using the Active Directory Users and Computers tool. See Chapter 5 for more information.

4. A, B, C, D. Before beginning the installation of a domain controller, you should have all of the information listed. See Chapter 2 for more information.

5. C. Permissions and Security settings cannot be made on Distribution groups. Distribution groups are used only for sending email. See Chapter 6 for more information.

6. D. Based on the business needs of an organization, a Windows 2000 Server computer can be configured in any of the above roles. See Chapter 1 for more information.

7. A, B, C, D. All of the trust configurations listed are possible. A one-way trust means that Domain A trusts Domain B, but not the reverse. A two-way trust means that both Domain A and Domain B trust each other automatically. Transitive trusts are implied, meaning that if Domain A trusts Domain B, and Domain B trusts Domain C, then Domain A trusts Domain C. See Chapter 3 for more information.

8. A. In general, you can accommodate your network infrastructure through the use of Active Directory sites. All of the other options should play a significant role when you go to design your OU structure. Permissions and Group Policy can both be applied at the domain or OU level. See Chapter 5 for more information.

9. C. Initialization ZAP files are used primarily to point to older programs that do not use the Windows Installer. .msi files are native Windows Installer files used with Windows Installer setup programs. The other file types do not apply to this situation. See Chapter 9 for more information.

10. B. Printer and Shared Folder objects within Active Directory can point to Windows NT 4 file and printer resources, as well as Windows 2000 and Server 2003 resources. See Chapter 6 for more information.

11. D. The number of sites in an Active Directory environment is independent of the domain organization. An environment that consists of three domains may have one or more sites, based on the physical network setup. See Chapter 4 for more information.

12. A. The purpose of auditing is to monitor and record actions taken by users. Auditing will not prevent users from attempting to guess passwords (although it might discourage them from trying, if they are aware it is enabled). See Chapter 6 for more information.

13. E.   In order to allow this permission at the OU level, the systems administrator must create a Group Policy object with the appropriate settings and link it to the OU. See Chapter 8 for more information.

14. A.   Assuming that the default settings are left in place, the Group Policy setting at the OU level will take effect. See Chapter 8 for more information.

15. B.   Delegation is the process by which administrators can assign permissions on the objects within an OU. This is useful when administrators want to give other users more control over administrative functions in Active Directory. See Chapter 5 for more information.

16. C.   The name of the server and the name of the share make up the UNC information required to create a Shared Folder object. See Chapter 5 for more information.

17. A, B, C, D.   All of the options listed are benefits of using Active Directory. See Chapter 1 for more information.

18. A, B, C, D.   One of the major design goals for DNS was support for scalability. All of the features listed can be used to increase the performance of DNS. See Chapter 2 for more information.

19. A, C.   Both the Active Directory Users and Computers tool and the Active Directory Sites and Services tool can be used to create GPO links toActive Directory. See Chapter 8 for more information.

20. B, C, D.   ADSI, CSVDE, and WSH are tools and scripting languages that can be used to automate common administrative tasks, such as the creation and management of user accounts. See Chapter 6 for more information.

21. B.   A page fault occurs when the operating system must retrieve information from disk instead of from RAM. If the number of page faults per second is high, then it is likely that the server would benefit from a RAM upgrade. See Chapter 7 for more information.

22. A.   User accounts and groups are used for setting security permissions, whereas OUs are used for creating the organizational structure within Active Directory. See Chapter 6 for more information.

23. A, B, C.   Of the choices listed, only the Schema Master applies to every domain in the forest. All of the other roles listed are configured individually for each domain within the Active Directory forest. See Chapter 3 for more information.

24. B.   DNS does not allow you to use more than one primary server per zone. See Chapter 2 for more information.

25. A.   By blocking policy inheritance on the OU, you can be sure that other settings defined at higher levels do not change the settings at the OU level. However, this will only work if the No Override option is not set at the site level. See Chapter 8 for more information.

26. C.   The Windows Server 2003 Backup utility does not include an operation for weekly backups. Weekly backups can be performed, however, by using the scheduling functionality of the Backup utility. See Chapter 7 for more information.

27. A, B, C, D. All of the descriptions listed are characteristics that are common to domain controllers within a single site. See Chapter 4 for more information.

28. C. Only Windows Server 2003 computers configured as domain controllers contain a copy of the Active Directory database. See Chapter 2 for more information.

29. A. The scope of Universal groups cannot be changed because they apply to more than one domain. See Chapter 6 for more information.

30. A. Remote Procedure Calls (RPCs) are used for intrasite replication. See Chapter 4 for more information.

Chapter

1

Overview of Active Directory

Managing users, computers, applications, and network devices can seem like a never-ending process. As a result, you need to be organized, especially when it comes to some of the most fundamental yet tedious tasks you perform every day. That's where the concept of directory services comes in.

Microsoft's Active Directory is designed to store information about all of the objects within your network environment, including hardware, software, network devices, and users. Furthermore, it is designed to increase capabilities while it decreases administration through the use of a hierarchical structure that mirrors a business's logical organization.

You've probably also heard that a great deal of planning and training is required to properly implement Active Directory's many features. In order to reap the true benefits of this new technology, you must be willing to invest the time and effort to get it right. From end users to executive management, the success of your directory services implementation will be based on input from the entire business. That's where the content of this book—and the Microsoft exam for which it will prepare you—comes in.

It's difficult to cover the various aspects of Windows Server 2003's most important administrative feature—Active Directory—even in a whole book. As was briefly mentioned in the introduction, Microsoft's main goal in Exam 70-294: Planning, Implementing, and Maintaining a Microsoft Windows Server 2003 Active Directory Infrastructure is to test your understanding of the various features of Active Directory. The problem is that it doesn't make much sense to begin implementing Active Directory until you understand the terms, concepts, and goals behind it.

Designing an entire directory services architecture that conforms to your business and technical requirements is beyond the scope of this book. In fact, it's such an important topic that Microsoft has decided to test those concepts under a separate exam: Exam 70-297: Designing a Microsoft Windows Server 2003 Active Directory and Network Infrastructure.

Once you have determined exactly what your Active Directory design should look like, it's time to implement it. Throughout this book, you'll learn about the various methods you can use to implement the tools and features of Windows Server 2003 based on your company's business and technical requirements. Despite the underlying complexity of Active Directory and all of its features, Microsoft has gone to great lengths to ensure that implementation and management of Active Directory are intuitive and straightforward; after all, no technology is useful if no one can figure out how to use it.

In this chapter, you'll look at some of the many benefits of using directory services and, specifically, Microsoft's Active Directory. You'll explore basic information regarding the various concepts related to Microsoft's Active Directory. The emphasis will be on addressing the concepts of a directory service, why directory services are needed, and how you can use one to improve operations in your environment. You'll then look at the various logical objects created in Active Directory and the ways in which you can configure them to work with your network environment. Finally, you'll learn the details related to mapping your organization's physical network infrastructure to the directory services architecture. The goal is to describe the framework on which Active Directory is based.

No specific exam objectives are covered in this chapter, but a basic understanding of why Active Directory was created and how it is structured is essential for performing well on the job and on the exam. If you've had little exposure to Active Directory, or if you want to know how Active Directory is different from the older Windows NT 4's flat domain model, which is called the New Technology Directory Service (NTDS), you should definitely read this chapter.

The Industry before Active Directory

Many production networks today are still operating without a single unified directory service. A number of small businesses and large global enterprises still store information in various disconnected systems instead of a centralized, hierarchical system such as Active Directory. For example, a company might record data about its employees (such as home addresses, phone numbers, and locations within the corporate entity) in a human resources database while network accounts reside on a Windows NT 4 Primary Domain Controller (PDC).

Other information, such as security settings for applications, resides within various other systems. And there are always the classic paper-based forms.

The main reason for this disparity was that no single flexible data storage mechanism was available. Implementing and managing many separate systems is a huge challenge for most organizations. Before you look at some potential solutions, you should examine Windows NT 4 further.

The Benefits of Windows NT 4

Microsoft designed the Windows 2000 Server and Server 2003 network operating system (NOS) platforms to succeed its highly successful Windows NT 4 Workstation and Server products. Because Windows 2000 Server and Server 2003 are both built upon NT's successful technology, you should understand the fundamental aspects of Windows NT's directory services before you dive into the new features available with Active Directory. Although it is built upon NT's previous success, Active Directory is a completely new technology introduced with Windows Server 2000, and improved upon in Windows Server 2003.

 The purpose of this introduction is to provide an overview of the functionality of Windows NT 4. For more details about the product, see www.microsoft.com/ntserver.

The goal of using an NOS like Windows NT 4 is to bring security, organization, and accessibility to information throughout a company's networked systems. Installing and using a Windows NT 4 server allows you to connect the desktop systems within your network, and it allows systems administrators to control access to centralized resources for end users who are looking to use them.

This model is referred to as a client/server model; the opposite would be a peer-to-peer model. In a peer-to-peer model, all data is stored on individual workstations and the security is controlled by the local workstation's owner. This can start to become unwieldy if your clients are numbered beyond 10, or if those same clients are located in multiple remote locations. Imagine having 100 files on 30 different workstations where one particular user goes on vacation and you cannot access a needed file on that particular workstation. In this scenario, we are talking about one file, one person, and one specific incident. Now imagine a network that contains 100 workstations in 5 locations. The peer-to-peer model is not scalable enough to accommodate the amount of users by location, so the client/server model is used so that all data can be stored on highly available server systems run by trained professionals. These professionals back up and secure the data as well as manage access to it among many other things. The client/server model is a much better approach and what Active Directory is essentially designed to deliver—centralized access to resources that can be secured and controlled.

For many years, the realm of network and systems management was one that was controlled by administrators who often worked with cryptic command-line interfaces. That is, only specialists managed information systems. Newer network operating systems, such as Novell NetWare and Windows NT, started making administration easier in the network computing world so that it no longer needed to be delegated to only a few individuals. For example, by bringing the intuitive graphical user interface (GUI) to the world of systems and network administration, Windows NT 4 opened up the doors to simplifying management while still providing the types of security required by most businesses. With these tools, managers and nontechnical staff could perform basic systems management functions.

Windows NT 4 Server and Workstation computers offered many benefits, including reliability, scalability, performance, and flexibility. In many cases, companies saw Windows NT 4 as a much more cost-effective solution than their existing client-server solutions. Other benefits of Windows NT included its compatibility with a large installed base of current software products. Application developers could, with a minimal amount of effort, develop programs that would run properly on various Windows-based platforms.

A major design goal for the Windows NT 4 operating system was to provide for a secure, yet flexible, network infrastructure. A few years ago, few technical and business professionals would have imagined that personal computers would make inroads into corporate server rooms and data centers. For many reasons, including cost-efficiency and price-performance ratios, they have done just that. Keep these characteristics in mind as you move forward into the discussion of the model used by Windows NT to organize users, secure resources, and learn about some of its shortcomings.

The Domain Model in Windows NT 4

The Windows NT 4 platform met many of the challenges of the networked world. However, like any technical solution, it had its limitations.

First and foremost, questions regarding the scalability of its rudimentary directory services prevented some potential inroads into corporate data centers. Windows NT used the concept of a *domain* to organize users and secure resources. A Windows NT 4 domain is essentially a centralized database of security information that allows for the management of network resources. A Windows-based domain is a logical grouping of computers that shares common security and user account information for the purpose of centralized security and administration. A domain is a logical entity applied to help secure and administer resources on your network. A domain is stored on a Domain Controller (DC), and when stored on NT 4 system, it is called either a PDC (Primary Domain Controller) or a BDC (Backup Domain Controller) even though they are no longer used except in NT–4 based configurations. With advancements in Windows 2000 and beyond, all servers that participate in sharing domain information are just called DCs.

A single domain constitutes a single administrative unit, and you can have multiple domains located within your organization although you will have a more complex administrative scenario. The domain database in Windows 2000 (and Windows Server 2003) is now stored in Active Directory. The domain controllers are now peers in a Windows 2000 configuration. They all replicate to each other so as to build reliability and high availability into the design.

As just mentioned, *domains* are implemented through the use of Windows NT 4 Server computers that function as either *Primary Domain Controllers (PDCs)* or *Backup Domain Controllers (BDCs)*. Every domain has exactly one PDC and may have one or more BDCs depending on your needs. All network security accounts are stored within a central database on the PDC. To improve performance and reliability in distributed environments, this database is replicated to BDCs. Although BDCs can help distribute the load of network logon requests and updates, there can be only one master copy of the accounts database. This primary copy resides on the PDC, and all user and security account changes must be recorded by this machine and transmitted to all other domain controllers. Figure 1.1 provides an example of such a topology.

In order to meet some of these design issues, several different Windows NT domain models have been used. Figure 1.2 provides an example of a multiple-master domain topology. In this scenario, user accounts are stored on one or more master domains. The servers in these domains are responsible primarily for managing network accounts. BDCs for these user domains are stored in various locations throughout the organization. Network files, printers, databases, and other resources are placed in resource domains with their own PDC and BDCs. The organization itself can create and manage these domains as needed, and it often administers them separately. In order for resources to be made available to users, each of the resource domains must have a trust relationship with the master domain(s). The overall process places all users from the master domains into global *groups*. These global groups are then granted access to network resources in the resource domains.

FIGURE 1.1   A Windows NT 4 domain topology using PDCs and BDCs

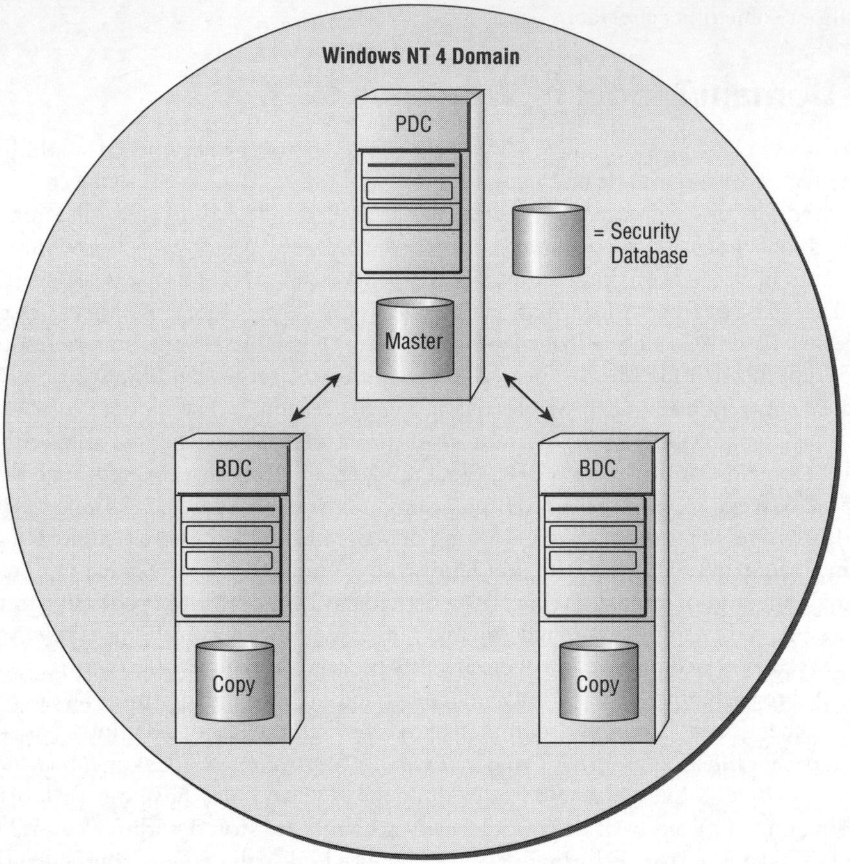

The Windows NT domain model works well for small- to medium and even large-sized organizations. It is able to accommodate thousands of users fairly well, and a single domain can handle a reasonable number of resources. These are just guidelines, however, and the network traffic created to keep domain controllers synchronized and the number of trust relationships to manage can present a challenge to network and systems administrators—especially on networks that are currently low on bandwidth. As the numbers of users grow, it can get much more difficult for the domains to accommodate large numbers of changes and network logon requests.

The Limitations of Windows NT 4

The Windows NT 4 domain model has several limitations that hinder its scalability to larger and more complex environments. One was already alluded to earlier—this domain model is not recommended when you need to accommodate the number of users supported by large organizations. When it comes to Windows NT 4, the larger the deployment, the more difficult and all-encompassing it is to design and implement it. With Active Directory, this has become a problem of the past.

FIGURE 1.2   A multiple-master domain topology

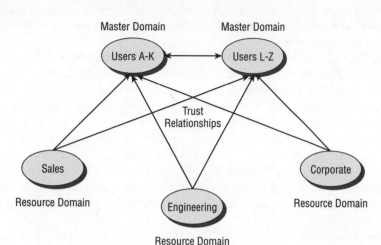

Although multiple domains can be set up to ease administration and network constraint issues, administering these domains can quickly become quite complicated and management-intensive. For example, trust relationships between the domains can quickly grow out of control if they are not managed properly, and providing adequate bandwidth for keeping network accounts synchronized can be a costly burden on the network. When working with Windows NT 4, you must make sure that you have the appropriate bandwidth on your network to satisfy the needs of the BDCs to communicate with PDCs for synchronization and replication reasons. Excessive traffic on wide area network (WAN) links that are undersized can cause a bottleneck. A bottleneck is an area within your network that, because of either poor design or excessive traffic, creates a choke point on your network where the transfer of data is dramatically slowed, or worse, stopped.

Consider a plumbing job where water needs to flow through four pipes to get from point A to point B. Three of the four pipes have the same diameter; the exception is the one by point B, which is much smaller than the others. When water is flowing from point A to point B, pressure builds because the water is being forced from a bigger pipe into a smaller one. Now, apply this to network communication media and the data that flows across it. What if you transferred a 200MB file across a 56K WAN link? You can start to see where any excessive traffic on undersized links can create problems.

As just mentioned, bottlenecks are areas of a network that can slow performance or even stop a process from being performed. You may even see KCC (Knowledge Consistency Checker) errors in your Event Viewer logs showing you replication problems—either way you find the errors. It is very important to consider network bandwidth and the ability of your Windows servers to synchronize and replicate to each other to maintain convergence of the centralized database so that those errors never occur in the first place. Too many problems on your network with your PDC and BDCs trying to communicate—and not being able to—are surefire ways to trigger corruption in your directory and cause even more problems for your users. Consider a situation where the PDC and BDC can't replicate and, as a result, account information becomes incorrect while you are trying to log in. Not only is this hard to pinpoint and diagnose, but it's also frustrating if you can't log in and do your work—or worse, if many users can't log in and do their work.

Bottlenecks are definite problem-causers; they can appear almost anywhere in the network infrastructure for a variety of reasons. To avoid misdiagnosing performance issues, it is imperative that you determine where these bottlenecks are before you deploy a directory services infrastructure. A network topology map can help you to locate bottlenecks easily, especially if transmission media speeds are listed in the documentation. For instance, if you see that your whole network runs on Fast Ethernet (at 100Mbps) and then you find out that all your server Network Interface Cards (NICs) operate at Ethernet speed (10Mbps). In this scenario, the servers' NICs are the bottleneck because they force 100Mbps down to 10Mbps. By upgrading your NICs to 100Mbps, you relieve this particular type of bottleneck. This is only one example; a more common example would be when you have a WAN link that is saturated or has failed altogether and you have no backup link to the headquarters site.

It is common for bottlenecks to occur with WAN links. A slow or unreliable link can cause network traffic to bog down to a point where data is prevented from flowing from its source to its intended destination. Now, consider what happens if that same WAN link connects one of your branch offices to a main site (the company headquarters) where the BDC is located. This BDC is used to authenticate users in the branch office so that they can log in and access resources on the server. What if this link becomes saturated to the point where data can no longer travel across it? Nobody in that branch office is able to work with resources on the server in the headquarters location because there is no way to communicate with the BDC that would have allowed the access to the resources. Once you can identify (and correct) the bottleneck, you can continue with your normal operations, although you should continue to keep an eye on the Event Viewer for more errors, as well as possibly using network-monitoring gear to help find and locate other bottlenecks that you may already have or that may occur. Another limitation of Windows NT, in addition to it being a bandwidth hog, is that the directory in use is completely flat and does not scale well in very large organizations. Because domains are flat entities used to organize and administer security information, they do not take into account the structure of businesses and cannot be organized in a hierarchical fashion (using subdomains for administrative purposes) as Active Directory can. Therefore, systems administrators are forced to place users into groups. Because groups cannot be nested (that is, have subgroups), it is not uncommon for many organizations to manage hundreds of groups within each domain. Setting permissions on resources (such as file and print services) can become an extremely tedious and error-prone process.

As far as security is concerned, administration is often delegated to one or more users of the Information Technology (IT) department. These individuals have complete control over the domain controllers and resources within the domain itself. This poses potential problems—both business and technology based. Because the distribution of administrator rights is extremely important, it is best to assign (or delegate) permissions to certain areas of the business.

However, the options available in the Windows NT 4 NOS were either difficult to implement or did not provide enough flexibility. All of this leads to a less-than-optimal configuration. For example, security policies are often set to allow users far more permissions than they need to complete their jobs.

If you have worked with Windows NT 4 domains in a medium- to large-sized environment, you are probably familiar with many of the issues related to the domain model.

Nevertheless, Windows NT 4 provides an excellent solution for many businesses and offers security, flexibility, and network management features unmatched by many of its competitors. As with almost any technical solution, however, there are areas in which improvements can be made.

Now that you've gone over the basics of Windows NT 4 and its directory structure, you can move on and examine how Windows Server 2003's Active Directory addresses some of these challenges.

The Benefits of Active Directory

Most businesses have created an organizational structure in an attempt to better manage their environments. For example, companies often divide themselves into departments (such as Sales, Marketing, and Engineering), and individuals fill roles within these departments (such as managers and staff). The goal is to add constructs that help coordinate the various functions required for the success of the organization as a whole.

The IT department in these companies is responsible for maintaining the security of the company's information. In modern businesses, this involves planning for, implementing, and managing various network resources. Servers, workstations, and routers are common infrastructure devices that are used to connect users with the information they need to do their jobs. In all but the smallest environments, the effort required to manage each of these technological resources can be great.

That's where Windows Server 2003 and Microsoft's *Active Directory* come in. In its most basic definition, a directory is a repository that records information and makes it available to users. The overall design goal for Active Directory is to create a single centralized (or decentralized with multiple domain controllers) repository of information that securely manages a company's resources. User account management, security, and applications are just a few of these areas. Active Directory is a data store that allows administrators to manage various types of information within a single distributed database. This is no small task, but many features of this directory services technology allow it to meet the needs of organizations of any size. Specifically, Active Directory's features include the following:

Hierarchical organization   In sharp contrast to the flat structure of the Windows NT 4 domain model, Active Directory is based on a hierarchical layout. Through the use of various organizational components (or objects), a company can create a network management infrastructure and directory structure that mirrors the business organization. This means that if a company has 10 major divisions, each of which has several departments (such as Sales and Human Resources), the directory services model can reflect this structure through the use of various objects within the directory. This structure can efficiently accommodate the physical and logical aspects of information resources, such as other databases, users, and computers. In addition to the hierarchical organization of objects within, Active Directory also integrates with the network naming service, the *Domain Name System (DNS)*. DNS provides for the hierarchical naming and location of resources throughout the company and on the public Internet.

Extensible schema   One of the foremost concerns with any type of database is the difficulty you encounter when you try to accommodate all types of information in one storage repository. That's why Active Directory has been designed with extensibility in mind. In this case, extensibility means the ability to expand (or extend) the directory schema. The *schema* is the actual structure of the database in terms of data types and location of the attributes. The schema is important because it allows applications to know where particular pieces of information reside. You cannot delete any portion of the schema, but you can change, modify, or alter it. The information stored within the structure of Active Directory can be expanded and customized through the use of various tools. One such tool is Active Directory Services Interface (ADSI), which is available on Microsoft's website `www.microsoft.com/ntworkstation/downloads/Other/ADSI25.asp` in the download section.

ADSI provides objects and interfaces that can be accessed from within common programming languages such as Visual Basic, Visual C#, and Active Server Pages (ASP). This feature allows Active Directory to adapt to special applications and to store additional information as needed. It also allows all of the various areas within an organization (or even between them) to share data easily based on the structure of Active Directory.

Centralized data storage   As mentioned earlier, all of the information within Active Directory resides within a single, yet distributed, data repository that allows users and systems administrators to easily access the information they need from wherever they may be within the company. This is one of the biggest design goals of the directory service in the first place—to be able to provide a secure and centralized location for all of your data. The benefits of centralized data storage include reduced administration requirements, less duplication, higher availability, and increased visibility and organization of data.

Replication   If server performance and reliability were not concerns, it might make sense to store the entire Active Directory on a single server. In the real world, however, accessibility of remote sites and cost constraints may require that the database be replicated throughout the network. Active Directory provides for this functionality. Through the use of replication technology, Active Directory's database can be distributed between many different servers in a network environment. The ability to define sites allows systems and network administrators to limit the amount of traffic between remote sites while still ensuring adequate performance and usability. Reliable data synchronization allows for multimaster replication—that is, all domain controllers can update information stored within Active Directory and can ensure its consistency at the same time.

Ease of administration   In order to accommodate various business models, Active Directory can be configured for centralized or decentralized administration. This gives network and systems administrators the ability to delegate authority and responsibilities throughout the organization while still maintaining security. Furthermore, the tools and utilities used to add, remove, and modify Active Directory objects are available with all Windows Server 2003 domain controllers. They allow for making company-wide changes with just a few mouse clicks.

Network security   Through the use of a single logon and various authentication and encryption mechanisms, Active Directory can facilitate security throughout an entire enterprise. Through the process of *delegation*, higher-level security authorities can grant permissions to other administrators. For ease of administration, objects in the Active Directory tree inherit permissions from their parent objects. Application developers can take advantage of many of these features to ensure that users are identified uniquely and securely. Network administrators can create and update permissions as needed from within a single repository, thereby reducing chances of inaccurate or outdated configuration.

Client configuration management   One of the biggest struggles for systems administrators comes with maintaining a network of heterogeneous systems and applications. A fairly simple failure—such as a hard disk crash—can cause hours of work in reconfiguring and restoring a workstation, especially an enterprise-class server. Hours of work can also be generated when users are forced to move between computers and they need to have all of their applications reinstalled and the necessary system settings updated. Many IT organizations have found that these types of operations can consume a great deal of IT staffers' time and resources. New technologies integrated with Active Directory allow for greatly enhanced control and administration of these types of network issues. The overall benefit is decreased downtime, a better end user experience, and reduced administration.

Scalability   Large organizations often have many users and large quantities of information to manage. Active Directory was designed with scalability in mind. Not only does it allow for storing up to millions of objects within a single domain, it also provides methods for distributing the necessary information between servers and locations. These features relieve much of the burden of designing a directory services infrastructure based on technical instead of business factors.

Searching functionality   One of the most important benefits of having all your network resources stored in a single repository is that it gives you the ability to perform accurate searches. Users often see NOSs as extremely complicated because of the naming and location of resources, but they shouldn't be that complicated. For example, if we need to find a printer, we should not need to know the name of the domain or print for that object. Using Active Directory, users can quickly find information about other users or resources, such as printers and servers, through an intuitive querying interface.

The technical chapters of this book cover the technical aspects of how Windows Server 2003 addresses all of these features. For now, keep in mind the various challenges that Active Directory was designed to address. The scope of this chapter is limited to introducing only the technical concepts on which Active Directory is based. In order to better understand this topic, you'll now see the various areas that make up the logical and physical structure of Active Directory.

Active Directory's Logical Structure

Database professionals often use the term *schema* to describe the structure of data. A schema usually defines the types of information that can be stored within a certain repository and special rules on how the information is to be organized. It can also be manipulated with the right tools, such as ADSI, mentioned earlier in the chapter. Within a *relational database* or Microsoft Excel spreadsheet, for example, we might define tables with columns and rows. Similarly, the Active Directory schema specifies the types of information that are stored within a directory.

The schema itself also describes the structure of the information stored within the Active Directory data store. The Active Directory data store, in turn, resides on one or more domain controllers that are deployed throughout the enterprise. In this section, you'll see the various concepts used to specify how Active Directory is logically organized.

Components and Mechanisms of Active Directory

In order to maintain the types of information required to support an entire organization, Active Directory must provide for many different types of functionality. Active Directory is made up of various components. Each of these components must work with the others to ensure that Active Directory remains accessible to all of the users that require it and to maintain the accuracy and consistency of its information.

In the following sections, you'll see each of the components that make up Active Directory.

Data Store

When you envision Active Directory from a physical point of view, you probably imagine a set of files stored on the hard disk that contain all of the objects within it. The term *data store* is used to refer to the actual structure that contains the information stored within Active Directory. The data store is implemented as just that—a set of files that resides within the filesystem of a domain controller. This is the fundamental structure of Active Directory.

The data store itself has a structure that describes the types of information it can contain. Within the data store, data about objects is recorded and made available to users. For example, configuration information about the domain topology, including trust relationships (which are covered later in this chapter), are contained within Active Directory. Similarly, information about users, groups, and computers that are part of the domain are also recorded.

 The Active Directory data store is also commonly referred to as the Active Directory database.

Schema

The Active Directory schema consists of rules on the types of information that can be stored within the directory. The schema is made up of two types of objects: attributes and classes. Attributes define a single granular piece of information stored within Active Directory. First Name and Last Name, for example, are considered attributes, which may contain the values of Bob and Smith. Classes are objects that are defined as collections of attributes. For example, a class called Employee could include the First Name and Last Name attributes.

It is important to understand that classes and attributes are defined independently and that any number of classes can use the same attributes. For example, if we create an attribute called Nickname, this value could conceivably be used to describe a User class and a Computer class. By default, Microsoft has included several different schema objects. In order to support custom data, however, applications developers can extend the schema by creating their own classes and attributes. As you'll see in Chapter 3, "Installing and Managing Trees and Forests," the entire schema is replicated to all of the domain controllers within the environment to ensure data consistency between them.

The overall result of the schema is a centralized data store that can contain information about many different types of objects—including users, groups, computers, network devices, applications, and more.

Global Catalog

The *Global Catalog* is a database that contains all of the information pertaining to objects within all domains in the Active Directory environment. One of the potential problems with working in an environment that contains multiple domains is that users in one domain may want to find objects stored in another domain, but they may not have any additional information about those objects.

The purpose of the Global Catalog is to index information stored in Active Directory so that it can be more quickly and easily searched. In order to store and replicate all of this information, the Global Catalog can be distributed to servers within the network environment. That is, network and systems administrators must specify which servers within the Active Directory environment will contain copies of the Global Catalog. This decision is usually made based on technical considerations (such as network links) and organizational considerations (such as the number of users at each remote site). You can think of the Global Catalog as a universal phone book. Much like the local phone book you may keep in your house, an object such as the Global Catalog would be quite large and bulky, but just like the phone book, it would also be very useful in helping you find and locate information. Your goal (as a systems administrator) would be to find a balance between maintaining copies of the phone book and making potential users of the book travel long distances to use it.

This distribution of Global Catalog information allows for increased performance during company-wide resource searches and can prevent excessive traffic across network links. Because the Global Catalog includes information about objects stored in all domains within the Active Directory environment, its management and location should be an important concern for network and systems administrators.

Searching Mechanisms

The best-designed data repository in the world is useless if users can't access the information stored within it. Active Directory includes a search engine that can be queried by users to find information about objects stored within it. For example, if a member of the Human Resources (HR) department is looking for a color printer, they can easily query Active Directory to find the one located closest to them. Best of all, the query tools are already built into Windows Server 2003 operating systems and are only a few mouse clicks away.

Replication

Although it is theoretically possible to create a directory service that involves only one central computer, there are several problems with this configuration. First, all of the data is stored on one machine. This server would be responsible for processing all of the logon requests and search queries associated with the objects that it contained. Although this scenario might work well for a small network, it would create a tremendous load on a single server in a very large environment. Furthermore, clients that are located on remote networks would experience slower response times due to the pace of network traffic. If this server became unavailable (due to a failed power supply, for example), network authentication and other vital processes could not be carried out. To solve these problems, Active Directory has been designed with a replication engine. The purpose of *replication* is to distribute the data stored within the directory throughout the organization for increased availability, performance, and data protection. Systems administrators can tune replication to occur based on their physical network infrastructure and other constraints.

An Overview of Active Directory Domains

As mentioned earlier, in a Windows Server 2003 Active Directory deployment, a domain is considered a logical security boundary that allows for the creation, administration, and management of related resources. You can think of a domain as a logical division, such as a neighborhood within a city. Although each neighborhood is part of a larger group of neighborhoods (the city), it may carry on many of its functions independently of the others. For example, resources such as tennis courts and swimming pools may be made available only to members of the neighborhood, whereas resources such as electricity and water supplies would probably be shared between neighborhoods. So, think of a domain as a grouping of objects that utilizes resources exclusive to its domain, but keep in mind that those resources can also be shared between domains.

Although the names and fundamental features are the same, Active Directory domains vary greatly from those in Windows NT. As we mentioned earlier, an Active Directory domain can store many more objects than a Windows NT domain. Furthermore, Active Directory domains can be combined together into trees and forests to form more complex hierarchical structures. If you think of a domain as a neighborhood, you can think of a group of similar domains (a tree) as a suburb and a group of disparate domains that trust each other (a forest) as a city. This is in contrast to Windows NT domains, which treat all domains as peers of each other (that is, they are all on the same level and cannot be organized into trees and forests). Before going into the details, let's discuss the concept of domains.

Within most business organizations, network and systems administration duties are delegated to certain individuals and departments. For example, a company might have a centralized IT department that is responsible for all implementation, support, and maintenance of network resources throughout the organization. In another example, network support may be largely decentralized—that is, each department, business unit, or office may have its own IT support staff. Both of these models may work well for a company, but implementing such a structure through directory services requires the use of logical objects.

Domains are composed of a collection of computers and resources that share a common security database. An Active Directory domain contains a logical partition of users, groups, and other objects within the environment. Objects within a domain share several characteristics, including the following:

Group Policy and security permissions Security for all of the objects within a domain can be administered based on one set of policies. Thus, a domain administrator can make changes to any of the settings within the domain. These settings can apply to all of the users, computers, and objects within the domain. For more granular security settings, however, permissions can be granted on specific objects, thereby distributing administration responsibilities and increasing security. Domains are configured as a single security entity. Objects, permissions, and other settings within a domain do not automatically apply to other domains.

Hierarchical object naming   All of the objects within an Active Directory container share a common namespace. When domains are combined together, however, the namespace is hierarchical. For example, a user in one department might have an object name called janedoe@engineering.microsoft.com while a user in another department might have one called johndoe@sales.microsoft.com. The first part of the name is determined by the name of the object within the domain (in these examples, the usernames janedoe and johndoe). The suffix is determined by the organization of the domains, in this case engineering.microsoft.com and sales.microsoft.com. The hierarchical naming system allows each object within Active Directory to have a unique name.

Hierarchical properties   Containers called *organizational units (OUs)* (described later, in the section titled "Creating a Domain Structure with Organizational Units") can be created within a domain. These units are used for creating a logical grouping of objects within Active Directory. The specific user settings and permissions that are assigned to these objects can be inherited by lower-level objects. For example, if we have an organizational unit for the North America division within our company, we can set user permissions on this object. All of the objects within the North America object (such as the Sales, Marketing, and Engineering departments) would automatically inherit these settings. This makes administration easier, but inheritance is an important concept to remember when implementing and administering security because it results in the implicit assignment of permissions. The proper use of hierarchical properties allows systems administrators to avoid inconsistent security policies (such as a minimum password length of six characters in one object and a minimum password length of eight characters in another).

Trust relationships   In order to facilitate the sharing of information between domains, trust relationships are automatically created between them. Additionally, the administrator can break and establish trust relationships based on business requirements. A trust relationship allows two domains to share security information and objects, but it does not automatically assign permissions to these objects. *Trusts* allow users who are contained within one domain to be granted access to resources in other domains. To make administrating trust relationships easier, Microsoft has made transitive two-way trusts the default relationship between domains. As shown in Figure 1.3, if Domain A trusts Domain B and Domain B trusts Domain C, Domain A implicitly trusts Domain C.

> Generally, triangles are used to represent Active Directory domains (thereby indicating their hierarchical structure), and circles are used to represent flat domains (such as those in Windows NT).

Overall, the purpose of domains is to ease administration while providing for a common security and resource database.

FIGURE 1.3   Transitive two-way trust relationships

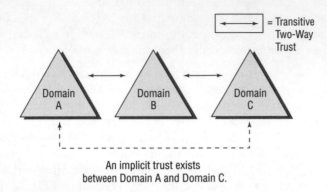

An implicit trust exists
between Domain A and Domain C.

Using Multiple Domains

Although the flexibility and power afforded by the use of an Active Directory domain will meet the needs of many organizations, there are reasons for which companies might want to implement more than one domain. We'll cover these planning issues in Chapter 3. For now, however, it is important to know that domains can be combined together into domain trees.

Domain trees are hierarchical collections of domains that are designed to meet the organizational needs of a business (see Figure 1.4). Trees are defined by the use of a contiguous namespace. For example, the following domains are all considered part of the same tree:

- `microsoft.com`
- `sales.microsoft.com`
- `research.microsoft.com`
- `us.sales.microsoft.com`

Notice that all of these domains are part of the `microsoft.com` domain. Domains within trees still maintain separate security and resource databases, but they can be administered together through the use of trust relationships. By default, trust relationships are automatically established between parent and child domains within a tree.

Although single companies will often want to configure domains to fit within a single namespace, noncontiguous namespaces may be used for several reasons. You'll look at several of these reasons in Chapter 3. When domain trees are combined together into noncontiguous groupings, they are known as *forests* (see Figure 1.5). Forests often contain multiple noncontiguous namespaces consisting of domains that are kept separate for technical or political reasons. Just as trust relationships are created between domains within a tree, trust relationships are also created between trees within a forest so that resources can be shared between them. New to Windows Server 2003, trusts can be established between forests as well.

FIGURE 1.4   A domain tree

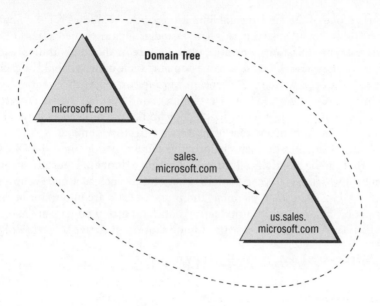

FIGURE 1.5   An Active Directory forest

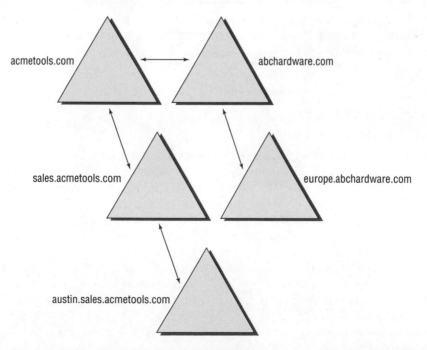

Physically, domains are implemented and managed by the use of domain controllers. This topic is covered later in this chapter in the section "Server Roles within Active Directory."

Creating a Domain Structure with Organizational Units

As we mentioned earlier, one of the fundamental limitations of the Windows NT 4 domain organization is that it consists of a flat structure. All users and groups are stored as part of a single namespace. Real-world organizations, however, often require further organization within domains. For example, we may have 3000 users in one domain. Some of these should be grouped together in an Engineering group. Within the Engineering group, we might also want to further subdivide users into other groups (for example, Development and Testing). Active Directory supports this kind of hierarchy. Figure 1.6 provides a depiction of the differences between the structure of a Windows NT 4 domain and that of an Active Directory domain.

The fundamental unit of organization within an Active Directory domain is the OU. OUs are container objects that can be hierarchically arranged within a domain. Figure 1.7 provides an example of a typical OU setup. OUs can contain other objects such as users, groups, computers, and even other OUs. The proper planning and usage of OUs are important because they are generally the objects to which security permissions and group policies are assigned. A well-designed OU structure can greatly ease the administration of Active Directory objects.

FIGURE 1.6   Windows NT 4 vs. Active Directory domains

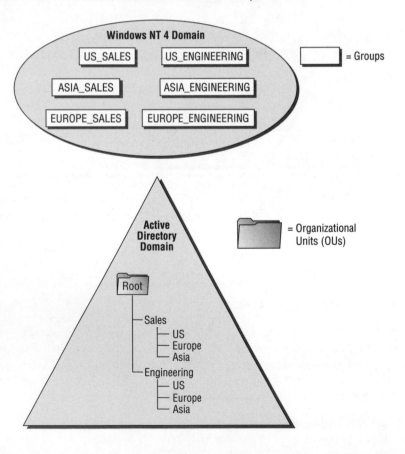

FIGURE 1.7   Two different OU hierarchy models

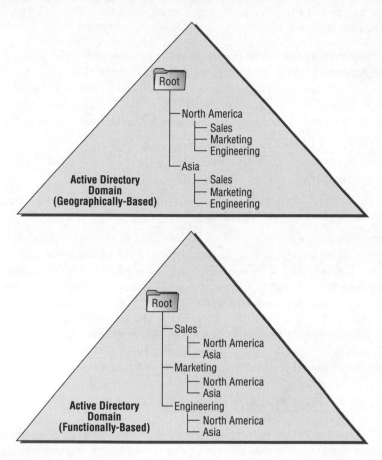

OUs can be organized based on various criteria. For example, we might choose to implement an OU organization based on the geographic distribution of our company's business units.

You'll look at various planning issues for OUs in Chapter 5, "Administering Active Directory."

Active Directory Object Names

A fundamental feature of a directory service is that each object within the directory should contain its own unique name. For example, your organization may have two different users named John Smith (who may or may not be in different departments or locations within the company). There should be some unique way for us to distinguish these users (and their corresponding user objects).

Generally, this unique identifier is called the *distinguished name (DN)*. Within Active Directory, each object can be uniquely identified using a long name that specifies the full path to the object. Following is an example of a DN:

```
/O=Internet/DC=Com/DC=MyCompany/DC=Sales
/CN=Managers/CN=John Smith
```

In this name, we have specified several different types of objects:

Organization (O)   The company or root-level domain. In this case, the root level is the Internet.

Domain component (DC)   A portion of the hierarchical path. DCs are used for organizing objects within the directory service. The DCs specify that the user object is located within the `sales.mycompany.com` domain.

Common name (CN)   Specifies the names of objects in the directory. In this example, the user John Smith is contained within the Managers container.

When used together, the components of the DN uniquely identify where the user object is stored. Instead of specifying the full DN, you might also choose to use a *relative distinguished name (RDN)*. This name specifies only part of the preceding path and is relative to another object. For example, if your current context is already the Managers group within the `sales.mycompany.com` domain, you could simply specify the user as `CN=John Smith`.

Note that if you change the structure of the domain, the DN of this object would also change. A change might happen if you rename one of the containers in the path or move the user object itself. This type of naming system allows for flexibility and the ability to easily identify the potentially millions of objects that might exist in Active Directory.

User, Computer, and Group Objects

The real objects that you will want to control and manage with Active Directory are the users, computers, and groups within your network environment. These are the types of objects that allow for the most granular level of control over permissions and allow you to configure your network to meet business needs.

User accounts are used to enforce the security within the network environment. These accounts define the login information and passwords that are used to receive permissions to network objects. Computer objects allow systems administrators to configure the functions that can be performed on client machines throughout the environment. Both User accounts and Computer objects enable security to be maintained at a granular level.

Although security can be enforced by placing permissions directly on User and Computer objects, it is much more convenient to combine users into groups. For example, if there are three users who will require similar permissions within the Accounting department, you could place all of them in one group. If users are removed or added to the department, you could easily make changes to the group without having to make any further changes to security permissions. Figure 1.8 shows how groups can be used to easily administer permissions.

FIGURE 1.8   Using groups to administer security

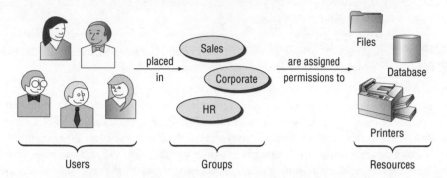

There are two main types of groups within Active Directory: security groups and distribution groups. Security groups are used to administer permissions. All members of a security group receive the same security settings. Distribution groups, on the other hand, are used only to send email and other messages to several different users at once. They do not involve the maintenance of security permissions but can be helpful in handling multiple users.

Overall, the proper use of groups assists greatly in implementing and managing security and permissions within Active Directory.

Active Directory's Physical Structure

So far, the discussion has focused on the logical units that make up Active Directory. That is, the ideas presented so far are designed to bring organization to the structure of the network. What you haven't examined is exactly how domains, trees, forests, and Active Directory itself are created and managed. In this section, you'll see how various servers and network devices can be used to implement and manage the components of Active Directory.

Server Roles within Active Directory

Active Directory data store is stored on one or more computers within an organization's network environment. Windows Server 2003 can participate in Active Directory domains under the following roles:

Domain controllers   The heart of Active Directory's functionality resides on domain controllers. These machines are responsible for maintaining the Active Directory data store, including all of its objects, and for providing security for the entire domain. Although an Active Directory configuration may involve only one domain controller, it is much more likely that organizations will have more servers in order to increase performance and establish fault tolerance. All of the information that resides within Active Directory is synchronized between the domain controllers, and most changes can be made at any of these servers. This functionality is referred to as multimaster replication and is the basis upon which Active Directory information is distributed throughout an organization.

In Active Directory, there is no distinction between PDCs and BDCs. Every domain controller is simply called a domain controller.

Member servers   Often, you will want to have servers that function as part of the domain but are not responsible for containing Active Directory information or authenticating users. Common examples include file and print servers, and web servers. A Windows Server 2003 computer that is a member of a domain but is not a domain controller itself is referred to as a *member server*. By using member servers, systems administrators can take advantage of the centralized security database of Active Directory without dedicating server processing and storage resources to maintaining the directory information.

Standalone servers   It is possible to run Windows Server 2003 computers in a workgroup environment that does not include Active Directory functionality at all. These machines are known as standalone servers. They maintain their own security database and are administered independently of other servers because no centralized security database exists. Stand-alone servers might be used for functions such as public web servers or in situations in which only a few users require resources from a machine and the administrative overhead for managing security separately on various machines is acceptable.

A major benefit in the Windows Server 2003 operating system is the ability to easily promote and demote domain controllers after the operating system has been installed. Unlike the situation with Windows NT 4, reinstallation of the entire operating system is no longer required to change the role of a server. Furthermore, by properly promoting and demoting domain controllers, you can effectively move them between domains, trees, and forests.

In addition to the various types of server roles that the Windows Server 2003 platform can take on within Active Directory domains, Active Directory requires systems administrators to assign specific functionalities to other servers. In discussing replication, certain servers might be referred to as masters. Masters contain copies of a database and generally allow both read and write operations. Some types of replication may allow multiple masters to exist, while others specify that only a single master is allowed. Certain tasks within Active Directory work well using multimaster replication.

For example, the ability to update information at one or more of the domain controllers can speed up response times while still maintaining data integrity through replication. Other functions, however, better lend themselves to being defined centrally. These operations are referred to as single-master operations because the function only supports modification on a single machine in the environment. These machines are referred to as Operations Masters servers. The role of these servers is to handle operations that are required to ensure consistency within an Active Directory environment. Some of these are unique within a domain, and others are unique within the tree or forest. The changes made on these machines are then propagated to other domain controllers, as necessary.

The various roles for Operations Masters servers within Active Directory include the following:

Schema Master   As we mentioned earlier, one of the benefits of Active Directory schema is that it can be modified. All changes to the schema, however, are propagated to all domain controllers within the forest. In order for the information to stay synchronized and consistent, it is necessary for one machine within the entire tree or forest to be designated as the Schema Master. All changes to the schema must be made on this machine. By default the first domain controller installed in the tree or forest is the Schema Master.

Domain Naming Master   When creating, adding, or removing domains, it is necessary for one machine in the tree or forest to serve as a central authority for the Active Directory configuration. The Domain Naming Master ensures that all of the information within the Active Directory forest is kept consistent and is responsible for registering new domains.

Within each Active Directory domain, the following roles can be assigned to domain controllers:

Relative ID (RID) Master   A fundamental requirement of any directory service is that each object must have a unique identifier. All users, groups, computers, and other objects within Active Directory, for example, are identified by a unique value. The RID Master is responsible for creating all of these identifiers within each domain and for ensuring that objects have unique IDs between domains by working with RID Masters in other domains.

PDC Emulator   In order to support Windows NT, Windows Server 2003 must have the ability to serve as a Windows NT PDC. Microsoft has made a conscious decision to allow networks to work in a mixed mode of Windows NT domains and Active Directory domains in order to facilitate the migration process. As long as there are computers in the environment running Windows NT 4, the PDC Emulator will allow for the transmission of security information between domain controllers. This provides for backward compatibility while an organization moves to Windows Server 2003 and Active Directory.

Infrastructure Master   Managing group memberships is an important role fulfilled manually by systems administrators. In a potentially distributed Active Directory environment, though, it is important to make sure that group and user memberships stay synchronized throughout the network. In order to understand how information might become inconsistent, look at an example using two domain controllers named DC1 and DC2. Suppose you make a change to a user's settings on DC1. At the same time, suppose another systems administrator makes a change to the same user account but on DC2. There must be some way to determine which change takes precedence over the other. More important, all domain controllers should be made aware of these changes so that the Active Directory database information remains consistent. The role of the Infrastructure Master is to ensure consistency between users and their group memberships as changes, additions, and deletions are made.

WARNING   If there is more than one domain controller in the domain, the Global Catalog should not reside on the same server as the Infrastructure Master. This would prevent it from seeing any changes to the data and would result in replication not occurring between the various domain controllers.

It is important to note that the above assignments are *roles* and that a single machine may perform multiple roles. For example, in an environment in which only a single domain controller exists, that server will assume all of the above roles by default. On the other hand, if multiple servers are present, these functions can be distributed between them for business and technical reasons. By properly assigning roles to the servers in your environment, you'll be able to ensure that single-master operations are carried out securely and efficiently. Server roles are discussed in more detail in Chapter 3.

Accessing Active Directory through LDAP

In order to insert, update, and query information from within Active Directory, Microsoft has chosen to employ the worldwide Internet Engineering Task Force (IETF) standard protocol called the *Lightweight Directory Access Protocol (LDAP)*. LDAP is designed to allow for the transfer of information between domain controllers and to allow users to query information about objects within the directory.

Because LDAP is a standard, it also facilitates interoperability between other directory services. Furthermore, communications can be programmed using objects such as the ADSI. For data transport, LDAP can be used over TCP/IP, thus making it an excellent choice for communicating over the Internet, as well as over private TCP/IP-based networks.

Managing Replication with Sites

A common mistake made in planning Active Directory is to base its structure on the technical constraints of a business instead of on business practices. For instance, a systems administrator might recommend that a separate domain be placed at each of a company's three remote sites. The rationale for this decision is understandable—the goal is to reduce network traffic between potentially slow and costly remote links. However, the multiple domain structure may not make sense for organizations that have a centralized IT department and require common security settings for each of the three locations.

In order to allow Active Directory to be based on business and political decisions while still accommodating network infrastructure issues, Windows Server 2003 supports the concept of *sites*. Active Directory sites are designed to define the physical layout of a company's network by taking into account multiple subnets, remote access links, and other network factors. When performing vital functions between domain controllers, for example, you might want to limit bandwidth usage across a slow link. However, within your local area network (LAN) environment, you will want replication to occur as quickly as possible to keep machines synchronized.

Sites are usually defined as locations in which network access is quick and inexpensive. Windows Server 2003 uses sites to determine when and how information should be replicated between domain controllers and other machines within the environment. Figure 1.9 provides an example of how a distributed company might choose to implement sites.

It is important to understand the distinction between logical and physical components of Active Directory. When planning your objects and domains, you will want to take into account the business requirements of your organization. This will create the logical structure of the directory. In planning for the implementation of Active Directory, however, you must take into account your network infrastructure—the physical aspects. Sites provide a great way to isolate these two requirements.

FIGURE 1.9   A typical site configuration

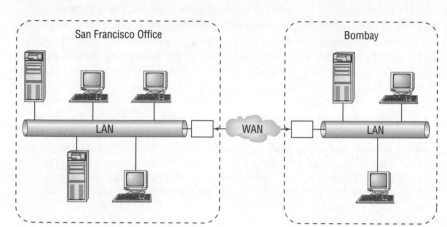

Site #1   Site #2

Active Directory Names and DNS

The DNS is a distributed database built upon an Internet standard that is used to resolve friendly, hierarchical names to TCP/IP network addresses. Systems administrators who have to remember many server IP addresses will easily recall the need for DNS—it can be quite a difficult and error-prone process to remember all of these numbers. For example, if you have a server on the Internet with an IP address of 24.133.155.7, you may want to give it a friendly name, such as sales.mycompany.com. Instead of typing the IP address every time you need to access the resource, you could specify the fully qualified name of the machine and leave it to the DNS servers on the Internet to resolve the address.

Understanding TCP/IP is vital to understanding the use of almost any modern network operating system. If you're planning to deploy a Windows Server 2003 environment, be sure you take the time to learn the details of working with TCP/IP. For more information, see the *MCSA/MCSE: Windows Server 2003 Network Infrastructure Implementation, Management, and Maintenance Study Guide (70-291), Second Edition* by Steve Suehring and James Chellis (Wiley, 2006).

The Windows Server 2003 Active Directory relies on DNS for finding DCs and naming and accessing Active Directory objects. Windows Server 2003 includes a DNS server service that can be used to automatically update records that store machine names to IP address mappings.

DNS offers many advantages. First, it is the primary name resolution method used on the Internet. Therefore, it has widespread support in all modern operating systems and works well between various operating system platforms. Second, DNS is designed with fault tolerance and distributed databases in mind. If a single DNS server does not have the information required to fulfill a request for information, it automatically queries another DNS server for this information. Systems administrators are only responsible for maintaining the DNS entries for their own machines. Through the use of efficient caching, the load of performing world-wide queries on large networks can be minimized.

> The various technical details related to DNS are beyond the scope of this book. For more information, see *MCSA/MCSE: Windows Server 2003 Network Infrastructure Implementation, Management, and Maintenance Study Guide (70-291), Second Edition* by Steve Suehring with James Chellis (Wiley, 2006) and *MCSE: Windows Server 2003 Network Infrastructure Planning and Maintenance Study Guide (70-293), Second Edition*, by Mark Foust with James Chellis (Wiley, 2006).

 Real World Scenario

Upgrading Windows NT Domains to Active Directory

You are a consultant doing work for an organization that has decided to move its environment to Active Directory. However, before the upgrade can begin, you must first design a suitable Active Directory. You have several choices that need to be made and many considerations to take into account. Factors that should affect your decision include the following:

Political issues   How does the current business operate—as single, independent business units, or as a centralized environment? Who will be responsible for administering portions of the network?

Network issues   What types of network connections are present between your remote offices? How reliable are these connections? Also, what are the domain name requirements for this environment?

Organizational structure   How are various areas of the business structured? For example, do the departments operate individually, with separate network administrators for each department? Or is the environment much more centralized?

Based on the answers to these questions, you might choose to implement only a single domain. This method provides for simple administration and should meet most requirements. You may, however, have other concerns (such as the need to support multiple DNS namespaces). In any case, the best solution will be based on the specific needs of the environment.

Summary

In this chapter we covered Active Directory fundamentals. Within the chapter, you were given a high-level overview of many concepts related to Active Directory and how it is logically laid out. We initially covered the benefits of deploying Active Directory. Some of these benefits include hierarchical organization, extensible schema, centralized data storage, replication, ease of administration, network security, client configuration management, scalability and performance, and searching functionality.

We also learned about how the Active Directory compares to Windows NT's domain model. Windows NT 4 uses a flat domain model, whereas Active Directory is hierarchical and can grow way beyond the limitations of the old model. As you have learned, Active Directory is robust and can scale beyond what NT 4 is able to offer.

In addition, we learned about the logical components of Active Directory, such as forests, domains, trees, and objects. We also learned how multiple Active Directory domains can be created and the reasons for doing so, such as keeping two companies' internal system models separate, for instance, if you have a merger and acquisition and want to keep the internal domain structures intact and separate. Within the chapter's sections, we also covered the importance of how you name Active Directory objects and how domain naming affects the planning of Active Directory. Lastly, we covered the physical components that make up an Active Directory environment, such as domain controllers, member servers, Operations Masters, and sites. In the next chapter, we will cover planning and installing Active Directory.

Exam Essentials

Understand the problems that Active Directory is designed to solve. The creation of a single, centralized directory service can make network operations and management much simpler. Active Directory solves many shortcomings in Windows NT's domain model.

Understand Active Directory design goals. Active Directory should be structured to mirror an organization's logical structure. Understand the factors that you should take into account, including business units, geographic structure, and future business requirements.

Understand features of Active Directory. Understand how and why Microsoft has included features that allow for extensibility, centralized data storage, replication, ease of administration, security, and scalability. Remember the Operations Master server roles that are required in an Active Directory environment. Operations Master roles are vital to the proper operations of Active Directory. Some of these roles must be present in each Active Directory domain while others require only one for the entire Active Directory environment.

Understand the basic domain structure for an Active Directory environment. An Active Directory environment can consist of only a single domain or it can include multiple domains that form a tree. Multiple trees can be combined into a forest.

Review Questions

1. Which of the following is not a feature of Active Directory?
   A. The use of LDAP for transferring information
   B. Reliance on DNS for name resolution
   C. A flat domain namespace
   D. The ability to extend the schema

2. Domains provide which of the following functions?
   A. Creating security boundaries to protect resources and ease of administration
   B. Easing the administration of users, groups, computers, and other objects
   C. Providing a central database of network objects
   D. All of the above

3. Which of the following types of servers contain copies of the Active Directory database?
   A. Member servers
   B. Domain controllers
   C. Standalone servers
   D. None of the above

4. Which of the following objects are used to create the logical structure within Active Directory domains?
   A. Users
   B. Sites
   C. Organizational units (OUs)
   D. Trees
   E. None of the above

5. Which of the following is *false* regarding the naming of Active Directory objects?
   A. Active Directory relies on DNS for name resolution.
   B. Two objects can have the same relative distinguished name.
   C. Two objects can have the same distinguished name.
   D. All objects within a domain are based on the name of the domain.

6. Which of the following are *true* regarding Active Directory trust relationships?
   A. Trusts are transitive.
   B. By default, trusts are two-way relationships.
   C. Trusts are used to allow the authentication of users between domains.
   D. All of the above.

7. Which of the following protocols is used to query Active Directory information?

   A. LDAP

   B. NetBEUI

   C. NetBIOS

   D. IPX/SPX

8. Which of the following is not true regarding the Windows NT domain namespace?

   A. Windows NT domains have a hierarchical namespace.

   B. Windows NT domains allow thousands of users.

   C. Windows NT domains can be implemented as master domains.

   D. Windows NT domains can be implemented as resource domains.

   E. All of the above.

9. Which of the following is a possible role for a Windows Server 2003?

   A. Member server

   B. Primary Domain Controller

   C. Backup Domain Controller

   D. Standalone server

   E. Both A and D

10. Which of the following statements is true regarding domain controllers?

   A. All Active Directory domain controllers are automatically configured as Windows NT domain controllers.

   B. Windows NT domain controllers can host a copy of the Active Directory database.

   C. Windows Server 2003 domain controllers can be configured to provide the functionality of Windows NT domain controllers.

   D. None of the above.

11. Which of the following is not a characteristic of DNS?

   A. Built-in redundancy

   B. Reliance on proprietary technologies

   C. Scalability

   D. Distributed databases

12. An organization uses 12 Active Directory domains in a single forest. How many Schema Masters must this environment have?

   A. 0

   B. 1

   C. 12

   D. More than 12

   E. None of the above

13. An organization has three remote offices and one large central one. How many sites should this environment contain?

   A. 0

   B. 1

   C. 3

   D. 4

   E. Not enough information

14. Which of the following features of Active Directory allows information between domain controllers to remain synchronized?

   A. Replication

   B. The Global Catalog

   C. The schema

   D. None of the above

15. Jane is a systems administrator for a large, multidomain, geographically distributed network environment. The network consists of a large, central office and many smaller remote offices located throughout the world. Recently, Jane has received complaints about the performance of Active Directory–related operations from remote offices. Users complain that it takes a long time to perform searches for network resources (such as Shared Folders and Printers). Jane wants to improve the performance of these operations. Which of the following components of Active Directory should she implement at remote sites to improve the performance of searches conducted for objects in *all* domains?

   A. Data store

   B. Global Catalog

   C. Schema

   D. None of the above

16. What is the name of the server that is a repository that stores Active Directory topology and schema information for Active Directory?

   A. The Domain Partition

   B. The Schema Master

   C. The Global Catalog

   D. None of the above

17. From the list of answers, choose the role associated with the server that ensures that names of newly created domains adhere to naming conventions associated with your infrastructure.

   A. The Domain Naming Master

   B. The PDC Emulator

   C. The Schema Master

   D. The Global Catalog

18. You are the network administrator for your company. You have been asked to install Windows Server 2003 systems into your current environment. You have a domain that contains Windows NT 4 servers. You need to ensure that both Windows NT 4 and Windows Server 2003 systems function in the same environment. What role handles replicating changes from Windows NT systems to 2003 systems?

A. The Domain Naming Master

B. The PDC Emulator

C. The Schema Master

D. The Global Catalog

19. You are the administrator for your company's domain. You need to subdivide groups in your organization within Active Directory. If you wanted to separate Sales from Marketing as an example, what could you use as a system of organizing this subdivision and any others that you need to divide?

A. Create OUs.

B. Use Users and Groups.

C. Create a Sites and Services subnet grouping.

D. Build a container in LM manager.

20. You are the network administrator for a 200-node network. You are currently looking at creating software packages to roll out to your network users. When the users log in, they will automatically install needed updates. You only need to roll out a specific set of updates to 30 of those nodes. What could you create so that you can separate those 30 from the 200 and roll out updates only to that group?

A. Create a policy that deploys only to those 30 members.

B. Create a group assignment through Administrative Tools.

C. Create an organizational unit (OU) for those 30 users.

D. None of the above.

Answers to Review Questions

1. C. Active Directory uses a hierarchical namespace for managing objects.

2. D. All of these options are features of domains and are reasons for their usefulness.

3. B. Only domain controllers contain a copy of the Active Directory database. Member servers rely on Active Directory but do not contain a copy of the database, and standalone servers do not participate in Active Directory at all.

4. C. OUs are used for creating a hierarchical structure within a domain. Users are objects within the directory, sites are used for physical planning, and trees are relationships between domains.

5. C. The distinguished name of each object in Active Directory must be unique, but the relative distinguished names may be the same. For example, we might have a User object named Jane Doe in two different containers.

6. D. Trusts are designed for facilitating the sharing of information and have all of the above features.

7. A. LDAP is the IETF standard protocol for accessing information from directory services. It is also the standard used by Active Directory.

8. A. The Windows NT namespace is a flat model because groups cannot contain other groups and there is no hierarchical structure within a domain. The components of Active Directory domains, on the other hand, allow for the use of organizational units (OUs) in order to create a manageable hierarchy within a domain.

9. E. Primary Domain Controllers and Backup Domain Controllers are only used in Windows NT domains.

10. C. Through the use of the PDC Emulator functionality, Windows Server 2003 domain controllers can provide services for Windows NT domains.

11. B. DNS is a worldwide standard that is widely supported in all modern operating systems.

12. B. Only one Schema Master is allowed in an Active Directory environment, regardless of the number of domains.

13. E. The site topology is completely independent from domain architecture—a domain can span many sites, and many domains can be part of the same site. The fact that the organization has four locations does not necessarily mean that it should use a specific number of sites. Rather, this determination should be made based on physical network characteristics.

14. A. Replication ensures that information remains synchronized between domain controllers.

15. B. The Global Catalog contains information about multiple domains, and additional Global Catalog servers can greatly increase the performance of operations such as searches for shared folders and printers. The other options are features of Active Directory, but they are not designed for fast searching across multiple domains.

16. C. The Global Catalog is a repository that stores the Active Directory topology and schema information for Active Directory directories. The Global Catalog contains information about multiple domains, and additional Global Catalog servers can greatly increase the performance of operations such as searches for shared folders and printers. The other options are features of Active Directory, but they are not designed for fast searching across multiple domains.

17. A. The Domain Naming Master role associated with the server ensures that names of newly created domains adhere to naming conventions associated with your infrastructure.

18. B. The PDC Emulator is responsible for helping keep Windows NT 4 systems and Windows 2000 Server and Server 2003 systems working together. Items such as time synchronization and replication can be handled by the PDC Emulator.

19. A. An OU is an organizational unit and is a container object that is an Active Directory administrative partition. OUs can contain users, groups, resources, and other OUs. You can use OUs to help build organization into your directory so that you can roll out software updates to groupings of users, and computers. OUs enable the delegation of administration to very distinct subtrees of the directory. OUs can be departments or groups. They are used to structure and manage your network in a way that reflects a company's business organization.

20. C. An OU is a container object that is an Active Directory administrative partition. OUs can contain users, groups, resources, and other OUs. You can use OUs to help build organization into your directory so that you can roll out software updates and so on to groupings of users, computers, and so on. OUs enable the delegation of administration to very distinct subtrees of the directory. OUs can be departments or groups. They are used to structure and manage your network in a way that reflects a company's business organization.

Chapter

2

Planning and Installing Active Directory

MICROSOFT EXAM OBJECTIVES COVERED IN THIS CHAPTER:

✓ **Implement an Active Directory directory service forest and domain structure.**

- Create and configure Application Data Partitions.

- Install and configure an Active Directory domain controller.

- Set an Active Directory forest and domain functional level based on requirements.

In the previous chapter, you saw the various factors you need to take into account when planning for Active Directory, such as your company's physical and logical structure and the need for centralized or decentralized administration. The time you spend understanding these concepts is very important because the success of your Active Directory implementation depends on them.

Now that you are familiar with the basics, you need to start looking at exactly how Active Directory can be implemented. You will begin by examining the necessary steps and conditions you need to follow to prepare to install Active Directory on your network. First, you need to prepare for the Domain Name System (DNS), since Active Directory cannot be installed without the support of a DNS server. You also need to verify that the computer you upgrade to a domain controller (also known and simply referred to as a DC) meets the basic file system and network connectivity requirements you need so that Active Directory runs smoothly and efficiently in your organization.

Next, you'll explore the new concept of domain functional levels, which essentially determine what sorts of domain controllers you can use in your environment. For instance, in Windows 2000 mixed domain functional level, you can include Server 2003, 2000 Server, and NT 4 Server domain controllers, but the functionality of the domain is severely limited.

Once you understand how to properly plan for your domain environment, you will learn how to install Active Directory, which you accomplish by promoting a Windows Server 2003 computer to a domain controller. You will also learn how to verify the installation by testing Active Directory from a client computer.

After the initial Active Directory installation, you will learn how to install and configure Application Directory partitions, which provide replicable data repositories using the Active Directory replication paradigm but don't actually store any security principals, such as users or groups.

As the name implies, Application Directory partitions are primarily used to store data generated by applications that need to be replicated throughout your network environments independently of the rest of Active Directory.

The final section deals with integrating DNS with Active Directory, which is a very important topic since Active Directory cannot function without the support of DNS, as you will see.

Preparing for Active Directory Installation

All too often, systems and network administrators implement hardware and software without first taking the time to evaluate the prerequisites. For example, you will not be able to implement a tape backup solution without first ensuring that the appropriate network connectivity and attachment interface are available on servers. Installation and configuration of Active Directory is no exception.

The main physical components that form the basis of Active Directory are Windows Server 2003 domain controllers. Before you begin installing domain controllers to set up your Active Directory environment, you should ensure that you are properly prepared to do so. In the following sections, you'll see some of the prerequisites and types of information you'll need to successfully install and configure an Active Directory environment.

> The technical information and exercises in this chapter are based on the assumption that you will be using Microsoft's implementation of DNS (such as Unix- and Linux-based BIND), unless otherwise noted. If you are using other types of DNS servers in your environment, you may not be able to take advantage of all the features mentioned in this chapter.

Planning and Installing DNS

It is vital that you understand DNS in order to deploy Active Directory and install and configure domain controllers. A common mistake systems administrators make is underestimating the importance and complexity of DNS. Active Directory relies on DNS to find clients, servers, and network services that are available throughout your environment. Clients rely on DNS to find the file, print, and other resources they require to get their jobs done. Fully understanding DNS is not an easy task, especially if you have limited experience with the *Transmission Control Protocol/Internet Protocol (TCP/IP)* suite of protocols. However, you must understand and properly implement DNS if you want to use Active Directory successfully.

In the following section, you will learn about DNS and its importance in Active Directory.

> Although Microsoft has not defined any specific DNS-related exam objectives on Exam 70-294, it's definitely important for you to understand how DNS works (and how it relates to Active Directory). Further details about DNS are covered in *MCSA/MCSE: Windows Server 2003 Network Infrastructure Implementation, Management, and Maintenance Study Guide* by James Chellis, Paul Robichaux, and Matt Sheltz (Sybex, 2003) and *MCSE: Windows Server 2003 Network Infrastructure Planning and Maintenance Study Guide* by Suzan Sage London with James Chellis (Sybex, 2003).

DNS Overview

The Domain Name System (DNS) is a service designed to resolve Internet Protocol (IP) addresses to host names. One of the inherent complexities of working in networked environments involves working with various protocols and network addresses. Thanks largely to the tremendous rise in popularity of the Internet, however, most environments have transitioned to use TCP/IP as their primary networking protocol. Microsoft is no exception when it comes to supporting TCP/IP in its workstation and server products. All current versions of Microsoft's operating systems support it, as do most other modern operating systems. Since the introduction of Windows NT 4, TCP/IP has been the default protocol installed.

The TCP/IP protocol suite is actually a collection of different technologies (protocols and services) that allow computers to function together on a single network. Some of the major advantages of this protocol include widespread support for hardware, software, and network devices; reliance on a system of standards; and scalability.

TCP/IP is not the simplest protocol suite to understand, however. Because it was designed to support large, heterogeneous networks (because DNS is a separate service, and so is TCP, and IP where DNS handles name resolution), TCP handles tasks such as sequenced acknowledgments and IP involves many issues such as logical subnet assignment and routing. It is beyond the scope of this chapter to fully describe the intricacies of working with TCP/IP; it is generally covered in standalone volumes because it goes so in depth. However, this chapter does cover the information you need to understand DNS as it relates to Windows Server 2003 and Active Directory.

TCP/IP and DNS are based on a series of standards ratified by the Internet Engineering Task Force (IETF), a global standards organization. The job of this committee is to consider submissions for new features to TCP/IP and other related communications methods. Standards that are approved by the IETF are covered in Requests for Comments (RFCs). If you are looking for in-depth technical information on various Internet protocols and standards, see www.ietf.org. Also, more detailed coverage of networking is presented in the *MCSA/MCSE: Windows Server 2003 Network Infrastructure Implementation, Management, and Maintenance Study Guide* and the *MCSE: Windows Server 2003 Network Infrastructure Planning and Maintenance Study Guide.*

An IP address is simply a logical number that uniquely identifies a computer on a TCP/IP network. The address takes the form of four octets (eight binary bits), each of which is represented by a decimal number between 0 and 255. Decimal points logically separate each of the decimally represented numbers. For example, all of the following are valid IP addresses:

- 128.45.23.17

- 230.212.43.100

- 10.1.1.1

The dotted decimal notated representation was created to make it easier for users to deal with IP addresses. Obviously, this idea did not go far enough, hence the development of another abstraction layer of using names to represent the dotted decimal notation. For example, 11000000 10101000 00000001 00010101 maps to 192.168.1.21, which maps to `server1.company.org`, which is how the address is usually presented to the user or application.

Nowadays, most computer users are quite familiar with navigating to DNS-based resources, such as www.microsoft.com. In order to resolve these friendly names to TCP/IP addresses that the network stack can use, you must have some method for mapping them. Originally, ASCII flat files (often called HOSTS files as seen in Figure 2.1) were used for this purpose (in some cases, they are still used today in very small networks and can be used as a tool too help in the troubleshooting process when tyring to resolve names and you have resolution problems). But, as the number of machines and network devices grew, it became unwieldy for administrators to manage all of the manual updates that were required to enter new mappings to a master HOSTS file and distribute it or have everyone make the change themselves. Clearly, a better system was needed.

FIGURE 2.1   Sample HOSTS file

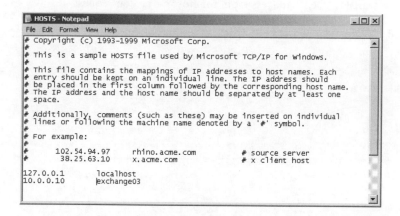

As you can see from this sample HOSTS file, you can conduct a quick test of the email server's name resolution. Do this by first entering the HOSTS file and adding the IP address–to–host name mapping and then by trying to ping the server by host name to verify that that you can reach it by an easy-to-remember name. This should drive home the concept of DNS for you because you can see it working to make your life easier—now you don't have to remember 10.0.0.10; you only need to remember exchange03. You can also see how this can become unwieldy if your have many hosts looking to use easy-to-remember names instead of IP addresses to locate resources on your network. It's imperative that you understand DNS in order to continue on with the chapter because Active Directory relies on it completely to be able to function properly.

When dealing with large networks, both users and network administrators must be able to locate the resources they require with minimal searching. Users don't care about the actual physical or logical network address of the machine; they just want to be able to connect to it using a simple name that they can remember. From a network administrator's standpoint, however, each machine must have its own logical address that makes it part of the network on which it resides. Therefore, some scalable and easy-to-manage method for resolving a machine's logical name to an IP address is required. DNS was created for this purpose.

DNS is a hierarchical naming system that contains a distributed database of name-to-IP address mappings. A DNS name is much friendlier and easier to remember than an IP address. For example, every time you enter a URL (such as www.microsoft.com), your computer, if configured to use a DNS server, will make a query to a DNS server that then resolves it to an

IP address. From then on, all communications between your computer and Microsoft's web server take place using the IP address, but users do not see this. The scalability and reliability of DNS can easily be inferred by its widespread use on the Internet. An example of how this works in a production environment can be seen in Figure 2.2. As you can see, the workstation that would like to access a file server on its LAN segment wants to do so by host name, not by IP address. When the workstation is booted on the local area network (LAN), the Dynamic Host Configuration Protocol (DHCP) server assigns not only an IP address to the workstation, but also a DNS server, so that when it accesses the file server, it can do so by using the DNS server assigned to translate the IP address from the host name you request.

FIGURE 2.2   Viewing how DNS and DHCP interoperate

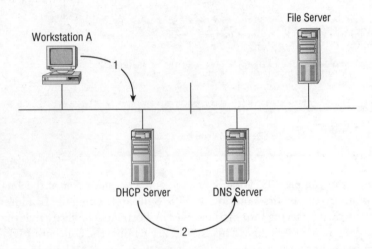

If you're new to DNS, the following sections will provide a lot of useful information on how DNS works. If you're a seasoned DNS veteran, you should still read about Windows Server 2003's DNS, which includes several additional features and enhancements that are not present in all DNS implementations.

DNS Namespace

If the world could run on only one flat network, things might be easier. We wouldn't need sub-nets, routers, and switches to isolate connections from each other. In the real world, however, technological and other limitations force network and systems administrators to create and adhere to their own specific set of names and network addresses. Furthermore, hierarchical names are extremely useful and necessary for computers participating in a worldwide global network such as the Internet. For example, if you have a computer called Workstation A, you must have some way to distinguish it from another computer with the same name at a different company. Similar to the way Active Directory uses hierarchical names for objects, DNS allows you to use a virtually unlimited number of machines. In the following sections, you'll look at how these hierarchical names are structured.

The Anatomy of a DNS Name

DNS names take the form of a series of alphanumeric strings separated by decimal points. Together, the various portions of a DNS name form what is called the *DNS namespace*, and each address within it is unique. All of the following examples are valid DNS names:

- `microsoft.com`
- `www.microsoft.com`
- `sales.microsoft.com`
- `engineering.microsoft.com`

The leftmost portion of the DNS name is the most specific portion, and it may refer to the name of a machine or a service. The remaining portions are part of the domain name and uniquely specify the network on which the host resides. The full name is referred to as the fully qualified domain name (FQDN). For example, the host name might be `engineering`, whereas the FQDN is `engineering.microsoft.com`.

Here are several features and limitations to note about a DNS name:

The name is hierarchical.   The domains listed at the right-most side of the address are higher-level domains. As you move left, each portion zooms in on the actual machine or service that is specified by the address. In other words, as you read from left to right, you are moving from a more specific name through its various containers.

The name is case-insensitive.   Although DNS names are sometimes printed in mixed-case for clarity, the case of the characters has no relevance. Therefore, `www.mycompany.com` and `www.MyCompany.com` are considered the same.

Each FQDN on a given network must be unique.   No two machines on the same network may have the same FQDN. This requirement ensures that each machine can be uniquely identified.

Only certain characters are allowed.   Each portion of the DNS name may include only standard English characters, decimal numbers, and dashes.

There are maximum lengths for addresses.   A DNS address can have a maximum length of 255 characters, and each name within the full name can have up to 63 characters.

Figure 2.3 shows an example of a valid hierarchical domain name.

FIGURE 2.3   A sample DNS namespace

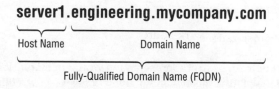

Now that you know the structure of a DNS name, you should see how the name is actually composed.

The Root

In order to be able to resolve friendly names to IP addresses, you must have some starting point. On a closed network, this would be fairly simple, since the "root" could be defined as a name created for the company. However, when you are dealing with the global Internet, you must make sure that names remain unique and that users throughout the world can resolve names for publicly available resources.

All Internet DNS names originate from one address known as the root. This address typically does not have a name and is represented in the DNS as a ".". Many organizations worldwide require domain names to be resolved starting at the root. That is the purpose of the top-level domains. On the Internet, there are several established top-level domains. Table 2.1 provides a list of some of the common North American ones. The standard top-level domains with which most people are familiar are registered in the root servers. Each domain namespace is reserved for a particular type of use, also shown in the table.

TABLE 2.1   Some North American Top-Level Domain Names

Top-Level Domain	Typical Users
.com	The top-level domain of .com represents the word "commercial." It is, hands down, the most widely used and accepted domain name in use today, worldwide. An example that uses this domain is www.wiley.com.
.net	The top-level domain of .net represents the word "network." It is most commonly used by Internet Service Providers (ISPs), hosting companies, or other businesses that are directly involved in the infrastructure of the Internet. An example is www.rsnetworks.net.
.org	The top-level domain of .org represents the word "organization." It is mostly used by not-for-profit groups. Here's an example: www.comptia.org.
.edu	The top-level domain of .edu represents the word "education." It is mostly used for colleges, universities, and education facilities worldwide. www.harvard.edu is an example of this type.
.gov	The top-level domain of .gov represents the word "government." It is mostly used by government agencies and departments. An example would be www.us.gov.
.int	International organizations.
.mil	The top-level domain of .mil represents the word "military." It is mostly used to denote branches of the military such as the United States Navy and the Marine Corps (www.usmc.mil).

TABLE 2.1   Some North American Top-Level Domain Names *(continued)*

Top-Level Domain	Typical Users
.biz	The top-level domain of .biz represents the word "business." It is mostly used to show a small business website, although most times, .com is preferred, only because it's more well-known to the general public.
.info	The top-level domain of .info represents the word "information." It is mostly used to show informational-based websites such as directories, phone books, or any other form of service that provides information to the general public or private groups.

In addition to these top-level domain names, there are many country codes for top-level domains throughout the world. Each is managed by its own authority. For example, an organization that is based in the United Kingdom may have a domain name of mycompany.co.uk. If you require a foreign domain name registration, you should inquire with the country's name service provider.

In order for an organization's own domain name to be resolved on the Internet, it must request that a second-level domain name be added to the global top-level DNS servers. Several registrars can perform this function worldwide.

For more information on registering a domain name for your own organization, see www.internic.net. There you will find a list of common registrars available worldwide. There is a nominal charge for each domain name you register, and a "lease" on a name is generally valid only for a limited time.

The name that is registered on the Internet is known as a second-level domain name. Company1.com, for example, would be considered a second-level domain name. Within an organization, however, all of the domain names would be subdomains of this one. Figure 2.4 provides an example of how the various levels of DNS domain names form a hierarchy.

A major consideration of DNS namespace configuration is whether or not you want to trust public ISPs for name resolution. If you do not, the alternative is to host your own domain name (which can consist of any top-level domain name you choose), but your servers cannot be made directly accessible on the Internet. For example, you might choose to use the names sales.mycompany and engineering.mycompany. Although these are perfectly valid DNS names for internal use, Internet users will not be able to access them if they are not listed on global Internet top-level DNS servers. On the other hand, you could trust public Internet authorities and use names such as sales.mycompany.com and engineering.mycompany.com (as long as you are the registered owner of the mycompany.com domain name). In this case, you would need to rely on the DNS servers managed by your ISP for external name resolution.

FIGURE 2.4 A DNS name hierarchy

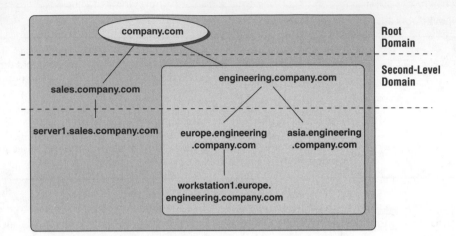

How DNS Maintains and Resolves Names

Once an organization has registered its own domain name, it must list that name on a DNS server. This might be a server controlled by the organization, or it might be one controlled by a third party such as an ISP that hosts the name. In either case, systems and network administrators can start adding names to their DNS servers using this top-level domain name.

If, for example, you have three computers that you want to make available on the Internet, you would first need to register a second-level domain name, such as mycompany.com. You could then choose to add your own domain names, such as the following:

- www.mycompany.com

- mail.mycompany.com

- computer1.northamerica.sales.mycompany.com

Each of these domain names must be listed on the DNS server as a *resource record (RR)*. The records themselves consist of a domain name–to–IP address mapping. When users try to access one of these machines (through a web browser, for example), the name will be resolved with the appropriate TCP/IP address. Computer 1 will have a unique IP address and a unique computer1.sales.mycompany.com in the DNS hierarchy—both resolvable to different IP addresses.

DNS servers are responsible for carrying out various functions related to name resolution. One of these functions is related to fulfilling DNS name mapping requests. If a DNS server has information about the specific host name specified in the request, it simply returns the appropriate information to the client that made the request. If, however, the DNS server does not have information about the specific host name, it must obtain that information from another DNS server. In this case, a process called name resolution is required. In order to resolve names of which it has no knowledge, DNS servers query other DNS servers for that information. As a result, you can see how a worldwide network of names can be formed. In Figure 2.5, we view this in action. Workstation A needs to make a request of its local DNS server. The local DNS server, when requested by the client, cannot locate the resource record it needs to service the client, so it queries a server it's configured to forward to. In this example, the query is sent to the ISP so that its DNS server can service the request.

FIGURE 2.5   How a DNS server queries a forward upstream DNS server for information

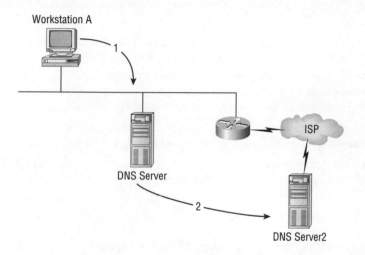

There can also be primary, secondary, and tertiary assignments within who to forward requests to; just in case a server is not available, the others can help it out by servicing the client request for them. In this example, we see how fault tolerance can be important, especially if you rely on your DNS the way Active Directory does.

Planning a DNS Structure

Planning is one of the most overlooked, yet critically important steps you need to implement a successful network of connected systems. It is extremely important for your organization to choose intuitive and consistent names when planning its DNS infrastructure. These are the names that users throughout the world will use to access your resources. The *root domain* name is especially important since it will be a part of the FQDN of all the machines on your network. For example, many users are accustomed to accessing a company's main web servers via the host name www, and they may find it difficult to access your main web servers if you use another host name. In this section, you'll look at several issues related to selecting internal and external DNS names.

Selecting a DNS Root Name

The first step in establishing a DNS structure for your organization involves selecting a top-level domain name. The most common choice for a top-level domain is .com (for commercial companies). Usually, you would then want to reserve a second-level domain name based on the name of your company. Currently, however, due to the large number of registered domains, it may be difficult to reserve that name. In any case, you should inquire with the Internet Network Information Center (InterNIC) at www.internic.net to find a usable domain name. A good name would be one that is easy to remember and that people will quickly associate with your company. If your company has a long name or its name consists of multiple words, you might want to abbreviate it. For example, users might find ComputerTechnologiesInc.com difficult to type, whereas CompTech.com is much simpler. Some common guidelines for choosing a suitable name include the following:

- Choose a name that is similar to the name of your company. This is a good practice if you want something easy to remember and something that you can brand, but if you are into securing your infrastructure and keeping your internal network private from your external one, it's recommended by security experts that you keep the your internal name different from the external public domain name.

- Use a name that will not usually change. Department or product names, for example, might change over time, whereas company names will remain relatively static.

- Ensure that you have the approval of your company's management and marketing staff before registering and using a name.

- Consult with your company's legal department (or a legal service) to ensure that the domain name is not currently being used and that a trademark on the name is not currently held by another company. If you know what to look for and how to search for it, run your own search for the information online and save yourself some money.

Once you have found a name, the process of registering it is quite simple and can be carried out entirely online. To start the registration process, connect to www.internic.net and follow the links for registering a new domain name. You will need to choose from among several official registrars and then follow the instructions provided.

 During the rise in popularity of the World Wide Web (WWW), many people rushed to reserve domain names based, for example, on the names of popular companies. These people (sometimes affectionately referred to as cyber-squatters) planned to sell the domain names to the companies that owned the copyright for the name. Today organizations exist to prevent third parties from using trademarked names as domain names. To inquire into the process of regaining a domain name to which you may have rights, see www.internic.net.

In order for your computers to be accessible via the Internet, you need to have a worldwide-registered domain name. As part of the name registration process, you will be required to provide technical information about the DNS server(s) that will host your domain name. If you have your own DNS servers, you can simply provide their IP addresses. Otherwise, you can receive this service from many commercial ISPs (for a fee). Figure 2.6 shows how DNS names are resolved with company domain names.

FIGURE 2.6   How root-level servers are related to private DNS servers

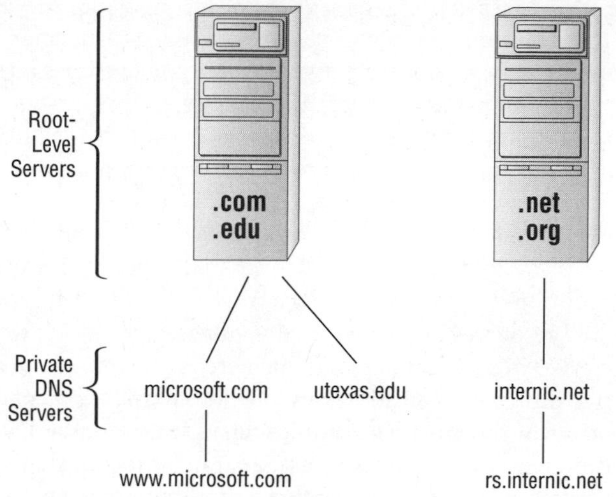

Root-
Level
Servers

.com
.edu

.net
.org

Private
DNS
Servers

microsoft.com   utexas.edu

internic.net

www.microsoft.com

rs.internic.net

Choosing Internal and External Names

So far, we have been talking about choosing an Internet root domain name. This external name is designed to make computers accessible publicly on the Internet. You will also need to choose a domain name for your internal network. The internal domain name may be the same as the external one, or it may be different. When you're managing internal names, you can choose any name that meets your own standards. You should, however, ensure that any external domain name you use has been properly registered with the Internet name authorities. Figure 2.7 provides an example of how different internal and external DNS names can be used.

FIGURE 2.7   Using different internal and external DNS names

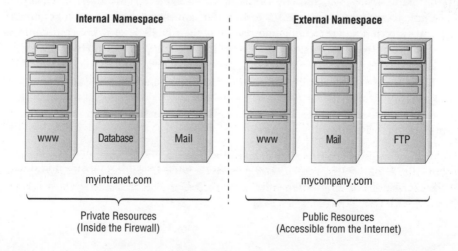

Internal Namespace

www   Database   Mail

myintranet.com

Private Resources
(Inside the Firewall)

External Namespace

www   Mail   FTP

mycompany.com

Public Resources
(Accessible from the Internet)

As was touched on earlier in the chapter, there are several pros and cons you should consider when you are deciding whether or not to use the same domain name for internal and external resources. One of the advantages of using the same name is consistency between internal and external resources. This means that users will be able to use the same email address for internal and external communications. However, if you choose to have the same name, you need to take great care in how you name resources and configure DNS servers. A small mistake in the naming, for instance, may result in an internal server being made available on the public Internet. Similarly, you must tell users which resources are only available from the internal network and which machines are accessible from the public Internet.

If you choose separate internal and external names, you will be able to easily determine which resources are publicly accessible and which ones are restricted to your private network. This practice also simplifies routing and DNS settings, since you can be sure that resources in the public domain are public and resources in the private domain are private. However, this method may require you to reserve two domain names (which are getting more and more difficult to find!) and give users two different email addresses (one for internal email and one for email sent by users located outside of the private network, such as Internet users).

You should base your decision regarding whether to use separate or identical internal and external namespaces on your organization's business and technical requirements.

Designing a Namespace

In this section, we will take a look at how namespace design is critical to solid DNS functionality so that you can achieve solid Active Directory performance and functionality. Remember, DNS is critical to Active Directory—they go hand in hand. Now that you understand what a namespace is, you may need to design a namespace for your company. Because most companies do business on the public Internet, most business have a web presence and have domains registered so that they are publicly viewable by anyone with an Internet connection.

At this point, the same design question always comes up: "Should we use the same name on the Internet that we use on the internal domain with Active Directory?" Let's discuss your options.

Using Different (separate) internal and external namespaces   If you choose to use separate or different namespaces, that's fine. As a matter of fact, it's recommended. Let's take a look at an example to see why it's important to consider namespace design. Take a company that uses separate internal and external namespaces for their DNS design. Say your company's name is wiley.com (represented as external.com in Figure 2.8); most likely you would advertise it as such on the public Internet. That does not mean you would use this name for your internal DNS infrastructure design, however. Instead, you'd select a different name, such as internal.com or anything else you wanted, just as long as you didn't select the same name you were planning to use on the public Internet. This way, you can have a separation at the firewall if you host the website internally in your company. Figure 2.8 shows what this looks like.

The company you see in Figure 2.8 uses separate internal and external namespaces. What is nice about this design is that since there are separate names used both inside and outside the company, you can keep the internal namespace a secret.

Remember to make sure that you reserve your DNS names with a registration authority. You can also reserve your private names so that they can't be used by others on the public Internet. If you fail to reserve and register the internal name, in the future, internal clients may be prevented from accessing this namespace on the public Internet; this is simply because the client won't be able to tell the difference between the internally selected name and the publicly assigned name via the registrar.

You can set up zones for the external and internal namespaces. Zones are covered shortly in the text.

FIGURE 2.8   The different internal and external namespaces

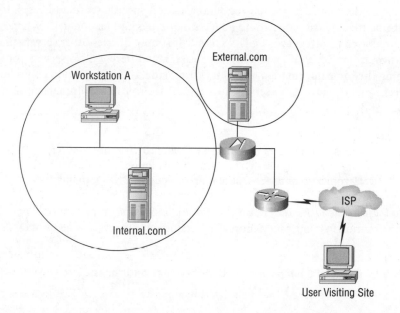

Using the same internal and external namespace names   If you choose to use the same internal and external namespace names, you will have a setup similar to the one in Figure 2.8, except that both names will be identical and you will need to make significant configuration changes to ensure proper functionality of the DNS.

Getting internal clients to utilize publicly available resources is a challenge. Same namespace names are not recommended because of the amount of configuration work you have to do to implement this design so that all your clients have access to public resources such as web-based servers on the public Internet. To get this to happen, you may have to implement a proxy. Unless you are sure you must have this type of design, it's always better to go with different namespaces. So just remember that though this is not a recommended configuration, it can be done.

Overview of DNS Zones

DNS servers work together to resolve hierarchical names. If they already have information about a name, they simply fulfill the query for the client; otherwise, if configured to do so, they query other DNS servers for the appropriate information. The system works well because it distributes the authority of separate parts of the DNS structure to specific servers. A DNS *zone* is a portion of the DNS namespace over which a specific DNS server has authority. In this section, you'll see how the concept of zones is used to ensure accurate name resolution on the Internet.

Purpose and Function of DNS Zones

In order to ensure that naming remains accurate in a distributed network environment, one DNS server must be designated as the master database for a specific set of addresses. It is on this server that updates to host name–to–IP address mappings can be updated. Whenever a DNS server is unable to resolve a specific DNS name, it simply queries other servers that can provide the information. Zones are necessary because many different DNS servers could otherwise be caching the same information. If changes are made, this information could become outdated. Therefore, one central DNS server must assume the role of the ultimate authority for a specific subset of domain names.

 There is an important distinction between DNS zones and Active Directory domains. Although both use hierarchical names and require name resolution, DNS zones do not necessarily map directly to DNS domains.

As shown in Figure 2.9, a zone may be an entire domain or it may represent only part of one. With this information in mind, take a more detailed look at the actual process of DNS name resolution.

FIGURE 2.9   The relationship between DNS domains and zones

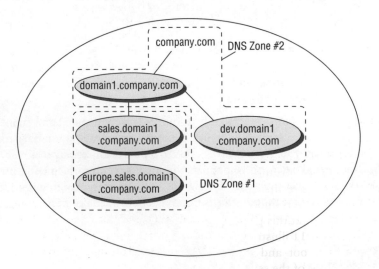

DNS Name Resolution

When you are using the Internet, DNS queries are extremely common. For example, every time you click a link to visit a new website, your computer makes a DNS query. In the simplest scenario, the client computer requests a DNS address from its designated DNS server. The DNS server has information about the IP address for the specified host name, it returns that information to the client, and the client then uses the IP address to initiate communications with the host. The client then uses that IP address information for subsequent requests to the same resource. This process is shown in Figure 2.10.

FIGURE 2.10   A simple DNS name resolution process

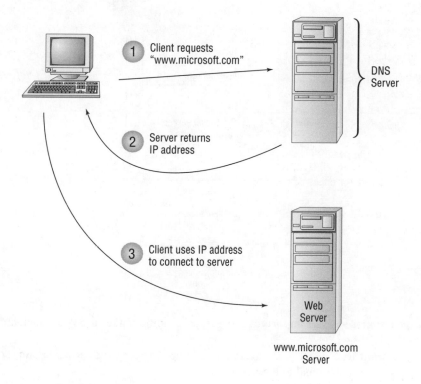

1 Client requests "www.microsoft.com"

2 Server returns IP address

3 Client uses IP address to connect to server

DNS Server

Web Server

www.microsoft.com Server

RECURSIVE QUERIES

If the DNS server does not contain information about the specific host requested, it initiates a query to another DNS server. This second DNS server thereby assumes responsibility for ultimately resolving the name. If it is unable to fulfill the request, it, in turn, queries another server. This process is known as *recursion*. The name resolution process usually begins with a query to the top-level DNS servers and continues downward through the domain hierarchy until the resource is reached. If, at this point, the name still cannot be resolved, an error is returned to the client. Figure 2.11 illustrates the process of recursion. Usually, DNS servers include information about the root- and top-level DNS servers. This information is entered in during the initial configuration of the server.

FIGURE 2.11   DNS name resolution through recursion

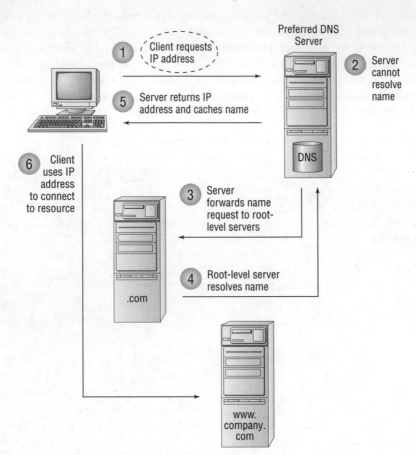

Because recursion is such an important process, you should make sure you understand the following example.

Suppose you want to connect to the DNS name Computer1.sales.somecompany.com. The following steps occur to make this happen:

1. The client requests information from its preferred DNS server.

2. The preferred DNS server is unable to find a resource record for this information in its own cache and must therefore query another server. The preferred DNS server first queries a root server and then it sends a query to the top-level domain server and requests information about the server that has authority over the somecompany.com domain.

3. Once it obtains this information, the preferred DNS server then queries the `somecompany.com` DNS server for information about the `Computer1` host name within the sales domain.

4. The client's preferred DNS server then returns the IP address of the host name to the client. The client can then use the IP address to communicate with the host. The preferred DNS server may choose to cache a copy of the resource record information just in case additional requests for the domain name are made.

ITERATIVE QUERIES

A client may also be configured to query multiple DNS servers for names. This process is known as *iteration*. Iteration is normally used when a client queries DNS servers, but it instructs them not to use recursion. Alternatively, systems administrators may configure DNS servers not to perform recursion. For example, you may configure all DNS servers to forward resolution requests to one DNS server on your network. This directs all DNS traffic through this one server, thereby reducing network traffic and allowing you to secure DNS requests.

In the iteration process, the DNS server fulfills a request if it is able to do so based on the information in its own database. If it cannot, it either returns an error or it points the client to another DNS server that may be able to resolve the name. Iteration requires the client to remain responsible for ultimately resolving the name request.

DNS FORWARDING

Usually, the client is configured with multiple DNS servers that are utilized according to a certain search order. This order is useful if different DNS servers are required to resolve intranet and Internet names. For example, a client may use one DNS server to resolve names for a specific department within the organization and another DNS server to resolve names of public websites. This method places the burden of finding the right name server on the client. In certain configurations, though, you may want to reduce network traffic with DNS *forwarding*, which allows you to specify exactly which DNS servers will be used for resolving names. For example, if you have multiple DNS servers located on a fast network (such as a local area network[LAN]), you may want each of them to request DNS information from only a few specific DNS servers that can then gain information from other DNS servers on the network. Figure 2.12 provides an example of how DNS forwarding can be used.

CACHING

Another feature of DNS servers is their ability to cache information. As you can imagine, going through the recursion process each time a DNS query is initiated can place a significant load on servers worldwide. In order to limit some of this traffic, DNS servers usually save information about mapped domain names in their own local database. If future requests are made for the same host and domain names, this cached information is usually used. To ensure that the cached information is reasonably up-to-date, a Time to Live (TTL) value is attached to each cached DNS record. Typical TTL values range from three to seven days. Once this time limit is exceeded, the cached value is no longer used, and the next request for the information will result in the DNS server going through the entire recursion process again.

FIGURE 2.12 Using DNS forwarding to reduce network traffic

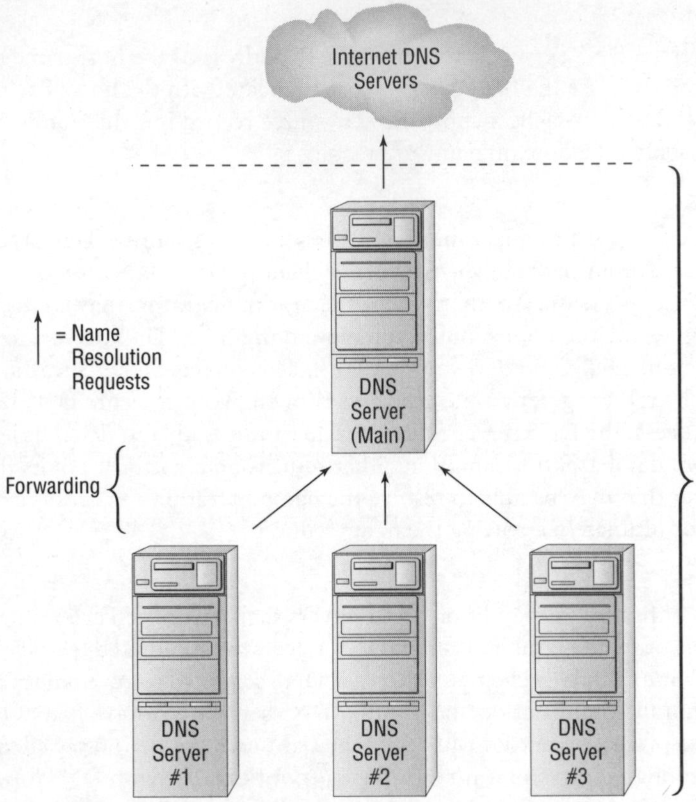

NOTE

Since DNS names are updated on a pull basis, it can take time for some DNS servers to update their databases. If you must make changes to a DNS entry, be sure to allow sufficient time for all of the name servers on the Internet to be updated by their peers. Usually, this should take only a few days, but, in some cases, it may take more than a week.

LOAD BALANCING

The Windows Server 2003 implementation of DNS supports load balancing through the use of round robin and netmask ordering. Load balancing distributes the network load between multiple network cards if they are available. You can create multiple resource records with the same host name but different IP addresses for multihomed computers. Depending on the options that you select, the DNS server responds with one of the multihomed computer's addresses.

If round robin is enabled, the first address entered in the database is returned to the resolver and then sent to the end of the list. The next time a client attempts to resolve the name, the DNS server returns the second name in the database (which is now the first name) and then sends it to the end of the list, and so on.

If netmask ordering is enabled, the DNS server uses the first IP address in the database that matches the subnet of the resolver. If none of the IP addresses match the subnet of the resolver, then the DNS server reverts to round robin. If round robin is disabled, the DNS server simply returns the first IP address in the database.

If neither round robin nor netmask ordering is enabled, then the DNS server always returns the first IP address in the database. This usually isn't very helpful, so fortunately round robin and netmask ordering are both enabled by default.

REVERSE LOOKUPS

Although the most common DNS functions involve the mapping of DNS names to IP addresses, certain applications might require the opposite functionality—the resolution of an IP address to a DNS name. This is handled through a *reverse lookup zone* in the DNS server. Reverse lookup zones start with a special Internet authority address and allow the DNS server to resolve queries for specific TCP/IP addresses.

In order to determine from which DNS server-specific information can be found, you must use zones. Now you'll examine the process of establishing authority for specific DNS zones.

Delegating Authority in DNS Zones

Every DNS server can be configured to be responsible for one or more DNS domains. The DNS server is then known as the authoritative source of address information for that zone. Generally, if you use only a single DNS domain, you have only one zone. Remember that there can be a many-to-many relationship between domains (which are used to create a logical naming structure) and zones (which refer primarily to the physical structure of a DNS implementation).

When you add subdomains, however, you have two options: you can allow the original DNS server to continue functioning as the authority for the *parent* and *child domains*, or you can choose to create another DNS zone and give a different server authority over it. The process of giving authority for specific domains to other DNS servers is known as *delegation*. Figure 2.13 shows how delegation can be configured.

The main reasons for using delegation are improving performance and simplifying administration. Using multiple DNS servers in a large network can help distribute the load involved in resolving names. It can also help administer security by allowing only certain types of records to be modified by specified systems administrators.

DNS Server Roles

One of the potential problems with configuring specific DNS servers as authorities for their own domains is fault tolerance. If an authoritative server becomes unavailable, normally this means that none of the names for the resources in that zone could be resolved to network addresses. This could be a potentially serious problem for networks of any size. For example, if the primary server for the sales.mycompany.com zone becomes unavailable (and there are no secondary servers in that zone), users will not be able to find resources such as `server1.sales.mycompany.com` or `workstation1.sales.mycompany.com`. In order to prevent the potential network problems caused by a single failed server, the DNS specification allows multiple servers to be supported per zone.

FIGURE 2.13   Delegating DNS authority to multiple DNS servers

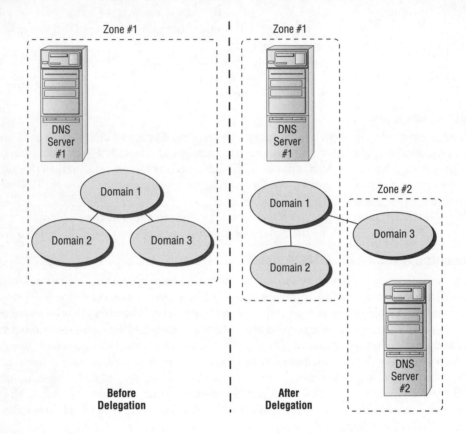

To maintain a distributed and hierarchical naming system, DNS servers can assume several different roles at once. In this section, we'll look at the various roles that DNS servers can assume within a zone.

Primary server   Each DNS zone must have one *primary DNS server*. The primary server is responsible for maintaining all of the records for the DNS zone, and it contains the primary copy of the DNS database. Additionally, all record updates occur on the primary server. You will want to create and add primary servers whenever you create a new DNS domain. When creating child domains, however, you may want to use the primary server from the parent domain.

Secondary server   A *secondary DNS server* contains a database of all of the same information as the primary name server and can be used to resolve DNS requests. The main purpose of a secondary server is to provide for fault tolerance, so if the primary server becomes unavailable, name resolution can still occur using the secondary server. Therefore, it is a good general practice to ensure that each zone has at least one secondary server to protect against failures.

Secondary DNS servers can also increase performance by offloading some of the traffic that would otherwise go to the primary server. Secondary servers are also often placed within the parts of an organization that have high-speed network access. This prevents DNS queries from having to run across slow wide area network (WAN) connections. For example, if there are two remote offices within the mycompany.com organization, you may want to place a secondary DNS server in each remote office. This way, when clients require name resolution, they will contact the nearest server for this IP address information, thus preventing unnecessary WAN traffic.

Although it is a good idea to have secondary servers, having too many of them can cause increases in network traffic due to replication (especially if DNS changes are fairly frequent). Therefore, you should always weigh the benefits and drawbacks and properly plan for secondary servers.

Master server *Master DNS servers* are used when DNS data is replicated between primary and secondary servers. Usually, the primary server also serves as the master server, but these tasks can be separated for performance reasons. The master server is responsible for propagating any changes in the DNS database to all secondary servers within a particular zone.

Caching-only server *Caching-only DNS servers* serve the same function as primary DNS servers in that they help clients resolve DNS names to network addresses. The only difference is that caching-only servers are not authoritative for any DNS zones, and they don't contain copies of the zone files. They only contain mappings as a result of resolved queries and, in fact, they lose all of their mapping information when the server shuts down, therefore, they are installed only for performance reasons. A caching-only DNS server may be used at sites that have slow connectivity to DNS servers at other sites.

Zone Transfers

Similar to the situation with domain controllers and Active Directory, it is important to ensure that DNS zone information is consistent between the primary and secondary servers. The process used to keep the servers synchronized is known as a *zone transfer*. When a secondary DNS server is configured for a zone, it first performs a zone transfer during which it obtains a copy of the primary server's address database. This process is known as an all-zone transfer (AXFR).

In order to ensure that information is kept up to date after the initial synchronization, DNS servers use incremental zone transfers (IXFRs). Through this process, the changes in the DNS zone databases are communicated between primary and secondary servers. IXFRs use a system of serial numbers to determine which records are new or updated. This system ensures that the newest DNS record is always used, even if changes were made on more than one server.

🌐 Real World Scenario

Optimizing DNS Performance

As the DNS administrator for your network environment, you are responsible for ensuring that DNS is working optimally. Recently, you've received several complaints that DNS queries are taking a long time and that sometimes client applications time out when they try to reach a remote server. The network is fairly large and includes 3 large offices and 25 remote sites.

So far, you have attempted to keep the DNS infrastructure design as simple as possible to ease administration. The current DNS environment consists of a single forward lookup zone that includes a primary server and two secondary servers. The primary server is located in one large office, and each of the secondary servers is located in the other two large offices. This design is simple and easy to administer, but the performance problem must be solved. So, what's the easiest way to do this?

Fortunately, DNS has been designed from the ground up to offer scalability and high performance for even the most widely distributed networks. In this example, you could choose to redesign the DNS infrastructure. For example, you could break a single zone down into multiple smaller zones and then implement additional DNS servers for those zones. However, this would require a considerable amount of effort for planning, design, and implementation. It might also be more difficult to administer. Since performance is currently the only complaint, let's look at another solution.

Another option involves creating additional secondary servers and placing them in areas where users are complaining about the performance of DNS queries. For example, you might decide that you need to deploy DNS servers in several of the larger remote offices and remote offices that are located across slow or unreliable WAN links. There is a potential problem with implementing additional secondary servers: doing so can increase the amount of network traffic that flows between the DNS servers when you make updates. However, you'll probably find that it's a worthwhile trade-off.

There's one more option that's easy to implement and can help increase performance: caching-only DNS servers. These servers are particularly helpful in environments that consist of multiple DNS zones. They're easy to administer since they don't contain authoritative copies of your DNS databases, and they can improve performance by providing a quicker way to resolve DNS queries for remote clients.

As you can see, DNS is powerful and flexible enough to offer you many different types of solutions to performance problems. Be sure to keep this in mind as you work with DNS in the real world!

Not all DNS servers support IXFRs. Windows NT 4's DNS services and earlier implementations of other DNS services require a full-zone transfer of the entire database in order to update their records. This can sometimes cause significant network traffic. As with any software implementation, you should always verify the types of functionality supported before you deploy it.

Zone transfers may occur in response to the following different events:

- The zone refresh interval has been exceeded.
- A master server notifies a secondary server of a zone change.
- A secondary DNS server service is started for the zone.
- A DNS zone transfer is manually initiated (by a systems administrator) at the secondary server.

An important factor to be aware of when you are dealing with zone transfers is that secondary servers always initiate them. This type of replication is commonly known as a pull operation. Normally, a zone transfer request is made when a refresh interval is reached on the secondary server. The request is sent to a master server, which then sends any changes to the secondary server. Usually the primary server is also configured as a master server, but this can be changed for performance reasons.

One of the problems with pull replication is that the information stored on secondary servers can remain out of date for a significant period of time. For example, suppose an IXFR occurs today, but the refresh interval is set to three days. If you make a change on the primary DNS server, this change will not be reflected on the secondary server for several days. One potential way to circumvent this problem is to set a very low refresh interval (such as a few hours). However, this can cause a lot of unnecessary network traffic and increased processing overhead.

In order to solve the problems associated with keeping resource records up to date, a feature known as DNS notify was developed. This method employs push replication to inform secondary servers whenever a change is made. When secondary servers receive the DNS notify message, they immediately initiate IXFR requests. Figure 2.14 shows how DNS notify is used to keep secondary servers up to date.

Managing DNS Resource Records

So far, we have looked at various ways in which DNS servers remain synchronized with each other. Now, it's time to look at the actual types of information stored within the DNS database.

When you're building a DNS infrastructure, once you have the top-level domain, the second-level domain, and a zone database created on the DNS server, it's important to add records to the infrastructure. Resource records are nothing more than files that hold data that the DNS server queries. Each domain that is created will always have resource records that contain information about the DNS infrastructure you are managing, especially by default. Some records are made by default when you install DNS for the first time.

FIGURE 2.14   Using DNS notify to update secondary servers

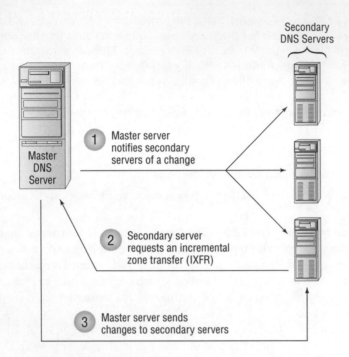

There are many types of DNS database records, with the most common database record being the A (Address) record, which does nothing more than map a host name and an IP address—this is the primary method of DNS resolution. A records are responsible for most of the DNS communication and resolution in use when you use DNS. The DNS forward lookup zones are populated with a variety of resource records.

Table 2.2 lists the types of records that are used within the DNS database. Each of these records is important for ensuring that the proper type of resource is made available. For example, if a client is attempting to send email, the DNS server should respond with the IP address corresponding to the Mail Exchanger (MX) record of the domain.

In addition to the DNS zone file parameters, certain conventions are often used on the Internet. For example, the host names `mail`, `www`, `ftp`, and `news` are usually reserved for email, World Wide Web, File Transfer Protocol, and Usenet news servers, respectively.

Now that you understand the purpose and methods of DNS, take a look at how Microsoft's DNS service operates.

Planning an Active Directory DNS Environment

So far, you've seen a lot of information regarding DNS concepts. Now that you've covered the DNS namespace and how DNS servers interact with each other, you should understand the name resolution infrastructure Active Directory requires. If you are still unclear on some of the concepts related to planning a DNS structure for an organization, be sure to review the information presented earlier in this chapter.

TABLE 2.2   DNS Resource Record Types

Resource Record Type	Meaning	Description
A	Address	Used to map host names to IP addresses. Multiple A records may be used to map to a single IP address.
CNAME	Canonical Name	Used as an alias or a nickname for a host (in addition to the A record).
MX	Mail Exchanger	Specifies the Simple Mail Transfer Protocol (SMTP) email server address for the domain.
NS	Name Server	Specifies the IP address of DNS servers for the domain.
PTR	Pointer	Used for reverse lookup operations. This file is just a pointer to another location.
RP	Responsible Person	Specifies information about the individual that is responsible for maintaining the DNS information.
SOA	Start of Authority	Specifies the authoritative server for a zone.
SRV	Service	Specifies server services available on a host; used by Active Directory to identify domain controllers. The standard for SRV records has not yet been finalized.

One of the major benefits of using Microsoft DNS is that it lets you manage and replicate the DNS database as a part of Active Directory. As a result, you can automate much of the administration of the DNS service and still keep information up to date.

With respect to your DNS environment, you'll want to plan to use various DNS servers. As was mentioned earlier in this chapter, there are several possible roles for DNS servers, including primary, secondary, master, and caching-only servers. With respect to Active Directory, DNS services are absolutely vital. If DNS isn't functioning properly, Active Directory clients and servers will not be able to locate each other, and network services will be severely impacted.

Let's look at how you can plan to use DNS zones and servers with Active Directory.

Planning DNS Zones

The first step in planning for DNS server deployment is determining the size and layout of your DNS zones. In the simplest configurations, you will have a single Active Directory domain and a single DNS zone. This configuration usually meets the needs of single-domain environments.

When you consider multiple domains, you generally need to make some choices when planning for DNS. In some environments, you might choose to use only a single zone that spans over all of the domains. In other cases, you might want to break zones apart for administrative and performance reasons.

The DNS zone configuration you choose is largely independent of the Active Directory configuration. That is, for any given Active Directory configuration, you could use any zone setup, as long as all names can be properly resolved. That said, make no mistake—the proper functioning of DNS zones is critical to how Active Directory functions.

Planning Server Roles

First and foremost, DNS servers are extremely important in the Active Directory environment. In order to provide for fault tolerance for DNS servers, you should ensure that each DNS zone you configure consists of one primary DNS server and at least one secondary server. If the primary DNS computer fails, the secondary server can still carry out name resolution operations, and most operations will continue normally. This is, however, a temporary solution since you will need to restore or replace the primary DNS server in order to make updates to the DNS zone information.

Generally, you will want to make the primary DNS server the master server for the zone. If it is necessary for performance reasons, however, you can choose to use a separate machine for DNS services.

You generally use caching-only servers when you want to make DNS information available for multiple computers that do not have a fast or reliable connection to the main network. You typically plan caching-only servers around the physical network because they do not have any authority over specific zones.

Figure 2.15 shows a representative DNS server configuration for an Active Directory domain. Notice that a single domain spans multiple locations, and the remote offices use secondary servers.

Installing DNS

It should come as no surprise that DNS must be properly designed, installed, and configured before you can install an Active Directory domain. If it is not already installed on the system, you should install the DNS service by using the Manage Your Server tool, which appears by default after you restart the computer (see Figure 2.16). By clicking Add Or Remove A Role, you start the Configure Your Server Wizard, which you can use to quickly and easily enable DNS on the server. You can then use DNS to perform name resolution to other domain controllers or resources on your network (if any).

If you haven't yet installed DNS, you will be prompted to do so as part of the configuration of a domain controller. In some cases, this provides an easy way to configure DNS with the appropriate options for Active Directory. It's not the right choice for every environment, however. Unless you are setting up Active Directory in a test environment or on a network that doesn't yet have DNS services, you may find it easier to test and verify the DNS configuration before you start installing Active Directory.

FIGURE 2.15   Arranging servers for Active Directory

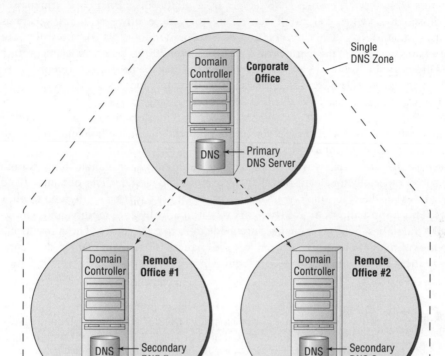

FIGURE 2.16   The Manage Your Server tool

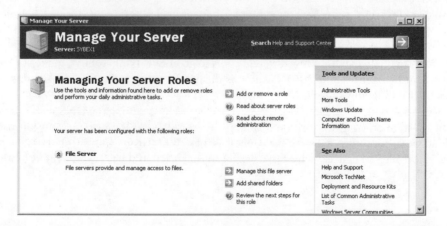

Although DNS servers must be present on your network, you do not have to use Microsoft's DNS service. If other DNS servers are available on the network, you may choose to use those servers when you install Active Directory. Note, however, that if you're using other implementations of DNS servers (such as Unix or Windows NT 4), you will not be able to take advantage of all of the features of Windows Server 2003's DNS and its integration with Active Directory. In addition, you will be required to enter the proper SRV records manually because most current DNS servers do not support dynamic updates.

Dynamic updates enable DNS client workstations to register and update their resource records (RRs) with a DNS server when changes occur. If implemented, zone RR maintenance drops to nearly nothing. Windows Server 2003 supports dynamic update functionality as seen in RFC 2136 (`www.faqs.org/rfcs/rfc2136.html`).

If you use this functionality, you can reduce the requirement for manual administration of zone records, especially for clients that frequently move and use DHCP to obtain an IP address.

Once DNS has been installed, you should ensure that it has been configured to allow updates. This option allows Active Directory to automatically add, modify, and remove RRs to the DNS database whenever changes are made in Active Directory. The Allow Updates option is extremely useful because it reduces the chances for error in manual data entry and greatly reduces the administration effort required.

> If you plan to work through the exercises presented in this chapter, be sure that you have either already installed DNS or are at least planning to do so as part of Active Directory installation process. Installing and configuring DNS is described in detail in *MCSA/MCSE: Windows Server 2003 Network Infrastructure Implementation, Management, and Maintenance Study Guide (70-291), Second Edition* by Steve Suehring and James Chellis (Wiley, 2006).

Verifying the DNS Configuration

To verify DNS configuration, you can use the ping tool to quickly test DNS resolution.

You can use the `ping` command with the `-a` switch. Let's consider a problem where you have to test DNS resolution. Say, for example, that a user can't get to an Internet website. First you should check the client. Make sure you run the ipconfig utility with its assigned DNS-related switches. If you can ascertain that there's definitely something wrong with the DNS resolution, then you can use a few different tools to go about fixing it. First, make sure it's not a local client problem. The local DNS cache is flushed by using `ipconfig /flushdns`, which purges the DNS Resolver cache.

You can use ping to troubleshoot DNS-related issues by querying the DNS server. If you try to ping a system on your network by host name, it should work. If you want, you can also ping the IP address using the `-a` switch mentioned earlier. When using this particular switch, you can solve problems such as "why can't we get to that URL, `http://www.sybex.com?`"

You have to see if DNS resolution is working. You can see if the DNS server you configured to query knows what it's talking about. Use the nslookup command to shows this information:

```
> www.sybex.com
Server:  ns3.srv.hcvlny.cv.net
Address:  167.206.112.3

Non-authoritative answer:
Name:    www.sybex.com
Address:  63.99.198.12
```

When I query my local DNS server, I can see that sybex.com has an IP address that I can ping.

Now, it's possible to ping with the -a switch to also verify if DNS resolution is working. Pinging Sybex's IP address with the -a switch produces the DNS name of the system. As you can see in the following code, the Internet Control Message Protocol (ICMP) packet is blocked, so although DNS is working, you got a false positive. Let's try the same test via nslookup, and ping -a with www.yahoo.com. After getting Yahoo's public IP address, we run a quick test successfully. DNS resolution works. This works beautifully when you are inside your corporate network and are using internal DNS servers that are forwarding to external ones. You now know that you have verifiable DNS inside your organization and out.

```
>ping -a 216.109.118.74
Pinging p11.www.dcn.yahoo.com [216.109.118.74] with 32 bytes of data:

Reply from 216.109.118.74: bytes=32 time=22ms TTL=51
Reply from 216.109.118.74: bytes=32 time=25ms TTL=51
Reply from 216.109.118.74: bytes=32 time=27ms TTL=51
Reply from 216.109.118.74: bytes=32 time=32ms TTL=51

Ping statistics for 216.109.118.74:
    Packets: Sent = 4, Received = 4, Lost = 0 (0% loss),
Approximate round trip times in milli-seconds:
    Minimum = 22ms, Maximum = 32ms, Average = 26ms
```

You should also verify that DNS forward and reverse lookup zones have been created properly. These zones will be used to resolve names to network addresses and are extremely important for the successful setup of Active Directory.

Verifying the File System

When planning your Active Directory deployment, the file system the operating system uses is an important concern for many reasons. First, the file system can provide the ultimate level of security for all of the information stored on the server itself. Second, the file system is responsible for managing and tracking all of this data. Furthermore, certain features are available only on certain file systems. These features include encryption support, remote file access, remote storage, disk redundancy, and disk quotas.

The Windows Server 2003 platform allows the use of multiple file systems, including the following:

- *File Allocation Table (FAT)* file system
- File Allocation Table 32 (FAT32) file system
- *Windows New Technology File System (NTFS)*
- Windows New Technology File System 5 (NTFS 5)

The fundamental difference between FAT and NTFS partitions is that NTFS allows for file system–level security. Support for FAT and FAT32 is mainly included in Windows Server 2003 for backward compatibility. Specifically, these file systems are required in order to accommodate multiple boot partitions. For example, if you wanted to configure a single computer to boot into Windows 98 and Windows Server 2003, you would need to have at least one FAT or FAT32 partition. Although this is a good solution for situations such as training labs and test environments, you should strongly consider using only NTFS partitions on production server machines.

Windows Server 2003 uses an updated version of the NTFS file system called NTFS 5. There are many other benefits to using the NTFS 5 file system, including support for the following:

Disk quotas   In order to restrict the amount of disk space used by users on the network, systems administrators can establish disk quotas. By default, Windows Server 2003 supports disk quota restrictions at the volume level. That is, you can restrict the amount of storage space a specific user uses on a single disk volume. Third-party solutions that allow more granular quota settings are also available.

File system encryption   One of the fundamental problems with network operating systems (NOSs) is that systems administrators are often given full permission to view all files and data stored on hard disks. In some cases, this is necessary. For example, in order to perform backup, recovery, and disk management functions, at least one user must have all permissions. Windows Server 2003 and NTFS 5 address these issues by allowing for file system encryption. Encryption essentially scrambles all of the data stored within files before they are written to the disk. When an authorized user requests the files, they are transparently decrypted and provided. By using encryption, you can prevent the data from being used in the case where it is stolen or intercepted by an unauthorized user.

Dynamic volumes   Protecting against disk failures is an important concern for production servers. Although earlier versions of Windows NT supported various levels of Redundant Array of Independent Disks (RAID) technology, there were shortcomings with software-based solutions. Perhaps the most significant was that administrators needed to perform server reboots to change RAID configurations. Also, you could not make some configuration changes without completely reinstalling the operating system. With the support for dynamic volumes in Windows Server 2003, systems administrators can change RAID and other disk configuration settings without needing to reboot or reinstall the server. The end result is greater data protection, increased scalability, and increased uptime.

Mounted drives   By using mounted drives, systems administrators can map a local disk drive to an NTFS 5 directory name. This helps them organize disk space on servers and increase manageability. By using mounted drives, you could mount the C:\Users directory to an actual physical disk. If that disk became full, you could copy all of the files to another, larger drive without changing the directory path name or reconfiguring applications.

Remote storage   Systems administrators often notice that as soon as they add more space, they must plan the next upgrade. One way to recover disk space is to move infrequently used files to tape. However, backing up and restoring these files could be quite difficult and time consuming. Systems administrators can use the Remote Storage features supported by NTFS 5 to automatically off-load seldom-used data to tape or other devices, but the files remain available to users because they haven't been removed from the machine. If a user requests an archived file, Windows Server 2003 can automatically restore the file from a remote storage device and make it available. Using remote storage like this frees up systems administrators' time and allows them to focus on other tasks.

Although these reasons probably compel most systems administrators to use the NTFS 5 file system, there are more reasons that make using it mandatory. The most important reason is that the Active Directory data store must reside on an NTFS 5 partition. Therefore, before you begin installing Active Directory, make sure that you have at least one NTFS partition available. Also, be sure you have a reasonable amount of disk space available (at least 1GB). Because the size of the Active Directory data store will grow as you add objects to it, be sure you have adequate space for the future.

Exercise 2.1 shows you how to use the administrative tools to view and modify disk configuration.

WARNING   Before you make any disk configuration changes, be sure you completely understand their potential effects; then, perform the test in a lab environment and make sure you have good, verifiable backups handy. Changing partition sizes and adding and removing partitions can result in a total loss of all information on one or more partitions.

If you want to convert an existing partition from FAT or FAT32 to NTFS, you'll need to use the CONVERT command-line utility. For example, the following command converts the C: partition from FAT to NTFS:

```
CONVERT c: /fs:ntfs
```

EXERCISE 2.1

Viewing Disk Configuration

1. Open the Computer Management icon in the Administrative Tools program group.

2. Under the Storage branch, click Disk Management.

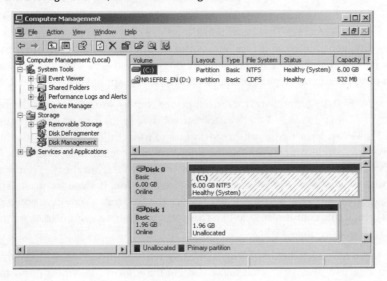

3. The Disk Management program shows you the logical and physical disks that are currently configured on your system. Note that information about the size of each partition is also displayed. By using the View menu, you can choose various depictions of the physical and logical drives in your system.

4. To modify partition settings, right-click any of the disks or partitions and choose from the available options. This step is optional.

WARNING
Windows Server 2003 allows you to convert existing FAT or FAT32 partitions to NTFS. However, this is a one-way process. You cannot convert an NTFS partition to any other file system without losing data. If this conversion is required, the recommended process involves backing up all existing data, deleting and reformatting the partition, and then restoring the data.

If the partition you are trying to convert contains any system files or the Windows Server 2003 virtual memory page file, a command-line message will inform you that the conversion will take place during the next reboot of the machine. After the partition is converted to NTFS, the computer will automatically reboot again, and you will be able to continue using the system.

Only the Windows NT, Windows 2000, Windows XP, and Windows Server 2003 operating systems (all based on the original NT architecture) can read and write to and from NTFS partitions. Therefore, if you are using other operating systems on the same computer, be sure you fully understand the effects of converting the file system.

Verifying Network Connectivity

Although a Windows Server 2003 computer can exist on a network by itself (or without a network card at all), you will not harness much of the potential of the operating system without network connectivity. Because the fundamental purpose of a network operating system is to provide resources to users, you must verify network connectivity.

Before you begin to install Active Directory, you should perform several checks of your current configuration to ensure that the server is configured properly on the network. You should test the following:

Network adapter   At least one network adapter should be installed and properly configured on your server. A quick way to verify that a network adapter is properly installed is to use the Computer Management administrative tool. Under the Network Adapters branch, you should have at least one network adapter listed. If you do not, use the Add/Remove Hardware icon in the Control Panel to configure hardware.

TCP/IP   Make sure TCP/IP is installed, configured, and enabled on any necessary network adapters. The server should also be given a valid IP address and subnet mask. Optionally, you may need to configure a default gateway, DNS servers, WINS servers, and other network settings. If you are using DHCP, be sure that the assigned information is correct. It is always a good idea to use a static IP address for servers because IP address changes can cause network connectivity problems if they are not handled properly.

Understanding TCP/IP is essential to the use of Windows Server 2003 and Active Directory. See *MCSA/MCSE: Windows Server 2003 Network Infrastructure Implementation, Management, and Maintenance Study Guide (70-291), Second Edition* (Sybex, 2006) to learn more about TCP/IP.

Internet access   If the server should have access to the Internet, verify that it is able to connect to external web servers and other machines outside the LAN. If the server is unable to connect, you might have a problem with the TCP/IP configuration.

LAN access   The server should be able to view other servers and workstations on the network. You can quickly verify this type of connectivity by using the My Network Places icon on the Desktop. If other machines are not visible, ensure that the network and TCP/IP configuration is correct for your environment.

Client access   Network client computers should be able to connect to your server and view any shared resources. A simple way to test connectivity is to create a share and test to see if other machines are able to see files and folders within it. If clients cannot access the machine, ensure that both the client and server are configured properly.

WAN access   If you're working in a distributed environment, you should ensure that you have access to any remote sites or users that will need to connect to this machine. Usually, this is a simple test that can be performed by a network administrator.

In some cases, verifying network access can be quite simple. You might have some internal and external network resources with which to test. In other cases, it might be more complicated. There are several tools and techniques you can use to verify that your network configuration is correct:

Using the ipconfig utility   By typing `ipconfig/all` at the command prompt, you can view information about the TCP/IP settings of a computer. Figure 2.17 shows the types of information you'll receive.

FIGURE 2.17   Viewing TCP/IP information with the ipconfig utility

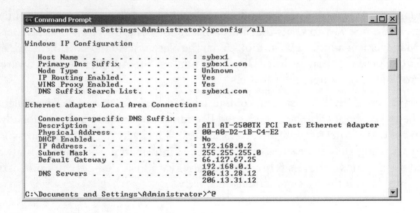

Using the ping command   The `ping` command was designed to test connectivity to other computers. You can use `ping` by simply typing **ping** and then an IP address or host name at the command line. The following are some steps for testing connectivity using the `ping` command.

Ping other computers on the same subnet.   You should start by pinging a known active IP address on the network to check for a response. If you receive one, then you have connectivity to the network. Next, check to see if you can ping another machine using its host name. If this works, then local name resolution works properly.

Ping other computers on different subnets.   In order to ensure that routing is set up properly, you should attempt to ping computers that are local on other subnets (if any exist) on your network. If this test fails, try pinging the default gateway. Any errors may indicate a problem in the network configuration or a problem with a router.

Some firewalls, routers, or servers on your network or on the Internet might prevent you from receiving a successful response from a `ping` command. This is usually for security reasons because malicious users might attempt to disrupt network traffic using excessive `ping`s as well as redirects and smurf attacks. Just because you do not receive a response, do not assume that the service is not available. Instead, try to verify connectivity in other ways. For example TRACERT can be used to demonstrate connectivity beyond your subnet even if other routers ignore ICMP responses. Since the display of a second router implies connectivity, the path to an ultimate destination shows success even if it does not display the actual names and addresses.

Browsing the network   To ensure that you have access to other computers on the network, be sure that they can be viewed using the Network Neighborhood icon. This verifies that your name resolution parameters are set up correctly and that other computers are accessible. Also, try connecting to resources (such as file shares or printers) on other machines. Because Master Brower issues are common and the Network Neighborhood is known to be unreliable based on how the browsing system works, its recommended that you use the Search feature and look for the computer by IP address or name in the directory.

Browsing the Internet   You can quickly verify whether your server has access to the Internet by visiting a known website, such as www.microsoft.com. This ensures that you have access outside of your network. If you do not have access to the Web, you might need to verify your proxy server settings (if applicable) and your DNS server settings.

By performing these simple tests, you can ensure that you have a properly configured network connection and that other network resources are available.

Determining the Domain Functional Level

Windows Server 2003 Active Directory introduces a new concept called domain and forest functionality. This is similar to the idea of mixed mode and native mode in Windows 2000 Active Directory, so much so that those two modes are actually included as a part of domain and forest functionality. However, Microsoft refers to these modes as *functional levels*, and adds a third functional level appropriately called *Windows Server 2003 functional level*. When you are installing a Windows Server 2003 domain controller, you must determine which functional level you will support: Windows 2000 Mixed, Windows 2000 Native, or Windows Server 2003.

Windows 2000 Mixed domain functional level is the default option when you are installing a domain controller. It is designed to allow backward compatibility with Windows NT 4 and earlier domain models. If you need to support Windows NT domain controllers for one or more domains within your environment, you should choose Windows 2000 Mixed domain functional level for those domains. However, as long as you are using Windows 2000 Mixed domain functional level, certain Active Directory features (such as universal groups and group nesting) are unavailable.

If your environment does not require support for Windows NT domain controllers within any of your domains but does require support for Windows 2000 domain controllers, then you can choose to implement your domains in Windows 2000 Native domain functional level. Windows 2000 Native domain functional level allows for most of the functionality of Active Directory for all domain controllers, but it does not allow for backward compatibility with Windows NT 4. Since this means that Windows NT domain controllers cannot be used in Windows 2000 Native domain functional level Active Directory domains, deciding whether or not to use Windows 2000 Native domain functional level is an important decision. Note also that domains cannot be converted from Windows 2000 Native domain functional level back to Windows 2000 Mixed domain functional level. Windows 2000 Native domain functional level does not offer the full functionality of Active Directory supported by Windows Server 2003, so you should consider upgrading all of your domain controllers if you want to use any of the new features of Active Directory.

If you know that you will only be running Windows Server 2003 domain controllers, you can install Active Directory in the Windows Server 2003 domain functional level. This level adds all of the functionality of Active Directory in Windows Server 2003, as shown in Table 2.3.

TABLE 2.3   Comparing Domain Functional Levels

Domain Functional Feature	Windows 2000 Mixed	Windows 2000 Native	Windows Server 2003
Ability to rename domain controllers.	Disabled	Disabled	Enabled
Logon Time stamp updates.	Disabled	Disabled	Enabled
Kerberos KDC key version numbers.	Disabled	Disabled	Enabled
InetOrgPerson objects can have passwords.	Disabled	Disabled	Enabled
Converts NT groups to domain local and global groups.	Disabled	Enabled	Enabled
SID history.	Disabled	Enabled	Enabled
Group nesting.	Enabled for Distribution Groups, disabled for Security Groups(note that Domain Local Security Groups can still have Global Groups as Members)	Enabled	Enabled
Universal Groups.	Enabled for Distribution Groups, Disabled for Security Groups	Enabled	Enabled

In addition to domain functional levels, Windows Server 2003 includes added forest functionality over Windows 2000. Forest functionality applies to all of the domains in a forest. There are two levels of forest functionality: Windows 2000 and Windows Server 2003. Windows 2000 forest functionality is the default and supports Windows NT 4, Windows 2000, and Windows Server 2003 domain controllers. All of the new forest functionality features of Windows Server 2003 are supported exclusively by Windows Server 2003. The new features include these:

Global Catalog replication enhancements   When an administrator adds a new attribute to the Global Catalog, only the changes are replicated to other global catalogs in the forest. This can significantly reduce the amount of network traffic generated by replication.

Defunct schema classes and attributes   You can never permanently remove classes and attributes from the Active Directory schema, but you can mark them as defunct so that they cannot be used. When forest functionality is raised to Windows Server 2003, you can redefine the defunct schema attribute so that it occupies a new role in the schema.

Forest trusts   Previously, system administrators had no easy way of granting permission on resources in different forests. Windows Server 2003 resolves some of these difficulties by allowing trust relationships between separate Active Directory forests. Forest trusts act much like domain trusts, except that they extend to every domain in two forests. Note that all forest trusts are intransitive.

Linked value replication   Windows Server 2003 introduces a new concept called linked value replication. In Windows 2000, if changes were made to a member of a group, the entire group would be replicated during the replication process. With linked value replication, only the user record that has been changed is replicated. This can significantly reduce network traffic associated with replication.

Renaming domains   Although the Active Directory domain structure was originally designed to be flexible, there were several limitations. Due to mergers, acquisitions, corporate reorganizations, and other business changes, you may need to rename domains. You can now change the DNS and NetBIOS names for any domain, as well as reposition a domain within a forest. Note that this operation is not nearly as simple as just issuing a rename command. Instead, there's a specific process you must follow to make sure that the operation is successful. Fortunately, when you properly follow the procedure, Microsoft supports domain renaming.

Other features   In addition to the Windows Server 2003 forest functional features just listed, Windows Server 2003 also supports improved replication algorithms and dynamic auxiliary classes. These improvements are designed to increase performance, scalability, and reliability.

Newer features within Active Directory are provided via a plethora of hot fixes, and via Service Pack 1 (SP1), and R2 (also known as Release 2), which is basically a rollup of SP1 and some additional functionality.

Within Active Directory, the following features are incorporated as of R2.

Active Directory Federation Services (ADFS, aka "Trustbridge"), which is nothing more than federated identity management. Federated identity management is a standards-based technology and information technology process that enables distributed identification, authentication, and authorization across organizational and platform boundaries. The ADFS solution in Windows Server 2003 R2 helps administrators address these challenges by enabling organizations to securely share a user's identity information.

Active Directory Application Mode (ADAM) is a new R2-based feature as well. Microsoft developed ADAM with Windows Server 2003 Active Directory so organizations that require flexible support for directory-enabled applications get it with this mode. ADAM uses the Lightweight Directory Access Protocol (LDAP) and is a directory service that adds flexibility and helps organizations avoid increased infrastructure costs.

Many of the concepts related to domain and forest functional features are covered in greater detail later in this book.

Planning the Domain Structure

Once you have verified the technical configuration of your server for Active Directory, it's time to verify the Active Directory configuration for your organization. Since the content of this chapter focuses on installing the first domain in your environment, you really only need to know the following information prior to beginning setup:

- The DNS name of the domain
- The computer name or the NetBIOS name of the server (which will be used by previous versions of Windows to access server resources)
- Whether the domain will operate in mixed mode or native mode
- Whether or not other DNS servers are available on the network
- What type of DNS servers are available on the network and how many

However, if you will be installing additional domain controllers in your environment or will be attaching to an existing Active Directory structure, you should also have the following information:

- If this domain controller will join an existing domain, you should know the name of that domain. You will also either require a password for a member of the Enterprise Administrators group for that domain or have someone with those permissions create a domain account before promotion.
- Whether the new domain will join an existing tree and, if so, the name of the tree it will join.
- The name of a forest to which this domain will connect (if applicable).

For more information on planning domain structure, review the information in Chapter 1, "Overview of Active Directory." We'll cover the details of working in multidomain Active Directory environments (including the creation of new trees and participating in an existing forest) in Chapter 3, "Installing and Managing Trees and Forests."

Installing Active Directory

Installing Active Directory is an easy and straightforward process as long as you planned adequately and made the necessary decisions beforehand. In this section, you'll look at the actual steps required to install the first domain controller in a given environment.

With previous versions of the Windows Server operating system, you had to determine the role of your server as it related to the domain controller or member server during installation. Choices included making the machine a Primary Domain Controller (PDC), a Backup Domain Controller (BDC), or a member server. This was an extremely important decision because, even though you could promote a BDC to a PDC, you had to completely reinstall the operating system to make any changes to the server's role between a domain controller and a member server.

Instead of forcing you to choose whether or not the machine will participate as a domain controller during setup, Windows Server 2003 allows you to promote servers after you install Active Directory. Therefore, at the end of the setup process, all Windows Server 2003 computers are configured as either member servers (if they are joined to a domain) or standalone servers (if they are part of a workgroup). The process of converting a member server to a domain controller is known as *promotion*. Through the use of a simple and intuitive wizard, systems administrators can quickly configure servers to be domain controllers after installation.

Later in this section, you'll follow the steps you need to take to install Active Directory by promoting the first domain controller in the domain. These steps are done using Active Directory *Installation Wizard (DCPROMO)*. This tool is designed to be used after a server has been installed in the environment. As part of the promotion process, the server creates or receives information related to Active Directory configuration.

The first step in installing Active Directory is promoting a Windows Server 2003 computer to a domain controller. The first domain controller in an environment serves as the starting point for the forest, trees, domains, and the Operations Master roles.

Exercise 2.2 shows the steps you need to follow to promote an existing Windows Server 2003 to a domain controller. In order to complete the steps in this exercise, you must have already installed and configured a Windows Server 2003 computer and a DNS server that supports SRV records. If you do not have a DNS server available, the Active Directory Installation Wizard automatically configures one for you.

Installing Windows Server 2003 is covered in more detail in the *MCSA/MCSE: Windows Server 2003 Environment Management and Maintenance Study Guide (70-290), Second Edition* (Sybex, 2006). DNS is covered in more detail in the *MCSA/MCSE: Windows Server 2003 Network Infrastructure Implementation, Management, and Maintenance Study Guide (70-291)* by James Chellis, Paul Robichaux, and Matt Sheltz (Sybex, 2006).

EXERCISE 2.2

Promoting a Domain Controller

1. Open the Manage Your Server utility, which is located in the Administrative Tools program group.

2. Click Add Or Remove A Role and then click Next to begin the process. For the server role, select Domain Controller (Active Directory) and then click Next. Finally, click Next once more to start the Active Directory Installation Wizard. Alternatively, you can start the Active Directory Installation Wizard by clicking Start ➢ Run and typing **dcpromo**.

3. Click Next on the Welcome To The Active Directory Installation Wizard page of the wizard to begin the domain controller promotion process. The Operating System Compatibility page of the wizard provides you with an important note about operating system compatibility. Click Next to continue.

4. On the Domain Controller Type page, specify the type of domain controller this server will be. To choose the domain controller type, select Domain Controller For A New Domain and click Next.

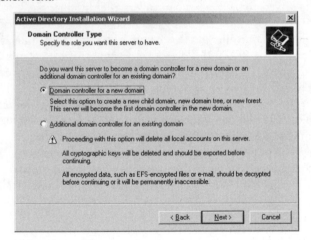

EXERCISE 2.2

5. On the Create New Domain page, choose whether the new domain tree is part of an existing forest or a new one that you create. Since this is the first tree in the forest, select Domain In A New Forest and click Next.

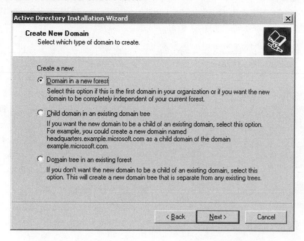

6. On the New Domain page, specify a name for the new domain by typing in the full name of the DNS domain. For example, you can type **test.mycompany.com**. If you are not working in a test environment, be sure that you have chosen a root domain name that is consistent for your organization, and doesn't overlap with others. For example, you might choose ActiveDirectory.test, since it is unlikely to conflict with other existing domains and DNS namespaces. Once you've selected a name, click Next.

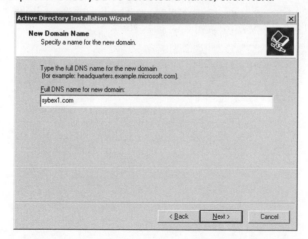

7. On the NetBIOS Domain Name page, type in the NetBIOS name for this machine and click Next. In order to preserve backward compatibility with earlier versions of Windows, you must provide a NetBIOS computer name. A NetBIOS name can be up to 15 characters. To make it easier to remember and type the name, you should limit yourself to the English alphabet characters and Arabic numbers.

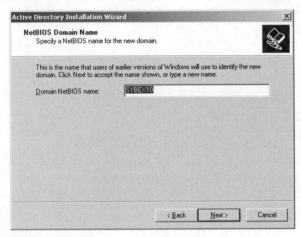

8. In the Database And Log Folders page, specify the file system locations for the Active Directory database and log file. Microsoft recommends that these files reside on separate physical devices in order to improve performance and to provide for recoverability. The default file system location is in a directory called NTDS located within the system root. However, you can choose any folder located on a FAT, FAT32, or NTFS partition. After you've specified the file system locations, click Next.

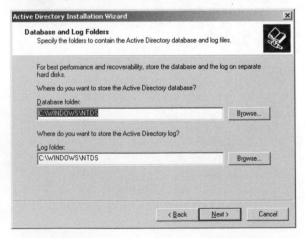

EXERCISE 2.2

9. On the Shared System Volume page, select a shared system volume location. The system volume folder is used to store domain information that is replicated to all of the other domain controllers in the domain. This folder must be stored on an NTFS 5 partition. The default location is in a directory called SYSVOL within the system root, but you can change this path based on your server configuration. Click Next.

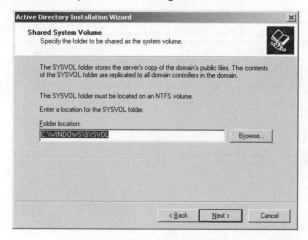

10. As part of the promotion process, Windows Server 2003 needs you to set permissions on user and group objects, which is done on the Permissions page. If you're running in a Windows 2000 Mixed domain functional level environment, choose Permissions Compatible With Pre-Windows 2000 Servers. If you are sure you will not be supporting non-Windows 2000 or newer machines, however, you should choose Permissions Compatible Only With Windows 2000 Or Windows Server 2003 Operating Systems. Although this option will not allow compatibility with previous operating systems, it will implement stronger security settings. Once you have made the appropriate selection, click Next.

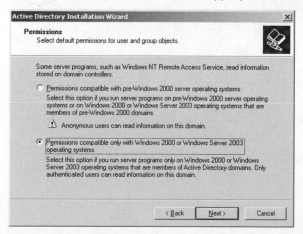

EXERCISE 2.2

11. On the Directory Services Restore Mode Administrator Password page, provide a Directory Services Restore Mode Administrator password. This password is used to restore Active Directory in the event of its loss or corruption. Note that this password does not have to correspond with passwords set for any other account. Once you've selected and confirmed the password, click Next.

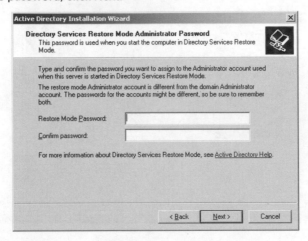

12. Based on the installation options you've selected, the Active Directory Installation Wizard presents a summary of your choices. It is a good idea to copy and paste this information into a text file to refer to later. Verify the options, and then click Next to begin the Active Directory installation process. When the necessary operations are complete, the wizard prompts you to click Finish.

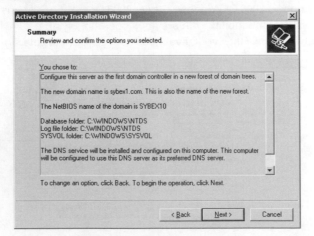

Once Active Directory has been installed, you are prompted to reboot the system. After the reboot, you can access the administrative tools that are related to the configuration and management of Active Directory.

Verifying Active Directory Installation

Once you have installed and configured Active Directory, you'll want to verify that you have done so properly. In the following sections, you'll look at methods for doing this.

Using Event Viewer

The first (and perhaps most informative) way to verify the operations of Active Directory is to query information stored in the Windows Server 2003 event log. You can do this using the Windows Server 2003 Event Viewer. Exercise 2.3 walks you through this procedure. Entries seen with the Event Viewer include errors, warnings, and informational messages. In order to complete the steps in this exercise, you must configure the local machine as a domain controller.

EXERCISE 2.3

Viewing the Active Directory Event Log

1. Open the Event Viewer snap-in from the Administrative Tools program group.

2. In the left pane, select Directory Service.

3. In the right pane, notice that you can sort information by clicking column headings. For example, you can click the Source column to sort by the service or process that reported the event.

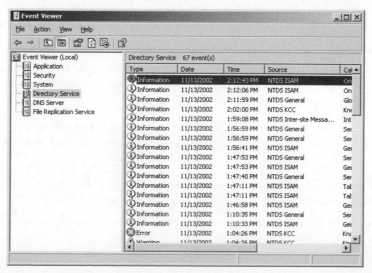

EXERCISE 2.3

4. Double-click an event in the list to see the details for that item. Note that you can click the Copy button to copy the event information to the Clipboard. You can then paste the data into a document for later reference. Also, you can move between items using the up and down arrows. Click OK when you are done viewing an event.

5. Filter an event list by right-clicking the Directory Service item in the left pane, selecting Properties, and then selecting the Filter tab. Note that filtering does not remove entries from the event logs—it only restricts their display.

6. To verify Active Directory installation, look for events related to the proper startup of Active Directory, such as Event ID 1000 (Active Directory Startup Complete) and 1394 (Attempts To Update The Active Directory Database Are Succeeding). Also, be sure to examine any Error or Warning messages because these could indicate problems with DNS or other necessary services.

7. When you're done viewing information in the Event Viewer, close the application.

 Real World Scenario

Gaining Insight through Event Viewer

Although its simple user interface and somewhat limited GUI functionality may make you overlook it, in the real world, the Event Viewer tool can be your best ally in isolating and troubleshooting problems with Windows Server 2003. The Event Viewer allows you to view information that is stored in various log files that are maintained by the operating system. This list of logs includes the following:

Application   Stores messages that are generated by programs that are running on your system. For example, SQL Server 2000 might report the completion of a database backup job within the Application log.

Security   Contains security-related information, as is defined by your auditing settings. For example, you could see when users have logged onto the system or when particularly sensitive files have been accessed.

System   Contains operating system–related information and messages. Common messages might include a service startup failure, or information about when the operating system was last rebooted.

Directory service   Stores messages and events related to how Active Directory functions. For example, details related to replication might be found here.

DNS server   Contains details about the operations of the DNS service. This log is useful for troubleshooting replication or name resolution problems.

Other log files   Contain various features of Windows Server 2003 and the applications that may run on this operating system that can create additional types of logs. This allows you to view more information about other applications or services through the familiar Event Viewer tool.

Additionally, developers can easily send custom information from their programs to the Application log. Having all of this information in one place really makes it easy to analyze operating system and application messages. Also, many third-party tools and utilities are available for analyzing log files.

Although the Event Viewer GUI does a reasonably good job of letting you find the information you need, you might want to extract information to analyze other systems or applications. One especially useful feature of the Event Viewer is its ability to save the log file in various formats. You can access this feature by clicking Action ➤ Save As. You'll be given the option of saving in various formats, including tab- and comma-delimited text files. These files can then be opened in other applications (such as Microsoft Excel) for additional data analysis.

Overall, in the real world, the Event Viewer can be an excellent resource for monitoring and troubleshooting your important servers and workstations!

In addition to providing information about the status of events related to Active Directory, you should make it a habit to routinely visit the Event Viewer to find information about other system services and applications.

Using Active Directory Administrative Tools

After a server has been promoted to a domain controller, you will see various tools added to the Administrative Tools program group (see Figure 2.18). These include the following:

Active Directory Domains and Trusts   You use this tool to view and change information related to the various domains in an Active Directory environment. This tool is covered in more detail in Chapter 3, "Installing and Managing Trees and Forests."

Active Directory Sites and Services   You use this tool to create and manage Active Directory sites and services to map to an organization's physical network infrastructure. Sites and services are covered in detail in Chapter 4, "Configuring Sites and Managing Replication."

Active Directory Users and Computers   User and computer management is fundamental for an Active Directory environment. The Active Directory Users and Computers tool allows you to set machine- and user-specific settings across the domain. This tool appears throughout many chapters in this book.

FIGURE 2.18 Some of the many Windows Server 2003 administrative tools

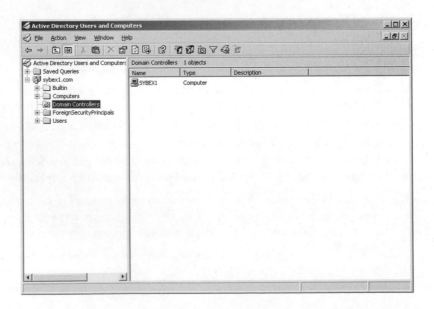

A good way make sure that Active Directory is functioning properly and is accessible is to run the Active Directory Users And Computers tool. When you open the tool, you should see a configuration similar to that shown in Figure 2.19. Specifically, you should make sure that the name of the domain you created appears in the list. You should also click the Domain Controllers folder and ensure that the name of your local server appears in the right pane. If your configuration passes these two checks, Active Directory is present and configured.

FIGURE 2.19 Viewing Active Directory information

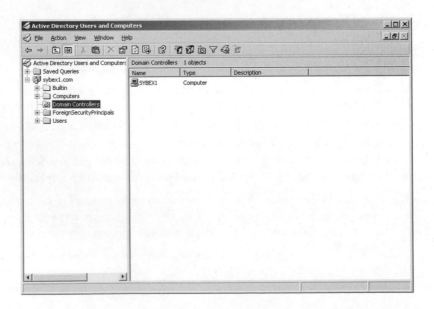

Testing from Clients

The best test of any solution is to simply verify that it works the way you had intended in your environment. When it comes to using Active Directory, a good test is to ensure that clients can view and access the various resources presented by Windows Server 2003 domain controllers. In the following sections, you'll look at several ways to verify that Active Directory is functioning properly.

Verifying Client Connectivity

Perhaps the most relevant way to test Active Directory is by testing client operations. Using previous versions of Windows (such as Windows NT 4 or Windows 95/98), you should be able to see your server on the network. Earlier versions of Windows-based clients recognize the NetBIOS name of the domain controller. Windows 2000 and newer computers should also be able to see resources in the domain, and users can browse for resources using the My Network Places icon.

If you are unable to see the recently promoted server on the network, it is likely due to a network configuration error. If only one or a few clients are unable to see the machine, the problem is probably related to client-side configuration. To fix this, make sure the client computers have the appropriate TCP/IP configuration (including DNS server settings) and that they can see other computers on the network.

If, however, the new domain controller is unavailable from any of the other client computers, you should verify the proper startup of Active Directory using the methods mentioned earlier in this chapter. If Active Directory has been started, ensure that the DNS settings are correct. Finally, test network connectivity between the server and the clients by accessing the My Network Places icon.

For more information on configuring client computers, see the *MCSA/MCSE: Windows XP Professional Study Guide, Third Edition* by Lisa Donald with James Chellis (Sybex, 2005).

Joining a Domain

If Active Directory has been properly configured, clients and other servers should be able to join the domain. Exercise 2.4 outlines the steps you need to take to join a Windows XP Professional computer to the domain. In order to complete this exercise, you must have already installed and properly configured at least one Active Directory domain controller and a DNS server that supports SRV records in your environment. In addition to the domain controller, you need at least one other Windows 2000, Windows XP Professional (Windows XP Home Edition cannot join a domain), or Windows Server 2003 computer that is not configured as a domain controller.

Once clients are able to successfully join the domain, they should be able to view Active Directory resources using the My Network Places icon. This test validates the proper functioning of Active Directory and ensures that you have connectivity with client computers.

EXERCISE 2.4

Joining a Computer to an Active Directory Domain

1. On the Desktop of the computer that is to be joined to the new domain, right-click the My Computer icon and click Properties (or, select System from the Control Panel).

2. Select the Network Identification tab. You will see the current name of the local computer as well as information on the workgroup or domain to which it belongs.

3. Click Change to change the settings for this computer.

4. If you want to change the name of the computer, you can make the change here. This is useful if your domain has a specific naming convention for client computers. Otherwise, continue to the next step.

5. In the Member Of section, choose the Domain option. Type the name of the Active Directory domain that this computer should join. Click OK.

6. When prompted for the username and password of an account that has permissions to join computers to the domain, enter the information for an administrator of the domain. Click OK to commit the changes. If joining the domain was successful, you will see a dialog box welcoming you to the new domain.

7. You will be notified that you must reboot the computer before the changes take place. Select Yes when prompted to reboot.

Creating and Configuring Application Data Partitions

Organizations store many different kinds of information in various places. For the IT departments that support this information, it can be difficult to ensure that the right information is available when and where it is needed. Windows Server 2003 introduces a new feature, called application data partitions, that allows systems administrators and application developers to store custom information within Active Directory. The idea behind *application data partitions* is that, since you already have a directory service that can replicate all kinds of information, you might as well use it to keep track of your own information.

Developing distributed applications that can, for example, synchronize information across an enterprise is not a trivial task. You have to come up with a way to transfer data between remote sites (some of which are located across the world), and you have to ensure that the data is properly replicated. The main benefit of storing application information in Active Directory is that you can take advantage of its storage mechanism and replication topology. Application-related information stored on domain controllers benefits from having fault-tolerance features and availability.

Take a look at the following simple example to understand how this can work. Suppose your organization has developed a customer Sales Tracking and Inventory application. The company needs to make the information that is stored by this application available to all of its branch offices and users located throughout the world. However, the goal is to do this with the least amount of IT administrative effort. Assuming that Active Directory has already been deployed throughout the organization, developers can build support into the application for storing data within Active Directory. They can then rely on Active Directory to store and synchronize the information between various sites. When users request updated data from the application, the application can obtain this information from the nearest domain controller that hosts a replica of the Sales Tracking and Inventory data.

Other types of applications can also benefit greatly from the use of application data partitions. Now that we have a good idea of what application data partitions are, let's take a look at how they can be created and managed using Windows Server 2003 and Active Directory.

Creating Application Data Partitions

By default, after creating an Active Directory environment, you will not have any customer application data partitions. Therefore, the first step in making this functionality available is to create a new application data partition. There are several tools you can used to do this:

Third-party applications or application-specific tools   Generally, if you are planning to install an application that can store information in the Active Directory database, you'll receive some method of administering and configuring that data along with the application. For example, the set up process for the application might assist you in the steps you need to take to set up a new application data partition and to create the necessary structures for storing data.

 The creation and management of application data partitions is an advanced Active Directory-related function. Be sure that you have a solid understanding of the Active Directory schema, Active Directory replication, LDAP, and your applications' needs before you attempt to create new application data partitions in a live environment.

Active Directory Services Interface (ADSI)   ADSI is a set of programmable objects that can be accessed through languages such as Visual Basic Scripting Edition (VBScript), Visual C#, Visual Basic .NET, and many other language technologies that support the Component Object Modeling (COM) standard. Through the use of ADSI, developers can create, access, and update data stored in Active Directory and in any application data partitions.

LDP   You can view and modify the contents of the Active Directory schema using LDAP-based queries. The LDP tool allows you to view information about application data partitions. In order to use this utility, you must first install the Windows Server 2003 Support Tools. The installer for this collection of utilities is located within the Windows Server 2003 installation media in the \Support\Tools folder. You'll need to run the SupTools.msi file in order to install the tools. Once the installation is complete, you can access the utility by clicking Start ➢ Run and typing **ldp.exe**. Figure 2.20 shows an example of connecting to a domain controller and browsing Active Directory information. For further details on using LDP, click the Support Tools Help icon (located within the Windows Support Tools program folder in the Start Menu). Additional details about working with the LDP tool are also available in the LDP.doc file, which is located within the folder into which you installed the Support Tools.

FIGURE 2.20 Using the LDP tool to view Active Directory schema information

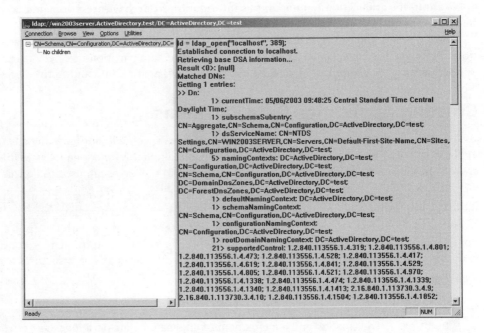

ntdsutil The ntdsutil utility is the main method by which systems administrators can create and manage application data partitions on their Windows Server 2003 domain controllers. This utility's specific commands are covered later in this section.

 The creation and management of application data partitions can be fairly complex, and the success of such a project will depend on the quality of the architecture design. This is a good example of where IT staff and application developers must cooperate to ensure that data is stored effectively and that it is replicated efficiently.

An application data partition can be created in one of three different locations within an Active Directory forest:

As a new tree in an Active Directory forest In this location, the new application data partition functions as a new tree within the Active Directory forest.

As a child of an Active Directory domain partition   Application partitions can be children of existing Active Directory domain partitions. For example, you can create an Accounting application data partition within the `Finance.MyCompany.com` domain.

As a child of another application data partition   This method allows you to create a hierarchy of application data partitions.

As you might expect, you must be a member of the Enterprise Admins or Domain Admins group in order to be able to create application data partitions. Alternatively, you can be delegated the appropriate permissions to create new partitions.

Now that we have a good idea of the basic ways in which application data partitions can be created, let's look at how replicas (copies of application data partition information) are handled.

Managing Replicas

Unlike the basic information that is stored in Active Directory, application partitions cannot contain security principals. Also, not all domain controllers automatically contain copies of the data stored in an application data partition. A replica is a copy of any data stored within Active Directory. In relation to application data, systems administrators can define which domain controllers host copies of the application data. This is a very important feature, since, if it's used effectively, administrators can find a good balance between replication traffic and data consistency. For example, suppose that 3 of your organization's 30 locations require up-to-date accounting-related information. You might choose to only replicate the data to domain controllers located in the places that require the data.

Replication is the process by which replicas are kept up to date. Similarly to how basic Active Directory information (such as users and groups) is synchronized between domain controllers, application data can be stored and updated on designated servers. Application data partition replicas are managed using the Knowledge Consistency Checker (KCC) that ensures that the designated domain controllers receive update replica information. Additionally, the KCC uses all of Active Directory sites and connection objects (covered in Chapter 4) that you create to determine the best method to handle replication.

Removing Replicas

When you demote a domain controller, that server can no longer host an application data partition. If a domain controller contains a replica of application data partition information, you must first remove the replica from the domain controller before it can be demoted. If a domain controller is the machine that hosts a replica of the application data partition, then the entire application data partition is removed and will be permanently lost. Generally, you want to do this only after you're absolutely sure that your organization no longer needs access to the data stored in the application data partition.

Using ntdsutil to Manage Application Data Partitions

The primary method by which systems administrators create and manage application data partitions is through the ntdsutil command-line tool. You can launch this tool by simply entering **ntdsutil** at a command prompt. The ntdsutil command is both interactive and context-sensitive. That is, once you launch the utility, you'll see an ntdsutil command prompt. At this prompt, you can enter various commands that set your context within the application. For example, if you enter the domain management command, you'll be able to enter in domain-related commands. Several operations also require you to connect to a domain, a domain controller, or an Active Directory object before you perform a command.

 For complete details on using ntdsutil see the Windows Server 2003 Help and Support Center.

Table 2.4 provides a list of the domain management commands supported by the ntdsutil tool. You can access this information by typing the following sequence of commands at a command prompt.

- ntdsutil
- domain management
- help

TABLE 2.4   ntdsutil Domain Management Commands

ntdsutil Domain Management Command	Purpose
Help or ?	Displays information about the commands that are available within the Domain Management menu of the ntdsutil command.
Connection or Connections	Allows you to connect to a specific domain controller. This will set the context for further operations that are performed on specific domain controllers.
Create NC *PartitionDistinguishedName DNSName*	Creates a new application directory partition.
Delete NC *PartitionDistinguishedName*	Removes an application data partition.
List NC Information *PartitionDistinguishedName*	Shows information about the specified application data partition.

TABLE 2.4   ntdsutil Domain Management Commands *(continued)*

ntdsutil Domain Management Command	Purpose
List NC Replicas *PartitionDistinguishedName*	Returns information about all replicas for the specific application data partition.
Precreate *PartitionDistinguishedName ServerDNSName*	Precreates cross-reference application data partition objects. This allows the specified DNS server to host a copy of the application data partition.
Remove NC Replica *PartitionDistinguishedName DCDNSName*	Removes a replica from the specified domain controller.
Select Operation Target	Selects the naming context that will be used for other operations.
Set NC Reference Domain *PartitionDistinguisedName DomainDistinguishedName*	Specifies the reference domain for an application data partition.
Set NC Replicate NotificationDelay *PartitionDistinguishedName FirstDCNotificationDelay OtherDCNotificationDelay*	Defines settings for how often replication will occur for the specified application data partition.

The commands listed in this table are all case-insensitive. Mixed-case was used to make them easier to read. Also, if you're wondering what the NC stands for, it's "naming context" (referring to the fact that this is a partition of the Active Directory schema).

Instead of focusing on those details of specific commands and syntax related to ntdsutil, be sure that you really understand application directory partitions and how they and their replicas can be used.

Figure 2.21 provides an example of working with ntdsutil. The following commands were entered to set the context for further operations:

- ntdsutil
- domain management
- connections

- `connect to server localhost`
- `connect to domain ADTest`
- `quit`
- `list`

FIGURE 2.21   Viewing naming contexts on the local domain controller

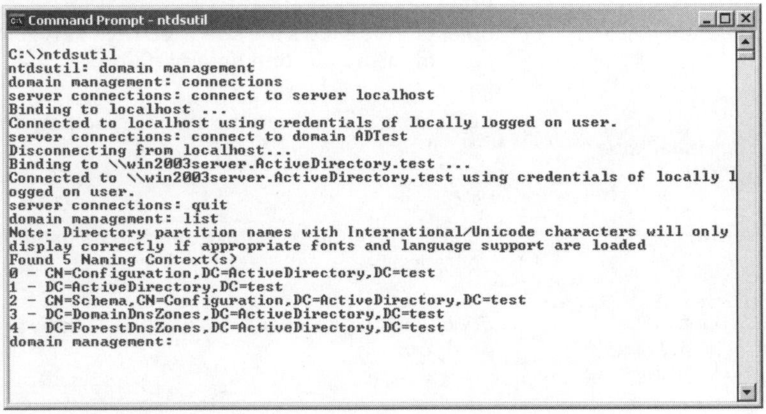

```
Command Prompt - ntdsutil                                              _|□|×|
C:\>ntdsutil
ntdsutil: domain management
domain management: connections
server connections: connect to server localhost
Binding to localhost ...
Connected to localhost using credentials of locally logged on user.
server connections: connect to domain ADTest
Disconnecting from localhost...
Binding to \\win2003server.ActiveDirectory.test ...
Connected to \\win2003server.ActiveDirectory.test using credentials of locally l
ogged on user.
server connections: quit
domain management: list
Note: Directory partition names with International/Unicode characters will only
display correctly if appropriate fonts and language support are loaded
Found 5 Naming Context(s)
0 - CN=Configuration,DC=ActiveDirectory,DC=test
1 - DC=ActiveDirectory,DC=test
2 - CN=Schema,CN=Configuration,DC=ActiveDirectory,DC=test
3 - DC=DomainDnsZones,DC=ActiveDirectory,DC=test
4 - DC=ForestDnsZones,DC=ActiveDirectory,DC=test
domain management:
```

Configuring DNS Integration with Active Directory

There are many benefits to integrating Active Directory and DNS services. First, you can configure and manage replication along with other Active Directory components. Second, you can automate much of the maintenance of DNS resource records through the use of dynamic updates. Additionally, you will be able to set specific security options on the various properties of the DNS service. Exercise 2.5 shows the steps that you can take to ensure that these integration features are enabled. Before you begin this exercise, make sure that the local machine is configured as an Active Directory domain controller and that DNS services have been properly configured. In this exercise, you'll look at the various DNS functions that are specific to interoperability with Active Directory.

If you instructed the Active Directory Installation Wizard to automatically configure DNS, many of the settings mentioned in this section may already be enabled. However, you should verify the configuration and be familiar with how the options can be set manually.

EXERCISE 2.5

Configuring DNS Integration with Active Directory

1. Open the DNS snap-in from the Administrative Tools program group.

2. Right-click the icon for the local DNS Server, and select Properties. Click the Security tab. Notice that you can now specify which users and groups have access to modify the configuration of the DNS server. Make any necessary changes, and click OK.

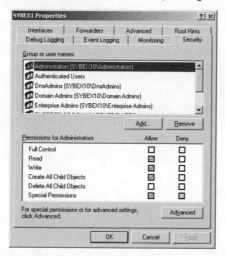

3. Expand the local server branch and the Forward Lookup Zones folder.

4. Right-click the name of the Active Directory domain you created, and select Properties.

5. On the General tab, verify that the type is Active Directory-Integrated and that the Data Is Stored In Active Directory message is displayed. If this option is not currently selected, you can change it by clicking the Change button next to Type.

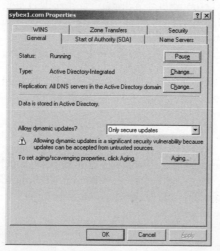

6. Verify that the Allow Dynamic Updates? option is set to Only Secure Updates. This ensures that all updates to the DNS resource records database are made through authenticated Active Directory accounts and processes. The other options are Yes (to allow both secure and nonsecure dynamic updates) and No (to disallow dynamic updates).

7. Finally, notice that you can define the security permissions at the zone level by clicking the Security tab. Make any necessary changes, and click OK.

Summary

In this chapter, we covered the basics for implementing an Active Directory forest and domain structure, creating and configuring application data partitions, and setting the functional level of your domain and forest.

You are now familiar with how Active Directory can be implemented. We carefully examined all the necessary steps and conditions you need to follow to install Active Directory on your network. First, you need to prepare for the Domain Name System (DNS) since Active Directory cannot be installed without the support of a DNS server. You also need to verify that the computer you upgrade to a domain controller (DC) meets some basic file system and network connectivity requirements so that Active Directory can run smoothly and efficiently in your organization. These are some of the most common things you will have to do when you deploy Active Directory.

We also covered the concept of domain functional levels, which essentially determine the kinds of domain controllers you can use in your environment. For instance, in the Windows 2000 Mixed domain functional level, you can include Server 2003, 2000 Server, and NT 4 Server domain controllers, but the functionality of the domain is severely limited.

In this chapter we also learned to install Active Directory, which you accomplish by promoting a Windows Server 2003 computer to a domain controller using DCPROMO. You also learned how to verify the installation by testing Active Directory from a client computer.

This chapter was limited in scope to examining the issues related to installing and configuring the first domain in an Active Directory environment. In later chapters, you'll see how to create and manage more complex configurations.

Exam Essentials

Know the prerequisites for promoting a server to a domain controller. You should understand the tasks that you must complete before you attempt to upgrade a server to a domain controller. Also, you should have a good idea of the information you need in order to complete the domain controller promotion process.

Understand the steps of the Active Directory Installation Wizard.   When you run the Active Directory Installation Wizard, you'll be presented with many different choices. You should understand the effects of the various options provided in each step of the wizard.

Be familiar with the tools that you will use to administer Active Directory.   There are three main administrative tools that are installed when you promote a Windows Server 2003 to a domain controller. Be sure you know which tools to use for which types of tasks.

Understand the purpose of application data partitions.   The idea behind application data partitions is that, since you already have a directory service that can replicate all kinds of security information, you can also use it to keep track of application data. The main benefit of storing application information in Active Directory is that you can take advantage of its storage mechanism and replication topology. Application-related information stored on domain controllers benefits from having fault-tolerance features and availability.

Review Questions

1. A system administrator is trying to determine which file system to use for a server that will become an Active Directory domain controller. Her company's requirements include the following:

   - The file system must allow for file-level security.
   - The file system must make efficient use of space on large partitions.
   - The file system must allow for auditing of logons and access to sensitive files.

   Which of the following file systems meets these requirements?

   A. FAT

   B. FAT32

   C. HPFS

   D. NTFS

2. What is the maximum number of domains that a Windows 2003 Server computer, configured as a domain controller, may participate in at one time?

   A. 0

   B. 1

   C. 2

   D. Any number of domains

3. In order to support Windows NT backup domain controllers in an Active Directory domain, which of the following modes must be used?

   A. Native mode

   B. Mixed mode

   C. Low-security mode

   D. Backward-compatibility mode

4. The process of converting a Windows Server 2003 computer to a domain controller is known as

   A. Advertising

   B. Reinstallation

   C. Promotion

   D. Conversion

5. DNS server services can be configured using which of the following tools?

   A. The DNS administrative tool

   B. Computer Management

   C. Network Properties

   D. Active Directory Users And Computers

6. You are the systems administrator for the XYZ Products, Inc. Windows Server 2003–based network. You are upgrading a Windows Server 2003 computer to an Active Directory domain controller and need to decide the initial domain name. Your business has the following requirements:

- The domain name must be accessible from the Internet.

- The domain name must reflect your company's proper name.

Which two of the following domain names meet these requirements?

A. XYZProducts.com

B. XYZProducts.domain

C. Server1.XYZProducts.org

D. XYZProductsServer2003

7. Recently, you have received several alerts that Server1 is running low on disk space. Server1 primarily stores users' home directories. This problem has occurred several times in the past, and you want to restrict the amount of space that users can use on one of the volumes on the server. Which NTFS 5 feature can you implement to limit the amount of disk space occupied by users?

A. Quotas

B. Encryption

C. Dynamic disks

D. Remote storage

E. Shared Folder Policy Objects

8. A system administrator is trying to determine which file system to use for a server that will become a Windows Server 2003 file server. His company's requirements include the following:

- The file system must allow for share-level security from within Windows 2000 Server.

- The file system must make efficient use of space on large partitions.

- For testing purposes, the machine must be able to dual-boot between Windows Me and Windows 2000.

Which of the following file systems meets these requirements?

A. FAT

B. FAT32

C. HPFS

D. NTFS

9. For security reasons, you have decided that you must convert the system partition on your Windows Server 2003 from the FAT32 file system to NTFS. Which two of the following steps must you take in order to convert the file system?

A. Run the command CONVERT /FS:NTFS from the command prompt.

B. Rerun Windows Server 2003 Setup and choose to convert the partition to NTFS during the reinstallation.

C. Boot Windows Server 2003 Setup from the installation CD-ROM and choose Rebuild File System.

D. Reboot the computer.

10. You are attempting to join various machines on your network to an Active Directory domain. Which of the following scenarios describe machines that can be added to the domain? Choose all that apply.

A. The machine is running Windows XP Professional.

B. The machine is a member of another domain.

C. The machine is running Windows Server 2003.

D. The machine is a member of a workgroup.

11. Which of the following operations is not supported by the Active Directory Installation Wizard?

A. Promoting a server to a domain controller

B. Demoting a domain controller to a server

C. Moving servers between domains

D. Starting the DNS Installation Wizard

12. Windows Server 2003 requires the use of which two of the following protocols or services in order to support Active Directory?

A. DHCP

B. TCP/IP

C. NetBEUI

D. IPX/SPX

E. DNS

13. You are promoting a Windows Server 2003 computer to an Active Directory domain controller for test purposes. This server will act alone on the network and does not need to be accessible from other machines. Which of the following domain names is a valid choice for the initial Active Directory domain? Choose all that apply.

A. mycompany.com

B. test.mycompany.com

C. mycompany.org

D. activedirectory.test

14. You are promoting a Windows Server 2003 computer to an Active Directory domain controller for test purposes. The new domain controller will be added to an existing domain. While you are using Active Directory Installation Wizard, you receive an error message that prevents the server from being promoted. Which of the following might be the cause of the problem? Choose all that apply.

A. The system does not contain an NTFS 5 partition on which the SYSVOL directory can be created.

B. You do not have a Windows Server 2003 DNS server on the network.

C. The TCP/IP configuration on the new server is incorrect.

D. The domain has reached its maximum number of domain controllers.

15. You are installing the first domain controller in your Active Directory environment. Where would you click next in the following exhibit in order to begin the Active Directory Installation Wizard?

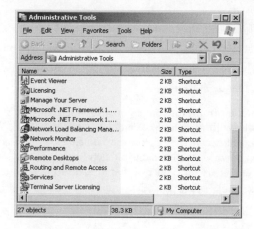

A. Remote Desktops

B. Services

C. Licensing

D. Manage Your Server

16. You are the network administrator for a large company that creates widgets. You are asked by management to implement a new R2-related feature on your Windows Server 2003 system. You need to implement Trustbridge so that you can implement federated identity management. Which of the following will help you do this?

A. Active Directory Federation Services

B. Active Directory DNS Services

C. Active Directory IIS Services

D. Active Directory IAS Services

17. You are the systems administrator responsible for your company's infrastructure. You need to quickly test DNS on a local machine. You think you have an issue with name resolution and you need to verify that you are using the correct host name. You want to test DNS on the local system and need to see if the host name "server-1" resolves to the IP address 10.1.1.1. Which of the following answers provides a solution to the problem?

   A. Add a DNS server to your local subnet.

   B. Add the mapping for the host name "server-1" to the IP address 10.1.1.1 in the local system's HOSTS file.

   C. Add an A record to your local WINS server.

   D. Add an MX record to your local DNS server.

18. As the lead administrator for 123 Inc., you are asked to solve a complex problem. Nobody on your staff can figure out why `server1.yourcompany.com` and `server1.yourcompany.com` can't communicate properly across the WAN. Choose the most likely cause of the problem from the following answers.

   A. There is a firewall blocking the traffic.

   B. There is a router access list assigned to the WAN port and it is blocking traffic.

   C. There is no route between the workstations.

   D. There needs to be unique FQDNs.

19. You are the network administrator for your company, which consists of 3 new Windows Server 2003 servers and 40 workstations running Windows XP Professional. You design a new name for your domain while deploying Active Directory. You consider DNS and how your clients will use it. Because you don't own your DNS name publicly, only privately, what is your next step if you want to ensure that you are the owner of that domain for the future?

   A. Make a lease offer and hold the domain.

   B. Make a list of similar domain names to use.

   C. Register the name with a registration authority.

   D. Use a reverse lookup zone to configure this functionality.

20. You are the systems administrator for 123 Inc. You are in charge of your company's DNS infrastructure. You want to ensure that naming remains accurate in a distributed network environment. Choose the proper way to ensure that DNS will stay accurate across the enterprise from the following options.

   A. You must designate one DNS server as the master database for a specific set of addresses.

   B. You need to implement round robin ordering.

   C. You need to implement a secondary transfer zone server to ensure accuracy.

   D. You must open Port 52 on all firewalls and access control lists enterprise-wide.

Answers to Review Questions

1. D. Only NTFS provides for this level of security and auditing functionality. FAT and FAT32 are rarely used in Server operating systems because they don't provide any native security features. Option C is incorrect because Windows Server 2003 does not support HPFS partitions.

2. B. A domain controller can contain Active Directory information for only one domain. If you want to use a multidomain environment, you must use multiple domain controllers configured in either a tree or forest setting.

3. B. In order to support Windows NT domain controllers, mixed-mode domains must be used. Note that in this configuration, several Windows 2000 Server and Windows Server 2003 Active Directory features will not be available. Choices C and D are incorrect because they are not modes that are supported by Active Directory.

4. C. Promotion is the process of making a Windows Server 2003 computer a new domain controller. This is the only way to install Active Directory.

5. A. The DNS administrative tool is designed to configure settings for the DNS server service. DNS zone files can also be manually edited using a standard text file editor.

6. A, C. Both of these domain names are based on the standard DNS top-level domain names and can therefore be made accessible over the Internet. Although you could use other top-level domain names (such as those provided in choices B and D), these names would not be automatically resolvable over the Internet.

7. A. Quotas allow systems administrators to place restrictions on the amount of disk space used on NTFS volumes. Quotas are native to NTFS and cannot be implemented on FAT or FAT32 drives. Options B, C, and D are available on NTFS partitions, but they cannot be used to restrict disk space. Option E is not an option related to disk storage management.

8. B. FAT32 partitions are compatible with other versions of Windows (such as Windows 95/98/Me), and make fairly efficient usage of disk space. If this machine was to be configured as a domain controller, the configuration would have required at least one NTFS partition in order to store the SYSVOL information.

9. A, D. In order to convert the system partition to NTFS, you must first use the CONVERT command-line utility and the reboot the server. During the next boot, the file system will be converted.

10. Answers: A, B, C, D. All of the above configurations can be joined to a domain. Note that if a machine is a member of another domain, it must first be removed from that domain before it can be joined to another one. Join it to a workgroup to remove it from the old domain, then join it to the new domain.

11. C. The only way to move a domain controller between domains is to demote it from its current domain and then promote it into another domain. You cannot move a domain controller automatically using any of the built-in tools included with Windows Server 2003.

12. Answers: B, E. The use of LDAP and TCP/IP is required to support Active Directory. TCP/IP is the network protocol that is favored by Microsoft, so they determined that all Active Directory communication would occur on TCP/IP. DNS is required because Active Directory is inherently dependent upon the domain model. Option A is used for automatic address assignment, and is not required. Similarly, options C and D, while they are available network protocols in Windows Server 2003, are not required by Active Directory.

13. Answers: A, B, C, D. All of the domain names listed may be used. Although it is recommended, a registered Internet domain name is not required for installing Active Directory.

14. Answers: A, C. The SYSVOL directory must be created on an NTFS 5 partition. If such a partition is not available, you will not be able to promote the server to a domain controller. An error in the network configuration might prevent the server from connecting to another domain controller in the environment.

15. D. You typically use the Configure Your Server Wizard, launched from the Manage Your Server tool, to begin the process of promoting a server to a domain controller.

16. A. You'll need to use Active Directory Federation Services (ADFS) in order to implement Trustbridge. Federated identity management is a standards-based technology and information technology process that will enable distributed identification, authentication, and authorization across organizational and platform boundaries. The ADFS solution in Windows Server 2003 R2 helps administrators address these challenges by enabling organizations to securely share a user's identity information.

17. B. The HOSTS file is a text file–based database of mappings between host names and IP addresses.

18. D. Each fully qualified domain name (FQDN), such as server1.yourcompany.com, must be unique. No two machines on the same network may have the same FQDN. This requirement ensures that each machine can be uniquely identified. The WAN link only connects what is still considered one network.

19. C. Ensure that you reserve your DNS names with a registration authority. You can also reserve your private names so that they cannot be used on the public Internet. Failure to reserve your internal name may prevent internal clients from accessing this namespace on the public Internet in the future; this is simply because then the client would not be able to tell the difference between the internally selected name and the publicly assigned name via the registrar. You can set up zones for both the external and internal namespaces.

20. A. In order to ensure that naming remains accurate in a distributed network environment, one DNS server must be designated as the master database for a specific set of addresses. It is on this server that updates to host name–to–IP address mappings can be updated. Whenever a DNS server is unable to resolve a specific DNS name, it simply queries other servers that can provide the information.

Chapter 3

Installing and Managing Trees and Forests

MICROSOFT EXAM OBJECTIVES COVERED IN THIS CHAPTER:

✓ **Plan flexible operations master role placement.**

- Plan for business continuity of operations master roles.
- Identify operations master role dependencies.

✓ **Implement an Active Directory directory service forest and domain structure.**

- Create the forest root domain.
- Create a child domain.
- Establish trust relationships. Types of trust relationships might include external trusts, shortcut trusts, and cross-forest trusts.

✓ **Manage an Active Directory forest and domain structure.**

- Manage trust relationships.
- Manage schema modifications.
- Add or remove a UPN suffix.

✓ **Troubleshoot Active Directory.**

- Diagnose and resolve issues related to operations master role failure.

So far, you have seen the steps you need to take to plan for Active Directory and to implement the first Active Directory domain. Although you were briefly introduced to the concepts related to multidomain Active Directory structures, the focus was on a single domain and the objects within it. Many businesses find that using a single domain provides an adequate solution to meet their business needs. By working with *trees* and *forests*, however, organizations can use multiple domains to better organize their environments.

This chapter begins by covering some reasons why you should create more than one Active Directory domain. Then, it moves on to look at the exact processes involved in creating a domain tree and joining multiple trees together into a domain forest. In addition, you will learn how to demote a domain controller and manage multiple domains after you've created trees and forests.

Reasons for Creating Multiple Domains

Before you look at the steps you must take to create multiple domains, you should become familiar with the reasons why an organization might want to create them. In general, you should always try to reflect your organization's structure within a single domain. Through the use of organizational units (OUs) and other objects, you can usually create an accurate and efficient structure within one domain, and creating and managing a single domain is usually much simpler than managing a more complex environment, which would consist of multiple domains. That said, this section of the text looks at some real benefits and reasons for creating multiple domains as well as some drawbacks of using them.

Reasons for Using Multiple Domains

There are several reasons why you might need to implement multiple domains. These reasons include such considerations as:

Scalability   Although Microsoft has designed Active Directory to accommodate millions of objects, this number may not be practical for your current environment. Supporting many thousands of users within a single domain places higher disk space, CPU (central processing unit), and network burdens on your *domain controllers*. Determining the scalability of Active Directory is something you have to plan, design, test, and analyze within your own environment.

Reducing replication traffic   All the domain controllers of a domain must keep an up-to-date copy of the entire Active Directory database. For small- to medium-sized domains, this is not generally a problem. Windows Server 2003 and Active Directory manage all of the details of transferring the database behind the scenes. Other business and technical limitations might, however, affect Active Directory's ability to perform adequate replication. For example, if you have two sites that are connected by a very slow network link (or a sporadic link, or no link at all), replication is not practical. In this case, you would probably want to create separate domains to isolate replication traffic. Sporadic coverage across the wide area network (WAN) link would come from circuit switching technologies such as Integrated Services Digital Network (ISDN) technologies. If you didn't have a link at all, then you would have a service provider outage or some other type of disruption. Separate domains would, of course, separate replication traffic, but if this is the case, the amount of administrative overhead is increased significantly.

Because it's common to have WAN links in your business environment, you will always need to consider how your users authenticate to a domain controller (DC) so a DC at a remote site is commonly seen to authenticate users locally to their local area network (LAN). This setup is the design you will most likely see at any given location or business that has used Microsoft TechNet as a reference tool. The most common design involves putting a DC at each remote site to keep authentication traffic from traversing the WAN. If it were the other way around, the authentication traffic that may cause the WAN may cause users problems if WAN utilization is high or if the link is broken and no other way to the central site is available. This design has many flaws, so the design most likely seen is one where each server must now replicate its database of information to each other server so that the network and its systems converge.

As just mentioned, is important to realize that the presence of slow WAN links alone is *not* a good reason to break an organization into multiple domains and because of this, the most common solution is to set up site links with the Site and Services Microsoft Management Console (MMC). When you use this MMC, you can manage replication traffic and fine tune independently of the domain architecture. We'll cover these topics in detail in Chapter 4, "Configuring Sites and Managing Replication."

There following are the reasons why you would want to use a multidomain architecture, such as when two companies merge through an acquisition.

Meeting business needs   There are several business needs that might justify the creation of multiple domains. Business needs can be broken down even further into organizational and political needs.

One of the organizational reasons for using multiple domains is to avoid potential problems associated with the Domain Administrator account. At least one user needs to have permissions at this level. If your organization is unable or unwilling to place this level of trust with all business units, then multiple domains may be the best answer. Since each domain maintains its own security database, you can keep permissions and resources isolated. Through the use of trusts, however, you can still share resources.

A political reason might arise if you had two companies that merged with two separate but equal management staffs, and two sets of officers. In such a situation, you might need to have Active Directory split into two separate databases to keep the security of the two groups separate. Some such organizations may need to keep the internal groups separate by law. If this is the case, a multidomain architecture is born to provide exactly this type of pristinely separate environment.

Many levels of hierarchy   Larger organizations tend to have very complex internal and external business structures that dictate the need for many different levels of organization. For example, two companies might merge and need to keep two sets of officers who are managed under two different logical groupings. As you will see in Chapter 5, "Administering Active Directory," OUs are used to help group different branches of the company so that you can assign permissions, or delegations, or whatever else you can think of without affecting anyone else. Management of data becomes much easier when you're using OUs, and if designed correctly, will help you control your network right from one console. You may only need one level of management—your company may be small enough to warrant the use of the default OU structure you see when Active Directory is first installed. If, however, you find that you need many levels of OUs to manage resources (or if there are large numbers of objects within each OU), it might make sense to create additional domains. Each domain would contain its own OU hierarchy and serve as the root of a new set of objects.

Varying security policies   All of the objects within the domain share many characteristics, one of which is the use of a security policy. A domain is designed to be a single security entity. If configured properly, the use of a domain will allow the assignment of usernames and password restrictions to apply to all of its objects located within. If you set a password length restriction to seven characters, then you can assign that same restriction to every object in the domain. If your organization requires separate security policies for different groups of users, you should consider creating multiple domains.

Decentralized administration   There are two main models of administration that are commonly used: a centralized administration model and a decentralized administration model. In the centralized administration model, a single IT organization is responsible for managing all of the users, computers, and security permissions for the entire organization. In the decentralized administration model, each department or business unit might have its own IT department. In both cases, the needs of the administration model can play a significant role in whether or not you decide to use multiple domains.

Consider, for example, a multinational company that has a separate IT department for offices in each country. Each IT department is responsible for supporting only the users and computers within its own region. Since the administration model is largely decentralized, creating a separate domain for each of these major business units might make sense from a security and maintenance standpoint.

Multiple DNS or domain names   Another reason why you may need to use a multidomain architecture would arise if you wanted or planned to use multiple DNS names within your organization. If you use multiple DNS names or domain names you must create multiple domains. Each domain can have only one fully qualified domain name (FQDN). A FQDN is the full name of a system that consists of a local host, a second-level domain name, and a top-level domain (TLD). For example, www.wiley.com is a FQDN. .com is the TLD, www is the host, and wiley is the domain name (second-level). Although not seen, a "." exists at the end of .com; it represents the root.

To apply this to our example of a business need, let's consider two groups within a company: Sales and Engineering. For example, if you need some of your users within the sales.mycompany.com namespace and others in the `engineering.mycompany.com` namespace, you must use multiple domains. If the domain names are noncontiguous, you will need to create multiple domain trees (a topic you'll see covered later in this chapter).

Drawbacks of Multiple Domains

Although there are many reasons why it makes sense to have multiple domains, there are also reasons why you should *not* break an organizational structure into multiple domains, many of which are related to maintenance and administration. Some of the drawbacks to using multiple domains include the following:

Administrative inconsistency   One of the fundamental responsibilities of most systems administrators is implementing and managing security. When you are implementing Group Policy and security settings in multiple domains, you must be careful to ensure that the settings are consistent. As mentioned previously, security policies can be different between domains. If this is what is intended, then it is not a problem. If, however, the organization wishes to make the same settings apply to all users, then each domain will require similar security settings.

Increased management challenges   Managing servers, users, and computers can become a considerable challenge when you are also managing multiple domains because many more administrative units are required. In general, you need to manage all user, group, and computer settings separately for the objects within each domain. The hierarchical structure provided by OUs, on the other hand, provides a much simpler and easier way to manage permissions.

Decreased flexibility   Creating a domain involves the *promotion* of a domain controller (DC) to the new domain. Although the process is quite simple, it is much more difficult to rearrange the domain topology within an Active Directory environment than it is to simply reorganize OUs. When planning domains, you should ensure that the domain structure will not change often, if at all.

Now that you have examined the pros and cons related to creating multiple domains, it is time to see how to create trees and forests.

Creating Domain Trees and Forests

So far this chapter has covered some important reasons for using multiple domains in a single network environment; now it's time to look at how to create multidomain structures like domain trees and domain forests.

Regardless of the number of domains you have in your environment, you always have a tree and a forest. This might surprise those of you who generally think of domain trees and forests as Active Directory environments that consist of multiple domains. However, recall that when you install the first domain in an Active Directory environment, that domain automatically creates a new forest and a new tree.

In the following sections, you will learn how to plan trees and forests as well as see how to actually promote domain controllers to establish a tree and forest environment.

Planning Trees and Forests

You have already seen several reasons why you must have multiple domains within a single company. What you haven't yet seen is how multiple domains can be related to each other and how their relationships can translate into domain forests and trees.

A fundamental commonality between the various domains that exist in trees and forests is that they all share the same Active Directory Global Catalog (GC). This means that if you modify the Active Directory schema, these changes must be propagated to all of the domain controllers in *all of the domains*. This is an important point because adding and modifying the structure of information in the GC can have widespread effects on replication and network traffic. Also, you need to ensure that any system you use in the Global Catalog role can handle it by sizing the system's hardware requirements up. This is especially true if there are multiple domains.

Every domain within an Active Directory configuration has its own unique name. For example, even though you might have a sales domain in two different trees, their complete names will be different (such as `sales.company1.com` and `sales.company2.com`).

In the following sections, you'll look at how you can organize multiple Active Directory domains based on business requirements.

Using a Single Tree

The concept of domain trees was created to preserve the relationship between multiple domains that share a common contiguous namespace. For example, you might have the following DNS domains (based on Internet names):

- `mycompany.com`
- `sales.mycompany.com`
- `engineering.mycompany.com`
- `europe.sales.mycompany.com`

Note that all of these domains fit within a single contiguous namespace. That is, they are all direct or indirect children of the `mycompany.com` domain. In this case, `mycompany.com` is called the *root* domain. All of the direct children (such as `sales.mycompany.com` and `engineering.mycompany.com`) are called *child* domains. Finally, *parent* domains are the domains that are directly above one domain. For example, `sales.mycompany.com` is the parent domain of `europe.sales.mycompany.com`. Figure 3.1 provides an example of a domain tree.

In order to establish a domain tree, you must create the root domain for the tree first. Then, you can add child domains off this root. These child domains can then serve as parents for further subdomains. Each domain must have at least one domain controller, and domain controllers can participate in only one domain at a time. However, domain controllers can be moved between domains. To do this, you must first demote a domain controller to a member server and then promote it to a domain controller in another domain.

FIGURE 3.1   A domain tree

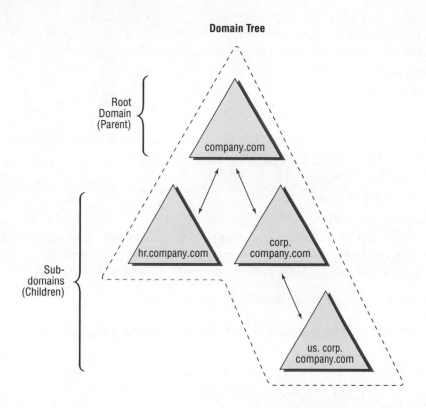

Domain Tree

Root Domain (Parent)

company.com

hr.company.com

corp. company.com

Sub-domains (Children)

us. corp. company.com

You will learn how to demote a domain controller later in this chapter, in the section titled "Demoting a Domain Controller."

Domains are designed to be security boundaries. The domains within a tree are, by default, automatically bound together using a two-way trust relationship, which allows resources to be shared between domains through the use of the appropriate user and group assignments. Because trust relationships are transitive, all of the domains within the tree trust each other. Note, however, that a trust by itself does not grant any security permissions to users or objects between domains. Trusts are designed only to *allow* resources to be shared; you must still go through the process of sharing and managing them. Administrators must explicitly assign security settings to resources before users can access resources between domains.

Using a single tree makes sense when your organization maintains only a single contiguous namespace. Regardless of the number of domains that exist within this environment and how different their security settings are, they are related by a common name. Although domain trees make sense for many organizations, in some cases, the network namespace may be considerably more complicated. You'll look at how forests address these situations next.

Using a Forest

Active Directory forests are designed to accommodate multiple noncontiguous namespaces. That is, they can combine domain trees together into logical units. An example might be the following tree and domain structure:

- Tree: Organization1.com
  - Sales.Organization1.com
  - Marketing.Organization1.com
  - Engineering.Organization1.com
  - NorthAmerica.Engineering.Organization1.com
- Tree: Organization2.com
  - Sales.Organization2.com
  - Engineering.Organization2.com

Figure 3.2 provides an example of how multiple trees can fit into a single forest. Such a situation might occur in the acquisition and merger of companies or if a company is logically divided into two or more completely separate and autonomous business units.

FIGURE 3.2   A single forest consisting of multiple trees

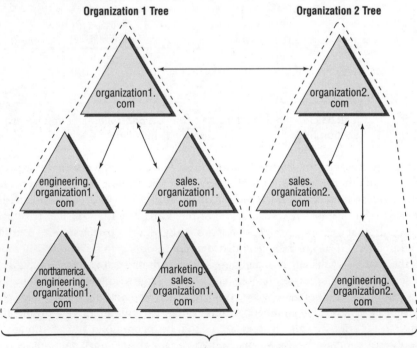

All of the trees within a forest are related through a single forest root domain. This is the first domain that is created in the Active Directory environment. The root domain in each tree creates a transitive trust with the forest root domain. The result is a configuration in which all of the trees within a domain and all of the domains within each tree trust each other. Again, as with domain trees, the presence of a trust relationship does not automatically signify that users have permissions to access resources across domains. It only allows objects and resources to be shared. Authorized network administrators must set up specific permissions.

All of the domains within a single Active Directory forest have the following features in common:

Schema   The schema is the Active Directory structure that defines how the information within the data store is structured. In order for the information stored on various domain controllers to remain compatible, all of the domain controllers within the entire Active Directory environment must share the same schema. For example, if you add a field for an employee's benefits plan number, all domain controllers throughout the environment need to recognize this information before you can share information between them.

Global Catalog   One of the problems associated with working in large network environments is that sharing information across multiple domains can be costly in terms of network and server resources. Fortunately, Active Directory uses the Global Catalog (GC), which serves as a repository for information about a subset of all objects within *all* Active Directory domains in a forest. Systems administrators can determine what types of information should be added to the defaults in the GC. Generally, they decide to store commonly used information, such as a list of all of the printers, users, groups, and computers. In addition, they can configure specific domain controllers to carry a copy of the GC. Now, if you go back to the question of where all the color printers in the company can be found, all that you need to do is to contact the nearest GC server.

Configuration information   Some roles and functions must be managed for the entire forest. When you are dealing with multiple domains, this means that you must configure certain domain controllers to perform functions for the entire Active Directory environment. Some specifics of this will be discussed later in this chapter.

The main purpose of allowing multiple domains to exist together is to allow them to share information and other resources. Now that you've seen the basics of domain trees and forests, take a look at how domains are actually created.

The Promotion Process

A domain tree is created when a new domain is added as the child of an existing domain. This relationship is established during the promotion of a Windows Server 2003 computer to a domain controller. Although the underlying relationships can be quite complicated in larger organizations, the *Active Directory Installation Wizard (DCPROMO)* makes it easy to create forests and trees.

Using the Active Directory Installation Wizard, you can quickly and easily create new domains by promoting a Windows Server 2003 standalone server or a member server to a domain controller. When you install a new domain controller, you can choose to make it part of an existing domain, or you can choose to make it the first domain controller in a new domain. In the following sections and exercises, you'll become familiar with the exact steps you need to take to create a domain tree and a domain forest when you promote a server to a domain controller.

> The promotion process involves many steps and decisions, the details of which were covered in Chapter 2, "Planning and Installing Active Directory." If you are unfamiliar with the process and ramifications related to promoting a server to a domain controller, review that chapter before you continue.

Creating a Domain Tree

In the previous chapter, you saw how to promote the first domain controller in the first domain in a forest, also known as the root. If you don't promote any other domain controllers, then that domain controller simply controls that one domain and no trees are created. To create a new domain tree, you need to promote a Windows Server 2003 computer to a domain controller. In the Active Directory Installation Wizard, select the option that makes this domain controller the first machine in a new domain that is a child of an existing domain. As a result, you will have a new domain tree that contains two domains—a parent and a child.

Before you can create a new child domain, you need the following information:

- The name of the parent domain (the one you created in the previous chapter)
- The name of the child domain (the one you are planning to install)
- The file system locations for the Active Directory database, logs, and shared system volume
- DNS configuration information
- The NetBIOS name for the new server
- A domain administrator username and password

Exercise 3.1 walks you through the process of creating a new child domain using the Active Directory Installation Wizard. This exercise assumes that you have already created the parent domain and that you are using a server in the domain that is not a domain controller.

EXERCISE 3.1

Creating a New Subdomain

1. Log on to the computer as a member of the Administrators group and open the Active Directory Installation Wizard by clicking Start ➢ Run, and typing **dcpromo**. Click Next to begin the wizard.

2. You will see a message that states that Windows 95 and Windows NT 4.0 computers running Service Pack 3 or earlier will be unable to communicate with Windows Server 2003
computers. Read the information and then click Next to continue.

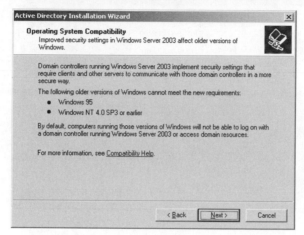

3. On the Domain Controller Type page, select Domain Controller For A New Domain.
Click Next.

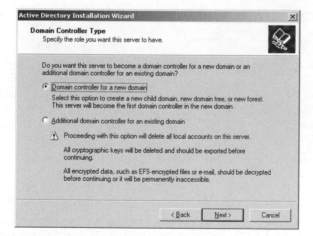

4. On the Create New Domain page, choose Child Domain In An Existing Domain Tree. Click Next.

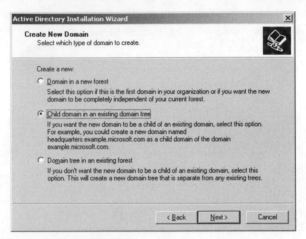

5. On the Network Credentials page, enter the username and password for the domain administrator of the domain you wish to join. You will also need to specify the full name of the domain. After you have entered the appropriate information, click Next.

6. If the information you entered was correct, you will see the Child Domain Installation page. Here, you will be able to confirm the name of the parent domain and then enter the domain name for the child domain. If you want to make a change, you can click the Browse button and search for a domain. The Complete DNS Name Of New Domain field will show you the FQDN for the domain you are creating. Click Next to continue.

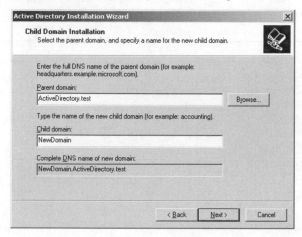

7. On the NetBIOS Domain Name page you'll be prompted for the NetBIOS name for this domain controller. This is the name that will be used by previous versions of Windows to identify this machine. Choose a name that is up to 15 characters in length and includes only alphanumeric characters. Click Next to continue.

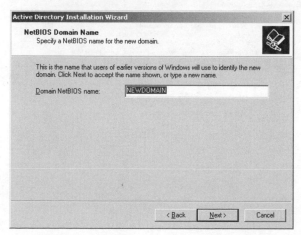

8. On the Database And Log Folders page, you'll need to specify the database and log locations. These settings specify where the Active Directory database resides on the local machine. As mentioned previously, it is good practice to place the log files on a separate physical hard disk because this increases performance. Enter the path for a local directory, and click Next.

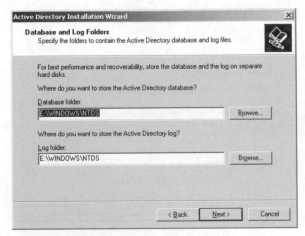

9. On the Shared System Volume page, specify the folder in which Active Directory public files will reside. This directory must be on an NTFS 5 partition. Choose the path, and then click Next.

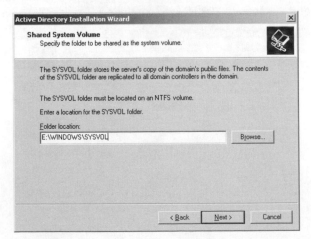

10. If you have not yet installed and configured the DNS service, or if you are getting a con-figuration error, the Active Directory Installation Wizard prompts you about whether or not the DNS service on the local machine should be configured automatically. Since Active Directory and client computers rely on DNS information for finding objects, gen-erally you will want the wizard to automatically configure DNS. Click Next to continue.

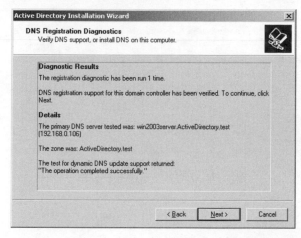

11. On the Permissions page, select whether or not you want to use permissions that are compatible with Windows NT domains. If you will be supporting any Windows NT Server computers or if you have existing Windows NT domains, you should choose Permissions Compatible With Pre–Windows 2000 Server Operating Systems. Otherwise, choose Per-missions Compatible Only With Windows 2000 Or Windows Server 2003 Operating Sys-tems. Click Next.

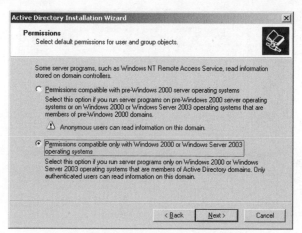

12. In order to be able to recover this server in the event of a loss of Active Directory information, you will need to provide a password on the Directory Services Restore Mode Administrator Password page. This password will allow you to use the built-in recovery features of Windows Server 2003 in the event that the Active Directory database is lost or corrupted. Enter a password, confirm it, and then click Next.

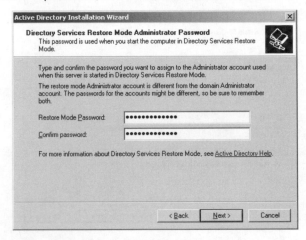

13. On the Summary page, you will be given a brief listing of all the choices you made in the previous steps. It's a good idea to copy this information and paste it into a text document for future reference. Click Next to continue on.

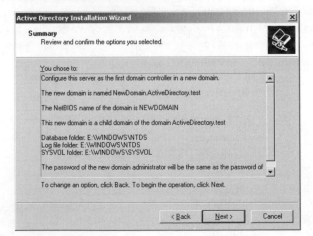

14. The Active Directory Installation Wizard will automatically begin performing the steps required to create a new domain in your environment. Note that you can press Cancel if you want to abort this process. When the process has completed, you will be prompted to reboot the system. After the system has been rebooted, the local server will be the first domain controller in a new domain. This domain will also be a subdomain of an existing one.

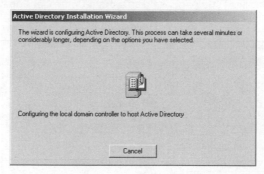

Joining a New Domain Tree to a Forest

A forest is formed by joining two or more domains or trees that do not share a contiguous namespace. For example, you could join the `organization1.com` and `organization2.com` domains together to create a single Active Directory environment.

Any two independent domains can be joined together to create a forest, as long as the two domains have noncontiguous namespaces. (If the namespaces were contiguous, you would actually need to create a domain tree.) The process of creating a new tree to form or add to a forest is as simple as promoting a server to a domain controller for a new domain that does *not* share a namespace with an existing Active Directory domain.

In Exercise 3.2, you will use the Active Directory Installation Wizard to create a new domain tree to add to a forest. In order to add a new domain to an existing forest, you must already have at least one other domain, which is the root domain. Keep in mind that the entire forest structure is destroyed if the original root domain is ever entirely removed. Therefore, you should have at least two domain controllers in the Active Directory root domain; the second serves as a backup in case you have a problem with the first, and it can also serve as a backup solution for disaster recovery and fault tolerance purposes. Such a setup provides additional protection for the entire forest in case one of the domain controllers fails. In order to complete this exercise, you must have already installed another domain controller that serves as the root domain for a forest, and you must use a server in the domain that is not a domain controller.

EXERCISE 3.2

Creating a New Domain Tree in the Forest

1. Open the Active Directory Installation Wizard by clicking Start ➢ Run, and typing **dcpromo**. Click Next to begin the wizard, and then click Next again to continue past the Operating System Compatibility screen.

2. On the Domain Controller Type page, select Domain Controller For A New Domain. Click Next.

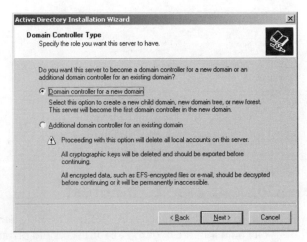

3. On the Create New Domain page, choose Domain In A New Forest. Click Next.

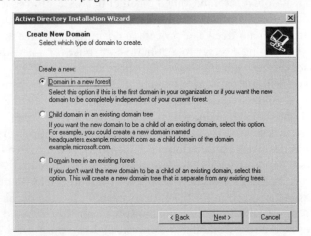

4. On the New Domain Name page, you need to specify the full name of the new domain you wish to create. Note that this domain may not share a contiguous namespace with any other existing domain. Once you have entered the appropriate information, click Next.

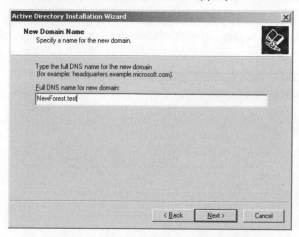

5. On the NetBIOS Domain Name page, you are prompted for the NetBIOS name of the domain controller. This is the name previous versions of Windows use to identify this machine. Choose a name that is up to 15 characters in length and includes only alphanumeric characters. Click Next to continue.

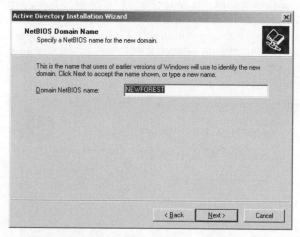

6. On the Database and Log Folders page, specify the database and log locations. These settings specify where the Active Directory database resides on the local machine. Enter the path for a local directory, and click Next.

7. On the Shared System Volume page, specify the folder in which Active Directory public files reside. This directory must be located on an NTFS 5 partition. Choose the path, and then click Next.

8. If you have not yet configured the DNS service, you are prompted to do so. Since Active Directory and client computers rely on DNS information for finding objects, generally you want the wizard to automatically configure DNS. Click Next to continue.

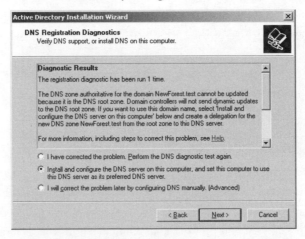

9. On the Permissions page, select whether or not you want to use permissions that are compatible with Windows NT domains. If you will be supporting any Windows NT Server computers or have existing Windows NT domains, you should choose Permissions Compatible With Pre–Windows 2000 Server Operating Systems. Otherwise, choose Permissions Compatible Only With Windows 2000 Or Windows Server 2003 Operating Systems. Click Next.

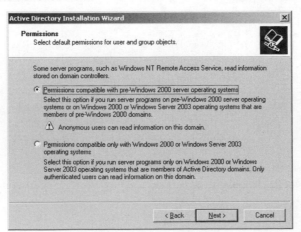

10. In order to be able to recover this server in the event of a loss of Active Directory information, you need to provide a Directory Services Restore Mode Administrator password. This password allows you to use the built-in recovery features of Windows Server 2003 if the Active Directory database is lost or corrupted. Enter a password, confirm it, and then click Next.

11. On the Summary page, you are given a brief listing of all of the choices you made in the previous steps. Click Next to continue.

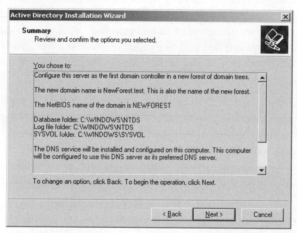

12. The Active Directory Installation Wizard automatically begins performing the steps required to create a new domain tree based on the information you provided. Note that you can press Cancel if you want to abort this process. When the setup is complete, you are prompted to reboot the system. Go ahead and do so, and once the process is finished, you will have a new domain tree.

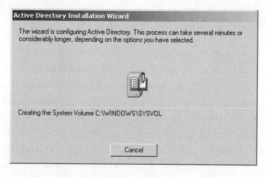

Adding Additional Domain Controllers

In addition to the operations you've already performed, you can use the Active Directory Installation Wizard to create additional domain controllers for any of your domains. There are two main reasons to create additional domain controllers:

Fault tolerance and reliability   As mentioned earlier in the chapter, you should always consider the theory of disaster recovery (DR) and have a plan, sometimes referred to as a Disaster Recovery Plan (DRP). In organizations that rely upon their network directory services infrastructures, you need Active Directory to provide security and resources for all users. For this reason, downtime and data loss are very costly. Through the use of multiple domain controllers, you can ensure that if one of the servers goes down, another one is available to perform the necessary tasks, such as user authentication and resource browsing. Additionally, data loss (perhaps from hard disk drive failure) will not result in the loss or unavailability of network security information since you can easily recover Active Directory information from the remaining, still functional domain controller.

Performance   The burden of processing login requests and serving as a repository for security permissions and other information can be quite extensive, especially in larger businesses that are massive in size. By using multiple domain controllers, you can distribute this load across multiple systems. Additionally, by strategically placing domain controllers, you can greatly increase response times for common network operations, such as authentication and browsing for resources.

As a rule of thumb, you should always plan and design your infrastructure to have at least two domain controllers per domain. For many organizations, this provides a good balance between the cost of servers and the level of reliability and performance. For larger or more distributed organizations, however, additional domain controllers greatly improve performance. Chapter 4 covers these issues in detail.

 Real World Scenario

Planning for Domain Controller Placement

You're the Senior Systems Administrator for a medium-sized Active Directory environment. Currently, the environment consists of only one Active Directory domain. Your company's network is spread out through 40 different sites within North America. Recently, you've received complaints from users and other system administrators about the performance of Active Directory–related operations. For example, users report that it takes several minutes to log on to their machines in the morning between the hours of 9 and 10 AM when activity is at its highest. Simultaneously, systems administrators complain that updating user information within the OUs for which they are responsible can take longer than expected.

One network administrator, who has a strong Windows NT 4 domain background but little knowledge of Active Directory design, suggests that you create multiple domains to solve some of the performance problems. However, you know that this would significantly change the environment and could make administration more difficult. Furthermore, the company's business goals involve keeping all company resources as unified as possible.

Fortunately, Active Directory's distributed domain controller architecture allows you to optimize performance for this type of situation without making dramatic changes to your environment. You decide that the quickest and easiest solution is to deploy additional domain controllers throughout the organization. The domain controllers are generally placed within areas of the network that are connected by slow or unreliable links. For example, a small branch office in Des Moines, Iowa receives its own domain controller. The process is quite simple: you install a new Windows Server 2003 computer and then run the Active Directory Installation Wizard (DCPROMO) to make the new machine a domain controller for an existing domain. Once the initial directory services data is copied to the new server, it is ready to service requests and updates of your domain information.

Note that there are potential drawbacks to this solution; for instance, you have to manage additional domain controllers and the network traffic generated from communications between the domain controllers. It's important that you monitor your network links to ensure that you've reached a good balance between replication traffic and overall Active Directory performance. In later chapters, you'll see how you can configure Active Directory sites to better map Active Directory operations to your physical network structure.

Demoting a Domain Controller

In addition to being able to promote member servers to domain controllers, the Active Directory Installation Wizard can do the exact opposite—demote domain controllers.

You might choose to demote a domain controller for a couple of reasons. First, if you have determined that the role of a server should change (for example, from a domain controller to a member or standalone server you might make into a web server), you can easily demote it to make this happen. Another common reason to demote a domain controller is if you wish to move the machine between domains. Because you cannot do this in a single process, you need to first demote the existing domain controller to remove it from the current domain. Then, you can promote it into a new domain. The end result is that the server is now a domain controller for a different domain.

To demote a domain controller, simply access the Active Directory Installation Wizard. The wizard automatically notices that the local server is a domain controller and when it does, you will be asked by the wizard to verify each step you take, as you are for most things you do in Windows. You are prompted to decide whether or not you really want to remove this machine from the current domain (see Figure 3.3). Note that if the local server is a Global Catalog server, you will be warned that at least one copy of the Global Catalog must remain available so that you can perform logon authentication.

FIGURE 3.3   Demoting a domain controller using the Active Directory Installation Wizard

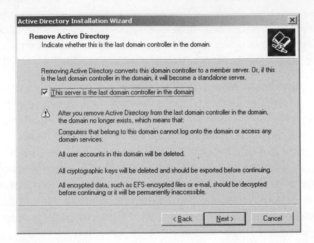

In order for a domain to continue to exist, there must be at least one remaining domain controller in that domain. As noted in the dialog box in Figure 3.3, you must take some very important considerations into account if you are removing the last domain controller from the domain. Because all of the security accounts and information will be lost, you should ensure that the following requirements are met before you remove a domain's last domain controller:

Computers no longer log on to this domain.   Ensure that computers that were once members of this domain have changed domains. If computers are still attempting to log on, they will not be able to use any of the security features, including any security permissions or logon accounts. Users will, however, still be able to log on to the computer using cached authenticated information.

No user accounts are needed.   All of the user accounts that reside within the domain (and all of the resources and permissions associated with them) will be lost when the domain is destroyed. Therefore, if you have already set up usernames and passwords, you need to transfer these accounts to another domain; otherwise, you will lose all of this information.

All encrypted data is decrypted.   You need the security information (including User, Computer, and Group objects) stored within the Active Directory domain database to access any encrypted information. Once the domain fails to exist, the security information stored within it will no longer be available, and any encrypted information stored in the file system will become permanently inaccessible. So, decrypt any encrypted data before you begin the demotion process so that you can make sure you can access this information afterward. For example, if you have encrypted files or folders that reside on NTFS volumes, you should decrypt them before you continue with the demotion process.

Back up all cryptographic keys.   If you are using cryptographic keys to authenticate and secure data, you should export the key information before you demote the last domain controller in a domain. Because this information is stored in the Active Directory database, any resources locked with these keys become inaccessible once the database is lost as a result of the demotion process.

WARNING   Removing a domain from your environment is not an operation that should be taken lightly. Before you plan to remove a domain, make a list of all the resources that depend on the domain and the reasons why the domain was originally created. If you are sure your organization no longer requires the domain, then you can safely continue. If you are not sure, think again because the process cannot be reversed and you could lose critical information!

By now, you've probably noticed a running theme—a lot of information disappears when you demote the last domain controller in a domain. The Active Directory Installation Wizard makes performing potentially disastrous decisions very easy. Be sure that you understand these effects before you demote the last domain controller for a given domain.

By default, at the end of the demotion process, the server is joined as a member server to the domain for which it was previously a domain controller. If you demote the last domain controller in the domain, the server becomes standalone.

Managing Multiple Domains

You can easily manage most of the operations that must occur *between* domains by using the Active Directory Domains And Trusts administrative tool. If, on the other hand, you want to configure settings *within* a domain, you should use the Active Directory Users And Computers tool. In the following sections, you'll look at ways to perform two common domain management functions with the tools just mentioned: managing *single master operations* and managing trusts. We'll also look at ways to manage UPN suffixes to simplify user accounts, and we'll examine Global Catalog servers in more detail.

Managing Single Master Operations

For the most part, Active Directory functions in what is known as multimaster replication. That is, every domain controller within the environment contains a copy of the Active Directory database that is both readable and writable. This works well for most types of information. For example, if you want to modify the password of a user, you can easily do this on *any* of the domain controllers within a domain. The change is then automatically propagated to the other domain controllers.

However, some functions are not managed in a multimaster fashion. These operations are known as *operations masters*. You must perform single-master operations on specially designated machines within the Active Directory forest. There are five main single-master functions: two that apply to an entire Active Directory forest and three that apply to each domain.

The following single-master operations apply to the entire forest:

Schema Master   Earlier, you learned that all of the domain controllers within a single Active Directory environment share the same schema. This ensures information consistency. Developers and systems administrators can, however, modify the Active Directory schema by adding custom information. A trivial example might involve adding a field to employee information that specifies a user's favorite color.

When you need to make these types of changes, you must perform them on the domain controller that serves as the *Schema Master* for the environment. The Schema Master is then responsible for propagating all of the changes to all of the other domain controllers within the forest.

Domain Naming Master   The purpose of the *Domain Naming Master* is to keep track of all the domains within an Active Directory forest. You access this domain controller whenever you need to add new domains to a tree or forest.

Within each domain, at least one domain controller must fulfill each of the following roles:

Relative ID (RID) Master   Every object within Active Directory must be assigned a unique identifier so that it is distinguishable from other objects. For example, if you have two OUs named IT that reside in different domains, you must have some way to easily distinguish between them. Furthermore, if you delete one of the IT OUs and then later re-create it, the system must be able to determine that it is not the same object as the other IT OU. The unique identifier for each object is made up of a domain identifier and a relative identifier (RID). RIDs are always unique within an Active Directory domain and are used for managing security information and authenticating users. The *RID Master* is responsible for creating these values within a domain whenever new Active Directory objects are created.

Primary Domain Controller (PDC) Emulator Master   Within a domain, the *Primary Domain Controller (PDC) Emulator Master* is responsible for maintaining backward compatibility with Windows NT domain controllers. When running in mixed-mode domains, the PDC Emulator is able to process authentication requests and serve as a PDC with Windows NT Backup Domain Controllers (BDCs).

When running in Windows 2000 Native or Windows Server 2003 domain functional level (which does not support the use of pre–Windows 2000 domain controllers), the PDC Emulator Master serves as the default domain controller to process authentication requests if another domain controller is unable to do so. The PDC Emulator also receives preferential treatment whenever domain security changes are made.

Infrastructure Master   Whenever a user is added to or removed from a group, all of the other domain controllers should be made aware of this change. The role of the domain controller that acts as an *Infrastructure Master* is to ensure that group membership information stays synchronized within an Active Directory domain.

Now that you are familiar with the different types of single-master operations, Exercise 3.3 shows you how these roles can be assigned to servers within the Active Directory environment. In this exercise, you will assign single-master operations roles to various domain controllers within the environment. In order to complete the steps in this exercise, you only need one Active Directory domain controller.

EXERCISE 3.3

Assigning Single-Master Operations

1. Open the Active Directory Domains and Trusts administrative tool by clicking Start ➢ Administrative Tools ➢ Active Directory Domains and Trusts.

2. Right-click Active Directory Domains and Trusts, and choose Operations Master.

3. In the Change Operations Master dialog box, note that you can change the operations master by clicking the Change button. If you want to move this assignment to another computer, you first need to connect to that computer and then make the change. Click Close to continue without making any changes.

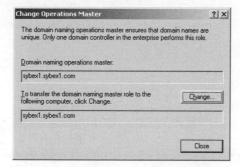

4. Close the Active Directory Domains and Trusts administrative tool.

5. Open the Active Directory Users and Computers administrative tool.

6. Right-click the name of a domain and select "Operations Masters". This brings up the RID tab of the Operations Master dialog box.

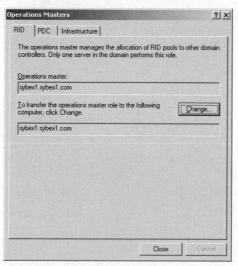

Notice that you can change the computer that is assigned to the role. In order to change the role, you first need to connect to the appropriate domain controller. Notice that the PDC and Infrastructure roles have similar tabs. Click Close to continue without making any changes.

7. When you are finished, close the Active Directory Users And Computers tool.

Note that you manage single-master operations with two different tools. You use the Active Directory Domains And Trusts tool to configure forest-wide roles, while you use the Active Directory Users And Computers snap-in to administer roles within a domain. Although this might not seem intuitive at first, it can help you remember which roles apply to domains and which apply to the whole forest.

Managing Trusts

Trust relationships make it easier to share security information and network resources between domains. As was already mentioned, standard transitive two-way trusts are automatically created between the domains in a tree and between each of the trees in a forest. Figure 3.4 shows an example of the default trust relationships in an Active Directory forest.

FIGURE 3.4   Default trusts in an Active Directory forest

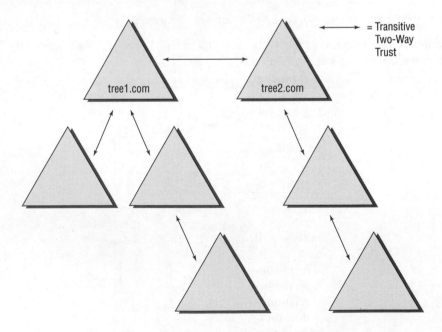

When configuring trusts, there are two main characteristics you'll need to consider:

Transitive trusts   By default, Active Directory trusts are *transitive trusts*. The simplest way to understand transitive relationships is through an example like the following: if Domain A trusts Domain B and Domain B trusts Domain C, then Domain A implicitly trusts Domain C. If you need to apply a tighter level of security, trusts can be configured as intransitive so that this type of behavior does not occur by default.

One-way vs. two-way   Trusts can be configured as one-way or two-way relationships. The default operation is to create *two-way trusts* or *bidirectional trusts*. This makes it easier to manage trust relationships by reducing the trusts you must create. In some cases, however, you might decide that you do not need two-way trusts. In one-way relationships, the trusting domain allows resources to be shared with the trusted domain.

When domains are added together to form trees and forests, an automatic transitive two-way trust is created between them. Although the default trust relationships work well for most organizations, there are some reasons why you might want to manage trusts manually. First, you may want to remove trusts between domains if you are absolutely sure that you do not want resources to be shared between domains. Second, because of security concerns, you may need to keep resources isolated. In addition to the default trust types, you can also configure the following types of special trusts:

External trusts   You use *external trusts* to provide access to resources on a Windows NT 4 domain or forest that cannot use a forest trust. Windows NT 4 domains cannot benefit from the other trust types that are new to Windows Server 2003, so in some cases, external trusts could be your only option. External trusts are always nontransitive, but they can be established in a one-way or two-way configuration.

Realm trusts   Similar to external trusts, you use *realm trusts* to connect to a non-Windows domain that uses Kerberos authentication. Realm trusts can be transitive or non-transitive, one-way or two-way.

Cross-forest trusts   *Cross-forest trusts* are used to share resources between forests. They can only be used with Windows Server 2003 domains and cannot be intransitive, but they can be established in a one-way or two-way configuration. Authentication requests in either forest can reach the other forest in a two-way cross-forest trust.

Shortcut trusts   In some cases, you may actually want to create direct trusts between two domains that implicitly trust each other. Such a trust is sometimes referred to as a *shortcut trust* and can improve the speed at which resources are accessed across many different domains.

Perhaps the most important aspect to remember regarding trusts is that creating them only *allows* you to share resources between domains. The trust does not grant any permissions between domains by itself. Once a trust has been established, however, systems administrators can easily assign the necessary permissions.

Exercise 3.4 walks you through the steps you need to take to manage trusts. In this exercise, you will see how to assign trust relationships between domains. In order to complete the steps in this exercise, you must have domain administrator access permissions.

EXERCISE 3.4

Managing Trust Relationships

1. Open the Active Directory Domains And Trusts administrative tool by clicking Start ➤ Administrative Tools ➤ Active Directory Domains And Trusts.

2. Right-click the name of a domain and select Properties.

3. Select the Trusts tab. You will see a list of the trusts that are currently configured. To modify the trust properties for an existing trust, highlight that trust and click Properties.

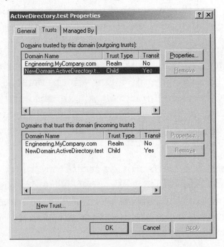

4. This screen displays information about the trust's direction, transitivity, and type, along with the names of the domains involved in the relationship. Click Cancel to exit without making any changes.

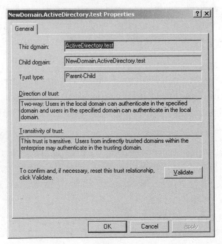

EXERCISE 3.4 *(continued)*

5. To create a new trust relationship, click the New Trust button on the Trusts tab. The New Trust Wizard appears. Click Next to proceed with the wizard.

6. On the Trust Name page, you are prompted for the name of the domain with which the trust should be created. Enter the name of the domain and click Next.

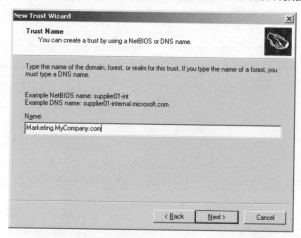

7. On the Trust Type page, you would normally choose the Trust With A Windows Domain option if you know that the other domain uses a Windows domain controller. In order to continue with this exercise (without requiring access to another domain), it is important to choose the Realm Trust option. This selection allows you to walk through the process of creating a trust relationship without needing an untrusted domain in the Active Directory environment. Select the Realm Trust option. Click Next when you are done.

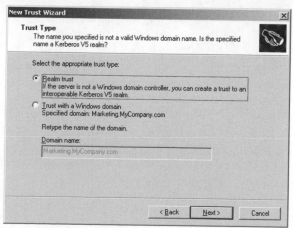

8. On the Transitivity Of Trust page, choose whether the trust is transitive or intransitive. Choose the Nontransitive option and click Next to continue.

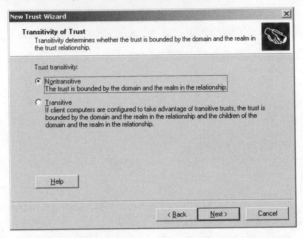

9. On the Direction Of Trust page, select the direction of the trust. If you want both domains to trust each other, select the two-way option. Otherwise select either One-Way: Incoming or One-Way: Outgoing, depending on where the affected users are located. For the sake of this exercise, choose One-Way: Incoming and then click Next.

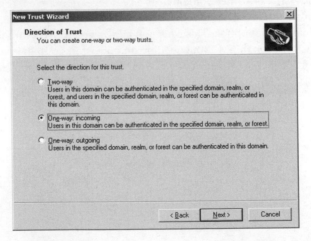

10. On the Trust Password page, specify a password that should be used to administer the trust. Note that if there is an existing trust relationship between the domains, the passwords must match. Click Next to continue.

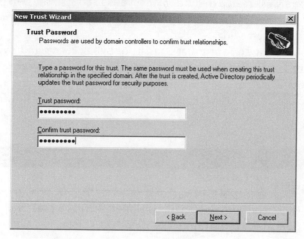

11. Now you see a summary page that recaps the selections you have made. Because this is an exercise, you don't actually want to establish this trust. Click Cancel on the Trust Selections Complete page to cancel the wizard without saving the changes.

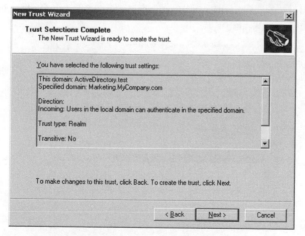

12. Exit the Trust properties for the domain by clicking Cancel.

Once you have established the trust relationships, you will be able to share resources between domains. You'll look at exactly how this is done in Chapter 6, "Planning Security for Active Directory."

Managing UPN Suffixes

User principal name (UPN) suffixes are the part of a user's name that appears after the @ symbol. So, for instance, the UPN suffix of james@sybex1.com would be sybex1.com. By default, the UPN suffix is determined by the name of the domain in which the user is created. In this example, the user james was created in the domain sybex1.com, so the two pieces of the UPN logically fit together. However, you might find it useful to provide an alternative UPN suffix to consolidate the UPNs forest-wide.

For instance, if you manage a forest that consists of sybex1.com and sybex2.com, you might want all of your users to adopt the more generally applicable sybex.com UPN suffix. By adding additional UPN suffixes to the forest, you can easily choose the appropriate suffix when it comes time to create new users. Exercise 3.5 shows you exactly how to add additional suffixes to a forest.

EXERCISE 3.5

Adding a UPN Suffix

1. Open the Active Directory Domains And Trusts administrative tool by clicking Start ➢ Administrative Tools ➢ Active Directory Domains And Trusts.

2. Right-click Active Directory Domains And Trusts in the left side of the window and select Properties.

3. On the UPN Suffixes tab of the Active Directory Domains And Trusts Properties dialog box, enter any alternate UPN suffix in the Alternate UPN Suffixes field. Click the Add button to add the suffix to the list.

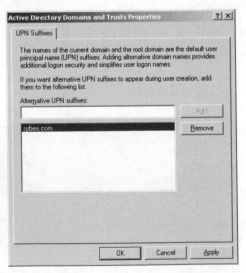

4. To remove a UPN suffix, select its name in the list and click the Remove button.

Managing Global Catalog Servers

One of the best features of a distributed directory service like Active Directory is that you can store different pieces of information throughout an organization. For example, a domain in Japan might store a list of users who operate within a company's Asian operations business unit, while one in New York would contain a list of users who operate within its North American operations business unit. This architecture allows systems administrators to place the most frequently accessed information on domain controllers in different domains, thereby reducing disk space requirements and replication traffic.

There is, however, a problem you may encounter when you deal with information that is segmented into multiple domains. The issue involves querying information stored within Active Directory. What would happen, for example, if a user wanted a list of all of the printers available in all domains within the Active Directory forest? In this case, the search would normally require information from at least one domain controller in each of the domains within the environment. Some of these domain controllers may be located across slow WAN links or may have unreliable connections. The end result would include an extremely long wait while retrieving the results of the query, that is, if any results came up without timing out.

Fortunately, Active Directory has a mechanism that speeds up such searches. You can configure any number of domain controllers to host a copy of the Global Catalog. The Global Catalog contains all of the schema information and a subset of the attributes for all domains within the Active Directory environment. Although a default set of information is normally included with the Global Catalog, systems administrators can choose to add additional information to this data store if needed. Servers that contain a copy of the Global Catalog are known as Global Catalog servers. Now, whenever a user executes a query that requires information from multiple domains, they need only contact the nearest Global Catalog server for this information. Similarly, when users must authenticate across domains, they do not have to wait for a response from a domain controller that may be located across the world. The end result is that the overall performance of Active Directory queries increases.

Exercise 3.6 walks you through the steps you need to take to configure a domain controller as a Global Catalog server. Generally, Global Catalog servers are only useful in environments that use multiple Active Directory domains. Chapter 4 covers the details of placing Global Catalog servers in a distributed environment.

EXERCISE 3.6

Managing Global Catalog Servers

1. Open the Active Directory Sites And Services administrative tool by clicking Start ➤ Administrative Tools ➤ Active Directory Sites And Services.

2. Find the name of the local domain controller within the list of objects (typically under Default First Site Name ➤ Servers), and expand this object. Right-click NTDS Settings and select Properties.

EXERCISE 3.6 *(continued)*

3. In the NTDS Settings Properties dialog box, type **Primary GC Server for Domain** in the Description field. Note that there is a checkbox that determines whether or not this computer contains a copy of the Global Catalog. If the box is checked, then this domain controller contains a subset of information from all other domains within the Active Directory environment. Select the Global Catalog checkbox, and then click OK to continue.

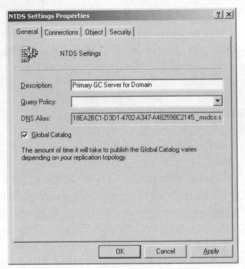

4. When you are finished, close the Active Directory Sites And Services administrative tool.

Summary

In this chapter, we covered the basics of creating multiple domains. We now know why we would want to plan for them and what the benefits and drawbacks are of either selecting to keep only one domain active, or having a multidomain environment. For example, you might select to have multiple domains if you have an acquisitions and mergers situation where you need to keep multiple administrators. In addition, by using multiple domains, organizations can retain separate security databases; however, they are also able to share resources between domains.

We also learned how to use multiple domains to provide two major benefits for the network directory services—security and availability. These benefits are made possible through Active Directory and the administrative tools that can be used to access it.

In addition, we covered how system administrators can simplify operations while still ensuring that only authorized users have access to their data, how multiple domains can interact to form Active Directory trees and forests, and how you can use the Active Directory Installation Wizard to create new Active Directory trees and forests.

In the next chapter, we cover how to use the components of Active Directory to manage replication operations and traffic by building sites and using site links.

Exam Essentials

Understand the reasons for using multiple domains.   There are seven primary reasons for using multiple domains: they provide additional scalability, they reduce replication traffic, they help with political and organizational issues, they provide many levels of hierarchy, they provide varying security policies, they allow for decentralized administration, and they allow for multiple DNS or domain names.

Understand the drawbacks of using multiple domains.   With multiple domains, maintaining administrative consistency is more difficult. The number of administrative units multiplies as well, which makes it difficult to keep track of network resources. Finally, it is much more difficult to rearrange the domain topology within an Active Directory environment than it is to simply reorganize OUs.

Know how to create a domain tree.   To create a new domain tree, you need to promote a Windows Server 2003 computer to a domain controller and select the option that makes this domain controller the first machine in a new domain that is a child of an existing one. The result is a new domain tree that contains two domains—a parent domain and a child domain.

Know how to join a domain tree to a forest.   Creating a new tree to form or add to a forest is as simple as promoting a server to a domain controller for a new domain that does *not* share a namespace with an existing Active Directory domain. In order to add a new domain to an existing forest, you must already have at least one other domain. This domain serves as the root domain for the entire forest.

Understand how to manage single-master operations.   Single-master operations must be performed on specially designated machines within the Active Directory forest. There are five main single-master functions: two that apply to an entire Active Directory forest (Schema Master and Domain Naming Master) and three that apply to each domain (Relative ID [RID] Master, Primary Domain Controller (PDC) Emulator Master, and Infrastructure Master).

Understand how to manage trusts.   When configuring trusts, you'll need to consider two main characteristics: transitivity and direction. The simplest way to understand transitive relationships is through an example like the following: If Domain A trusts Domain B and Domain B trusts Domain C, then Domain A implicitly trusts Domain C. Trusts can be configured as intransitive so that this type of behavior does not occur. In one-way relationships, the trusting domain allows resources to be shared with the trusted domain. In two-way relationships, both domains trust each other equally. Special trusts include external trusts, realm trusts, cross-forest trusts, and shortcut trusts.

Understand how to manage UPN suffixes.   By default, the name of the domain in which the user is created determines the UPN suffix. By adding additional UPN suffixes to the forest, you can easily choose more manageable suffixes when it comes time to create new users.

Understand how to manage Global Catalog (GC) servers.   You can configure any number of domain controllers to host a copy of the Global Catalog. The Global Catalog contains all of the schema information and a subset of the attributes for all domains within the Active Directory environment. Servers that contain a copy of the Global Catalog are known as Global Catalog servers. Whenever a user executes a query that requires information from multiple domains, they need only contact the nearest Global Catalog server for this information. Similarly, when users must authenticate across domains, they will not have to wait for a response from a domain controller that may be located across the world. The end result is increased overall performance of Active Directory queries.

Review Questions

1. You are a systems administrator for an environment that consists of two Active Directory domains. Initially, the domains were configured without any trust relationships. However, the business now needs to share resources between domains. You decide to create a trust relationship between Domain A and Domain B. Before you take any other actions, which of the following statements is true? Choose all that apply.

    A. All users in Domain A can access all resources in Domain B.

    B. All users in Domain B can access all resources in Domain A.

    C. Resources cannot be shared between the domains.

    D. Users in Domain A do not have permission to access resources in Domain B.

    E. Users in Domain B do not have permission to access resources in Domain A.

2. Jane is a systems administrator for a large Active Directory environment that plans to deploy four Active Directory domains. She is responsible for determining the hardware budget she needs to deploy the four domains. She has the following requirements:

    - The budget should minimize the number of servers to be deployed initially.

    - Each domain must implement enough fault tolerance to survive the complete failure of one domain controller.

    - If one domain controller fails, users in all domains should still have access to Active Directory information.

    In order to meet these requirements, what is the minimum number of domain controllers Jane can deploy initially?

    A. 0

    B. 1

    C. 2

    D. 4

    E. 8

3. Juan is a network administrator for three Active Directory domains that support offices based primarily in South America. His organization has recently decided to open several offices in North America and Asia, and many of the employees will be relocated to staff these offices. As part of the change, several offices in South America will either be closed or reduced in size.

    Currently, the environment consists of many Windows Server 2003 computers in different configurations. In order to conserve hardware resources, Juan plans to reassign some of the servers located in South America to support operations in North America and Asia, which will include the creation of new domains. Which of the following server configurations can be directly promoted to become a domain controller for a new domain? Choose all that apply.

    A. Member server

    B. Standalone server

    C. Domain controller

    D. Secondary domain controller

4. Monica is the systems administrator for a mixed-domain environment that consists of Active Directory domain controllers and Windows NT 4 domain controllers. The server roles are as follows:

Server1: Schema Master

Server2: RID Master

Server3: Windows NT 4 Backup Domain Controller

Server4: Infrastructure Master

Server5: PDC Emulator Master

When the business finishes migrating the entire environment to Windows Server 2003, which of the following machines will no longer be required?

A. Server1

B. Server2

C. Server3

D. Server4

E. Server5

5. Implicit trusts created between domains are known as which of the following?

A. Two-way trusts

B. Transitive trusts

C. One-way trusts

D. Intransitive trusts

6. You are a developer for a small organization that has deployed a single Active Directory domain. Your organization has begun using the Active Directory schema in order to store important information related to each of the company's 350 employees. Most of the fields of information you plan to support are already included with the basic Active Directory schema. However, one field—a "security clearance level" value—is not supported. You want to take advantage of the extensibility of Active Directory by adding this field to the properties of a User object. On which of the following servers can the change be made?

A. Any domain controller

B. Any member server

C. The Schema Master

D. The Global Catalog

7. What is a set of Active Directory domains that share a contiguous namespace called?

A. A forest

B. A domain hierarchy

C. A tree

D. A DNS zone

8. A junior systems administrator who was responsible for administering an Active Directory domain accidentally demoted the last domain controller of your `ADTest.com` domain. He noticed that after the demotion process was complete, no Active Directory–related operations could be performed by any machine on the network. He calls you to ask for advice about re-creating the domain. Your solution must meet the following requirements:

- No Active Directory security information can be lost.

- All objects must be restored.

- The process must not require the use of Active Directory or server backups because they were not being performed for the `ADTest.com` domain.

After the last domain controller in a domain has been demoted, how can the domain be re-created to meet these requirements?

A. By creating a new domain controller with the same name as the demoted one.

B. By creating a new domain with the same name.

C. By adding a new member server to the old domain.

D. None of the above solutions meets the requirements.

9. Which of the following item(s) does not depend on the DNS namespace? (Choose all that apply.)

A. Organizational Units (OUs)

B. Domains

C. Domain trees

D. Domain forests

E. DNS zones

F. Active Directory sites

10. Which of the following types of computers contain a copy of the Global Catalog?

A. All Windows NT domain controllers

B. All Active Directory domain controllers

C. Specified Active Directory domain controllers

D. Active Directory workstations

11. Which of the following pieces of information should you have before you use the Active Directory Installation Wizard to install a new subdomain? Choose all that apply.

A. The name of the child domain

B. The name of the parent domain

C. DNS configuration information

D. NetBIOS name for the server

12. Which type of trust is automatically created between the domains in a domain tree?

 A. Transitive

 B. Two-way

 C. Transitive two-way

 D. Intransitive two-way

13. The Active Directory Installation Wizard can be accessed by typing which of the following commands?

 A. `domaininstall`

 B. `domainupgrade`

 C. `dconfig`

 D. `dcinstall`

 E. `dcpromo`

14. A systems administrator wants to remove a domain controller from a domain. Which of the following is the easiest way to perform the task?

 A. Use the Active Directory Installation Wizard to demote the domain controller.

 B. Use the `DCPROMO /REMOVE` command.

 C. Reinstall the server over the existing installation, and make the machine a member of a workgroup.

 D. Reinstall the server over the existing installation, and make the machine a member of a domain.

15. Which of the following is *true* regarding the sharing of resources between forests?

 A. All resources are automatically shared between forests.

 B. A trust relationship must exist before resources can be shared between forests.

 C. Resources cannot be shared between forests.

 D. A transitive trust relationship must exist before resources can be shared between forests.

16. Your company is being bought by another company and you will be affected by the merger. You need to quickly connect the two companies. There are security reasons for keeping the two IT departments and the two forests separate. If you have a new domain to bring into the pre-existing forest, what is the easiest way to achieve this goal?

 A. Deploy another forest.

 B. Use a design with a single domain.

 C. Design a third domain with a new forest for the merger.

 D. Use a design with multiple domains.

17. You are the network administrator for your company's infrastructure. You need to merge a company into your current domain and forest. From the following selections, what is the best way to accomplish this task?

   A. Join the new domain to a new forest.

   B. Join the new domain to a current one.

   C. Create a new FQDN and use a secondary zone.

   D. Allow for a canonical name record to translate to the new domain.

18. As the systems engineer installing the new Active Directory domain, you need to consider where you will have your five main single-master functions. Of the five main single master functions, two apply to an entire Active Directory forest. What are the three that apply to just the domain?

   A. Domain Naming Master

   B. Relative ID (RID) Master

   C. Primary Domain Controller (PDC) Emulator Master

   D. Infrastructure Master

19. When deploying Active Directory, you decide to create a new domain tree. What do you need to do to create this?

   A. Demote a Windows Server 2003 computer to a member server and select the option that makes this tree master for the new domain.

   B. Use a Windows Server 2003 computer as a domain naming master and select the Tree Master option. This will force the selection.

   C. Use a system as a member server, promote it to a domain controller, and then select Use As Tree Master when prompted.

   D. Promote a Windows Server 2003 computer to a domain controller and select the option that makes this domain controller the first machine in a new domain that is a child of an existing one.

20. You are the network administrator for your company and are responsible for the current Active Directory layout. You are purchasing a new company soon and need to connect up the two seamlessly. You need to make sure there is no more administrative overhead than absolutely needed. You currently have two forests and two domains. You need to reduce administrative costs and the overhead and streamline Active Directory deployment. What is the best solution to this problem?

   A. Use multiple domains. Ensure that you are using the Active Directory Connector and make sure you set up QoS (quality of service) on the Active Directory Connector.

   B. Install a new domain controller and use it to offload processes.

   C. Do not use multiple domains. They increase overhead and shouldn't be used unless absolutely needed. Redesign your network to fall under one domain and one forest, then plan and cutover accordingly.

   D. Make sure that you use a third-party load balancer to speed up Active Directory convergence.

Answers to Review Questions

1. D, E. A trust relationship only allows for the *possibility* of sharing resources between domains; it does not explicitly provide any permissions. In order to allow users to access resources in another domain, you must configure the appropriate permissions.

2. E. Every domain must have at least one domain controller; therefore, Jane would need at least four domain controllers in order to create the domains. Furthermore, to meet the requirements for fault tolerance and the ability to continue operations during the failure of a domain controller, each of the four domains must also have a second domain controller. Therefore, Jane must deploy a minimum of eight servers configured as Active Directory domain controllers.

3. Answers: A, B. Both member servers and standalone servers can be promoted to domain controllers for new Active Directory domains. In order to "move" an existing domain controller to a new domain, the domain controller must first be demoted to a nondomain controller. It can then be promoted to a domain controller for a new domain. Secondary domain controllers do not exist in Active Directory.

4. C. The Windows NT Backup Domain Controller will no longer be necessary once the environment moves to a Windows Server 2003 platform (although it may be upgraded to a Windows Server 2003 domain controller). The PDC Emulator Master is used primarily for compatibility with Windows NT domains; however, it will still be required for certain domain-wide functions in a Windows Server 2003 environment.

5. B. Trusts between domains that have not been explicitly defined are known as transitive trusts. Transitive trusts can be either one-way or two-way.

6. C. The Schema Master is the only server within Active Directory on which changes to the schema can be made.

7. C. A domain tree is made up of multiple domains that share the same contiguous namespace.

8. D. Once the last domain controller in an environment has been removed, there is no way to re-create the same domain. If adequate backups had been performed, you may have been able to recover information by rebuilding the server.

9. A, F. OUs do not participate in the DNS namespace—they are used primarily for naming objects within an Active Directory domain. The naming for Active Directory objects, such as sites, does not depend on DNS names either.

10. C. Systems administrators can define which domain controllers in the environment contain a copy of the Global Catalog (GC). Although the GC does contain information about all domains in the environment, it does not have to reside on all domain controllers. In fact, by default, the GC is only contained on the domain controller that is the root of the forest.

11. A, B, C, D. Before beginning the promotion of a domain controller, you should have all of the information listed. You must specify all of these pieces of information in the Active Directory Installation Wizard.

12. C. A transitive two-way trust is automatically created between the domains in a domain tree.

13. E. The dcpromo command can be used to launch the Active Directory Installation Wizard. None of the other commands are valid in Windows Server 2003.

14. A. The Active Directory Installation Wizard allows administrators to remove a domain controller from a domain quickly and easily without requiring them to reinstall the operating system.

15. B. When you create trust relationships, resources can be shared between domains that are in two different forests. To simplify access to resources (at the expense of security), a systems administrator could enable the Guest account in the domains so that resources would be automatically shared for members of the Everyone group.

16. D. As an administrator, you may find times where you need to create multiple domains. When you use a design with multiple domains, you provide additional scalability to your design. Multiple domains also reduce replication traffic, help with political and organizational issues, provide many levels of hierarchy, provide varying security policies, allow for decentralized administration, and allow for multiple DNS or domain names.

17. B. Creating a new tree to form or add to a forest is as simple as promoting a server to a domain controller for a new domain that does not share a namespace with an existing Active Directory domain. In order to add a new domain to an existing forest, you must already have at least one other domain. This domain serves as the root domain for the entire forest.

18. B, C, and D. Single-master operations must be performed on specially designated machines within the Active Directory forest. The five main single-master functions are the following: two that apply to an entire Active Directory forest (Schema Master and Domain Naming Master) and three that apply to each domain (Relative ID [RID] Master, Primary Domain Controller [PDC] Emulator Master, and Infrastructure Master).

19. D. To create a new domain tree, you need to promote a Windows Server 2003 computer to a domain controller and select the option that makes this domain controller the first machine in a new domain that is a child of an existing one. The result is a new domain tree that contains two domains—a parent domain and a child domain.

20. C. With multiple domains, maintaining administrative consistency is more difficult. The number of administrative units multiplies as well, which makes it difficult to keep track of network resources.

Chapter

4

Configuring Sites and Managing Replication

MICROSOFT EXAM OBJECTIVES COVERED IN THIS CHAPTER:

✓ **Plan a strategy for placing global catalog servers.**

- Evaluate network traffic considerations when placing global catalog servers.

✓ **Implement an Active Directory site topology.**

- Configure site links.
- Configure preferred bridgehead servers.

✓ **Manage an Active Directory site.**

- Configure replication schedules.
- Configure site link costs.
- Configure site boundaries.

✓ **Monitor Active Directory replication failures. Tools might include Replication Monitor, Event Viewer, and support tools.**

- Monitor Active Directory replication.
- Monitor File Replication service (FRS) replication.

✓ **Troubleshoot Active Directory.**

- Diagnose and resolve issues related to Active Directory replication.

Microsoft has designed Active Directory to be an enterprise-wide solution for managing network resources. In previous chapters, you saw how to create Active Directory objects based on an organization's logical design. Domain structure and organizational unit (OU) structure, for example, should be designed based primarily on an organization's business needs.

Now it's time to learn how Active Directory can map to an organization's *physical* requirements. Specifically, you must consider network connectivity between sites and the flow of information between domain controllers under less than ideal conditions. These constraints determine how domain controllers can work together to ensure that the objects within Active Directory remain synchronized, no matter how large and geographically dispersed the network is.

Fortunately, through the use of the Active Directory Sites And Services administrative tool, you can quickly and easily create the various components of an Active Directory replication topology. Using this tool, you will create objects called sites, you can place servers in sites, and you can create connections between sites. Once you have configured Active Directory replication to fit your current network environment, you can sit back and allow Active Directory to make sure that information remains consistent across domain controllers.

This chapter covers the features of Active Directory that allow systems administrators to modify the behavior of replication based on their physical network design. Through the use of sites, systems and network administrators will be able to leverage their network infrastructure to best support Windows Server 2003 and Active Directory.

Overview of Active Directory Physical Components

In an ideal situation, a high-speed network would connect all computers and networking devices. In such a situation, you would be able to ensure that, regardless of the location of a network user, they would be able to quickly and easily access resources. When working in the real world, however, there are many other constraints to keep in mind. These include the following:

Network bandwidth Network bandwidth generally refers to the amount of data that can pass through a specific connection in a given amount of time. For example, when considering the wide area network (WAN), a T1 may have 1.544Mbps (megabits per second), or a standard analog modem may have a bandwidth of 56.6Kbps (kilobits per second) or less. Another example would be on your local area network (LAN), where an Ethernet connection may have a bandwidth of 100Mbps. Many different types of networks dictate all different speeds; even so, its imperative that you consider network bandwidth at all times when you're thinking of how to deploy domain controllers in your environment.

Network cost   Cost is perhaps the single biggest factor in determining a network design. If cost were not a constraint, organizations would clearly choose to use high-bandwidth connections for all of their sites. This is just as important as adding redundancy to your links (having multiple links) so that if in case of the loss of a single link, you can still connect to the site you want to communicate with. Realistically, trade-offs in performance must be made for the sake of affordability. Some of the factors that can affect the cost of networking include the distance between networks and the types of technology available at certain locations throughout the world. In locations that are underdeveloped or completely remote, you may not even be able to get Internet Service Provider (ISP)– or Telecom-based access beyond a satellite connection, and what is available can be quite costly. Network designers must keep these factors in mind and often they must settle for less-than-ideal connectivity.

Before we considered the monetary value of doing business, we now consider another definition of cost. When designing and configuring networks, you can require certain devices to automatically make data transport decisions based on an assigned network cost. These devices are commonly known as routers and use routing protocols to make routing decisions. One of the elements in configuring a routing protocol is the ability to adjust the cost of a route. In many cases, for example, there may be multiple ways to connect to a remote site, and a router may have multiple interfaces connected to it with different paths out of the network to which it is locally connected. When two or more routes are available, the one with the lower cost is automatically used first.

All of these factors listed play an important role when you make your Active Directory implementation decisions. When designing networks, systems and network administrators use the following terms to distinguish the types of connectivity between locations and servers:

Local area networks (LANs)   A *local area network (LAN)* is usually characterized as a high-bandwidth network. Generally, an organization owns all of its LAN network hardware and software. Ethernet is by far the most common networking standard. Ethernet speeds are generally at least 10Mbps and can scale to multiple gigabits per second. Currently, the standard for Ethernet is 10 Gigabit Ethernet, which runs 100 times the speed of Gigabit Ethernet (1 Gbps). Several LAN technologies, including routing and switching, are available to segment LANs and reduce contention for network resources.

Wide area networks (WANs)   The purpose of a *wide area network (WAN)* is similar to that of a LAN—to connect network devices together. Unlike LANs, however, WANs are usually leased from third-party telecommunications carriers and ISPs. Although extremely high-speed WAN connections are available, they are generally costly for organizations to implement through a distributed environment. Therefore, WAN connections are characterized by lower-speed connections and, sometimes, nonpersistent connections.

The Internet   To not have heard of the Internet, you would have had to be locked away in a server room (without network access) for a long time. The Internet is a worldwide public network infrastructure based on the *Internet Protocol (IP)*. Access to the Internet is available through organizations known as ISPs. Because it is a public network, there is no single "owner" of the Internet. Instead, large network and telecommunications providers are constantly upgrading the infrastructure of this network to meet growing demands.

Organizations now make regular use of the Internet. For example, it's rare nowadays to see advertisements that don't direct you to one website or another. Through the use of technologies such as Virtual Private Networks (VPNs), organizations can use encryption and authentication technology to enable secure communications across the Internet.

Regardless of the issues related to network design and technological constraints, network users have many different requirements and needs that must be addressed. First and foremost, network resources such as files, printers, and shared directories must be made available. Similarly, the resources stored within Active Directory—and, especially, its security information—are required for many operations that occur within domains.

 You can get more information on Windows Server 2003 networking technologies in the *MCSA/MCSE: Windows Server 2003 Environment Management and Maintenance Study Guide* by Lisa Donald, with Suzan Rupp and James Chellis (Sybex, 2003).

With these issues in mind, take a look at how you can configure Active Directory to reach connectivity goals using replication.

Active Directory Replication

Active Directory was designed as a scalable, distributed database that contains information about an organization's network resources. In previous chapters, we looked at how domains can be created and managed and how domain controllers are used to store Active Directory databases.

Even in the simplest of network environments, you generally need more than one domain controller. The major reasons for this include fault tolerance (if one domain controller fails, others can still provide services as needed) and performance (the workload can be balanced between multiple domain controllers). Windows Server 2003 domain controllers have been designed to contain read-write copies of the Active Directory database. However, the domain controllers must also contain knowledge that is created or modified on other domain controllers since a systems administrator may make changes on only one out of many domain controllers.

To keep information consistent between domain controllers, you use *Active Directory replication*. Replication is the process by which changes to the Active Directory database are transferred between domain controllers. The end result is that all of the domain controllers within an Active Directory domain contain up-to-date information and achieved convergence. Keep in mind that domain controllers may be located very near to each other (e.g., within the same server rack) or they may be located across the world from each other. Although the goals of replication are quite simple, the real-world constraints of network connections between servers cause many limitations that must be accommodated. If you had a domain controller on your local LAN, you may find that between your server connections you have Gigabit Ethernet, which runs at 1000Mbps, whereas you may have a domain controller on the other side or a WAN where the network link runs at a fraction of a T1, 56Kbps. Replication traffic must traverse each link to ensure convergence no matter what the speed or bandwidth available.

Throughout this chapter, you will look at the technical details of Active Directory replication and how the concept of sites and site links can be used to map the logical structure of Active Directory to a physical network topology to help it work efficiently, no matter what type of link you are working with.

Active Directory Site Concepts

One of the most important concepts you will come across when you are designing and implementing Active Directory focuses on separating the logical components from the physical components of the directory service. The logical components include the features that map to business requirements. For example, Active Directory domains, OUs, users, groups, and computers are all designed to map to the political requirements of a company and are made to help facilitate any business needs that can be thought of.

Active Directory physical components, on the other hand, are based on technical issues. These issues will crop up, for instance, when the question of how Active Directory can remain synchronized in a distributed network environment is covered. Active Directory uses the concept of sites to map to an organization's physical network. Stated simply, a *site* is a collection of well-connected computers. The technical implications of sites are defined later in this chapter.

It is important to understand that there is no specified relationship between Active Directory domains and Active Directory sites. An Active Directory site can contain many domains. Alternatively, a single Active Directory domain can span multiple sites. Figure 4.1 illustrates this very important characteristic of their relationship.

FIGURE 4.1   Potential relationships between domains and sites

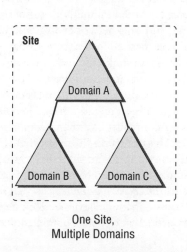

One Site,
Multiple Domains

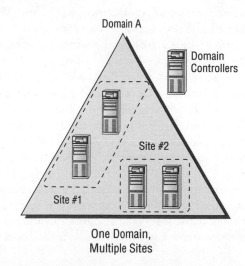

One Domain,
Multiple Sites

There are two main reasons to use Active Directory sites. We will look at these two reasons in the following sections.

Service Requests

Clients often require the network services of a domain controller. One of the most common reasons for this is that they need the domain controller to perform network authentication. Using Active Directory sites, clients can easily connect to the domain controller that is located closest to them. By doing this, they avoid many of the inefficiencies associated with connecting to distant domain controllers or to those that are located on the other side of a slow network connection. One such problem associated with services could include having a saturated network link, which might cause two domain controllers to be out of sync with each other.

Other network services include the Licensing service (for tracking licenses associated with Microsoft and other compatible products) and such applications as messaging (such as Exchange Server). All of these functions depend on the availability of network services. In the case of Active Directory, clients should try to connect to the domain controllers that are located closest to them. This reduces network utilization and results in increased performance.

Replication

As we mentioned earlier, the purpose of Active Directory replication is to ensure that the information stored on all domain controllers within a domain remains synchronized. In environments with many domains and domain controllers, there are multiple communication paths between them, which makes the synchronization process more complicated. One method of transferring updates and other changes to Active Directory would be for all of the servers to communicate directly with each other as soon as a change occurs; they can all update with the change and reach convergence again. This is not ideal, however, since it places high requirements on network bandwidth and is inefficient for many network environments that use slower and more costly WAN links, especially if all environments were to do it at the same time. In this case, the network connection at the core of your network could become saturated and actually decrease performance of the entire WAN.

Using sites, Active Directory can automatically determine the best methods for performing replication operations. Sites take into account an organization's network infrastructure and Active Directory uses them to determine the most efficient method for synchronizing information between domain controllers. Systems administrators can make their physical network design map to Active Directory objects. Based on the creation and configuration of these objects, the Active Directory service can then manage replication traffic in an efficient way.

Whenever a change is made to the Active Directory database on a domain controller, the change is given a logical sequence number. The domain controller can then propagate these changes to other domain controllers based on replication settings. In the event that the same setting (such as a user's last name) has been changed on two different domain controllers (before replication can take place), these sequence numbers are used to resolve the conflict.

Windows Server 2003 introduces a new feature called *linked value replication* that is only active when the domain is in Windows Server 2003 domain functional level. In Windows 2000, if a change was made to a member of a group, the entire group was replicated. With linked value replication, only the group member is replicated. This greatly enhances replication efficiency and cuts down on network traffic utilization. Linked value replication is automatically enabled in Windows Server 2003 domain functional level domains.

Planning Your Sites

Much of the challenge of designing Active Directory is related to mapping a company's business processes to the structure of a hierarchical data store. So far, you've seen many of these requirements. But what about the existing network infrastructure? Clearly, when you plan for and design the structure of Active Directory, you must take into account your LAN and WAN characteristics. Let's see how Active Directory sites can be used to manage replication traffic.

Synchronizing Active Directory is extremely important. In order to keep security permissions and objects within the directory consistent throughout the organization, you must use replication. Active Directory data store supports multimaster replication. That is, data can be modified at any domain controller within the domain because replication ensures that information remains consistent throughout the organization.

Ideally, every site within an organization has reliable, high-speed connections with one another. A much more realistic scenario, however, is one in which bandwidth is limited and connections are sometimes either sporadically available or completely unavailable.

Using sites, network and systems administrators can define which domain controllers are located on which areas of the network. These settings can be based on the bandwidth available between the areas of the network. Additionally, *subnets*—logically partitioned areas of the network—can be defined between them. Subnets are designed by subdividing IP addresses into usable blocks for assignment, and they are also objects found within the Sites and Services Microsoft Management Console (MMC) in the Administrative Tools folder. The Windows Server 2003 Active Directory services use this information to decide how and when to replicate data between domain controllers.

Directly replicating information between all domain controllers might be a viable solution for some companies. For others, however, this might result in a lot of traffic traveling over slow or undersized network links. One way to efficiently synchronize data between sites that are connected with slow connections is to use a bridgehead server. Bridgehead servers are designed to accept traffic between two remote sites and to then forward this information to the appropriate servers. Figure 4.2 provides an example of how a bridgehead server can reduce network bandwidth requirements and improve performance. Reduced network bandwidth requirements and improved performance can also be achieved by configuring replication to occur according to a predefined schedule if bandwidth usage statistics are available.

Bridgehead servers would not fit a normal hub and spoke WAN topology where you generally have a core site (usually company headquarters) and all of your remote sites are links that are one off from the core. You can use a bridgehead server design to fit a distributed star, where you have a hub and spoke topology design, with more spokes coming out of the first set of spokes. Doing so would make some of your spoke sites into smaller core sites; it is at these sites that you would place your bridgehead server. In the case Figure 4.2, you can see that your Asia headquarters site is also where you can connect up to India, China, and Hong Kong—thus making Asia headquarters the ideal site for the bridgehead server.

FIGURE 4.2   Using a bridgehead server

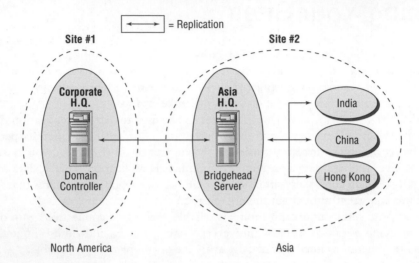

In addition to managing replication traffic, sites also offer the advantage of allowing clients to access the nearest domain controller. This prevents problems with user authentication across slow network connections and it can help find the shortest and fastest path to resources such as files and printers. Therefore, Microsoft recommends that you place at least one domain controller at each site that contains a slow link. Preferably, this domain controller also contains a copy of the Global Catalog so that logon attempts and resource search queries do not occur across slow links. The drawback, however, is that deploying more copies of the Global Catalog to servers increases replication traffic.

Through proper planning and deployment of sites, organizations can best use the capabilities of the network infrastructure while keeping Active Directory synchronized.

Implementing Sites and Subnets

Now that you have an idea of the goals of replication, look at the following quick overview of the various Active Directory objects that are related to physical network topology.

The basic objects that are used for managing replication include the following:

Subnets   A subnet is a partition of a network. As we started to discuss earlier, subnets are logical IP blocks usually connected to other IP blocks through the use of routers and other network devices. All of the computers that are located on a given subnet are generally well connected.

It is extremely important to understand the concepts of TCP/IP and the routing of network information when you are designing the topology for Active Directory replication. Although TCP/IP is not tested heavily in this exam, you should still generally understand it so that you know how to deploy sites properly. See *MCSA/MCSE: Windows Server 2003 Network Infrastructure Implementation, Management, and Maintenance Study Guide (70-291), Second Edition,* by Steve Suehring and James Chellis, (Wiley, 2006) for more information on this topic.

Sites   An Active Directory site is a logical object that can contain servers and other objects related to Active Directory replication. Specifically, a site is a grouping of related subnets. Sites are created to match the physical network structure of an organization.

Site links   *Site links* are created to define the types of connections that are available between the components of a site. Site links can reflect a relative cost for a network connection and can reflect the bandwidth that is available for communications.

Each of these components works together to determine how information is used to replicate data between domain controllers. Figure 4.3 provides an example of the physical components of Active Directory.

FIGURE 4.3   Active Directory replication objects

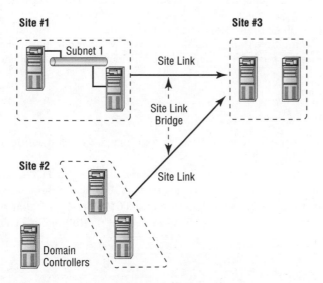

There are many issues related to configuring and managing sites; each is covered throughout this chapter. Overall, the use of sites allows you to control the behavior of Active Directory replication between domain controllers. With this background and goal in mind, let's look at how sites can be implemented to control Active Directory replication so that it is efficient and in sync. As you will learn, if you do not have replication set up properly, you will experience problems with your domain controllers after awhile. An example of a common replication problem may be Event Log event ID 1311, which states that the Windows NT Directory Services (NTDS) Knowledge Consistency Checker (KCC) has found (and reported) a problem with Active Directory replication. This error states that the replication configuration information in Active Directory does not accurately reflect the physical topology of the network. Although only an example, this is commonly found on ailing networks that have replication problems for one reason or another.

Creating Sites

The primary method for creating and managing Active Directory replication components is to utilize the Active Directory Sites And Services tool, or MMC found within the Administrative Tools folder. Using this administrative component, you can graphically create and manage sites in much the same way as you create and manage OUs. Exercise 4.1 walks you through the process of creating Active Directory sites. In order to complete this exercise, the local machine must be a domain controller. Also, this exercise assumes that you have not yet changed the default domain site configuration. Do not perform any testing on a production system or network—make sure you test site configuration in a lab setting only.

The exercises in this chapter have been designed to work through the use of a single domain controller and single Active Directory domain. Although you can walk through all of the steps required to create sites and related objects without using multiple domain controllers, real-world replication generally involve the use of multiple domain controllers in multiple physical sites.

Creating Subnets

Once you have created the sites that map to your network topology, it's time to define the subnets that define the site boundaries.

Subnets are based on TCP/IP address information and take the form of a TCP/IP address and a subnet mask. For example, the TCP/IP address may be 10.120.0.0, and the subnet mask may be 255.255.0.0. This information specifies that all of the TCP/IP addresses that begin with the first two octets are part of the same TCP/IP subnet. All of the following TCP/IP addresses would be within this subnet:

- 10.120.1.5
- 10.120.100.17
- 10.120.120.120

EXERCISE 4.1

Creating Sites

1. Open the Active Directory Sites And Services tool from the Administrative Tools program group.

2. Expand the Sites folder.

3. Right-click the Default-First-Site-Name item, and choose Rename. Rename the site to **CorporateHQ**. The Active Directory Sites And Services tool should now look like this:

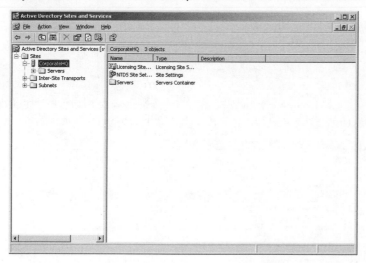

4. Create a new site by right-clicking the Sites object and selecting New Site.

5. On the New Object–Site dialog box, type **Austin** for the site name. Click the DEFAULTIP-SITELINK item, and then click OK to create the site. Note that you cannot include spaces or other special characters in the name of a site.

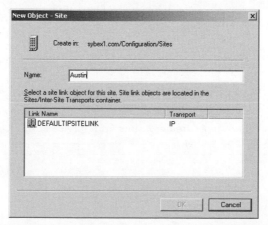

6. You will see a dialog box stating the actions that you should take to finish the configuration of this site. Click OK to continue.

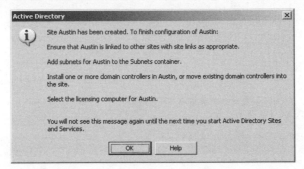

7. Create another new site and name it **NewYork**. Again, choose the DEFAULTIPSITELINK item. The Active Directory Sites And Services tool should now look like this:

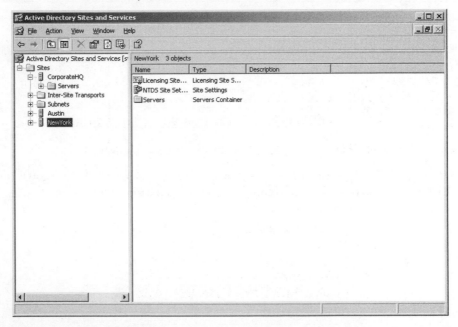

8. When finished, close the Active Directory Sites And Services tool.

The Active Directory Sites And Services tool expresses these subnets in a somewhat different notation. It uses the provided subnet address and appends a slash followed by the number of bits in the subnet mask. In the example in the previous paragraph, the subnet would be defined as 10.120.0.0/16.

Remember that sites typically represent distinct physical locations, and these locations almost always have their own subnets. The only way for a domain controller (DC) in one site to reach to a DC in another site is to add subnet information about the remote site. Generally, information regarding the definition of subnets for a specific network environment will be available from a network designer. Exercise 4.2 walks you through the steps you need to take to create subnets and assign subnets to sites. In order to complete the steps in this exercise, you must have first completed Exercise 4.1.

EXERCISE 4.2

Creating Subnets

1. Open the Active Directory Sites And Services tool from the Administrative Tools program group.

2. Expand the Sites folder. Right-click the Subnets folder, and select New Subnet.

3. In the New Object–Subnet dialog box, you are prompted for information about the TCP/IP details for the new subnet. For the address, type **100.1.1.0,** and for the mask, type **255.255.255.0**. You will see that the Name value has been automatically calculated as 100.1.1.0/24. Click the Austin site, and then click OK to create the subnet.

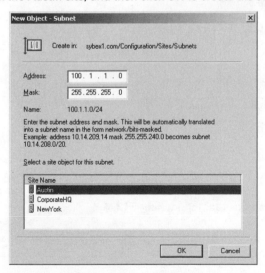

4. In the Active Directory Sites And Services tool, right-click the newly created 100.1.1.0/24 subnet object, and select Properties.

5. On the subnet Properties dialog box, type **Austin 100Mbit LAN** for the description. Click OK to continue.

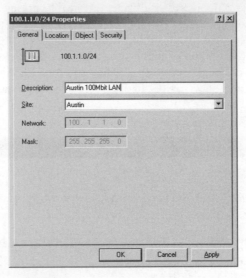

6. Create a new subnet using the following information:

Address: **160.25.0.0**

Mask: **255.255.0.0**

Site: **NewYork**

Description: **NewYork 100Mbit LAN**

7. Finally, create another subnet using the following information:

Address: **176.33.0.0**

Mask: **255.255.0.0**

Site: **CorporateHQ**

Description: **Corporate 100Mbit switched LAN**

EXERCISE 4.2 *(continued)*

The Active Directory Sites And Services tool should now look like this:

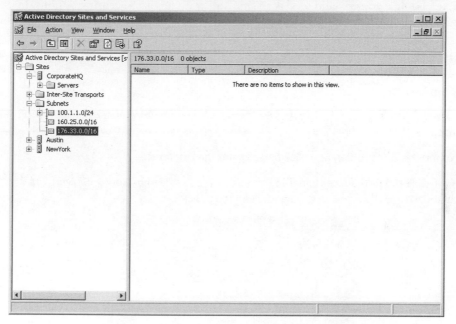

8. When finished, close the Active Directory Sites And Services tool.

So far, you have created the basic components that govern Active Directory sites: sites and subnets. You also linked these two components together by defining which subnets belong in which sites. These two steps—creating sites and subnets—form the basis of mapping the physical network infrastructure of an organization to Active Directory. Now, look at the various settings that you can make for sites.

Configuring Sites

Once you have created Active Directory sites and defined which subnets they contain, it's time to make some additional configurations to the site structure. Specifically, you'll need to assign servers to specific sites and configure the site licensing options. Placing servers in sites tells Active Directory replication services how to replicate information for various types of servers. Later in this chapter, you'll look at the details of working with replication within and between sites.

The purpose of a *licensing server* is to track the operating system and Microsoft BackOffice licenses within a domain. This is an important feature because it allows systems administrators to ensure that they have purchased the proper number of licenses for their network environment. Since servers must record licensing information, you can use the Active Directory Sites And Services tool to specify a License server for a site.

In Exercise 4.3, you will add servers to sites and configure site-licensing options. In order to complete the steps in this exercise, you must have first completed Exercises 4.1 and 4.2.

EXERCISE 4.3

Configuring Sites

1. Open the Active Directory Sites And Services tool from the Administrative Tools program group.

2. Expand the Sites folder, and click and expand the Austin site.

3. Right-click the Servers container in the Austin site, and select New ➤ Server. Type **AustinDC1** for the name of the server, and then click OK.

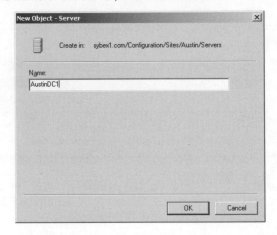

4. Create a new Server object within the CorporateHQ site, and name it **CorpDC1**. Note that this object also includes the name of the local domain controller.

5. Create two new Server objects within the NewYork site, and name them **NewYorkDC1** and **NewYorkDC2**. The Active Directory Sites And Service tool should now look like this:

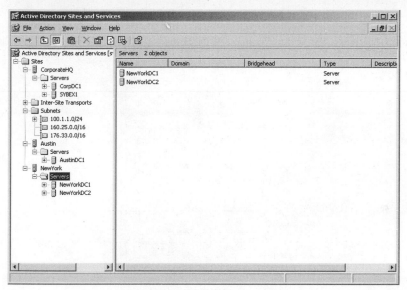

6. Right-click the NewYorkDC1 server object and select Properties. In the NewYorkDC1 Properties box, select the IP in the Transports Available For Inter-site Data Transfer box, and click Add to make this server a preferred IP bridgehead server. Click OK to accept the settings.

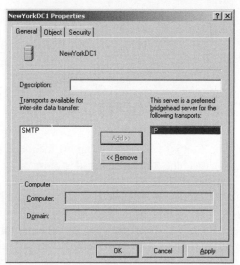

7.   To set the Licensing server for the CorporateHQ site, click the Austin container and look in the right windowpane. Right-click the Licensing Site Settings object, and select Properties. To change the computer that will act as the Licensing server for the site, click Change in the Licensing Site Settings Properties dialog box. Enter the name of the local domain controller and press Enter. To save the settings, click OK.

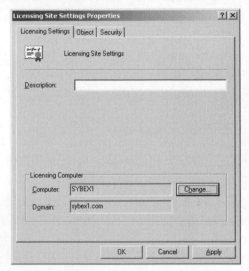

8.   When you are finished, close the Active Directory Sites And Services tool.

With the configuration of the basic settings for sites out of the way, it's time to focus on the real details of the site topology—creating site links and site link bridges.

Configuring Replication

Sites are generally used to define groups of computers that are located within a single geographic location. In most organizations, machines that are located in close physical proximity (for example, within a single building or branch office) are well connected. A typical example is a LAN in a branch office of a company. All of the computers may be connected together using Ethernet, and routing and switching technology may be in place to reduce network congestion.

Often, however, domain controllers are located across various states, countries, and even continents. In such a situation, network connectivity is usually much slower, less reliable, and more costly than that for the equivalent LAN. Therefore, Active Directory replication must accommodate accordingly. When managing replication traffic within Active Directory sites, you need to be aware of two main areas of synchronization:

Intrasite   *Intrasite replication* refers to the synchronization of Active Directory information between domain controllers that are located in the same site. In accordance with the concept of sites, these machines are usually well connected by a high-speed LAN.

Intersite   *Intersite replication* occurs between domain controllers in different sites. Usually, this means that there is a WAN or other type of low-speed network connection between the various machines. Intersite replication is optimized for minimizing the amount of network traffic that occurs between sites.

In the following sections, you'll look at ways to configure both intrasite and intersite replication. Additionally, you'll see features of Active Directory replication architecture that can be used to accommodate the needs of almost any environment.

Intrasite Replication

Intrasite replication is generally a simple process. One domain controller contacts the others in the same site when changes to its copy of Active Directory are made. It compares the logical sequence numbers in its own copy of Active Directory with that of the other domain controllers, then the most current information is chosen by the DC in question, and all domain controllers within the site use this information to make the necessary updates to their database.

Because you can assume that the domain controllers within an Active Directory site are well connected, you can pay less attention to exactly when and how replication takes place. Communications between domain controllers occur using the *Remote Procedure Call (RPC) protocol*. This protocol is optimized for transmitting and synchronizing information on fast and reliable network connections. The actual directory synchronizing information is not compressed; therefore, it provides for fast replication at the expense of network bandwidth, which is usually readily available because most LANs today are running on Fast Ethernet (100Mbps) at a minimum.

Intersite Replication

Intersite replication is optimized for low-bandwidth situations and network connections that have less reliability. Intersite replication offers several specific features that are tailored toward these types of connections. To begin with, two different protocols may be used to transfer information between sites:

RPC over IP   When connectivity is fairly reliable, IP is a good choice. IP-based communications require you to have a live connection between two or more domain controllers in different sites and let you transfer Active Directory information. RPC over IP was originally designed for slower WANs in which packet loss and corruption may occur often. As such, it is a good choice for low-quality connections involved in intersite replication.

Simple Mail Transfer Protocol (SMTP) *Simple Mail Transfer Protocol (SMTP)* is perhaps best known as the protocol that is used to send and receive email messages on the Internet. SMTP was designed to use a store-and-forward mechanism through which a server receives a copy of a message, records it to disk, and then attempts to forward it to another email server. If the destination server is unavailable, it holds the message and attempts to resend it at periodic intervals.

This type of communication is extremely useful for situations in which network connections are unreliable or not always available. If, for instance, a branch office in Peru is connected to the corporate office by a dial-up connection that is available only during certain hours, SMTP would be a good choice.

SMTP is an inherently insecure network protocol. Therefore, if you would like to ensure that you transfer replication traffic securely and you use SMTP for Active Directory replication, you must take advantage of Windows Server 2003's Certificate Services functionality.

Other intersite replication characteristics that are designed to address low-bandwidth situations and less reliable network connections include the compression of Active Directory information. This compression is helpful because changes between domain controllers in remote sites may include a large amount of information and also because network bandwidth tends to be less available and more costly. You can determine intersite replication topology by using site links and site link bridges. Replication can occur based on a schedule defined by systems administrators. All of these features give you a high degree of flexibility in controlling replication configuration.

You can configure intersite replication by using the Active Directory Sites And Services tool. Select the name of the site for which you want to configure settings. Then, right-click the NTDS Site Settings object in the right windowpane, and select Properties. By clicking the Change Schedule button in the NTDS Site Settings Properties dialog box, you'll be able to configure how often replication between sites will occur (see Figure 4.4).

 You will see how to set the replication schedule in Exercise 4.4.

FIGURE 4.4 Configuring intersite replication schedules

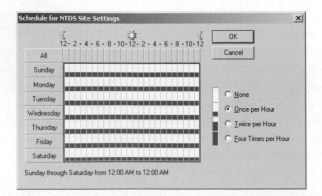

In the following sections, you will see how to configure site links and site link bridges, as well as how to manage connection objects and bridgehead servers.

Creating Site Links and Site Link Bridges

The overall topology of intersite replication is based on the use of site links and site link bridges. Site links are logical connections that define a path between two Active Directory sites. Site links can include several descriptive elements that define their network characteristics. *Site link bridges* are used to connect site links together so that the relationship can be transitive.

Figure 4.5 provides an example of site links and site link bridges.

FIGURE 4.5   An example of site links and site link bridges

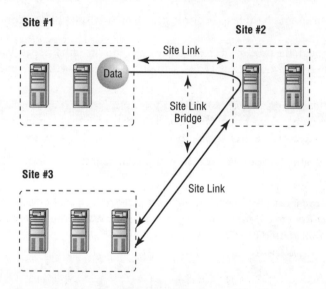

Both of these types of logical connections are used by Active Directory services to determine how information should be synchronized between domain controllers in remote sites. This information is used by the KCC, which forms a replication topology based on the site topology created. This service is responsible for determining the best way to replicate information within and between sites.

When creating site links for your environment, you'll need to consider the following factors:

Transporting information   You can choose to use either RPC over IP or SMTP for transferring information over a site link. The main determination will be based on your network infrastructure and the reliability of connections between sites.

Assigning a cost value   Multiple site links can be created between sites. Site links can be assigned a cost value based on the type of connection. The systems administrator determines the cost value, and the relative costs of site links are then used to determine the optimal path for replication. The lower the cost, the more likely the link is to be used for replication.

For example, a company may primarily use a T1 link between branch offices, but it may also use a slower and circuit-switched dial-up Integrated Services Digital Network (ISDN) connection for redundancy (in case the T1 fails). In this example, a systems administrator may assign a cost of 25 to the T1 line and a cost of 100 to the ISDN line. This ensures that the more reliable and higher-bandwidth T1 connection is used whenever it's available but that the ISDN line is also available.

Determining a replication schedule   Once you've determined how and through which connections replication will take place, it's time to determine *when* information should be replicated. Replication requires network resources and occupies bandwidth. Therefore, you need to balance the need for consistent directory information with the need to conserve bandwidth. For example, if you determine that it's reasonable to have a lag time of six hours between when an update is made at one site and when it is replicated to all others, you might schedule replication to occur once in the morning, once during the lunch hour, and more frequently after normal work hours.

Based on these factors, you should be able to devise a strategy that allows you to configure site links.

Exercise 4.4 walks you through the process of creating site links and site link bridges. In order to complete the steps in this exercise, you must have first completed Exercises 4.1, 4.2, and 4.3.

EXERCISE 4.4

Creating Site Links and Site Link Bridges

1. Open the Active Directory Sites And Services tool from the Administrative Tools program group.

2. Expand Sites, Inter-site Transports, IP object. Right-click the DEFAULTIPSITELINK item in the right pane, and select Rename. Rename the object **CorporateWAN**. The ActiveDirectory Sites And Services tool should now look like this:

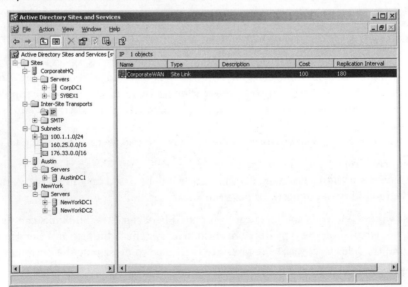

3. Right-click the CorporateWAN link, and select Properties. In the CorporateWAN Properties dialog box, type **T1 Connecting Corporate and NewYork Offices** for the description.
Remove the Austin site from the link by highlighting Austin and clicking Remove. For the
Cost value, type **50**, and specify that replication should occur every 60 minutes. To create
the site link, click OK.

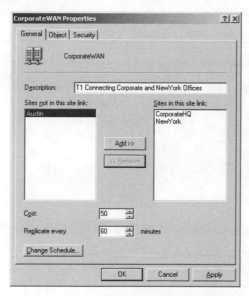

4. Right-click the IP folder, and select New Site Link. On the New Object–Site Link dialog
box, name the link **CorporateDialup**. Add the Austin and CorporateHQ sites to the site
link, and then click OK.

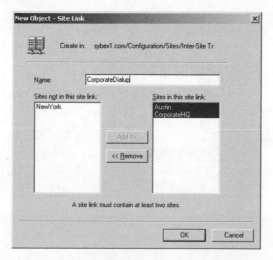

5. Right-click the CorporateDialup link, and select Properties. In the CorporateDialup Properties dialog box, type **ISDN Dialup between Corporate and Austin office** for the description. Set the Cost value to 100, and specify that replication should occur every 120 minutes. To specify that replication should occur only during certain times of the day, click the Change Schedule button.

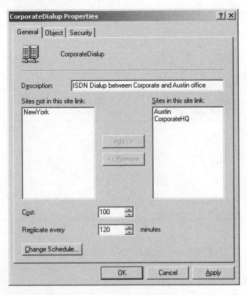

6. On the Schedule For CorporateDialup dialog box, highlight the area between 8:00 AM and 6:00 PM for the days Monday through Friday, and click the Replication Not Available option. This will ensure that replication traffic is minimized during normal work hours.

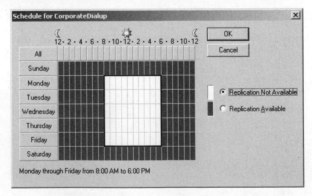

Click OK to accept the new schedule and then OK again to create the site link.

7. Right-click the IP object, and select New Site Link Bridge. On the New Object–Site Link Bridge dialog box, name the site link bridge **CorporateBridge**. Note that the Corporate-Dialup and CorporateWAN site links are already added to the site link bridge. Because there must be at least two site links in each bridge, you will not be able to remove these links. Click OK to create the site link bridge.

8. When finished, close the Active Directory Sites And Services tool. It should look like this now:

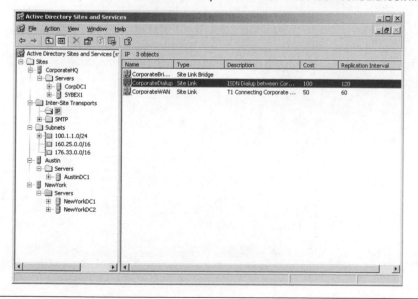

Creating Connection Objects

Generally, it is a good practice to allow Active Directory's replication mechanisms to automatically schedule and manage replication functions. In some cases, however, you may want to have additional control over replication. Perhaps you want to replicate changes on demand (when you create new accounts). Or you may want to specify a custom schedule for certain servers.

Connection objects provide you with a way to set up these different types of replication schedules. Connection objects can be created with the Active Directory Sites And Services tool by expanding a server object, right-clicking the NTDS Settings object, and selecting New Active Directory Connection (see Figure 4.6).

Within the properties of the connection object, which you can see in the right pane of the Active Directory Sites And Services tool, you can specify the type of transport to use for replication (RPC over IP or SMTP), the schedule for replication, and the domain controllers that participate in the replication (see Figure 4.7). Additionally, you have the ability to right-click the connection object and select Replicate Now. Always ensure that if you kick off a manual replication, you don't do it during business hours if you think you do not have the bandwidth available to accomplish it. If you do it during business hours, you will most likely create a network slow-down if you do not plan properly. It's always safe to plan a test during non-business hours or during times of very little activity on the network.

FIGURE 4.6   Creating a new connection object

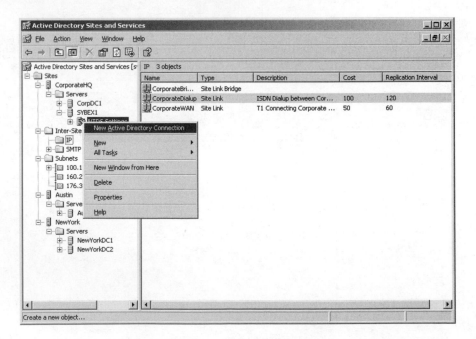

FIGURE 4.7   Viewing the properties of a connection object

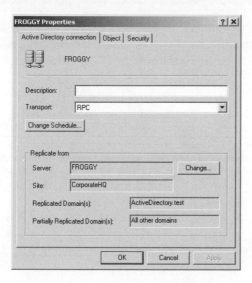

In Exercise 4.5, you create and configure a custom connection object to control Active Directory replication. Unlike previous exercises in this chapter, this exercise requires at least two domain controllers.

EXERCISE 4.5

Creating Connection Objects

1. Open the Active Directory Sites And Services tool.

2. Find the site that contains the local domain controller, and expand this object.

3. Expand the name of the local domain controller. Right-click NTDS Settings, and select New Active Directory Connection.

4. The Find Domain Controllers box appears showing a list of the servers that are available. Highlight the name of the server to which you want to connect, and click OK.

5. For the name of the connection object, type **Connection**. Click OK.

6. In the right pane of the Active Directory Sites And Services tool, right-click the Connection item, and select Properties.

7. When the Connection Properties dialog box appears, type **After-hours synchronization** in the description field. For the Transport, choose IP from the drop-down menu.

8. When you are finished, click OK to save the properties of the connection object.

---

9. To modify the allowed times for replication, click the Change Schedule button in the Active Directory Sites And Service tool. Highlight the area from 8:00 AM to 6:00 PM for all days, and then click the Once Per Hour item. This reduces the frequency of replication during normal business hours. Click OK to save the schedule.

10. Close the Active Directory Sites And Services tool.

Moving Server Objects between Sites

Using the Active Directory Sites And Services tool, you can easily move servers between sites. To do this, simply right-click the name of a domain controller and select Move. You can then select the site to which you want to move the domain controller object.

Figure 4.8 shows the screen that you see when you attempt to move a server. After the server is moved, all replication topology settings are updated automatically. If you want to choose custom replication settings, you need to manually create connection objects (as described earlier).

FIGURE 4.8   Choosing a new site for a specific server

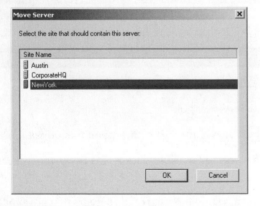

In Exercise 4.6, you move a server object between sites. In order to complete the steps in this exercise, you must have first completed the previous exercises in this chapter.

Creating Bridgehead Servers

By default, all of the servers in one site communicate with the servers in another site. You can, however, further control replication between sites by using *bridgehead servers*. As we mentioned earlier in the chapter, the use of bridgehead servers helps minimize replication traffic, especially in larger distributed star network topologies, and it allows you to dedicate machines that are better connected to receive replicated data. Figure 4.9 provides an example of how bridgehead servers work.

EXERCISE 4.6

Moving Server Objects between Sites

1. Open the Active Directory Sites And Services administrative tool.

2. Right-click the server named NewYorkDC1, and select Move.

3. In the Move dialog box, select the Austin site, and then click OK. This moves this server to the Austin site.

4. To move the server back, right-click NewYorkDC1 (now located in the Austin site) and then click Move. Select New York for the destination site.

5. When finished, close the Active Directory Sites And Services administrative tool.

FIGURE 4.9 A replication scenario using bridgehead servers

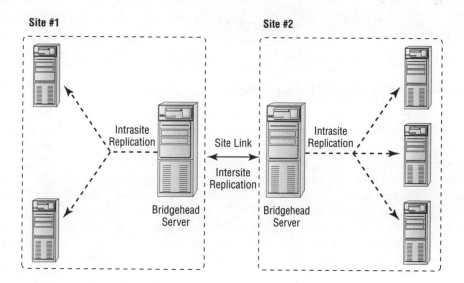

You can use a bridgehead server to specify which domain controllers are preferred for transferring replication information between sites. Different bridgehead servers can be selected for RPC over IP and SMTP replication, thus allowing you to balance the load. To create a bridgehead server for a site, simply right-click a domain controller and select Properties, which brings up the bridgehead server Properties dialog box (See Figure 4.10). To make the server a bridgehead server, just select one or both replication types from the left side of the dialog box and click the Add button to add them to the right side of the dialog box.

FIGURE 4.10 Specifying a bridgehead server

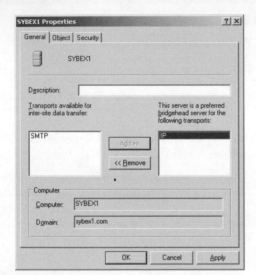

Configuring Server Topology

When you are using environments that require multiple sites, you must carefully consider where you place your servers. In doing so, you can greatly improve performance and the end user's experience by reducing the time they must spend performing common operations such as authentication or searching Active Directory for resources.

There are two main issues to consider when designing a distributed Active Directory environment. The first is how you should place domain controllers within the network environment. The second is how to manage the use of Global Catalog (GC) servers. Finding the right balance between servers, server resources, and performance can be considered an art form for network and systems administrators. In the following sections, you'll look at some of the important considerations that must be taken into account when you design a replication server topology.

Placing Domain Controllers

Microsoft highly recommends that you have at least two domain controllers in each domain of your Active Directory environment. As mentioned earlier in this chapter, the use of additional domain controllers provides increased network performance (since the servers can balance the burden of serving client requests) and provides for fault tolerance (in case one domain controller fails, the other still contains a valid and usable copy of the Active Directory database). Furthermore, if you place the domain controllers properly, you can increase overall network performance since clients can connect to the server closest to them instead of performing authentication and security operations across a slow WAN link.

As we just mentioned, having too few domain controllers can be a problem. However, there is also such a thing as *too many* domain controllers. Keep in mind that the more domain controllers you choose to implement, the greater the replication traffic. Because each domain controller must propagate any changes to all of the others, you can probably see how the compounding of services can result in increased network traffic.

Placing Global Catalog Servers

A *Global Catalog (GC) server* is a domain controller that contains a copy of all the objects contained in the forest-wide domain controllers that compose the Active Directory database. Making a domain controller a GC server is very simple, and you can change this setting quite easily. That brings us to the harder part—determining which domain controllers should also be GC servers.

Where you place domain controllers and GC servers is very important. Generally, you want to make GC servers available in every site that has a slow link. This means that the most logical place to put a GC server would be in every site and closest to the WAN link for the best possible connectivity. However, there is a trade-off that can make having too many GC servers a bad thing. The main issue is associated with replication traffic—you must keep each GC server within your environment synchronized with the other servers. In a very dynamic environment, using additional GC servers causes a considerable increase in additional network traffic. Therefore, you will want to find a good balance between replication burdens and GC query performance in your own environment.

To create a GC server, simply expand the Server object in the Active Directory Sites And Services tool, right-click NTDS settings, and select Properties to bring up the NTDS Properties dialog box (see Figure 4.11). To configure a server as a GC server, simply place a check mark in the Global Catalog box.

FIGURE 4.11   Enabling the Global Catalog on an Active Directory domain controller

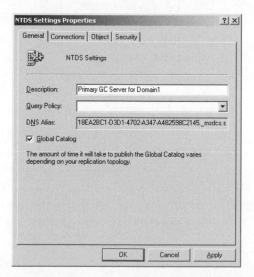

Real World Scenario

Accommodating a Changing Environment

You're a systems administrator for a medium-sized business that consists of many offices located throughout the world. Some of these offices are well connected because they use high-speed, reliable links, while others are not so fortunate. Overall, things are going well until your CEO announces that the organization will be merging with another large company and that the business will be restructured. The restructuring will involve opening new offices, closing old ones, and transferring employees to different locations. Additionally, changes in the IT budget will affect the types of links that exist between offices. Your job as the systems administrator is to ensure that the network environment and, specifically, Active Directory, keeps pace with the changes and ultimately outperforms them.

An important skill for any technical professional is the ability to quickly and efficiently adapt to a changing organization. When a business grows, restructures, or forms relationships with other businesses, often many IT-related changes must also occur. You may have to create new network links for example. Fortunately, Active Directory has been designed with these kinds of challenges in mind. For example, you can use the Active Directory Sites And Services administrative tool to reflect physical network changes in Active Directory topology. If a site that previously had 64Kbps of bandwidth was upgraded to a T1 connection, you could change those characteristics for the site link objects. Conversely, if a site that was previously well connected was reduced to a slow, unreliable link, you could reconfigure the sites, change the site link transport mechanisms (perhaps from IP to SMTP to accommodate a nonpersistent link), and create connection objects (which would allow you to schedule replication traffic to occur during the least busy hours). Or suppose that many of your operations move overseas to a European division. This might call for designating specific domain controllers as preferred bridgehead servers to reduce the amount of replication traffic over costly and slow overseas links.

Sweeping organizational changes inevitably require you to move servers between sites. For example, an office may be closed and its domain controllers may be moved to another region of the world. Again, you can accommodate this change by using Active Directory administrative tools. You may change your OU structure to reflect new logical and business-oriented changes, and you can move server objects between sites to reflect physical network changes.

Rarely can the job of mapping a physical infrastructure to Active Directory be "complete." In most environments, it's safe to assume that you will always need to make changes based on business needs. Overall, however, you should feel comfortable that the physical components of Active Directory are at your side to help you accommodate these changes.

Monitoring and Troubleshooting Active Directory Replication

For the most part, domain controllers handle the replication processes automatically. However, systems administrators still need to monitor the performance of Active Directory replication, since failed network links and incorrect configurations can sometimes prevent the synchronization of information between domain controllers.

There are several ways in which you can monitor the behavior of Active Directory replication and troubleshoot the process if problems occur.

Using System Monitor

The Windows Server 2003 System Monitor administrative tool was designed so that you can monitor many performance statistics associated with using Active Directory. Included within the various performance statistics that you may monitor are counters related to Active Directory replication.

We'll cover the details of working with the System Monitor tools of Windows Server 2003 in Chapter 7, "Active Directory Optimization and Reliability."

Troubleshooting Replication

A common symptom of replication problems is that information is not updated on some or all domain controllers. For example, a systems administrator creates a User account on one domain controller, but the changes are not propagated to other domain controllers. In most environments, this is a potentially serious problem because it affects network security and can prevent authorized users from accessing the resources they require.

You can take several steps to troubleshoot Active Directory replication; each of these is discussed in the following sections.

Verifying Network Connectivity

In order for replication to work properly in distributed environments, you must have network connectivity. Although ideally all domain controllers would be connected by high-speed LAN links, this is rarely the case for larger organizations. In the real world, dial-up connections and slow connections are common. If you have verified that your replication topology is set up properly, you should confirm that your servers are able to communicate. Problems such as a failed dial-up connection attempt can prevent important Active Directory information from being replicated.

Verifying Router and Firewall Configurations

Firewalls are used to restrict the types of traffic that can be transferred between networks. Their main use is to increase security by preventing unauthorized users from transferring information. In some cases, company firewalls may block the types of network access that must be available in order for Active Directory replication to occur. For example, if a specific router or firewall prevents data from being transferred using SMTP, replication that uses this protocol will fail.

Examining the Event Logs

Whenever an error in the replication configuration occurs, the computer writes events to the Directory Service and File Replication Service event logs. By using the Event Viewer administrative tool, you can quickly and easily view the details associated with any problems in replication. For example, if one domain controller is not able to communicate with another to transfer changes, a log entry is created. Figure 4.12 shows an example of the types of events you will see in the Directory Service log, and Figure 4.13 shows a specific example of a configuration error.

FIGURE 4.12   Viewing entries in the Directory Service event log

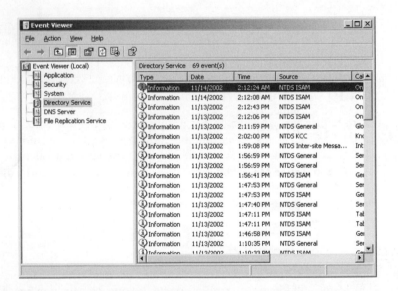

Monitoring Replication with the Replication Monitor

The Replication Monitor is not installed on Windows Server 2003 computers by default, but it is included on the Windows Server 2003 CD-ROM as part of the support tools package. After you install the support tools, you can access the Replication Monitor by entering **replmon** in the Run dialog box. The Replication Monitor window is initially empty; you must add one or more servers to the monitor window in order to derive any meaningful information from the tool. To add a server, right-click the Monitored Servers item in the left pane and select Add Monitored Server. The Add Monitored Server Wizard prompts you to enter or select a server from a list, which is a very straightforward process.

FIGURE 4.13   Examining the details of an event log entry

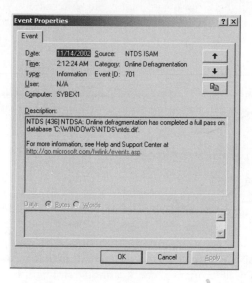

After you add a server to Replication Monitor, you can begin monitoring replication traffic. Figure 4.14 displays a single server in the left pane. You can see the different Active Directory partitions under the server name. You can use the Replication Monitor primarily for the following two purposes: checking for replication errors and initiating immediate domain controller synchronization.

FIGURE 4.14   The Replication Monitor

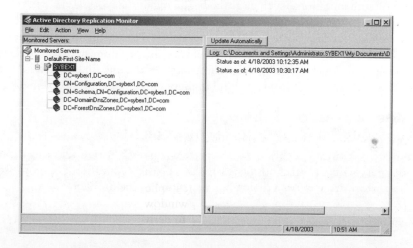

To check for replication errors, click the Action menu and select Domain ➤ Search Domain Controllers For Replication Errors. In the Search Domain Controllers For Replication Errors dialog box, click the Run Search button to search domain controllers in the domain for errors. Any errors are displayed in the main section of the dialog box.

To synchronize Active Directory immediately, right-click a server name and select Synchronize Each Directory Partition With All Servers from the pop-up menu. Alternately, you can synchronize partitions individually by clicking a partition name and selecting Synchronize This Directory Partition With All Servers from the pop-up menu.

Verifying Site Links

Before domain controllers in different sites can communicate with each other, the sites must be connected by site links. If replication between sites is not occurring properly, verify that the proper site links are in place.

Verifying That Information Is Synchronized

It's often easy to forget to perform manual checks regarding the replication of Active Directory information. One of the reasons for this is that Active Directory domain controllers have their own read/write copies of the Active Directory database. Therefore, if connectivity does not exist, you will not encounter failures while creating new objects.

It is important to periodically verify that objects have been synchronized between domain controllers. This process might be as simple as logging on to a different domain controller and looking at the objects within a specific OU. This manual check, although it might be tedious, can prevent inconsistencies in the information stored on domain controllers, which, over time, can become an administration and security nightmare.

Verifying Authentication Scenarios

A common replication configuration issue occurs when clients are forced to authenticate across slow network connections. The primary symptom of the problem is that users complain about the amount of time it takes them to log on to Active Directory (especially during times of high volume of authentications, such as at the beginning of the workday).

Usually, you can alleviate this problem by using additional domain controllers or reconfiguring the site topology. A good way to test this is to consider the possible scenarios for the various clients that you support. Often, walking through a configuration, such as "A client in Domain1 is trying to authenticate using a domain controller in Domain2, which is located across a slow WAN connection," can be helpful in pinpointing potential problem areas.

Verifying the Replication Topology

The Active Directory Sites And Services tool allows you to verify that a replication topology is logically consistent. You can quickly and easily perform this task by right-clicking the NTDS Settings within a Server object and choosing All Tasks ➤ Check Replication Topology (see Figure 4.15). If any errors are present, a dialog box alerts you to the problem.

FIGURE 4.15   Verifying Active Directory topology using the Active Directory Sites And Services tool

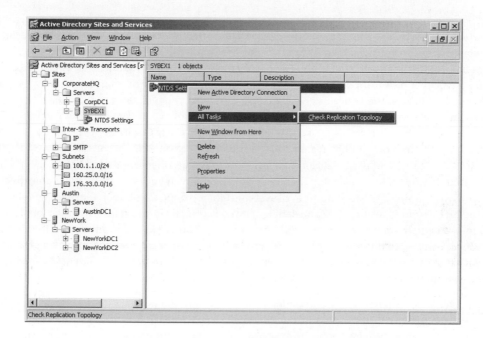

Here's a great online link that will help you troubleshoot replication problems: www.microsoft.com/technet/prodtechnol/windows2000serv/technologies/activedirectory/maintain/opsguide/part1/adogd12.mspx.

Summary

In this chapter we discussed the purpose of Active Directory replication. As we learned, replication is used to keep domain controllers synchronized and is important in Active Directory environments of all sizes. Replication is the process by which changes to the Active Directory database are transferred between domain controllers.

This chapter also covered the concepts of sites, site boundaries, and subnets.

As well as learning how to configure them, we learned that subnets define physical portions of your network environment. As well, sites are defined as collections of well-connected IP subnets. Site boundaries are defined by the subnet or subnets that you include in your site configuration.

Case Study: Troubleshooting Real-World Replication Problems

Designing and laying out Active Directory (and all its logical and physical components) properly is the key to your success. It is particularly important that you know how to use sites and why replication is so crucial to Active Directory health. Without a clean, consistent copy of the database (the heart and soul of your whole Microsoft systems infrastructure), you could be in for a world of hurt from problems that will surely come up. Poor or improper design leads to most, if not all, of the critical Active Directory problems you will see. For instance, Microsoft Exchange Server 2003 uses Active Directory and does not even install without it present. To connect to other directories, you can use the Active Directory Connector (ADC). Imagine replicating information to other systems that are also relying on a clean, consistent copy of that same database, and then realizing that your entire Active Directory directory service is corrupted. It only makes sense that if you have problems with your directory, you can expect them to be amplified by the number of systems that are dependent upon that same directory. Laying out your sites properly and setting them up correctly is going to save you a lot of problems—using the models and lessons learned in this chapter alone can save you a lot of headaches. Sticking to this methodology will ensure that you have a better chance of success with your deployment. Quite often, what those who are deploying miss is designing Active Directory while thinking of the future and the company's growth.

It is also very important that you understand the underlying network. If you are unfamiliar with the LAN and WAN (topology, bandwidth, logical addressing, and so on), you will surely encounter replication issues because you wouldn't have planned Active Directory without considering it first. Replication problems, if left unchecked, can cause a meltdown of your current setup causing many problems that fill up your event logs. In Windows Server 2003, the replication process is responsible for keeping each domain controller updated with the latest Active Directory information. If this process is flawed, you end up with an inconsistent database, which inevitably leads to the possible and somewhat inevitable corruption of Active Directory itself. Active Directory corruption can be avoided with proper planning, design, management, and maintenance. Therefore, remembering that Active Directory follows a multimaster replication scheme is important to your designs success. If your network can't support replication (or prevents it from occurring), inevitably you will have problems with your directory.

Troubleshooting real-world replication problems will teach you a lot about what Active Directory can do if it is designed and laid out incorrectly. Let's take a look at a real-world example of a company (123 Ltd.) that had a problem with their Active Directory deployment so you can see why all of these considerations are important.

123 Ltd. has one central core location, Chicago, where most of the company's resources are located. There are three remote sites, one in China, one in India, and one in Spain. Here is the company's network topology:

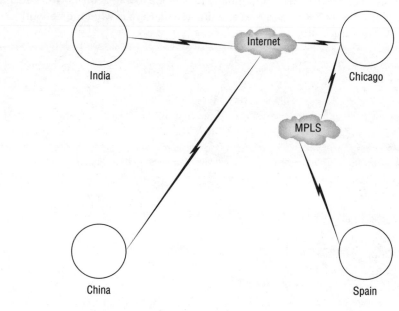

The company's goal, by its third quarter of operation, is to merge with another company based in China that also has headquarters in NY. As is the case with most companies, these mergers and acquisitions cause the network to grow. You are really lucky if you have all Microsoft systems available and all are currently running Windows Server 2003. Most times, this is not the case. If, however, you find yourself positioned with a merger that will bring a new company into the pre-existing one, then you must take a step back and look at the whole picture. Take into account the network layout and how Active Directory can be configured (with the Active Directory Sites And Services administrative tool) to mirror the network so that the best possible replication scheme is picked and fine-tuned. Here is what the network should look like after the acquisition.

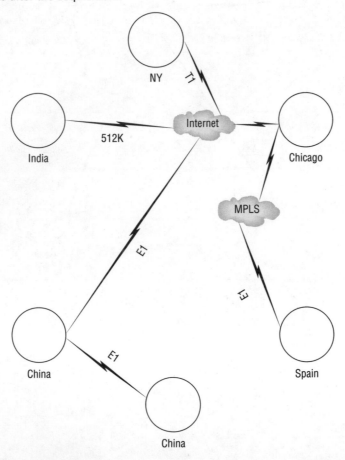

In this example, it was far cheaper to piggyback through the connection already established from China to Chicago and establish a separate T1 to connect the New York office to the core network in the 123 Ltd.'s headquarters, in Chicago.

If you ensure that the network is laid out properly beforehand and you know what that layout looks like, you can fine-tune Active Directory to work with your network, not against it. In this example, 123 Ltd. has a network that is properly sized to handle the current load on the network. This ensures efficient data transfer. Active Directory knows to minimize replication traffic by using state-based and pull replication. Active Directory is designed to send only the updates that are necessary, and with each new release, what is replication gets even more streamlined.

You also need to consider domain controller placement. As you now know, domain controllers all share Active Directory, and they all need to be able to converge. This is what keeps the database consistent and error free. If you follow this model and make sure that your network is able to handle your DC layout, then you will minimize the number of problems you will encounter. In this real-world example, 123 Ltd. has one domain. Each site has less than 15 to 20 users per site, and the headquarters in Chicago has about 50 users.

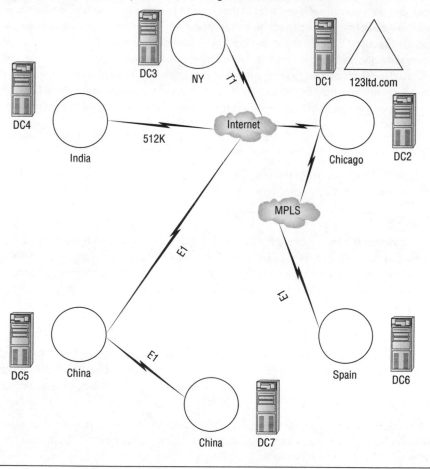

There are two domain controllers in Chicago for disaster recovery. If you want to plan for replication between all the domain controllers, you need to consider setting up site links (see information on this earlier in this chapter). Because every domain controller contains a writable copy of the Active Directory database, it's imperative that you set up a way for them to share it properly. Even so, errors will occur. Let's take a look at a few common ones caused by inconsistencies in the database.

In this case, a duplicate object is present in the Active Directory of the local domain controller's replication partner, so updating it is impossible. Intersite replication can have problems such as this. Because intersite replication is domain controller replication across two or more sites, all it takes is one problematic network link to cause problems between the domain controllers. For example, notice that the company uses the Internet as its method of WAN connectivity where there is a dedicated link in Spain via Multiprotocol Label Switching (MPLS). In an MPLS network, incoming packets are assigned a label that is used to help route the traffic efficiently (and usually with a class of service) so that you can rely on it. The Internet links (in this example) are connected and secured with IPSec, an encryption technology used to keep data secure across an unsecure network, such as the Internet. The Internet is also a best effort medium. You will not get a dedicated level of bandwidth on the Internet and because of that, you may have breaks in your network where you may not have connectivity between domain controllers. If this is the case, you may use backup links to provide a form of redundancy, much like the second domain controller's exact purpose—to keep Active Directory safe.

Once you have identified a problem (such as event ID 1083), the next step is to fix it.

Note: I omitted information from the graphics in this case study to protect the identity of the company that experienced this problem.

We also covered the basics of replication and the differences between intrasite and intersite replication. The purpose and use of bridgehead servers we also covered in depth. Although replication is a behind-the-scenes type of task, the optimal configuration of sites in distributed network environments will result in better use of bandwidth and faster response by network resources. For these reasons, you should be sure that you thoroughly understand the concepts related to managing replication for Active Directory.

We covered the placement of domain controllers and Global Catalog servers in the network and how when placed properly, can increase the performance of Active Directory operations.

We also learned how to monitor and troubleshoot replication. The Windows Server 2003 System Monitor administrative tool was designed so that you can monitor many performance statistics associated with using Active Directory.

Exam Essentials

Understand the purpose of Active Directory replication.   Replication is used to keep domain controllers synchronized and is important in Active Directory environments of all sizes. Replication is the process by which changes to the Active Directory database are transferred between domain controllers.

Understand the concept of sites, site boundaries, and subnets.   Subnets define physical portions of your network environment. Sites are defined as collections of well-connected IP subnets. Site boundaries are defined by the subnet or subnets that you include in your site configuration.

Understand the differences between intrasite and intersite replication.   Intrasite replication is designed to synchronize Active Directory information to machines that are located in the same site. Intersite replication is used to synchronize information for domain controllers that are located in different sites.

Understand the purpose of bridgehead servers.   Bridgehead servers are designed to accept traffic between two remote sites and to then forward this information to the appropriate servers. One way to efficiently synchronize data between sites that are connected with slow connections is to use a bridgehead server.

Implement site links, site link bridges, and connection objects.   All three of these object types can be used to finely control the behavior of Active Directory replication and to manage replication traffic. Site links are created to define the types of connections that are available between the components of a site. Site links can reflect a relative cost for a network connection and can reflect the bandwidth that is available for communications. Site link bridges are used to connect site links together so that the relationship can be transitive. Connection objects provide you with a way to set up special types of replication schedules such as immediate replication on-demand or specifying a custom schedule for certain servers.

Configure replication schedules and site link costs.   Multiple site links can be created between sites. Site links can be assigned a cost value based on the type of connection. The systems administrator determines the cost value, and the relative costs of site links are then used to determine the optimal path for replication. The lower the cost, the more likely the link is to be used for replication. Once you've determined how and through which connections replication will take place, it's time to determine *when* information should be replicated. Replication requires network resources and occupies bandwidth. Therefore, you need to balance the need for consistent directory information with the need to conserve bandwidth.

Determine where to place domain controllers and Global Catalog servers based on a set of requirements.   The placement of domain controllers and Global Catalog servers can increase the performance of Active Directory operations. However, in order to optimize performance, you should understand where the best places are to put these servers in a network environment that consists of multiple sites.

Monitor and troubleshoot replication.   The Windows Server 2003 System Monitor administrative tool was designed so that you can monitor many performance statistics associated with using Active Directory. In addition, you should always verify basic network connectivity and router and firewall connections, examine the event logs, and make use of the new Replication Monitor utility included in Windows Server 2003.

Review Questions

1. Daniel is responsible for managing Active Directory replication traffic for a medium-sized organization that has deployed a single Active Directory domain. Currently, the environment is configured with two sites and the default settings for replication. Each site consists of 15 domain controllers. Recently, network administrators have complained that Active Directory traffic is using a large amount of available network bandwidth between the two sites. Daniel has been asked to meet the following requirements:

   ▪ Reduce the amount of network traffic between domain controllers in the two sites.

   ▪ Minimize the amount of change to the current site topology.

   ▪ Require no changes to the existing physical network infrastructure.

   Daniel decides that it would be most efficient to configure specific domain controllers in each site that will receive the majority of replication traffic from the other site. Which of the following solutions meets the requirements?

   A. Create additional sites that are designed only for replication traffic and move the existing domain controllers to these sites.

   B. Create multiple site links between the two sites.

   C. Create a site link bridge between the two sites.

   D. Configure one server at each site to act as a preferred bridgehead server.

2. Which of the following must not be manually created when you are setting up a replication scenario involving three domains and three sites?

   A. Sites

   B. Site links

   C. Connection objects

   D. Subnets

3. Which of the following services of Active Directory is responsible for maintaining the replication topology?

   A. File Replication Service

   B. Knowledge Consistency Checker

   C. Windows Internet Name Service

   D. Domain Name System

4. Matt, a systems administrator for an Active Directory environment that consists of three sites, wants to configure site links to be transitive. Which of the following Active Directory objects is responsible for representing a transitive relationship between sites?

   A. Additional sites

   B. Additional site links

   C. Bridgehead servers

   D. Site link bridges

5. You have configured your Active Directory environment with multiple sites and have placed the appropriate resources in each of the sites. You are now trying to choose a protocol for the transfer of replication information between two sites. The connection between the two sites has the following characteristics:

   • The link is generally unavailable during certain parts of the day due to an unreliable network provider.

   • The replication transmission must be attempted whether the link is available or not. If the link was unavailable during a scheduled replication, the information should automatically be received after the link becomes available again.

   • Replication traffic must be able to travel over a standard Internet connection.

   Which of the following protocols meets these requirements?

   A. IP

   B. SMTP

   C. RPC

   D. DHCP

6. A network administrator has decided that it will be necessary to implement multiple sites in order to efficiently manage your company's large Active Directory environment. Based on her recommendations, you make the following decisions:

   • The best configuration involves the creation of four sites.

   • The sites will be connected with site links and site link bridges.

   • Two small offices must only receive replication traffic during non-business hours.

   • The organization owns a single DNS name: supercompany.com.

   • Administration should be kept as simple as possible, and you want to use the smallest possible number of domains.

   Based on this information, you must plan the Active Directory domain architecture. What is the minimum number of domains that must be created to support this configuration?

   A. 0

   B. 1

   C. 4

   D. 8

7. Andrew is troubleshooting a problem with Active Directory. One systems administrator has told him that she made an update to a User object and that another system administrator reported that he had not seen the changes appear on another domain controller. It has been over a week since the change was made. Andrew further verifies the problem by making a change to another Active Directory object. Within a few hours, the change appears on a few domain controllers, but not on all of them.

Which of the following are possible causes for this problem? Choose all that apply.

A. Network connectivity is unavailable.

B. Connection objects are not properly configured.

C. Sites are not properly configured.

D. Site links are not properly configured.

E. A WAN connection has failed.

F. Andrew has configured one of the domain controllers for manual replication updates.

8. A systems administrator suspects that there is an error in the replication configuration. How can he look for specific error messages related to replication?

A. By using the Active Directory Sites And Services administrative tool

B. By using the Computer Management tool

C. By going to Event Viewer ➢ System log

D. By going to Event Viewer ➢ Directory Service log

9. Christina is responsible for managing Active Directory replication traffic for a medium-sized organization. Currently, the environment is configured with a single site and the default settings for replication. The site contains over 50 domain controllers and the system administrators are often making changes to the Active Directory database. Recently, network administrators have complained that Active Directory traffic is consuming a large amount of network bandwidth between portions of the network that are connected by slow links. Ordinarily, the amount of replication traffic is reasonable, but recently users have complained about slow network performance during certain hours of the day.

Christina has been asked to alleviate the problem while meeting the following requirements:

▪ Be able to control exactly when replication occurs.

▪ Be able to base Active Directory replication on the physical network infrastructure.

▪ Perform the changes without creating or removing any domain controllers.

Which two of the following steps can Christina take to meet these requirements?

A. Create and define Connection objects that specify the hours during which replication will occur.

B. Create multiple site links.

C. Create a site link bridge.

D. Create new Active Directory sites that reflect the physical network topology.

E. Configure one server at each of the new sites to act as a bridgehead server.

10. Jason, a systems administrator, suspects that Active Directory replication traffic is consuming a large amount of network bandwidth. Jason is attempting to determine the amount of network traffic that is generated through replication. He wants to do the following:

- Determine replication data transfer statistics.
- Collect information about multiple Active Directory domain controllers at the same time.
- Measure other performance statistics, such as server CPU utilization.

Which of the following administrative tools is most useful for meeting these requirements?

A. Active Directory Users And Computers

B. Active Directory Domains And Trusts

C. Active Directory Sites And Services

D. Event Viewer

E. Performance

11. You are the administrator of a large, distributed network environment. Recently, your IT department has decided to add various routers to the environment to limit the amount of traffic going to and from various areas of the network. You need to reconfigure Active Directory replication to reflect the physical network changes. Which of the following Active Directory objects should you modify to define the network boundaries for Active Directory sites?

A. Site links

B. Site link bridges

C. Bridgehead servers

D. Subnets

12. You have recently created a new Active Directory domain by promoting several Windows Server 2003 computers to domain controllers. You then use the Active Directory Sites And Services tool to configure sites for the environment. You soon find that changes that are made on one domain controller may not appear in the Active Directory database on another domain controller. By checking the Directory Services log using the Event Viewer application, you find that one of the domain controllers at a specific site is not receiving Active Directory updates. Which of the following is/are a possible reason(s) for this? (Choose all that apply.)

A. Network connectivity has not been established for this server.

B. A firewall is preventing replication information from being transmitted.

C. There are not enough domain controllers in the environment.

D. There are too many domain controllers in the environment.

E. You chose to disable Active Directory replication during the promotion of the machine to a domain controller.

13. You administer a network that consists of one domain that spans three physical locations: San Jose, Chicago, and Austin. All three locations contain domain controllers. You have a T1 line between San Jose and Chicago, with an ISDN for backup. The ISDN line must have the default site link cost assigned to it. You want Austin to always use San Jose for its replication communication even though a link does exist between Austin and Chicago for other purposes.

In the following diagram, select and place the correct relative costs that should be assigned to the various site links. Each cost can only be used once.

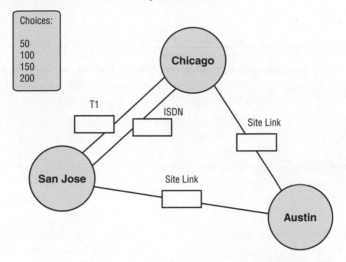

14. You need to create a new site named San Diego. Looking at the following screen, what would you do next in order to create the new site?

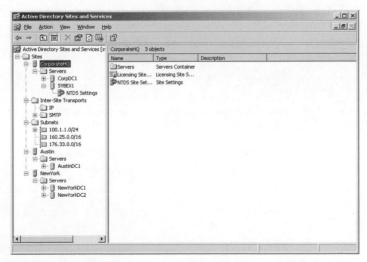

A. Right-click CorporateHQ.

B. Right-click Sites.

C. Double-click CorporateHQ.

D. Double-click Sites.

15. You administer a network with locations at two different sites. Both a T1 line (and a dial-up line used for redundancy) connect the sites. You want to ensure that replication normally occurs on the T1 line, but only uses the dial-up line as backup in case the T1 goes down. What should you do to meet these requirements? Choose all that apply.

   A. Lower the cost of the T1 line.

   B. Lower the cost of the dial-up line.

   C. Raise the cost of the T1 line.

   D. Raise the cost of the dial-up line.

16. You are the administrator for a network with locations at three different sites. You would like to specify the placement of the Global Catalog (GC) server. You have a central site located in New York, and two remote sites located in New Jersey and Connecticut. There are 100 users located in New York and 20 at each of the smaller locations. You have two full T1s connecting New Jersey and Connecticut to New York. What state would it make sense to put your GC in if you are only going to use one Global Catalog?

   A. Connecticut

   B. New Jersey

   C. New York

   D. All of the above

17. As the network administrator for RJS LLC, you are interested in specifying a bridgehead server at a location due to a recent merger. Your company just bought ABC Inc., and from this acquisition comes a large Active Directory domain. You need to bring up a new domain controller but need to specify the intrasite replication. How do you specify this server as a bridgehead server?

   A. In Sites and Services, right-click a domain controller and select Properties. Select one or both replication transports from the left and click Add.

   B. In the system Registry, change the enum_bridgehead value in HKEY_LOCAL_MACHINE to 1. Reboot the server.

   C. In Sites and Services, right-click a domain controller and select Properties. Choose Add from the bridgehead server tab.

   D. In the Control Panel, click the Active Directory Management Applet, and in the Sites tab, select the Make This Server A Bridgehead Server option.

18. You are the administrator for your company's Active Directory infrastructure. The company has three domain controllers, each of which has Knowledge Consistency Checker (KCC) errors consistently popping up in the directory services Event Viewer log. What does this indicate?

   A. Replication problems

   B. DNS problems

   C. Name resolution problems

   D. Global Catalog placement

19. You need to keep track of licensing with the licensing server. Where can you configure the licensing server so that as the system administrator you can ensure you are compliant?

  A. Configure licensing in the Control Panel under the Licensing Applet.

  B. Configure licensing in the Registry under the HKEY_ClASSES_ROOT key.

  C. Configure licensing in the Computer Management MMC.

  D. Configure licensing in the Sites And Services tool.

20. You are the network administrator responsible for deploying sites and subnets within your organization. You want to make sure you have set up your subnet objects correctly. From the following list, choose which subnet object cannot be used.

  A. 10.1.1.0

  B. 192.168.256.0

  C. 11.1.1.0

  D. 172.16.1.0

Answers to Review Questions

1. D. Preferred bridgehead servers receive replication information for a site and transmit this information to other domain controllers within the site. By doing this, Daniel can ensure that all replication traffic between the two sites is routed through the bridgehead servers and that replication traffic will flow properly between the domain controllers.

2. C. By default, Connection objects are automatically created by the Active Directory replication engine. You can, however, choose to override the default behavior of Active Directory replication topology by manually creating Connection objects, but this step is not required.

3. B. The Knowledge Consistency Checker (KCC) is responsible for establishing the replication topology and ensuring that all domain controllers are kept up to date.

4. D. Site link bridges are designed to allow site links to be transitive. That is, they allow site links to use other site links to transfer replication information between sites. By default, all site links are bridged. However, you can turn off transitivity if you want to override this behavior.

5. B. The Simple Mail Transfer Protocol (SMTP) was designed for environments in which persistent connections may not always be available. SMTP uses the store-and-forward method to ensure that information is not lost if a connection cannot be made.

6. B. Because there is no relationship between domain structure and site structure, only one domain is required. Generally, if there is only one domain, there will be many domain controllers with at least one in each site.

7. Answers: A, B, C, D, E, F. Misconfiguring any of these components of Active Directory may cause a failure in replication.

8. D. The Directory Service event log contains error messages and information related to replication. These details can be useful when you are troubleshooting replication problems.

9. Answers: A, D. By creating new sites, Christina can help define settings for Active Directory replication based on the environment's network connections. She can use Connection objects to further define the details of how and when replication traffic will be transmitted between the domain controllers.

10. E. Through the use of the Performance administrative tool, systems administrators can measure and record performance values related to Active Directory replication. Jason can also use this tool to monitor multiple servers at the same time and view other performance-related statistics.

11. D. Subnets define the specific network segments that are well connected.

12. A, B. Because replication is occurring between most of the domain controllers, it is likely that a network problem is preventing this domain controller from communicating with the rest. A lack of network connectivity or the presence of a firewall can also prevent replication from occurring properly. The number of domain controllers in an environment will not prevent the replication of information, nor can replication be disabled during the promotion process.

13. The ISDN line is required to have the default cost of 100. That means that the T1 line's cost must be lower than 100 for this connection to be used by preference, and the only choice is 50. That leaves costs of 150 and 200 for the Austin links. Because Austin will never get replication information from Chicago, that link's cost should be 200. That only leaves 150 for the cost of the link between Austin and San Jose.

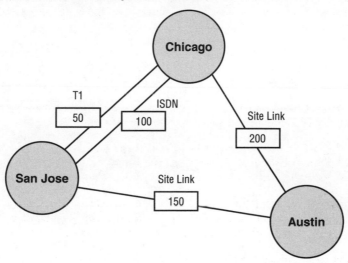

14. B. New sites can be created using the New Site action from the Sites contextual menu.

15. Answers: A, D. Lower costs are preferred over higher costs. However, if the lower cost connection fails for whatever reason, the higher cost link will be used.

16. C. Because you will only be using one Global Catalog (GC) server, it makes sense to position it centrally to the rest of the servers (New Jersey and Connecticut) on your network.

17. A. To make a bridgehead server, you simply need to right-click the domain controller you want to change to bridgehead server, select Properties, and add the transports.

18. A. Because of the nature of Knowledge Consistency Checker (KCC) errors, it's important to understand that they directly relate to replication problems, site linkage issues, and so on. KCC errors are indicative of replication problems.

19. D. As a systems administrator, you may want to use the Licensing Server to keep tabs on your compliance. You can do this in the Active Directory Sites And Services administration tool.

20. B. Answer B cannot be used as a subnet object because 192.168.256.0 is an invalid IP address.

Chapter

5

Administering Active Directory

MICROSOFT EXAM OBJECTIVES COVERED IN THIS CHAPTER:

✓ **Plan an administrative delegation strategy.**

 ▪ Plan an organizational unit (OU) structure based on delegation requirements.

✓ **Plan an OU structure.**

 ▪ Analyze the administrative requirements for an OU.

 ▪ Analyze the Group Policy requirements for an OU structure.

✓ **Implement an OU structure.**

 ▪ Create an OU.

 ▪ Delegate permissions for an OU to a user or to a security group.

 ▪ Move objects within an OU hierarchy.

In the previous chapter, you learned how to work with sites, but you still haven't been introduced to the lower-level objects that exist in Active Directory. In this chapter, you look at the structure of the various components within a domain. You'll see how an organization's business structure can be mirrored within Active Directory through the use of organizational units (OUs) for ease of use and to create a seamless look and feel. Because the concepts related to OUs are quite simple, some systems administrators may underestimate their importance and not plan to use them accordingly. Make no mistake—one of the fundamental components of a successful Active Directory installation is the proper design and deployment of OUs.

You'll also see the actual steps you need to take to create common Active Directory objects and then learn how these objects can be configured and managed. Finally, you'll look at ways to publish resources and methods for creating user accounts automatically.

An Overview of OUs

An *organizational unit (OU)* is a logical group of Active Directory objects, just as its name implies. OUs serve as containers within which other Active Directory objects can be created, but they do not form part of the DNS namespace. They are used solely to create organization within a domain.

OUs can contain the following types of Active Directory objects:

- Users
- Groups
- Computers
- Shared Folder objects
- Contacts
- Printers
- Other OUs

Perhaps the most useful feature of OUs is that they can contain *other* OU objects. As a result, systems administrators can hierarchically group resources and other objects according to business practices. The OU structure is extremely flexible and, as you will see later in this chapter, can easily be rearranged to reflect business reorganizations.

Each type of object has its own purpose within the organization of Active Directory domains. Later in this chapter, you'll look at the specifics of User, Computer, Group, and Shared Folder objects. For now, the focus is on the purpose and benefits of using OUs.

The Purpose of OUs

OUs are mainly used to organize the objects within Active Directory. Before you dive into the details of OUs, however, you must understand how OUs, users, and groups interact. Most importantly, you should understand that OUs are simply containers that you can use to logically group various objects. They are not, however, groups in the classical sense. That is, they are not used for assigning security permissions. Another way of stating this is that the user accounts, computer accounts, and group accounts that are contained in OUs are considered security principals while the OUs themselves are not.

OUs do not take the place of standard user and group permissions (this topic is covered in Chapter 6, "Planning Security for Active Directory"). A good general practice is to assign users to groups and then place the groups within OUs. This enhances the benefits of setting security permissions and of using the OU hierarchy for making settings. Figure 5.1 illustrates this concept.

FIGURE 5.1   Using users, groups, and OUs

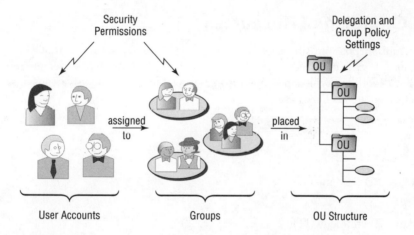

An OU contains objects only from within the domain in which it resides. As you'll see later in this chapter in the section titled "Delegation of Administrative Control," the OU is the finest level of granularity used for setting group policies and other administrative settings.

Benefits of OUs

There are many benefits of using OUs throughout your network environment:

- OUs are the smallest unit to which you can assign directory permissions.
- You can easily change the OU structure, and it is more flexible than the domain structure.
- The OU structure can support many different levels of hierarchy.
- Child objects can inherit OU settings.

- You can set Group Policy settings on OUs.
- You can easily delegate the administration of OUs and the objects within them to the appropriate users and groups.

Now that you have a good idea of why you should use OUs, take a look at some general practices you can use to plan the OU structure.

Planning the OU Structure

One of the key benefits of Active Directory is the way in which it can bring organization to complex network environments. Before you can begin to implement OUs in various configurations, you must plan a structure that is compatible with business and technical needs. In this section, you'll learn about several factors you should consider when planning for the structure of OUs.

Logical Grouping of Resources

The fundamental purpose of using OUs is to hierarchically group resources that exist within Active Directory. Fortunately, hierarchical groups are quite intuitive and widely used in most businesses. For example, a typical manufacturing business might divide its various operations into different departments like these:

- Sales
- Marketing
- Engineering
- Research and Development
- Support
- Information Technology (IT)

Each of these departments usually has its own goals and missions. In order to make the business competitive, individuals within each of the departments are assigned to various roles. Some types of roles might include the following:

- Managers
- Clerical staff
- Technical staff
- Planners

Each of these roles usually entails specific job responsibilities. For example, managers should provide direction to general staff members. Note that the very nature of these roles suggests that employees may fill many different positions. That is, one employee might be a manager in one department and a member of the technical staff in another. In the modern workplace, such situations are quite common.

All of this information helps you plan how to use OUs. First, the structure of OUs within a given network environment should map well to the business's needs, including the political and logical structure of the organization, as well as its technical needs. Figure 5.2 shows how a business organization might be mapped to the OU structure within an Active Directory domain.

FIGURE 5.2   Mapping a business organization to an OU structure

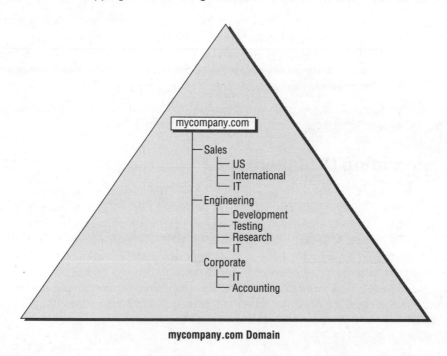

mycompany.com Domain

When naming OUs for your organization, you should keep several considerations and limitations in mind:

Keep the names and descriptions simple.   The purpose of OUs is to make administration and usage of resources simple. Therefore, it's always a good idea to keep the names of your objects simple and descriptive. Sometimes, finding a balance between these two goals can be a challenge. For example, although a printer name like "The LaserJet located near Bob's cube" might seem descriptive, it is certainly difficult to type. Also, imagine the naming changes that you might have to make if Bob moves (or leaves the company)!

Pay attention to limitations.   The maximum length for the name of an OU is 65 characters. In most cases, this should adequately describe the OU. Remember, the name of an OU object does not have to uniquely describe it because the OU is generally referenced as part of the overall hierarchy. For example, you can choose to create an IT OU within two different parent OUs. Even though the OUs have the same name, users and administrators are able to distinguish them based on their complete path name.

Pay attention to the hierarchical consistency. The fundamental basis of an OU structure is its relationship to a hierarchy. From a design standpoint, this means that you cannot have two OUs with the same name at the same level. However, you can have OUs with the same name at different levels. For example, you could create a Corporate OU within both the North America OU and the South America OU. This is because the fully qualified name includes information about the hierarchy. When an administrator tries to access resources in the Corporate OU, they must specify which Corporate OU they mean.

If, for example, you create a North America OU, the Canada OU should logically fit under it. If you decide that you want to separate them into completely different containers, then you might want to use other, more appropriate names. For example, you could change North America to U.S. Users and administrators depend on the hierarchy of OUs within the domain, so make sure that it remains logically consistent.

Based on these considerations, you should have a good idea of how to best organize the OU structure for your domain.

Understanding OU Inheritance

When you rearrange OUs within the structure of Active Directory, you can change several settings. When they are moving and reorganizing OUs, systems administrators must pay careful attention to automatic and unforeseen changes in security permissions and other configuration options. By default, OUs inherit the permissions of their new parent container when they are moved. Note that by using the built-in tools provided with Windows Server 2003 and Active Directory, you can move or copy OUs only within the same domain.

If you need to move an entire OU structure between domains, you can use the `movetree` command supplied with the Windows Server 2003 resource kit. To learn how to use movetree, visit `http://support.microsoft.com/?kbid=238394`.

Delegation of Administrative Control

We already mentioned that OUs are the smallest component within a domain to which administrative permissions and group policies can be assigned by administrators. Now, you'll take a look at specifically how administrative control is set on OUs.

Delegation occurs when a higher security authority assigns permissions to a lesser security authority. As a real-world example, assume that you are the director of IT for a large organization. Instead of doing all of the work yourself, you would probably assign roles and responsibilities to other individuals. For example, if you worked within a multidomain environment, you might make one systems administrator responsible for all operations within the Sales domain and another responsible for the Engineering domain. Similarly, you could assign the permissions for managing all printers and print queues objects within your organization to one individual user while allowing another individual user to manage all security permissions for users and groups.

In this way, you can distribute the various roles and responsibilities of the IT staff throughout the organization. Businesses generally have a division of labor that handles all of the tasks involved in keeping the company's networks humming. Network operating systems (NOSs), however, often make it difficult to assign just the right permissions, or in other words, very granular permissions. Sometimes, this complexity is necessary to ensure that only the right permissions are assigned. A good general rule of thumb is to provide users and administrators the minimum permissions they require to do their jobs. This way you can ensure that accidental, malicious, and otherwise unwanted changes do not occur.

> You can also use auditing to log events to the Security log in the Event Viewer. This is another way to ensure that if accidental, malicious, and otherwise unwanted changes do occur, they are logged and traceable.

In the world of Active Directory, you use the process of delegation to define permissions for OU administrators. As a system administrator you will be occasionally tasked with having to delegate responsibility to others—you can't do it all, although sometimes some administrators believe that they can. If you do find yourself in a role to delegate, remember that Windows Server 2003 was designed to offer you the ability to do so. In its simplest definition, delegation allows a higher administrative authority to grant specific administrative rights for containers and subtrees to individuals and groups. What this essentially does is eliminate the need for domain administrators with sweeping authority over large segments of the user population. You can break up this control over branches within your tree, within each OU you create.

> To understand delegation and rights, you should first understand the concept of access control entries (ACEs). ACEs grant specific administrative rights on objects in a container to a user or group. The containers' access control list (ACL) is used to store ACEs.

When you are considering implementing delegation, there are two main concerns to keep in mind:

Parent-child relationships   The OU hierarchy you create will be very important when you consider the maintainability of security permissions. OUs can exist in a parent-child relationship, which means that permissions and group policies set on OUs higher up in the hierarchy (parents) can interact with objects in lesser OUs (children). When it comes to delegating permissions, this is extremely important. You can allow child containers to automatically inherit the permissions set on parent containers. For example, if the North America division of your organization contains 12 other OUs, you could delegate permissions to all of them by placing security permissions on the North America division, saving time, and reducing the likelihood of human error. This feature can greatly ease administration, especially in larger organizations, but it is also a reminder of the importance of properly planning the OU structure within a domain.

> You can delegate control only at the OU level and not at the object level within the OU.

Inheritance Settings   Now that you've seen how you can use parent-child relationships for administration, you should consider *inheritance*, the actual process of inheriting permissions. When you set permissions on a parent container, all of the child objects are configured to inherit the same permissions. You can override this behavior, however, if business rules do not lend themselves well to inheritance.

Applying Group Policy

One of the strengths of the Windows operating system is that it offers users a great deal of power and flexibility. From installing new software to adding device drivers, users can make many changes to their workstation configurations. However, this level of flexibility is also a potential problem. For instance, inexperienced users might inadvertently change settings, causing problems that can require many hours to fix.

In many cases (and especially in business environments), users only require a subset of the complete functionality the operating system provides. In the past, however, the difficulty associated with implementing and managing security and policy settings has led to lax security policies. Some of the reasons for this are technical—it can be very tedious and difficult to implement and manage security restrictions. Other problems have been political—users and management might feel that they should have full permissions on their local machines, despite the potential problems this might cause.

That's where the idea of group policies comes in. Simply defined, *group policies* are collections of permissions that you can apply to objects within Active Directory. Specifically, Group Policy settings are assigned at the site, domain, and OU levels, and they can apply to user accounts, computer accounts, and groups. Examples of settings that a systems administrator can make using group policies include the following:

- Restricting users from installing new programs

- Disallowing the use of the Control Panel

- Limiting choices for display and Desktop settings

 Chapter 8, "Planning, Implementing, and Managing Group Policy," covers the technical issues related to group policies.

Creating OUs

Now that you have looked at several different ways in which OUs can be used to bring organization to the objects within Active Directory, it's time to look at how you can create and manage them.

Through the use of the Active Directory Users And Computers administrative tool, also called an MMC (Microsoft Management Console), you can quickly and easily add, move, and change OUs. This graphical tool makes it easy to visualize and create the various levels of hierarchy an organization requires.

Figure 5.3 shows a geographically based OU structure that a multinational company might use. Note that the organization is based in North America and it has a corporate office located there. In general, all of the other offices are much smaller than the corporate office located in North America.

FIGURE 5.3   A geographically based OU structure

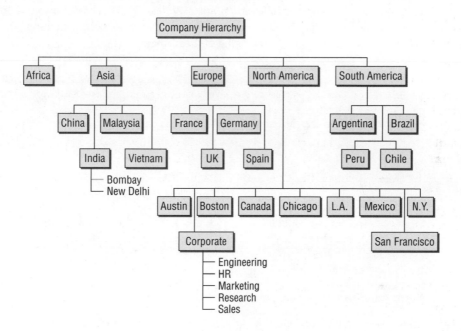

Also, it's important to note that this OU structure could have been designed in several different ways. For example, we could have chosen to group all of the offices located in the United States within a U.S. OU. However, due to the size of the offices, we chose to place these objects at the same level as the Canada and Mexico OUs. This prevents an unnecessarily deep OU hierarchy while still logically grouping the offices.

Exercise 5.1 walks you through the process of creating several OUs for a multinational business. You'll be using this OU structure in later exercises within this chapter.

 In order to perform the exercises included in this chapter, you must have administrative access to a Windows Server 2003 domain controller.

 Creating OUs and other Active Directory objects can be tedious, especially for large organizations. A good way to speed up the process is to use keyboard shortcuts to create objects instead of using the mouse. Also, learn the shortcuts for the context menus. For example, the *n* key automatically chooses the New selection, and the *o* key specifies that you want to create an OU.

EXERCISE 5.1

Creating an OU Structure

1.   Open the Active Directory Users And Computers administrative tool.

2.   Right-click the name of the local domain, and choose New ➤ Organizational Unit. You will see the dialog box shown in the following graphic. Notice that this box shows you the current context within which the OU will be created. In this case, you're creating a top-level OU, so the full path is simply the name of the domain.

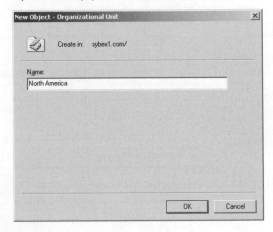

3.   Type **North America** for the name of the first OU. Click OK to create this object.

4.   Create the following top-level OUs by right-clicking the name of the domain and choosing New ➤ Organizational Unit:

       Africa

       Asia

       Europe

       South America

     Note that the order in which you create the OUs is not important. In this exercise, you are simply using a method that emphasizes the hierarchical relationship.

5.   Create the following second-level OUs within the North America OU by right-clicking the North America OU and selecting New ➤ Organizational Unit:

       Austin

       Boston

       Canada

Chicago

Corporate

Los Angeles

Mexico

New York

San Francisco

6. Create the following OUs under the Asia OU:

    China

    India

    Malaysia

    Vietnam

7. Create the following OUs under the Europe OU:

    France

    Germany

    Spain

    UK

8. Create the following OUs under the South America OU:

    Argentina

    Brazil

    Chile

    Peru

9. Create the following third-level OUs Under the India OU by right-clicking India within the Asia OU, and selecting New ➢ Organizational Unit:

    Bombay

    New Delhi

10. Within the North America Corporate OU, create the following OUs:

    Engineering

EXERCISE 5.1 *(continued)*

HR

Marketing

Research

Sales

11. When you have completed the creation of the OUs, you should have a structure that looks similar to the one in the following graphic.

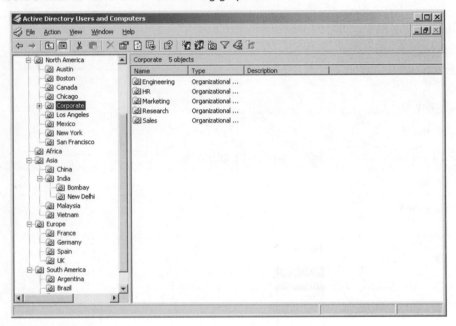

Managing OUs

Managing network environments would be challenging enough if things rarely changed. However, in the real world, business units, departments, and employee roles change frequently. As business and technical needs change, so should the structure of Active Directory.

Fortunately, changing the structure of OUs within a domain is a relatively simple process. In the following sections, you'll look at ways to delegate control of OUs and make other changes.

Moving, Deleting, and Renaming OUs

The process of moving, deleting, and renaming OUs is a simple one. Exercise 5.2 shows how you can easily change and reorganize OUs to reflect changes in the business organization. The specific scenario covered in this exercise includes the following changes:

- The Research and Engineering departments have been combined to form a department known as Research and Development (RD).

- The Sales department has been moved from the Corporate office to the New York office.

- The Marketing department has been moved from the Corporate office to the Chicago office.

This exercise assumes that you have already completed the steps in Exercise 5.1.

EXERCISE 5.2

Modifying OU Structure

1. Open the Active Directory Users And Computers administrative tool.

2. Right-click the Engineering OU (located within North America ➢ Corporate) and click Delete. When you are prompted for confirmation, click Yes. Note that if this OU contained objects, they all have been automatically deleted as well.

3. Right-click the Research OU and select Rename. Type **RD** to change the name of the OU and press Enter.

4. Right-click the Sales OU and select Move. In the Move dialog box, expand the North America branch and click the New York OU. Click OK to move the OU.

EXERCISE 5.2 *(continued)*

5. You will use an alternate method to move the Marketing OU. You can either drag the Marketing OU and drop it onto the Chicago OU, or you can select the Marketing OU and then Edit ➢ Cut (or Ctrl+X). Then select the Chicago OU and select Edit ➢ Paste (or Ctrl+V). Either method moves the Marketing OU into the Chicago OU.

6. When you have finished, you should see an OU structure similar to the one shown in the following graphic. Close the Active Directory Users And Computers administrative tool.

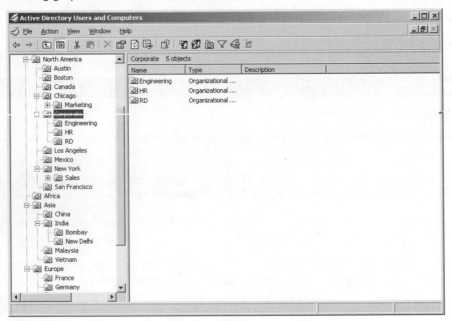

Administering Properties of OUs

Although OUs are primarily created for organizational purposes within the Active Directory environment, they have several settings that you can modify. To modify the properties of an OU using the Active Directory Users And Computers administrative tool, you can right-click the name of any OU and select Properties; when you do, the OU Properties dialog box appears. In the example shown in Figure 5.4, you see the options on the General tab.

In any organization, it helps to know who is responsible for managing an OU. This information can be set on the Managed By tab (see Figure 5.5). The information specified on this tab is very convenient because it is automatically pulled from the contact information on a user record. You should consider always having a contact for each OU within your organization so that users and other systems administrators know whom to contact if they need to make any changes.

FIGURE 5.4   The General tab of the OU Properties dialog box

FIGURE 5.5   The Managed By tab of the OU Properties dialog box

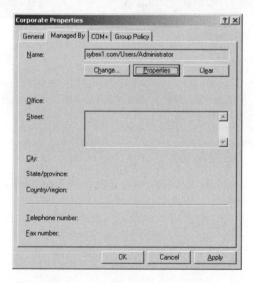

NOTE You can set Group Policy settings for the OU on the Group Policy tab. Chapter 8 covers this topic.

Delegating Control of OUs

In simple environments, one or a few systems administrators may be responsible for managing all of the settings within Active Directory. For example, a single systems administrator could manage all users within all OUs in the environment. In larger organizations, however, roles and responsibilities may be divided among many different individuals. A typical situation is one in which a systems administrator is responsible for objects within only a few OUs in an Active Directory domain. Or, one systems administrator might manage User and Group objects while another is responsible for managing file and print services.

Fortunately, using the Active Directory Users And Computers tool, you can quickly and easily ensure that specific users receive only the permissions they need. In Exercise 5.3, you will use the *Delegation of Control Wizard* to assign permissions to individuals. In order to successfully complete these steps, you must first have created the objects in the previous exercises of this chapter.

EXERCISE 5.3

Using the Delegation of Control Wizard

1. Open the Active Directory Users And Computers administrative tool.

2. Right-click the Corporate OU within the North America OU and select Delegate Control. This starts the Delegation of Control Wizard. Click Next to begin configuring security settings.

3. In the Users Or Groups page, click the Add button. In the Enter The Object Names To Select field, enter **Account Operators** and press Enter. Click Next to continue.

4. In the Tasks To Delegate page, select Delegate The Following Common Tasks and place a check mark next to the following items:

   Create, Delete, And Manage User Accounts

   Reset User Passwords And Force Password Change At Next Logon

   Read All User Information

   Create, Delete, And Manage Groups

   Modify The Membership Of A Group

Click Next to continue.

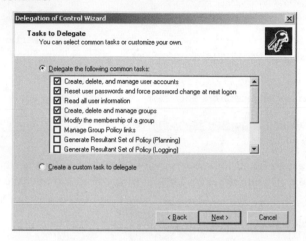

5. The Completing The Delegation of Control Wizard page then provides a summary of the operations you have selected. To implement the changes, click Finish.

Although the common tasks available through the wizard are sufficient for many delegation operations, you may have cases in which you want more control. For example, you might want to give a particular systems administrator permissions to modify only Computer objects. Exercise 5.4 uses the Delegation of Control Wizard to assign more granular permissions. In order to successfully complete these steps, you must first have completed the previous exercises in this chapter.

EXERCISE 5.4

Delegating Custom Tasks

1. Open the Active Directory Users And Computers administrative tool.

2. Right-click the Corporate OU within the North America OU and select Delegate Control. This starts the Delegation of Control Wizard. Click Next to begin making security settings.

3. In the Users Or Groups page, click the Add button. In the Enter The Object Names To Select field, enter **Server Operators** and press Enter. Click Next to continue.

4. In the Tasks To Delegate page, select the Create A Custom Task To Delegate radio button, and click Next to continue.

5. In the Active Directory Object Type page, choose Only The Following Objects In The Folder, and place a check mark next to the following items (you will have to scroll down to see them all):

> Computer Objects
>
> Contact Objects
>
> Group Objects
>
> Organizational Unit Objects
>
> Printer Objects
>
> User Objects

Click Next to continue.

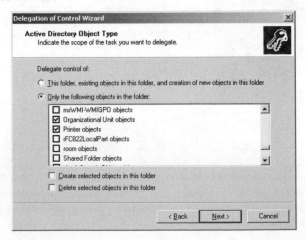

EXERCISE 5.4 *(continued)*

6. In the Permissions page, place a check mark next to only the General option. Note that if the various objects within your Active Directory schema had property-specific settings, you would see those options here. Place a check mark next to the following items:

> Create All Child Objects
>
> Read All Properties
>
> Write All Properties

Click Next to continue.

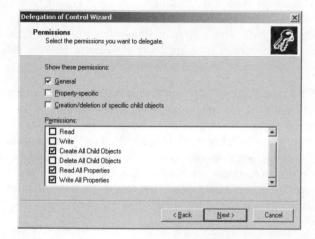

7. This gives the members of the Server Operators group the ability to create new objects within the Corporate OU and the permissions to read and write all properties for these objects. Click Next to continue.

8. The Completing The Delegation of Control Wizard page provides a summary of the operations you have selected. To implement the changes, click Finish.

In addition to the basic types of security options you set in the exercise, you can create custom tasks and place permissions on specific types of objects within a container. Chapter 6 covers security permissions in greater detail.

🌐 Real World Scenario

Delegation: Who's Responsible for What?

You're the IT director for a large, multinational organization. You've been with the company for quite a while—since the environment had only a handful of offices and a few network and systems administrators. But times have changed. Systems administrators must now coordinate the efforts of hundreds of IT staffers in 14 countries.

When the environment ran under a Windows NT 4 domain environment, the network was set up with many domains. For security, performance, and distribution of administration reasons, the computing resources in each major office were placed in their own domain. You have recently decided to move to Active Directory and to consolidate the numerous Windows NT domains into a single Active Directory domain. However, securely administering a distributed environment is still an important concern. So, the challenge involves determining how to coordinate the efforts of different systems administrators.

Fortunately, through the proper use of OUs and delegation, you are given a lot of flexibility in determining how to handle the administration. You can structure the administration in several ways. First, if you choose to create OUs based on geographic business structure, you could delegate control of these OUs based on the job functions of various systems administrators. For example, you could use one user account to administer the Europe OU. Within the Europe OU, this systems administrator could delegate control of offices represented by the Paris and London OUs. Within these OUs, you could further break down the administrative responsibilities for printer queue operators and security administrators.

Alternatively, the OU structure may create a functional representation of the business. For example, the Engineering OU might contain other OUs that are based on office locations such as New York and Paris. A systems administrator of the Engineering domain could delegate permissions based on geography or job functions to the lower OUs. Regardless of whether you build a departmental, functional, or geographical OU model, keep in mind that each model excludes other models. This is one of the most important decisions to make. When you are making this decision or modifying previous decisions, your overriding concern is how it will affect the management and administration of the network. The good news is that because Active Directory has so many features, the model you choose can be based on specific business requirements rather than imposed by architectural constraints.

Troubleshooting OUs

In general, you should find using OUs to be straightforward and relatively painless. With adequate planning, you'll be able to implement an intuitive and useful structure for OU objects.

The most common problems with OU configuration are related to the OU structure. When troubleshooting OUs, pay careful attention to the following factors:

Inheritance   By default, Group Policy and other settings are transferred automatically from parent OUs to child OUs and objects. Even if a specific OU is not given a set of permissions, objects within that OU might still get them from parent objects.

Delegation of administration   If you allow the wrong user accounts or groups to perform specific tasks on OUs, you might be violating your company's security policy. Be sure to verify the delegations you have made at each OU level.

Organizational issues   Sometimes, business practices do not easily map to the structure of Active Directory. A few misplaced OUs, user accounts, computer accounts, or groups can make administration difficult or inaccurate. In many cases, it might be beneficial to rearrange the OU structure to accommodate any changes in the business organization. In others, it might make more sense to change business processes.

If you regularly consider each of these issues when troubleshooting problems with OUs, you will be much less likely to make errors in the Active Directory configuration.

Creating and Managing Active Directory Objects

Now that you are familiar with the task of creating OUs, you should find creating and managing other Active Directory objects quite simple. The following sections look at the details.

Overview of Active Directory Objects

By default, after you install and configure a domain controller, you will see the following organizational sections within the Active Directory Users And Computers tool:

Built-In   The Built-In container includes all of the standard groups that are installed by default when you promote a domain controller. You can use these groups to administer the servers in your environment. Examples include the Administrators group, Backup Operators, and Print Operators.

Computers   By default, the Computers container contains a list of the workstations in your domain. From here, you can manage all of the computers in your domain.

Domain Controllers   The Domain Controllers container includes a list of all of the domain controllers for the domain.

Foreign security principals   *Foreign security principals* are any objects to which security can be assigned and that are not part of the current domain. Security principals are Active Directory objects to which permissions can be applied, and they can be used to manage permissions in Active Directory. Chapter 6 covers the details of working with security principals.

Users The Users container includes all of the security accounts that are part of the domain. When you first install the domain controller, there will be several groups in this container. For example, the Domain Admins group and the Administrator account are created in this container.

There are several different types of Active Directory objects that you can create and manage. The following are specific object types:

Computer Computer objects represent workstations that are part of the Active Directory domain. Every computer within a domain shares the same security database, including user and group information. Computer objects are useful for managing security permissions and enforcing Group Policy restrictions.

Contact *Contact objects* are usually used in OUs to specify the main administrative contact. Contacts are not security principals like users, but they are used to specify information about individuals within the organization.

Group *Group objects* are logical collections of users that are used primarily for assigning security permissions to resources. When managing users, you should place them into groups and then assign permissions to the group. This allows for flexible management and prevents systems administrators from having to set permissions for individual users.

Organizational Unit An OU object is created to build a hierarchy within the Active Directory domain. It is the smallest unit that can be used to create administrative groupings, and it can be used to assign group policies. Generally, the OU structure within a domain reflects a company's business organization.

Printer *Printer objects* map to printers.

Shared Folder *Shared Folder objects* map to server shares. They are used to organize the various file resources that may be available on file/print servers. Often, Shared Folder objects are used to give logical names to specific file collections. For example, systems administrators might create shared folders for common applications, user data, and shared public files. Shared Folder objects can be created and managed within Active Directory.

User A *User object* is the fundamental security principal on which Active Directory is based. User accounts contain information about individuals, as well as password and other permission information.

Chapter 6 covers the security aspects related to the use of Active Directory objects. For now, however, know that these objects are used to represent various items in your network environment. By using these objects, you will be able to manage the content of your Active Directory.

Exercise 5.5 walks you through the steps you need to take to create various objects within an Active Directory domain. In this exercise, you create some basic Active Directory objects. In order to complete this exercise, you must have access to at least one Active

Directory domain controller and you should have also completed the previous exercises in this chapter.

Creating Active Directory Objects

1. Open the Active Directory Users And Computers tool.

2. Expand the current domain to list the objects currently contained within it. For this exercise you will use the second- and third-level OUs contained within the North America top-level OU, as shown in the following graphic.

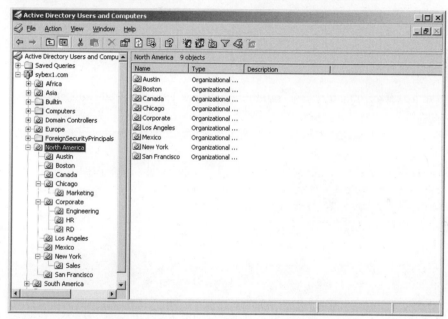

3. Right-click the Corporate OU, and select New ➢ User. Fill in the following information:

   First Name: **Monica**

   Initial: **D**

   Last Name: **President**

   Full Name: (leave as default)

   User Logon Name: **mdpresident** (leave default domain)

Click Next to continue.

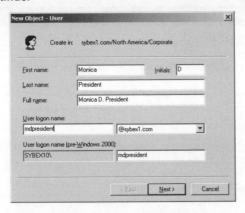

4. Enter in a password for this user, and then confirm it. Note that you can also make changes to password settings here. Click Next.

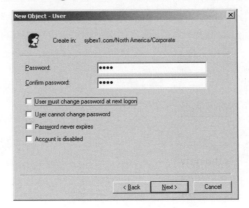

5. You will see a summary of the user information. Click Finish to create the new user.

6. Create another user in the RD container with the following information:

First Name: **John**

Initials: **Q**

Last Name: **Admin**

Full Name: (leave as default)

User Logon Name: **jqadmin** (leave default domain)

Click Next to continue.

7. Assign a password. Click Next, and then click Finish to create the user.

8. Right-click the RD OU, and select New ➢ Contact. Use the following information to fill in the properties of the Contact object:

First Name: **Jane**

Initials: **R**

Last Name: **Admin**

Display Name: **jradmin**

Click OK to create the new Contact object.

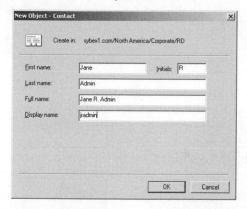

9. Right-click the RD OU, and select New ➢ Shared Folder. Enter **Software** for the name and **\\server1\applications** for the network path (also known as the Universal Naming Convention [UNC] path). Note that although this resource does not exist, the object can still be created. Click OK to create the Shared Folder object.

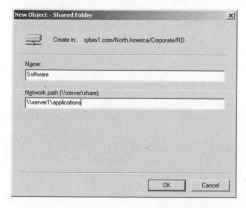

10. Right-click the HR OU, and select New ➢ Group. Type **All Users** for the group name (leave the Group Name (Pre–Windows 2000) field with the same value). For the Group Scope, select Global, and for the Group Type, select Security. To create the group, click OK.

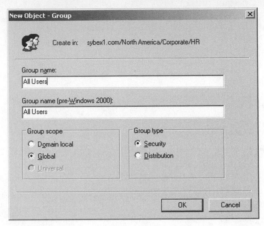

11. Right-click the Sales OU and select New ➢ Computer. Type **Workstation1** for the name of the computer. Notice that the pre–Windows 2000 name is automatically populated and that, by default, the members of the Domain Admins group are the only ones that can add this computer to the domain. Place a check mark in the Assign This Computer Account As A pre–Windows 2000 Computer box, and then click OK to create the Computer object.

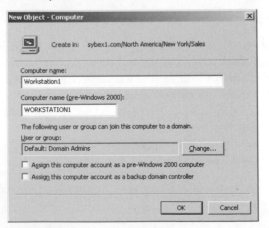

12. Close the Active Directory Users And Computers tool.

Managing Object Properties

Once you've created the necessary Active Directory objects, you'll probably need to make changes to their default properties. In addition to the settings you made when creating Active Directory objects, there are several more properties that can be configured. You can access object properties by right-clicking any object and selecting Properties from the pop-up menu.

Each object type contains a unique set of properties. The following properties are available for users:

- General: General account information about this user
- Address: The physical location information about this user
- Account: User logon name and other account restrictions, such as workstation restrictions and logon hours
- Profile: Information about the user's roaming profile settings
- Telephones: Telephone contact information for the user
- Organization: The user's title, department, and company information
- Member Of: Group membership information for the user
- Dial-In: Remote Access Service (RAS) permissions for the user
- Environment: Logon and other network settings for the user
- Sessions: Session limits, including maximum session time and idle session settings
- Remote Control: Remote control options for this user's session
- Terminal Services Profile: Information about the user's profile for use with Terminal Services
- COM+: Specifies a COM+ partition set for the user

As you can see from the following list of properties, computers have much different characteristics than users:

- General: Information about the name of the computer, the role of the computer, and its description. Note that you can enable an option to allow the Local System Account of this machine to request services from other servers. This is useful if the machine is a trusted and secure computer.
- Operating System: The name, version, and service pack information for the operating system running on the computer.
- Member Of: Active Directory groups that this Computer object is a member of.
- Location: A description of where the computer is physically located.
- Managed By: Information about the User or Contact object that is responsible for managing this computer.
- Dial-in: Sets dial-in options for the computer.

Exercise 5.6 walks you through setting various properties for Active Directory objects. In order to complete the steps in this exercise, you must have first completed Exercise 5.5.

Although it may seem somewhat tedious, it's always a good idea to enter as much information as you know about Active Directory objects when you create them. Although the name Printer1 may be meaningful to you, users will appreciate the additional information when they are searching for objects.

EXERCISE 5.6

Managing Object Properties

1. Open the Active Directory Users And Computers tool.

2. Expand the name of the domain, and select the **RD** container. Right-click the John Q. Admin user account, and select Properties.

3. Here, you will see the various Properties tabs for the User account. Make some configuration changes based on your personal preferences. Click OK to continue.

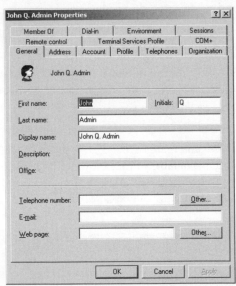

4. Select the HR OU. Right-click the All Users group, and click Properties. In the All Users Properties dialog box, you will be able to modify the membership of the group.

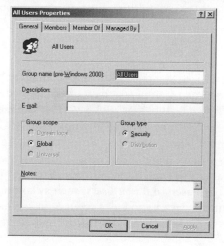

Click the Members tab, and then click Add. Add the Monica D. President and John Q. Admin User accounts to the Group. Click OK to save the settings and then OK to accept the group modifications.

5. Select the Sales OU. Right-click the Workstation1 Computer object. Notice that you can choose to disable the account or reset it (to allow another computer to join the domain under that same name). From the right-click menu, choose Properties. You'll see the properties for the Computer object.

Examine the various options and make changes based on your personal preference. After you have examined the available options, click OK to continue.

6. Select the Corporate OU. Right-click the Monica D. President User account, and choose Reset Password. You will be prompted to enter a new password and then asked to confirm it. Note that you can also force the user to change this password upon the next logon.

7. Close the Active Directory Users And Computers tool.

By now, you have probably noticed that there are a lot of common options for Active Directory objects. For example, Group and Computer objects both have a Managed By tab. Windows Server 2003 introduces a new feature that allows you to manage many user objects at once. You can select several user objects by holding down the Shift or Ctrl key while selecting. Right-click any one of the selected objects and select Properties to display the properties that are available for multiple users. Notice that not every user property is available, because some properties are unique to each user. You can also configure the description field for multiple object selections that include both users and non-users, such as computers and groups.

As was mentioned earlier, it's always a good idea to enter in as much information as possible about an object. This helps systems administrators and users alike.

Filtering and Advanced Active Directory Features

The Active Directory Users And Computers tool has a couple of other features that come in quite handy when you are managing many objects. You can access the Filter Options dialog box by clicking the View menu in the MMC and choosing Filter Options. You'll see a dialog box similar to the one shown in Figure 5.6. Here, you can choose to filter objects by their specific types within the display. For example, if you are an administrator who works primarily with user accounts and groups, you can select those specific items by placing check marks in the list. In addition, you can create more complex filters by choosing Create Custom Filter. That provides you with an interface that looks similar to that of the Find command.

FIGURE 5.6   The Filter Options dialog box

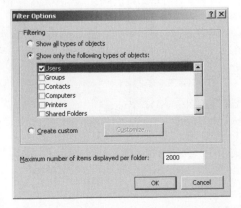

Another option in the Active Directory Users And Computers tool is to view Advanced options. You can enable the Advanced options by choosing Advanced Features in the View menu. This adds two top-level folders to the list under the name of the domain.

The System folder (shown in Figure 5.7) provides a list of some additional features that you can configure to work with Active Directory. For example, you can configure settings for the Distributed File System (DFS), IP Security (IPSec) policies, the File Replication Service, and more. In addition to the System folder, you'll see the LostAndFound folder. This folder contains any files that may not have been replicated properly between domain controllers. You should check this folder periodically for any files so that you can decide whether you need to move them or copy them to other locations.

FIGURE 5.7   Advanced Features in the System folder in the Active Directory Users And Computers tool

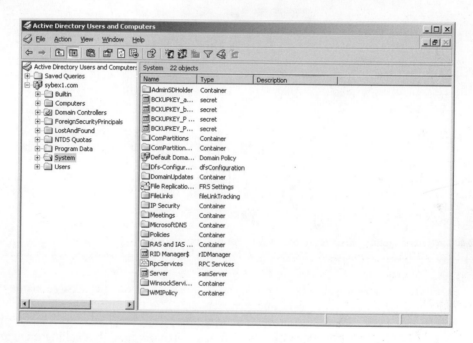

As you can see, managing Active Directory objects is generally a simple task. The Active Directory Users And Computers tool allows you to configure several objects. Let's move on to look at one more common administration function—moving objects.

Moving, Renaming, and Deleting Active Directory Objects

One of the extremely useful features of the Active Directory Users And Computers tool is its ability to easily move users and resources.

Exercise 5.7 walks you through the process of moving Active Directory objects. In this exercise, you will make several changes to the organization of Active Directory objects. In order to complete this exercise, you must have first completed Exercise 5.5.

EXERCISE 5.7

Moving Active Directory Objects

1. Open the Active Directory Users And Computers tool, and expand the name of the domain.

2. Select the Sales OU, right-click Workstation1, and select Move. A dialog box appears. Select the RD OU, and click OK to move the Computer object to that container.

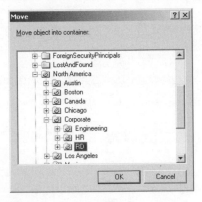

3. Click the RD OU, and verify that Workstation1 was moved.

4. Close the Active Directory Users And Computers tool.

In addition to moving objects within Active Directory, you can also easily rename them by right-clicking an object and selecting Rename. Note that this option does not apply to all objects. For example, in order to prevent security breaches, Computer objects cannot be renamed. You can also remove objects from Active Directory by right-clicking them and choosing Delete.

WARNING Deleting an Active Directory object is an irreversible action. When an object is destroyed, any security permissions or other settings made for that object are removed as well. Because each object within Active Directory contains its own security identifier (SID), simply re-creating an object with the same name does not place any permissions on it. Before you delete an Active Directory object, be sure that you will never need it again.

Resetting an Existing Computer Account

Every computer on the domain establishes a discrete channel of communication with the domain controller at logon time. The domain controller stores a randomly selected password (different from the user password) for authentication across the channel, which is updated every 30 days. Sometimes the computer's password and the domain controller's password don't match, and communication between the two machines fails.

Without the ability to reset the computer account, you wouldn't be able to connect the machine to the domain. Fortunately, you can use the Active Directory Users And Computers tool to reestablish the connection.

Exercise 5.8 shows you how to reset an existing computer account. You should have completed the previous exercises in this chapter before you begin this exercise.

EXERCISE 5.8

Resetting an Existing Computer Account

1. Open the Active Directory Users And Computers tool and expand the name of the domain.

2. Click the RD OU, and then right-click the Workstation1 computer account.

3. Select Reset Account from the context menu. Click Yes to confirm your selection. Click OK at the success prompt.

4. When you reset the account, you break the connection between the computer and the domain, so after performing this exercise, reconnect the computer if you want it to continue working on the network.

Publishing Active Directory Objects

One of the main goals of Active Directory is to make resources easy to find. Two of the most commonly used resources in a networked environment are server file shares and printers. These are so common, in fact, that most organizations have dedicated file and print servers. When it comes to managing these types of resources, Active Directory makes it easy to determine which files and printers are available to users.

With that said, take a look at how Active Directory manages to publish shared folders and printers.

Making Active Directory Objects Available to Users

An important aspect of managing Active Directory objects is that a systems administrator can control which objects users can see. The act of making an Active Directory object available is known as *publishing*. The two main publishable objects are Printer objects and Shared Folder objects.

The general process for creating server shares and shared printers has remained unchanged from previous versions of Windows. That is, the main method involves creating the various objects (a printer or a file system folder) and then enabling them for sharing. To make these resources available via Active Directory, however, there's an additional step: you must publish the resources. Once an object has been published in Active Directory, clients will be able to use it.

You can also publish Windows NT 4 resources through Active Directory by creating Active Directory objects as we did in Exercise 5.5. When you publish objects in Active Directory, you should know the server name and share name of the resource. When they use Active Directory objects, systems administrators can change the resource to which the object points without having to reconfigure or even notify clients. For example, if you move a share from one server to another, all you need to do is update the Shared Folder object's properties to point to the new location. Active Directory clients still refer to the resource with the same path and name as they used before.

Without Active Directory, Windows NT 4 shares and printers are accessible only by using NetBIOS-based shares. If you're planning to disable the NetBIOS protocol in your environment, you must be sure that these resources have been published or they will not be accessible.

Publishing Printers

Printers can be published easily within Active Directory. This makes them available to users in your domain.

Exercise 5.9 walks you through the steps you need to take to share and publish a Printer object by having you create and share a printer. In order to complete the printer installation, you need access to the Windows Server 2003 installation media (via the hard disk, a network share, or the CD-ROM drive).

EXERCISE 5.9

Creating and Publishing a Printer

1. Click Start ➢ Control Panel ➢ Printers And Faxes ➢ Add Printer. This starts the Add Printer Wizard. Click Next to begin.

2. In the Network Or Local Printer page, select Local Printer. Uncheck the Automatically Detect And Install My Plug And Play Printer box. Click Next.

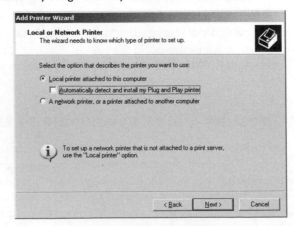

3. In the Select A Printer Port page, select Use The Following Port. From the list beside that option, select LPT1: Recommended Printer port. Click Next.

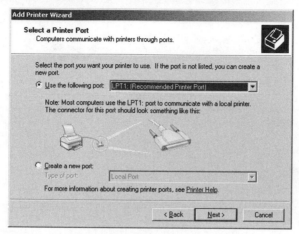

4. On the Install Printer Software page, select Generic for the manufacturer, and for the printer, highlight Generic /Text Only. Click Next.

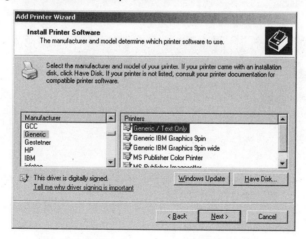

EXERCISE 5.9 *(continued)*

5.   On the Name Your Printer page, type **Text Printer**. Click Next.

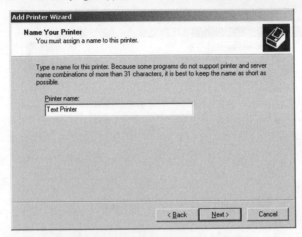

6.   On the Printer Sharing page, **select Share Name** and accept the default share name ofTextPrin. Click Next.

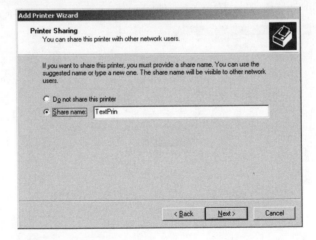

EXERCISE 5.9 *(continued)*

7. On the Location and Comment page, type **Building 203** and add the following comment: **This is a text-only printer.** Click Next.

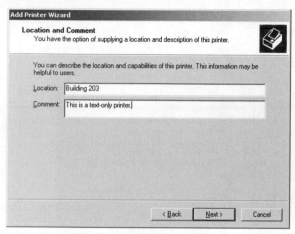

8. On the Print Test Page page, click No; then click Next.

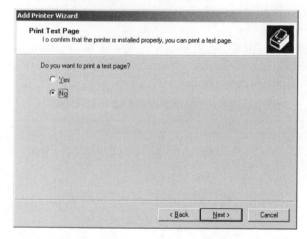

9. On the Completing The Add Printer Wizard page, you see a confirmation of the printer options you selected. Click Finish to create the printer.

10. Next, you need to verify that the printer will be listed in Active Directory. Click Start ➢ Control Panel ➢ Printers And Faxes, then right-click the Text Printer icon and select Properties.

11. Next, select the Sharing tab, and ensure that the List In The Directory box is checked. Note that you can also add additional printer drivers for other operating systems using this tab. Click OK to accept the settings.

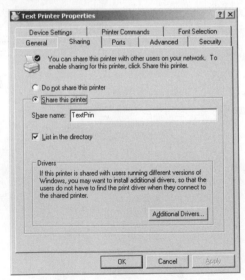

Note that when you create and share a printer this way, an Active Directory Printer object is not displayed within the Active Directory Users And Computers tool. The printer is actually associated with the Computer object to which it is shared. Printer objects in Active Directory are manually created for sharing printers from Windows NT 4 and earlier shared printer resources.

Publishing Shared Folders

Now that you've created and published a printer, you'll see how the same thing can be done to shared folders.

Exercise 5.10 walks through the steps required to create a folder, share it, and then publish it in Active Directory. This exercise assumes that you are using the C: partition; however, you may want to change this based on your server configuration. This exercise assumes that you have completed Exercise 5.5.

EXERCISE 5.10

Creating and Publishing a Shared Folder

1. Create a new folder in the root directory of your C: partition, and name it **Test Share**.

2. Right-click the Test Share folder, and select Sharing And Security.

3. On the Sharing tab, select Share This Folder. For the share name, type **Test Share,** and for the description, enter **Share used for testing Active Directory**. Leave the User Limit, Permissions, and Caching settings as their defaults. Click OK to create the share.

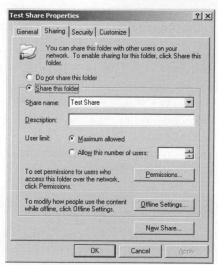

EXERCISE 5.10 *(continued)*

4. To verify that the share has been created, choose Start ➤ Run and type the UNC path for the local server. For instance, if the server is named sybex1, you would type **\\sybex1**. This connects you to the local computer, where you can view any available network resources. Verify that the Test Share folder exists, and then close the window.

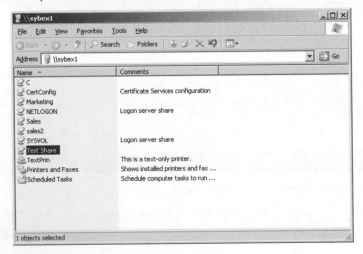

5. Open the Active Directory Users And Computers tool. Expand the current domain, and right-click the RD OU. Select New ➤ Shared Folder.

6. In the New Shared Folder dialog box, type **Shared Folder Test** for the name of the folder. Then type the UNC path to the share (for example, **\\sybex1\Test Share**). Click OK to create the share.

Once you have created and published the Shared Folder object, clients can use the My Network Places icon to find this object. The Shared Folder object will be organized based on the OU in which you created the Shared Folder object. When you use publication, you can see how this makes it easy to manage shared folders.

Once you have created resources, you will likely want to restrict their use to only certain users and groups. Chapter 6 covers ways to do this.

Querying Active Directory

So far you've created several Active Directory resources. One of the main benefits of having all of your resource information in Active Directory is that you should be able to easily find what you're looking for using the Find dialog box. Recall that we recommended that you should always enter as much information as possible when creating Active Directory objects. This is where that extra effort begins to pay off.

Exercise 5.11 walks you through the steps to find specific objects in Active Directory. In order to complete this exercise, you must have first completed Exercise 5.5.

EXERCISE 5.11

Finding Objects in Active Directory

1. Open the Active Directory Users And Computers tool.

2. Right-click the name of the domain and select Find.

3. On the Find dialog box, select Users, Contacts, And Groups from the Find drop-down list. For the In setting, choose Entire Directory. This searches the entire Active Directory environment for the criteria you enter. Note that if this is a production domain and if there are many objects, this may be a time-consuming and network-intensive operation.

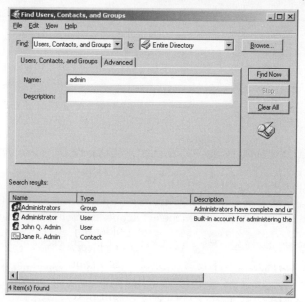

4. In the Name field, type **admin** and then click Find Now to obtain the results of the search.

5. Now that you have found several results, you can narrow down the list. Click the Advanced tab of the Find dialog box. In the Field drop-down list, select User ➢ Last Name. For Condition, select Starts With, and for Value, type **Admin**. Click Add to add this item to the search criteria. Click Find Now. Notice that this time, only the User and Contact that have the last name Admin are shown.

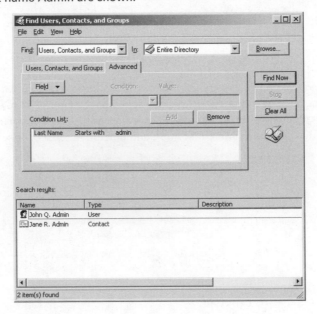

6. To filter the result set even further, click the View menu and select Filter. The filter is displayed in the row just above the Search Results windows. In the Name field, type **John** and press Enter. Notice that this filters the list to only the John Q. Admin User object.

7. To view more information about the User object, you can right-click it and select Properties.

8. To quickly view (and filter) more information about multiple objects, select the View menu and choose Select Columns. By selecting fields and clicking Add, you can view more information about the retrieved objects. Click OK to add the information.

9. When you have finished searching, close the Find dialog box and exit the Active Directory Users And Computers tool.

Using the many options available in the Find dialog box, you can usually narrow down the objects you're searching for quickly and efficiently. Users and systems administrators alike find this tool useful in environments of any size.

Summary

In this chapter, we covered the fundamentals of administering Active Directory. The most important part of administering Active Directory is learning about how to work with OUs. As a result, you should be aware of the purpose of OUs—they help you to organize and manage the directory. For instance, think of administrative control. If you wanted to delegate rights to another administrator (such as a Sales Manager), you could delegate that authority to that user within the SALES OU. As the Systems Administrator, you retain the rights to the castle.

We also looked at how to design an OU structure from an example. In our example, we looked at how to design proper OU layout. Once we finished designing, we looked at how to create, organize, and reorganize OUs if need be.

Lastly, we covered how to use the Active Directory Users And Computers tool to manage Active Directory objects. If you're responsible for day-to-day systems administration, there's a good chance that you are already familiar with this tool, but if not, you should be now. Using this tool, you learned how to work with Active Directory objects such as Users, Computers, and Groups.

In the next chapter, we look at how to plan security for Active Directory.

Exam Essentials

Understand the purpose of OUs. OUs are used to create a hierarchical, logical organization for objects within an Active Directory domain.

Know the types of objects that can reside within OUs. OUs can contain Active Directory User, Computer, Shared Folder, and other objects.

Understand how to use the Delegation of Control Wizard. The Delegation of Control Wizard is used to assign specific permissions at the level of OUs.

Understand the concept of inheritance. By default, child OUs inherit permissions and Group Policy assignments set for parent OUs. However, these settings can be overridden for more granular control of security.

Understand how Active Directory objects work. Active Directory objects represent some piece of information about components within a domain. The objects themselves have attributes that describe details about them.

Understand how Active Directory objects can be organized. By using the Active Directory Users And Computers tool, you can create, move, rename, and delete various objects.

Learn how resources can be published. A design goal for Active Directory was to make network resources easier for users to find. With that in mind, you should understand how using published printers and shared folders can simplify network resource management.

Review Questions

1. Gabriel is responsible for administering a small Active Directory domain. Recently, the Engineering department within his organization has been divided into two departments. He wants to reflect this organizational change within Active Directory and plans to rename various groups and resources. Which of the following operations can he perform using the Active Directory Users And Computers tool? Choose all that apply.

   A. Renaming an organizational unit

   B. Querying for resources

   C. Renaming a group

   D. Creating a computer account

2. You are a domain administrator for a large domain. Recently, you have been asked to make changes to some of the permissions related to OUs within the domain. In order to further restrict security for the Texas OU, you remove some permissions at that level. Later, a junior systems administrator mentions that she is no longer able to make changes to objects within the Austin OU (which is located within the Texas OU). Assuming no other changes have been made to Active Directory permissions, which of the following characteristics of OUs might have caused the change in permissions?

   A. Inheritance

   B. Group Policy

   C. Delegation

   D. Object properties

3. Isabel, a systems administrator, has created a new Active Directory domain in an environment that already contains two trees. During the promotion of the domain controller, she chose to create a new Active Directory forest. Isabel is a member of the Enterprise Administrators group and has full permissions over all domains. During the organization's migration to Active Directory, many updates have been made to the information stored within the domains. Recently, users and other system administrators have complained about not being able to find specific Active Directory objects in one or more domains (although they exist in others).

   In order to investigate the problem, Isabel wants to check for any objects that have not been properly replicated among domain controllers. If possible, she would like to restore these objects to their proper place within the relevant Active Directory domains.

   Which two of the following actions should she perform to be able to view the relevant information?

   A. Change Active Directory permissions to allow object information to be viewed in all domains.

   B. Select the Advanced Features item in the View menu.

   C. Promote a member server in each domain to a domain controller.

   D. Rebuild all domain controllers from the latest backups.

   E. Examine the contents of the LostAndFound folder using the Active Directory Users And Computers tool.

4. You are a consultant hired to evaluate an organization's Active Directory domain. The domain contains over 200,000 objects and hundreds of OUs. You begin examining the objects within the domain, but you find that the loading of the contents of specific OUs takes a very long time. Furthermore, the list of objects can be very large. You want to do the following:

- Avoid the use of any third-party tools or utilities and use the built-in Active Directory administrative tools.

- Be able to limit the list of objects within an OU to only the type of objects that you're examining (for example, only Computer objects).

- Prevent any changes to the Active Directory domain or any of the objects within it.

Which of the following actions meet the above requirements?

A. Use the Filter option in the Active Directory Users And Computers tool to restrict the display of objects.

B. Use the Delegation of Control Wizard to give yourself permissions over only a certain type of object.

C. Implement a new naming convention for objects within an OU and then sort the results using this new naming convention.

D. Use the Active Directory Domains And Trusts tool to view information from only selected domain controllers.

E. Edit the domain Group Policy settings to allow yourself to view only the objects of interest.

5. Your organization is currently planning a migration from a Windows NT 4 environment that consists of several domains to an Active Directory environment. Your staff consists of 25 systems administrators who are responsible for managing one or more domains. The organization is finalizing a merger with another company.

John, a technical planner, has recently provided you with a preliminary plan to migrate your environment to several Active Directory domains. He has cited security and administration as major justifications for this plan. Jane, a consultant, has recommended that the Windows NT 4 domains be consolidated into a single Active Directory domain. Which of the following statements provide a valid justification to support Jane's proposal? (Choose all that apply.)

A. In general, OU structure is more flexible than domain structure.

B. In general, domain structure is more flexible than OU structure.

C. It is possible to create a distributed systems administration structure for OUs by using delegation.

D. The use of OUs within a single domain can greatly increase the security of the overall environment.

6. Miguel is a junior-level systems administrator and has basic knowledge about working with Active Directory. As his supervisor, you have asked Miguel to make several security-related changes to OUs within the company's Active Directory domain. You instruct Miguel to use the basic functionality provided in the Delegation of Control Wizard. Which of the following operations are represented as common tasks within the Delegation of Control Wizard? (Choose all that apply.)

   A. Reset passwords on user accounts.

   B. Manage Group Policy links.

   C. Modify the membership of a group.

   D. Create, delete, and manage groups.

7. You are the primary systems administrator for a large Active Directory domain. Recently, you have hired another systems administrator to offload some of your responsibilities. This systems administrator will be responsible for handling help desk calls and for basic user account management. You want to allow the new employee to have permissions to reset passwords for all users within a specific OU. However, for security, reasons, it's important that the user not be able to make permissions changes for objects within other OUs in the domain. Which of the following is the best way to do this?

   A. Create a special administration account within the OU and grant it full permissions for all objects within Active Directory.

   B. Move the user's login account into the OU that he or she is to administer.

   C. Move the user's login account to an OU that contains the OU (that is, the parent OU of the one that he or she is to administer).

   D. Use the Delegation of Control Wizard to assign the necessary permissions on the OU that he or she is to administer.

8. You have been hired as a consultant to assist in the design of an organization's Active Directory environment. Specifically, you are instructed to focus on the OU structure (others will be planning for technical issues). You begin by preparing a list of information that you need to create the OU structure for a single domain. Which of the following pieces of information is not vital to your OU design?

   A. Physical network topology

   B. Business organizational requirements

   C. System administration requirements

   D. Security requirements

9. You want to allow the Super Users group to create and edit new objects within the Corporate OU. Using the Delegation of Control Wizard, you choose the Super Users group and arrive at the following screen. Where would you click in order to add the ability to create and edit new objects in the Corporate OU?

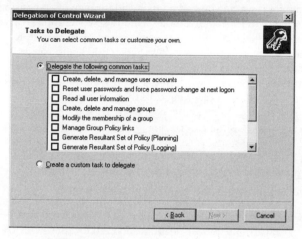

A. Create, Delete, And Manage User Accounts

B. Create, Delete, And Manage Groups

C. Manage Group Policy Links

D. Create A Custom Task To Delegate

10. A systems administrator is using the Active Directory Users And Computers tool to view the objects within an OU. He has previously created many users, groups, and computers within this OU, but now only the users are showing. What is a possible explanation for this?

A. Groups and computers are not normally shown in the Active Directory Users And Computers tool.

B. Another systems administrator may have locked the groups, preventing others from accessing them.

C. Filtering options have been set that specify that only User objects should be shown.

D. The Group and Computer accounts have never been used and are, therefore, not shown.

11. The company you work for has a multilevel administrative team that is segmented by departments and locations. There are four major locations and you are in the Northeast group. You have been assigned to the administrative group that is responsible for creating and maintaining network shares for files and printers in your region. The last place you worked was a large Windows NT 4 network, where you had a much wider range of responsibilities. You are excited about the chance to learn more about Windows Server 2003. For your first task, you have been given a list of file and printer shares that need to be created for the users in your region. You ask how to create them in Windows Server 2003, and you are told that the process of creating a share is the same as with Windows NT. You create the shares and use NET USE to test them. Everything appears to work fine, so you send out a message that the shares are available. The next day, you start receiving calls from users who say that they cannot see any of resources that you created. What is the most likely reason for the calls from the users?

A. You forgot to enable NetBIOS for the shares.

B. You need to force replication for the shares to appear in the directory.

C. You need to publish the shares in the directory.

D. The shares will appear within the normal replication period.

12. Wilford Products has over 1000 users in five locations across the country. The network consists of four servers and around 250 workstations in each location. One of the four servers in each location is a domain controller. As the new network administrator, you are now responsible for all aspects of the OUs within the directory. After meeting with the HR department, you have been informed that the vice president of sales has left the organization, and you are to remove his access to all resources on the network. You return to your office and remove his account from the directory. After you remove the account, you are immediately notified that you have been misinformed and the vice president of sales is not leaving the company. You quickly re-add him within the window of replication between the other domain controllers. What else must you do to reinstate his account and all his associated permissions?

A. Nothing. Since you re-created the account before the replication window opened, the account will remain in the directory.

B. Open the Tombstone folder and remove the object that is pending in order to remove the account before the replication window opens.

C. After replication occurs, you need to manually synchronize his account in the domain controllers.

D. You must re-establish every permission and setting manually.

13. You want to publish a printer to Active Directory. In the following screen, where would you click in order to accomplish this task?

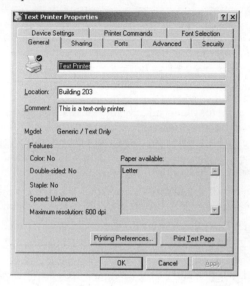

A. The Sharing tab

B. The Advanced tab

C. The Device Settings tab

D. The Printing Preferences button

14. You have inherited the administrator position of a network that has already completed its migration from Windows NT to Windows Server 2003. The network consists of a single domain that serves two locations with five servers at each site. The replication topology has proven to be solid, and the monitoring tasks that were in place when you arrived show no errors. Each site has two domain controllers for redundancy, each of which has a DNS server to support name resolution. Your first tasks are to learn how the directory has been designed and how the structure of the OUs is providing management capabilities to the domain. As you begin to settle in, you add some new users to the domain, but some of them complain that they cannot do what you have told them they could do. As you investigate the problem, you determine that Group Policy is not being applied when the users with the problems log on to the network. What are the possible reasons for this problem? (Choose all that apply.)

A. The policy has been blocked for the OU of which the users are members.

B. The users are not members of the OU that is subject to the Group Policy object.

C. The users are members of a security group whose Apply Group Policy ACE is set to Deny.

D. Policies must be applied to the specific OU that contains the users before they take effect.

15. A systems administrator creates a local Printer object, but it doesn't show up in Active Directory when a user executes a search for all printers. Which of the following are possible reasons for this? Choose all that apply.

A. The printer was not shared.

B. The List In Directory option is unchecked.

C. The client does not have permissions to view the printer.

D. The printer is malfunctioning.

16. As the network administrator for your company, you find that you need a plan for how to structure your OUs. You also need to accommodate the delegation of a few OUs to other administrators. Your current layout is as follows: you have a Sales department, a Marketing department, and an HR department. You need to plan and create OUs. You want to delegate control of each OU to each department supervisor. Which of the following solutions will help satisfy your plan?

A. Build an OU called ADMIN, and then create three OUs below it called SALES, MARKET, and HR. Delegate control of each OU to each respective department head.

B. Build an OU called SITEA, and then create two OUs below it called SALES and MARKET. Create a third OU under MARKET called HR. Delegate control of each OU to each respective department head.

C. Build an OU called ADMIN, and then create three OUs below it called SALES, MARKET, and HR. Create Administrator accounts for each OU and then allow each to control their respective OUs.

D. Build an OU called SITEA, and then create four OUs below it called SALES, ADMIN, MARKET, and HR. Delegate control of each OU to each respective department head and make sure that ADMIN keeps Executive Administrative privileges.

17. You are the Lead Administrator and Designer for your company. You have just installed the first of many Windows Server 2003 systems. You are building your infrastructure and now need to design the OU layout and implement it. You have to design an OU structure that includes the following departments: IT, HR, SALES, MARKETING, ENGINEERING, and CORPORATE. You also need to make sure that the supervisor within each department is able to be managed each OU you create. You will need to delegate permissions. What is the best way to design your OU structure?

A. Create an OU at the top level and call it DELEGATION. Create second-level OUs under DELEGATION and assign administrative rights to each. Create a policy that will allow each supervisor the right to manage the DELEGATION OU.

B. Create an OU at the top level. Call it ADMIN1. Create IT, HR, SALES, MARKETING, ENGINEERING, and CORPORATE under ADMIN1. Set up delegation to the proper users for each OU.

C. Design a top-level OU and create it with administrative rights. Name it US. Make an OU called COMP1 under US and then create SALES and MARKETING under it. Create a second OU called UK and create all the rest of the needed OUs under it. Rights will be assigned by default.

D. Create an OU at the top level. Call it TOP1. Create a Regional OU called US. Create IT1, HR1, SALES1, MARKETING1, ENGINEERING1, and CORPORATE1 under US1. Set up delegation to the proper users for each OU.

18. You are the network administrator responsible for administering and creating new OUs for your organization. You just changed an internal company name and need to make that change in Active Directory. From the list of choices, what is the easiest way to make this change?

A. Rename the OU to SALESFORCE1.

B. Delete the OU and re-create it.

C. Using the Active Directory Sites And Services tool, use the Name option to make the change.

D. Create a new OU, name it SALESFORCE1, and delete the old OU.

19. As the lead systems administrator for your company, you are asked to delegate permissions to a user within the SALES OU. What tool is used to achieve this functionality? (Choose only one).

A. In Active Directory Sites And Services, right-click the OU where you want to delegate permissions and choose Delegate Control.

B. In Active Directory Trusts And Domains, right-click the OU where you want to delegate permissions and choose Delegate Control.

C. In Active Directory Users And Computers, right-click the OU where you want to delegate permissions and choose Delegate Control.

D. In Active Directory Domains And Forests, right-click the OU where you want to delegate permissions and choose Delegate Control.

20. You are asked to deploy Windows Server 2003 in your organization. You need to consider creating a management structure that will allow you to apply policies. What logical Active Directory object will allow you this functionality?

A. Containers

B. Forests

C. Domains

D. Organizational units (OUs)

Answers to Review Questions

1. Answers: A, B, C, D. The Active Directory Users And Computers tool was designed to simplify the administration of Active Directory objects. All of the above operations can be carried out using this tool.

2. A. Inheritance is the process by which permissions placed on parent OUs affect child OUs. In this example, the permissions change for the higher-level OU (Texas) automatically caused a change in permissions for the lower-level OU (Austin).

3. Answers: B, E. Enabling the Advanced Features item in the View menu will allow Isabel to see the LostAndFound and System folders. The LostAndFound folder contains information about objects that could not be replicated among domain controllers.

4. A. Through the use of the filtering functionality, you can choose which types of objects you want to see using the Active Directory Users And Computers tool. Several of the other choices may work, but they require changes to Active Directory settings or objects.

5. A, C. You can easily move and rename OUs without having to promote domain controllers and make network changes. This makes OU structure much more flexible and a good choice since the company may soon undergo a merger. Because security administration is important, delegation can be used to control administrative permissions at the OU level.

6. Answers: A, B, C, D. All of the options listed are common tasks presented in the Delegation of Control Wizard.

7. D. The Delegation of Control Wizard is designed to allow administrators to set up permissions on specific Active Directory objects.

8. A. OUs are created to reflect a company's logical organization. Because your focus is on the OU structure, you should be primarily concerned with business requirements. Other Active Directory features can be used to accommodate the network topology and technical issues (such as performance and scalability).

9. D. When you choose to delegate custom tasks, you have many more options for what you can delegate control of and what permissions you can apply. To do this, you must first select the Create A Custom Task To Delegate radio button, and then select the custom tasks. In this case, you would delegate control of Organizational Unit objects and set the permissions to Create All Child Objects, Read All Properties, and Write All Properties.

10. C. The filtering options would cause other objects to be hidden (although they still exist). Another explanation (but not one of the choices) is that a higher-level systems administrator modified the administrator's permissions using the Delegation of Control Wizard.

11. C. You need to publish shares in the directory before they are available to the users of the directory. If NetBIOS is still enabled on the network, the shares will be visible to the NetBIOS tools and clients, but you do not have to enable NetBIOS on shares. Although replication must occur before the shares are available in the directory, it is unlikely that the replication will not have occurred by the next day. If this is the case, then you have other problems with the directory as well.

12. D. When you delete an object in the directory, such as a user, it is gone and cannot be brought back. You could use a tape backup to bring an object back, but this would be a major undertaking for something like that and you would lose any other changes that occurred since the last backup. The best way to deal with an employee leaving the organization is to disable the account and wait for a specified period before permanently removing it. In many cases, the person who replaces them will need the same resources, so you can then simply rename the account, change the password, and re-enable the account for the new user.

13. A. The Sharing tab contains a check box that you can use to list the printer in Active Directory.

14. Answers: A, B, C. If you or a previous administrator has blocked a policy from flowing to an OU, then it will not apply to users in the OU. If the users are not in an OU that is subject to the policy, then the users will not receive that policy. If the users are members of a security group with an ACE set to Deny The Apply Group Policy, then it will block the policy. In general, policies flow down the directory tree if they are not blocked, so you do not have to apply the policy to each individual OU.

15. Answers: A, B, C. The first three reasons listed are explanations for why a printer may not show up within Active Directory. The printer will appear as an object in Active Directory even if it is malfunctioning.

16. A. The easiest way to achieve a desired result that is both easy to manage and secure is to build an OU called ADMIN, and then create three OUs below it called SALES, MARKET, and HR. Delegate control of each OU to each respective department head. If you do this, then you can retain control over the ADMIN OU and still be able to maintain control over your systems.

17. B. To lay out the OU design properly, you should consider the easiest possible way to get it done. In this example, that would be to create an administrative top-level OU and then branch of from there. This way, you can maintain control while still being able to delegate as you see fit. Also, always keep it simple. You can make OUs by country code and so on—that is actually recommended—just ensure that you always spend some time beforehand considering the future so that you can prepare for it and not have to do double the work.

18. A. The easiest way to achieve the desired result is to simply rename the OU. Make sure you are comfortable with exactly what you can and can't do with OUs. OUs are not only heavily tested on Microsoft exams but are also something you will always have to deal with while working with the technology.

19. C. If you need to delegate control, you can use Active Directory Users And Computers, right-click the OU where you want to delegate permissions, and choose Delegate Control.

20. D. OUs are extremely important to Active Directory's logical design. OUs allow you to delegate permissions, apply security, and so on.

Chapter 6

Planning Security for Active Directory

MICROSOFT EXAM OBJECTIVES COVERED IN THIS CHAPTER:

- ✓ **Plan a strategy for placing global catalog servers.**
  - ▪ Evaluate the need to enable universal group caching.
- ✓ **Plan an administrative delegation strategy.**
  - ▪ Plan a security group hierarchy based on delegation requirements.
- ✓ **Plan a security group strategy.**
- ✓ **Plan a user authentication strategy.**
  - ▪ Plan a smart card authentication strategy.
  - ▪ Create a password policy for domain users.
- ✓ **Configure the user environment by using Group Policy.**
  - ▪ Configure user settings by using Group Policy.

One of the most fundamental responsibilities of any systems administrator is security management. Therefore, all network operating systems (NOSs) offer some way to grant or deny access to resources, such as files and printers. Active Directory is no exception. You can define fundamental security objects through the use of the users, groups, and computers security principals. Then you can allow or disallow access to resources by granting specific permissions to each of these objects.

In this chapter, you'll learn how to implement security within Active Directory. Through the use of Active Directory tools, you can quickly and easily configure the settings that you require in order to protect information. Note, however, that proper planning for security permissions is an important prerequisite. If your security settings are too restrictive, users may not be able to perform their job functions. Worse yet, they may try to circumvent security measures. They may even complain to their management teams, and eventually you will receive these complaints. You may continuously try to seek balance—to have enough security and, at the same time, be somewhat transparent to the end users, who simply want to do their jobs and not be bothered by what's between the lines. On the other end of the spectrum, if security permissions are too lax, users may be able to access and modify sensitive company resources. You should consider checking your security policy. If you don't have one, consider creating one that states what is expected of every computer user in your company. Fine-tuning Active Directory to comply with your security policy and allowing end users to function without an issue should be your goal.

You should know how to use Active Directory to apply permissions to resources on the network. Particular attention is placed on the evaluation of permissions when applied to different groups and the flow of permissions through the organizational units (OUs) via Group Policy, which is discussed in depth in Chapter 8, "Planning, Implementing, and Managing Group Policy." With all of this in mind, let's start looking at how you can manage security within Active Directory.

In order to complete the exercises in this chapter, you should understand the basics of working with Active Directory objects. If you are not familiar with creating and managing users, groups, computers, and OUs, you should review the information in Chapter 5, "Administering Active Directory," before continuing.

Active Directory Security Overview

One of the fundamental design goals for Active Directory is to define a single, centralized repository of users and information resources. Active Directory records information about all of the users, computers, and resources on your network. Each domain acts as a security boundary, and members of the domain (including workstations, servers, and domain controllers) share information about the objects within them.

The information stored within Active Directory determines which resources are accessible to which users. Through the use of *permissions* that are assigned to Active Directory objects, you can control all aspects of network security.

Many security experts state that 20 percent of real-world network security is a technical issue and that 80 percent of it is a process-and-policy one. Don't make the mistake of trying to solve all security problems through system(s) configurations. You also need to establish and enforce business rules, physically secure your resources, and ensure that users are aware of any restrictions. A security policy (as was mentioned earlier) is a written document used to dictate a set of laws, rules, and practices that regulate how an organization (quite possibly yours) manages, protects, and distributes data.

Throughout this chapter, you'll learn the details of security as it pertains to Active Directory. Note, however, that this is only one aspect of true network security. That is, you should always be sure that you have implemented appropriate access control settings for the file system, network devices, and other resources. Let's start by looking at the various components of network security: working with security principals, managing security and permissions, access control lists (ACLs), and access control entries (ACEs).

Understanding Security Principals

Security principals are Active Directory objects that are assigned *security identifiers (SIDs)*. A SID is a unique identifier that is used to manage any object to which permissions can be assigned. Security principals are assigned permissions to perform certain actions and access certain network resources.

The basic types of Active Directory objects that serve as security principals include the following:

User accounts   User accounts identify individual users on your network by including information such as the user's name and their password. User accounts are the fundamental unit of security administration.

Groups   There are two main types of groups: *security groups* and *distribution groups*. Both types can contain user accounts. Security groups are used for easing the management of security permissions. Distribution groups, on the other hand, are used solely for the purpose of sending email. Distribution groups are not considered security principals. You'll see the details of groups in the next section.

Computer accounts   Computer accounts identify which client computers are members of particular domains. Because these computers participate in the Active Directory database, systems administrators can manage security settings that affect the computer. Computer accounts are used to determine whether a computer can join a domain and for authentication purposes. As you'll see later in this chapter, systems administrators can also place restrictions on certain computer settings to increase security. These settings apply to the computer and, therefore, also apply to any user who is using it (regardless of the permissions granted to the user account).

Note that other objects—such as OUs—do not function as security principals. What this means is that you can apply certain settings (such as Group Policy) on all of the objects within an OU; however, you cannot specifically set permissions with respect to the OU itself. The purpose of OUs is to logically organize other Active Directory objects based on business needs, add a needed level of control for security, and create an easier way to delegate.

Security principals can be assigned permissions so that they can access various network resources, can be given user rights, and may have their actions tracked (through *auditing*, covered later in this chapter). The three types of security principals—user accounts, groups, and computer accounts—form the basis of the Active Directory security architecture. As a systems administrator, you will likely spend a portion of your time managing permissions for these objects.

It is also important to understand that, since a unique SID defines each security principal, deleting a security principal is an irreversible process. For example, if you delete a user account and then later re-create one with the same name, you need to reassign permissions and group membership settings for the new account.

The fundamental security principals that are used for security administration include users and groups. In the following sections, you'll learn how users and groups interact and about the different types of groups that you can create.

Types of Groups

When dealing with groups, you should make the distinction between local security principals and domain security principals. You use local users and groups to assign the permissions necessary to access the local machine. For example, you may assign the permissions you need to reboot a domain controller to a specific local group. Domain users and groups, on the other hand, are used throughout the domain. These objects are available on any of the computers within the Active Directory domain and between domains that have a trust relationship.

There are two main types of groups used in Active Directory:

Security groups   Security groups are considered security principals. They can contain user accounts. To make administration simpler, permissions are usually granted to groups. This allows you to change permissions easily at the Active Directory level (instead of at the level of the resource on which the permissions are assigned).

Security groups can be used for email purposes—that is, a systems administrator can automatically email all of the user accounts that exist within a group. Of course, the systems administrator must specify the email addresses for these accounts.

Active Directory Contact objects can also be placed within security groups, but security permissions will not apply to them.

Distribution groups   Distribution groups are not considered security principals and are used only for the purpose of sending email messages. You can add users to distribution groups just as you would add them to security groups. Distribution groups can also be placed within OUs for easier management. They are useful, for example, if you need to send email messages to an entire department or business unit within Active Directory.

Understanding the differences between security and distribution groups is important in an Active Directory environment. For the most part, systems administrators use security groups for daily administration of permissions. On the other hand, systems administrators who are responsible for maintaining email distribution lists generally use distribution groups to logically group members of departments and business units.

When working in Windows 2000 Native or Server 2003 functional level domains, you can convert security groups to or from distribution groups. When group types are running in a Windows 2000 Mixed domain functional level, they cannot be changed.

Group Scope

In addition to being classified by type, each group is also given a specific scope. The scope of a group defines two characteristics. First, it determines the level of security that applies to a group. Second, it determines which users can be added to the group. Group scope is an important concept in network environments because it ultimately defines which resources users are able to access.

The three types of group scope are as follows:

Domain local   The scope of *domain local groups* extends as far as the local machine. When you're using the Active Directory Users And Computers tool, domain local accounts apply to the computer for which you are viewing information. Domain local groups are used to assign permissions to local resources, such as files and printers. They can contain global groups, universal groups, and user accounts.

Global   The scope of *global groups* is limited to a single domain. Global groups may contain any of the users that are a part of the Active Directory domain in which the global groups reside. Global groups are often used for managing domain security permissions based on job functions. For example, if you need to specify permissions for the Engineering Department, you could create one or more global groups (such as EngineeringManagers and Engineering-Developers). You could then assign security permissions to each group for any of the resources within the domain.

Universal   *Universal groups* can contain users from any domains within an Active Directory forest. Therefore, they are used for managing security across domains. Universal groups are available only when you're running Active Directory in the Windows 2000 Native or Windows Server 2003 domain functional level. When managing multiple domains, it often helps to group global groups within universal groups. For instance, if you have an Engineering global group in the `research .mycompany.com` domain and an Engineering global group in the `asia.mycompany.com` domain, you could create a universal AllEngineers group that contains both of the global groups. Now, whenever security permissions must be assigned to all engineers within the organization, you need only assign permissions to the AllEngineers universal group.

In order for domain controllers to process authentication between domains, information about the membership in universal groups is stored in the Global Catalog (GC). Keep this in mind if you ever plan to place users directly into universal groups and bypass global groups because all of the users will be enumerated in the GC, which will impact size and performance.

Fortunately, universal group credentials are cached on domain controllers that universal group members use to log on. The cached data is obtained whenever universal group members log on, and it is retained on the domain controller for eight hours by default. This is especially useful for smaller locations, such as branch offices, that run less expensive domain controllers. Most domain controllers at these locations cannot store a copy of the entire GC, and frequent calls to the nearest GC would require an inordinate amount of network traffic.

When you create a new group using the Active Directory Users And Computers tool, you must specify the scope of the group. Figure 6.1 shows the New Object—Group dialog box and the available options for the group scope.

FIGURE 6.1   The New Object—Group dialog box

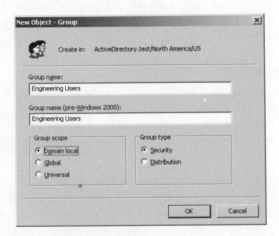

As you can see, the main properties for each of these group types are affected by whether Active Directory is running in Windows 2000 Mixed, Windows 2000 Native, or Server 2003 domain functional level. Each of these scope levels is designed for a specific purpose and will ultimately affect the types of security permissions that can be assigned to them.

There are several limitations on group functionality when running in Windows 2000 Mixed domain functional level. Specifically, the following limitations exist:

- Universal security groups are not available.

- Changing the scope of groups is not allowed.

- Limitations to group nesting exist. Specifically, the only nesting allowed is global groups contained in domain local groups.

When running in native-mode domains, you can make the following group scope changes:

- Domain local groups can be changed to a universal group. This change can be made only if the domain local group does not contain any other domain local groups.

- A global group can be changed to a universal group. This change can be made only if the global group is not a member of any other global groups.

Universal groups themselves cannot be converted into any other group scope type. Changing group scope can be helpful when your security administration or business needs change. You can change group scope easily using the Active Directory Users And Computers tool. To do so, access the properties of the group. As shown in Figure 6.2, you can make a group scope change by clicking one of the options.

FIGURE 6.2   The group Properties dialog box

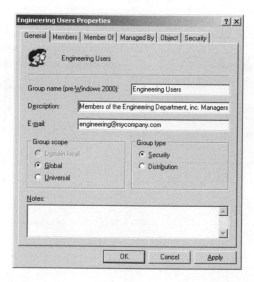

Built-In Domain Local Groups

Built-in domain local groups are used to perform administrative functions on the local server. Because they have preassigned permissions and privileges, they allow systems administrators to easily assign common management functions. Figure 6.3 shows the default built-in groups that are available on a Windows Server 2003 domain controller.

The list of built-in local groups includes the following:

Account Operators   These users are able to create and modify domain user and group accounts. Members of this group are generally responsible for the daily administration of Active Directory.

Administrators   Members of the Administrators group are given full permissions to perform any functions within the Active Directory domain and on the local computer. This includes the ability to access all files and resources that reside on any server within the domain. As you can see, this is a very powerful account.

In general, you should restrict the number of users who are included in this group because most common administration functions do not require this level of access.

FIGURE 6.3 The default built-in local groups

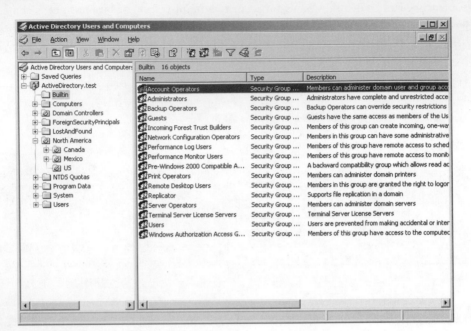

Backup Operators One of the problems associated with backing up data in a secure network environment is that there must be a way to bypass standard file system security in order to copy files. Although you could place users in the Administrators group, this usually provides more permissions than necessary. Members of the Backup Operators group are able to bypass standard file system security for the purpose of backup and recovery only. They cannot, however, directly access or open files within the file system.

Generally, the permissions assigned to the Backup Operators group are used by backup software applications and data.

Guests The Guests group is typically used for providing access to resources that generally do not require security. For example, if you have a network share that provides files that should be made available to all network users, you can assign permissions to allow members of the Guest group to access those files.

Print Operators Members of the Print Operators group are given permissions to administer all of the printers within a domain. This includes common functions such as changing the priority of print jobs and deleting items from the print queue.

Replicator The Replicator group was created to allow the replication of files among the computers in a domain. Accounts that are used for replication-related tasks are added to this group to provide those accounts with the permissions necessary to keep files synchronized across multiple computers.

Server Operators A common administrative task is managing server configuration. Members of the Server Operators group are granted the permissions they need to manage services, shares, and other system settings.

Users The Users built-in domain local group is used to administer security for most network accounts. Usually, this group is given minimal permissions and is used for the application of security settings that apply to most employees within an organization.

The remaining built-in groups, such as Network Configuration Operators and Performance Monitor, are beyond the scope of this book and are not part of the 70-294 exam. For more information, see *Mastering Windows Server 2003* by Mark Minasi.

Windows Server 2003 also includes many different default groups that can be found in the Users folder. As shown in Figure 6.4, these groups are of varying scopes, including domain local, global, and universal groups. You'll see the details of these groups in the next section.

FIGURE 6.4   Contents of the default Users folder

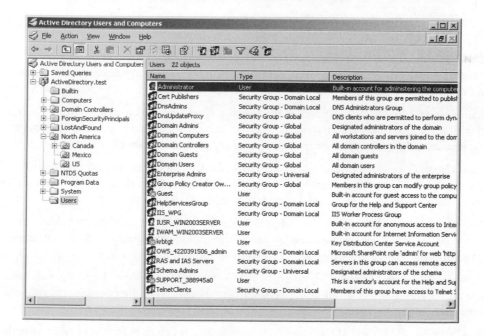

In addition, two important user accounts are created during the promotion of a domain controller. The first is the Administrator account. This account is assigned the password that is provided by a systems administrator during the promotion process, and it has full permissions to perform all actions within the domain. The second account is Guest, which is disabled by default. The purpose of the Guest account is to provide anonymous access to users who do not have an individual logon and password to use within the domain. Although the Guest account might be useful in some situations, it is generally recommended that this account be disabled to increase security.

Predefined Global Groups

As we mentioned earlier in this chapter, you use global groups to manage permissions at the domain level. Members of each of these groups are able to perform specific tasks related to managing Active Directory.

The following predefined global groups are installed in the Users folder:

Cert Publishers Certificates are used to increase security by allowing for strong authentication methods. User accounts are placed within the Cert Publishers group if they require the ability to publish security certificates. Generally, these accounts are used by Active Directory security services.

Domain Computers All of the computers that are members of the domain are generally members of the Domain Computers group. This includes any workstations or servers that have joined the domain but does not include the domain controllers.

Domain Admins Members of the Domain Admins group have full permissions to manage all of the Active Directory objects for this domain. This is a powerful account; therefore, you should restrict its membership to only those users who require full permissions.

Domain Controllers All of the domain controllers for a given domain are generally included within this group.

Domain Guests Generally, members of the Domain Guests group are given minimal permissions with respect to resources. Systems administrators may place user accounts in this group if they require only basic access or require temporary permissions within the domain.

Domain Users The Domain Users group usually contains all of the user accounts for the given domain. This group is generally given basic permissions to resources that do not require higher levels of security. A common example is a public file share.

Enterprise Admins Members of the Enterprise Admins group are given full permissions to perform actions within the entire domain forest. This includes functions such as managing trust relationships and adding new domains to trees and forests.

Group Policy Creator Owners Members of the Group Policy Creator Owners group are able to create and modify Group Policy settings for objects within the domain. This allows them to enable security settings on OUs (and the objects that they contain).

Schema Admins Members of the Schema Admins group are given permissions to modify the Active Directory schema. One example of what being a member of such a group can do is that as a member, you can create additional fields of information for user accounts. This is a very powerful function because any changes to the schema will be propagated to all of the domains and domain controllers within an Active Directory forest. Furthermore, changes to the schema cannot be undone (although additional options can be disabled).

In addition to these groups, you can create new ones for specific services and applications that are installed on the server (you'll notice Figure 6.4 includes more than just the ones in the preceding list). Specifically, services that run on domain controllers and servers will be created as security groups with domain local scope. For example, if a domain controller is running the DNS service, the DNSAdmins and DNSUpdateProxy groups become available. Similarly, if you install the DHCP service, it automatically creates the DHCPUsers and DHCPAdministrators groups. The purpose of these groups varies based on the functionality of the applications being installed.

Foreign Security Principals

In environments that consist of more than one domain, you may need to grant permissions to users who reside in multiple domains. Generally, you manage this using Active Directory trees and forests. However, in some cases, you may want to provide resources to users who are contained in domains that are not part of the same forest.

Active Directory uses the concept of *foreign security principals* to allow permissions to be assigned to users who are not part of the same Active Directory forest. This process is automatic and does not require the intervention of systems administrators. The foreign security principals can then be added to domain local groups, which, in turn, can be granted permissions for resources within the domain. You can view a list of foreign security principals by using the Active Directory Users And Computers tool. Figure 6.5 shows the contents of the ForeignSecurityPrincipals folder.

FIGURE 6.5   The ForeignSecurityPrincipals folder

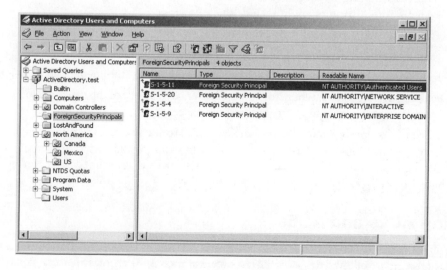

Managing Security and Permissions

Now that you understand the basic issues, terms, and Active Directory objects that pertain to security, it's time to look at how you can apply this information to secure your network resources. The general practice for managing security is to assign users to groups and then grant permissions and logon parameters to the groups so that they can access certain resources.

For management ease and to implement a hierarchical structure, you can place groups within OUs. You can also assign Group Policy settings to all of the objects contained within an OU. By using this method, you can combine the benefits of a hierarchical structure (through OUs) with the use of security principals. Figure 6.6 provides a diagram of this process.

FIGURE 6.6 An overview of security management

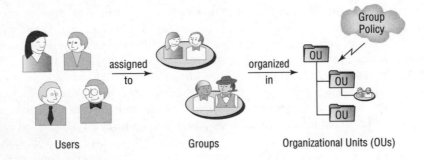

The primary tool used to manage security permissions for users, groups, and computers is the Active Directory Users And Computers tool. Using this tool, you can create and manage Active Directory objects and organize them based on your business needs. Common tasks for many systems administrators might include the following:

- Resetting a user's password (for example, in cases where they forget their password)

- Creating new user accounts (when, for instance, a new employee joins the company)

- Modifying group memberships based on changes in job requirements and functions

- Disabling user accounts (when, for example, users will be out of the office for long periods of time and will not require network resource access)

Once you've properly grouped your users, you need to set the actual permissions that affect the objects within Active Directory. The actual permissions available vary based on the type of object. Table 6.1 provides an example of some of the permissions that can be applied to various Active Directory objects and an explanation of what each permission does:

Using ACLs and ACEs

Each object in Active Directory has an access control list (ACL). The ACL is a list of user accounts and groups that are allowed to access the resource. For each ACL, there is an access control entry (ACE) that defines what a user or a group can actually do with the resource. Deny permissions are

TABLE 6.1   Permissions of Active Directory Objects

Permission	Explanation
Control Access	Changes security permissions on the object
Create Child	Creates objects within an OU (such as other OUs)
Delete Child	Deletes child objects within an OU
Delete Tree	Deletes an OU and the objects within it
List Contents	Views objects within an OU
List Object	Views a list of the objects within an OU
Read	Views properties of an object (such as a username)
Write	Modifies properties of an object

always listed first. This means that if users have Deny permissions through user or group membership, they will not be allowed to access the object, even if they have explicit Allow permissions through other user or group permissions. Figure 6.7 shows an ACL for the Sales OU.

The Security tab is only enabled if you selected the Advanced Features option from the View menu in the Active Directory Users And Computers tool.

FIGURE 6.7   ACL for an OU

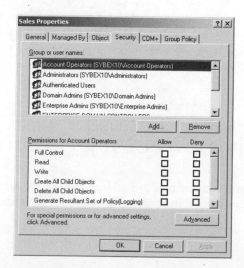

Using Groups Effectively

You are a new systems administrator for a medium-sized organization, and your network spans a single campus-type environment. The previous administrator whom you replaced was the main person who migrated the network from Windows NT 4 to Windows Server 2003. There are no real complaints about the network, and everyone seems happy with their new workstations. The environment is very collegial, with most employees on a first-name basis, and a great deal of your job is done in the hallway as you bump into people. As you familiarize yourself with the network, you soon realize that the previous administrator had a very ad hoc approach to administration. Many of the permissions to resources had been given to individual accounts as people asked for them. There doesn't seem to be any particular strategy in the design of the directory or the allocation of resources.

In one of your meetings with management, you are told that the company has acquired another company, and if this acquisition goes well, several more acquisitions will follow. You are informed of these sensitive plans because management does not want any hiccups in the information system as these new organizations are absorbed into the existing company.

You immediately realize that management practices of the past for this network have to vanish, and they need to be replaced with the best practices that have been developed for networks over the years. One of the fundamental practices in this type of environment is the use of groups to apply permissions and give privileges to users throughout the network.

Although it is quite simple to give permissions individually, and in some cases it seems like overkill to create a group, give permissions to the group, and then add a user to the group, it really pays off in the long run, regardless of how small your network is today. One constant in the networking world is that networks grow. And when they grow, it is much easier to add users to a well-thought-out system of groups and consistently applied policies and permissions than it is to patch these elements together for each individual user.

Don't get caught up in the "easy" way of dealing with each request as it comes down the pike. Take the time to figure out how the system will benefit from a more structured approach. Visualize your network as already large with numerous accounts, even if it is still small, and when it grows, you will be well positioned to manage the network as smoothly as possible.

Implementing Active Directory Security

So far, you have looked at many different concepts that are related to security within Active Directory. You began by exploring security principals and how they form the basis for administering Active Directory security. Then, you considered the purpose and function of groups, how group scopes can affect how these groups work, and how a list of the predefined users and groups is created for new domains and domain controllers. Based on all of this information, it's time to see how you can implement Active Directory security.

In this section, you'll take a look at how you can create and manage users and groups. The most commonly used tool for work with these objects is the Active Directory Users And Computers tool. Using this tool, you can create new user and group objects within the relevant OUs of your domain, and you can modify group membership and group scope.

In addition to these basic operations, you can use some additional techniques to simplify the administration of users and groups. One method involves using user templates. Additionally, you'll want be able to specify who can make changes to user and group objects. That's the purpose of delegation. Both of these topics are covered later in this section.

Let's start with the basics. In Exercise 6.1, you learn how to create and manage users and groups. If you are unfamiliar with basic Active Directory administration steps, review Chapter 5 before you walk through this exercise.

 This exercise involves the creation of new OUs and user accounts within an Active Directory domain. Be sure that you are working in a test environment to avoid any problems that might occur due to the changes that you make.

EXERCISE 6.1

Creating and Managing Users and Groups

1. Open the Active Directory Users And Computers tool.

2. Create the following top-level OUs:

    Sales

    Marketing

    Engineering

    HR

3. Create the following User objects within the Sales container (use the defaults for all fields not listed):

    a. First Name: **John**

        Last Name: **Sales**

EXERCISE 6.1 *(continued)*

User Logon Name: **JSales**

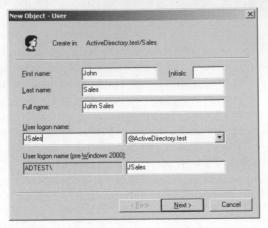

b.   First Name: **Linda**

Last Name: **Manager**

User Logon Name: **LManager**

4.   Create the following User objects within the Marketing container (use the defaults for all fields not listed):

a.   First Name: **Jane**

Last Name: **Marketing**

User Logon Name: **JMarketing**

b.   First Name: **Monica**

Last Name: **Manager**

User Logon Name: **MManager**

5.   Create the following User object within the Engineering container (use the defaults for all fields not listed):

First Name: **Bob**

Last Name: **Engineer**

User Logon Name: **BEngineer**

6. Right-click the HR container, and select New ➢ Group. Use the name **Managers** for the group, and specify Global for the group scope and Security for the group type. Click OK to create the group.

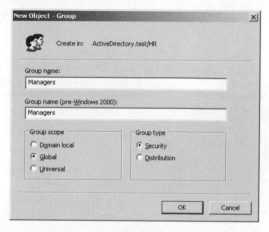

7. To assign users to the Managers group, right-click the Group object and select Properties. Change to the Members tab, and click Add. Enter Linda Manager and Monica Manager, and then click OK. You will see the group membership list. Click OK to finish adding the users to the group.

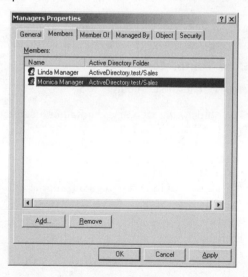

8. When you are finished creating users and groups, close the Active Directory Users And Computers tool.

Notice that you can add users to groups regardless of the OU in which they're contained. In Exercise 6.1, for example, you added two user accounts from different OUs into a group that was created in a third OU. This type of flexibility allows you to easily manage user and group accounts based on your business organization.

The Active Directory Users And Computers tool also allows you to perform common functions by simply right-clicking an object and selecting actions from the context menu. For example, we could right-click a user account and select Add Members To Group to quickly change group membership.

You may have noticed that creating multiple users can be a fairly laborious and a potentially error-prone process. As a result, you are probably ready to take a look at a better way to create multiple users, which is typically accomplished with user templates, as you will see in the next section.

Using User Templates

Sometimes you will need to add several users with the same security settings. Rather than creating each user from scratch and making configuration changes to each one manually, you can create one user template, configure it, and copy it as many times as necessary. Each copy retains the configuration, group membership, and permissions of the original, but you must specify a new username, password, and full name to make the new user unique.

In Exercise 6.2, you create a user template, make configuration changes, and create a new user based on the template. This exercise shows you that the new user you create will belong to the same group as the user template that you copied it from. You should have completed the previous exercise before you begin this one.

EXERCISE 6.2

Creating and Using User Templates

1. Open the Active Directory Users And Computers tool.

2. Create the following User object within the Sales container (use the defaults for all fields not listed):

    First Name: **Sales User**

    Last Name: **Template**

    User Logon Name: **SalesUserTemplate**

3. Create a new global security group called **Sales Users**, and add SalesUserTemplate to the group membership.

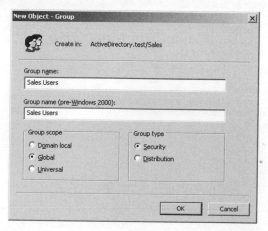

4. Right-click the SalesUserTemplate user object and select Copy from the context menu.

5. Enter the username, first name, and last name for the new "real" user. Click the Next button to move on to the password screen and enter the new user's password information. Close the Copy Object—User dialog box when you're done.

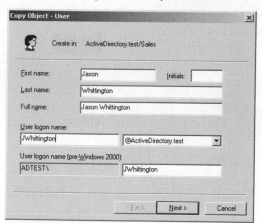

6. Right-click the user you created in step 5, select Properties, and click the Member Of tab.

7. Verify that the new user is a member of the Sales Users group.

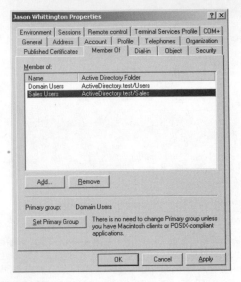

Delegating Control of Users and Groups

A common administrative function related to the use of Active Directory involves managing users and groups. OUs can be used to logically group objects so that they can be easily managed. Once you have placed the appropriate Active Directory objects within OUs, you are ready to delegate control of these objects.

Delegation is the process by which a higher-level security administrator assigns permissions to other users. For example, if Admin A is a member of the Domain Admins group, he is able to delegate control of any OU within the domain to Admin B. You can access the Delegation of Control Wizard through the Active Directory Users And Computers tool. You can use it to quickly and easily perform common delegation tasks. The wizard walks you through the steps of selecting for which object(s) you want to perform delegation, what permission you want to allow, and which users will have those permissions.

Exercise 6.3 walks through the steps required to delegate control of OUs. In order to complete the steps in this exercise, you must have already completed Exercise 6.1.

EXERCISE 6.3

Delegating Control of Active Directory Objects

1. Open the Active Directory Users And Computers tool.

2. Create a new user within the Engineering OU, using the following information (use the default settings for any fields not specified):

First Name: **Robert**

Last Name: **Admin**

User Logon Name: **radmin**

3. Right-click the Sales OU, and select Delegate Control. This starts the Delegation of Control Wizard. Click Next.

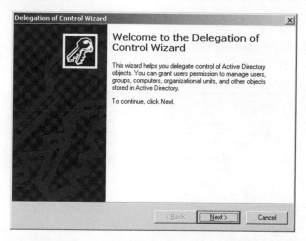

4. To add users and groups to which you want to delegate control, click the Add button. In the Add dialog box, enter **Robert Admin** for the name of the user to add. Note that you could specify multiple users or groups using this option. Click OK to add the account to the delegation list, which is shown in the Users Or Groups page. Click Next to continue.

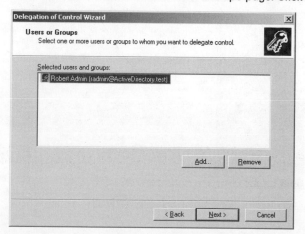

5. On the Tasks To Delegate page, you must specify which actions you want to allow the selected user to perform within this OU. Select the Delegate The Following Common Tasks option, and place a check mark next to the following options:

Create, Delete, And Manage User Accounts

Reset User Passwords And Force Password Change At Next Logon

Read All User Information

Create, Delete, And Manage Groups

Modify The Membership Of A Group

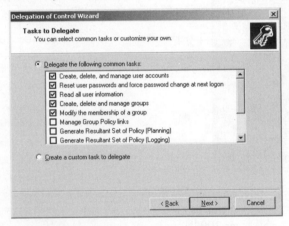

6. Click Next to continue. The wizard provides you with a summary of the selections that you have made on the Completing The Delegation Of Control Wizard page. To complete the process, click Finish to have the wizard commit the changes.

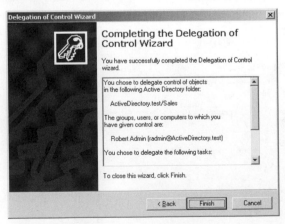

Now, when the user Robert Admin logs on (using "radmin" as his logon name), he will be able to perform common administrative functions for all of the objects contained within the Sales OU.

7. When you are finished, close the Active Directory Users And Computers tool.

Using Group Policy for Security

A very useful and powerful feature of Active Directory is a technology known as Group Policy. Through the use of Group Policy settings, systems administrators can assign literally hundreds of different settings and options for users, groups, and OUs. Specifically, in relation to security, there are many different options you can use to control how important features such as password policies, user rights, and account lockout settings can be configured.

The general process for making these settings is to create a Group Policy object (GPO) with the settings that you want, and to then link it to an OU or other Active Directory object.

We'll cover the details of creating, assigning, and managing Group Policy settings later in Chapter 8. The purpose of this section is to show the various Group Policy options that apply to Active Directory security.

Table 6.2 lists many Group Policy settings that are relevant to creating a secure Active Directory environment. Note that this list is not complete—there are many other options available through Windows Server 2003's administrative tools.

TABLE 6.2   Group Policy Settings Used for Security Purposes

Setting Section	Setting Name	Purpose
Account Policies ➤ Password Policy	Enforce PasswordHistory	Specifies how many passwords will be remembered. This option prevents users from reusing the same passwords, whenever they're changed.
Account Policies ➤ Password Policy	Minimum Password Length	Prevents users from using short, weak passwords by specifying the minimum number of characters that the password must include.

TABLE 6.2   Group Policy Settings Used for Security Purposes *(continued)*

Setting Section	Setting Name	Purpose
Account Policies ➢ Account Lockout Policy	Account LockoutDuration	Specifies how long an account will remain locked out after the account has been locked out (due, generally, to too many bad password attempts). By setting this option to a reasonable value (such as "15 minutes"), you can reduce administrative overhead while still maintaining fairly strong security.
Local Policies ➢ Security Options	Accounts: RenameAdministrator Account	Often, when trying to gain unauthorized access to a computer, individuals attempt to guess the Administrator password. One method for increasing security is to rename this account so that no password allows entry using this logon.
Local Policies ➢ Security Options	Domain Controller: Allow Server Operators To Schedule Tasks	This option specifies whether members of the built-in Server Operators group are allowed to schedule tasks on the server.
Local Policies ➢ Security Options	Interactive Logon: Do Not Display Last User Name	Increases security by not displaying the name of the last user who logged into the system.
Local Policies ➢ Security Options	Shutdown: Allow System To Be Shut Down Without Having To Log On	Allows systems administrators to perform remote shutdown operations without logging on to the server.

You can use several different methods to configure Group Policy settings using the tools included with Windows Server 2003. Exercise 6.4 walks through the steps required to create a basic Group Policy for the purpose of enforcing security settings. In order to complete the steps of this exercise, you must have already completed Exercise 6.1.

EXERCISE 6.4

Applying Security Policies by Using Group Policy

1. Open the Active Directory Users And Computers tool.

2. Right-click the domain name, and select Properties.

EXERCISE 6.4 *(continued)*

3. Change to the Group Policy tab, and select the Default Domain Policy.

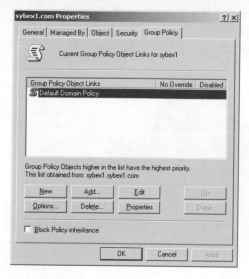

4. To specify the Group Policy settings, click Edit.

5. In the Group Policy window, open Computer Configuration, Windows Settings, Security Settings, Account Policies, Password Policy object.

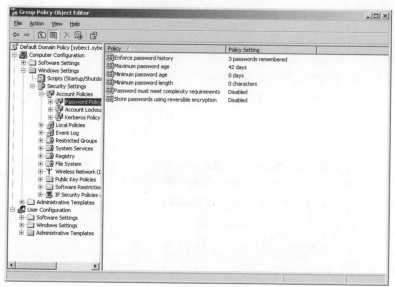

6. In the right pane, double-click the Minimum Password Length setting.

EXERCISE 6.4 *(continued)*

7. In the Security Policy Setting dialog box, place a check mark next to the Define This Policy Setting option. Increase the value to 7 characters. Click OK to return to the Group Policy Object Editor window.

8. Open User Configuration, Administrative Templates, Control Panel object. Double-click Prohibit Access To The Control Panel, select Enabled, and then click OK.

9. Close the Group Policy window to save the settings you chose. Click OK to enable the Security Group Policy.

10. To view the security permissions for a Group Policy object, right-click the domain name and select Properties. On the Group Policy tab, highlight the Default Domain Policy Group Policy object, and select Properties.

11. Select the Security tab of Default Domain Policy Properties dialog box. Click Add, and enter **Linda Manager**. Click OK to add this account to the list of users and groups that will be affected by these Group Policy settings. This takes you back to the Default Domain Policy Properties dialog box. Highlight Linda Manager, and allow this user the Read and Write permissions.

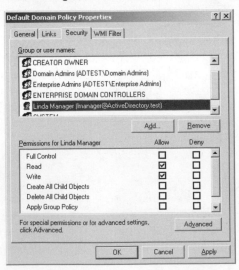

EXERCISE 6.4 *(continued)*

12. Click OK twice to save the changes. Linda Manager will now be able to view and change information for objects in the Sales OU.

13. When finished, close the Active Directory Users And Computers tool.

The settings that you specify apply to all of the security principals included within the OU to which the Group Policy applies.

 We will cover using the Group Policy Management Console (GPMC) in Chapter 8 where we learn more about how to configure Group Policy.

Understanding Smart Card Authentication

In the previous section, we discussed password policies and account lockout policies that increase security over the default Windows Server 2003 settings. However, the standard account logon process is still fairly insecure due to the fact that a malicious attacker only needs a single piece of information—a password—to log on to the network. This problem is compounded by the fact that users or administrators probably would not detect a stolen password until after it had been used by a hacker to break into the system. Smart cards, which are similar in appearance to credit cards, solve both of these problems.

Smart cards store user certificate information in a magnetic strip on a plastic card. As an alternative to the standard username and password logon process, users can insert a smart card into a special smart card reader attached to the computer and enter a unique PIN on the keyboard. This provides the system with a double-verification secure logon (the smart card and the PIN) and reduces the likelihood that a user's authentication method will be stolen without detection.

To deploy a smart card solution in the enterprise you must have a certificate authority (CA) and a public key infrastructure (PKI) on your intranet. In each domain, you must configure the security permissions of the Smart Card User, Smart Card Logon, and Enrollment Agent certificate templates to allow smart card users to enroll for certificates. You must also set up the certification authority to issue smart card certificates and Enrollment Agent certificates.

 Microsoft certificate services are beyond the scope of this book and are covered in more detail in the *MCSE: Windows Server 2003 Network Infrastructure Planning and Maintenance Study Guide* by Suzan Sage London and James Chellis (Sybex, 2003).

After you've configured your certificate server to meet the requirements for smart card authentication, you can set up a smart card enrollment station and begin issuing smart cards to users. Most organizations that use smart card authentication don't allow standard authentication at all, so Microsoft provides a Group Policy setting that requires the use of smart cards.

Preparing a Smart Card Certificate Enrollment Station

To begin issuing smart cards, you must prepare a smart card certificate enrollment station where you physically transfer the authentication information to smart cards. You need to install a smart card reader on the enrollment station, which in this case doubles as a smart card writer. Smart card readers are available from a variety of manufacturers, so you should always make sure that any smart card reader your company purchases is listed on the Windows Server 2003 hardware compatibility list (HCL). After you've properly installed the smart card reader, you need to install an Enrollment Agent certificate on the enrollment station, which you obtain from your CA.

Exercise 6.5 walks you through the process of configuring an enrollment station. Note that you must have access to a company CA configured in the manner described in the preceding paragraph in order to complete this exercise.

EXERCISE 6.5

Preparing a Smart Card Certificate Enrollment Station

1. Log on as the user or administrator who will issue the smart card certificates.

2. Open a Microsoft Management Console (MMC) by selecting Start ➢ Run and entering **mmc** in the Run dialog box.

3. Add the Certificates snap-in by selecting File ➢ Add/Remove Snap-in. Click Add in the Add Standalone Snap-in dialog box. Select the Certificates snap-in and click the Add button. Click Close and then click OK to return to the MMC and display the newly added snap-in.

4. Double-click the Certificates—Current User node in the MMC window.

5. Right-click the Personal node and select All Tasks ➢ Request New Certificate.

6. In the Certificate Request Wizard, select the Enrollment Agent certificate template. Enter a name and description for the template. When prompted, click Install Certificate.

After you've prepared the enrollment station to enroll smart cards certificates, you can actually begin writing certificate information to the physical cards. Follow the steps in Exercise 6.6 to enroll a smart card for user logon. Note that you must complete Exercise 6.5 before continuing. In addition, you must have a smart card reader and at least one blank smart card available.

EXERCISE 6.6

Setting Up a Smart Card for User Logon

1. Log on to the computer as the user or administrator that you configured in the previous exercise.

2. Open Internet Explorer by selecting Start ➤ All Programs ➤ Internet Explorer.

3. In the Address field, enter the address of the CA that issues smart card certificates and press Enter.

4. In the Internet Explorer (IE) window, click Request a Certificate, and then click Advanced Certificate Request.

5. Click Request A Certificate For A Smart Card On Behalf Of Another User Using The Smart Card Certificate Enrollment Station. If prompted, click Yes to accept the smart card signing certificate.

6. Click Smart Card Logon on the Smart Card Certificate Enrollment Station web page.

7. Under Certification Authority, select the CA you want to issue the smart card certificate.

8. Under Cryptographic Service Provider, select the cryptographic service provider of the smart card's manufacturer.

9. Under Administrator Signing Certificate, click the Enrollment Agent certificate from the previous exercise.

10. Under User To Enroll, click Select User. Select the user to enroll and click Enroll.

11. When prompted, insert the smart card into the smart card reader and click OK. When prompted, enter a new PIN for the smart card.

Now that you've seen how to configure a smart card enrollment station and set up smart cards for user logon, you should begin to think about Group Policy settings for enforcing smart card logon. One of the most common mistakes that administrators make when administering a smart card policy is to not require smart card logon at all. This means that users with smart cards can log on with either their smart cards or through the standard username and password procedure, which defeats the point of issuing smart cards in the first place! Exercise 6.7 shows you how to configure Group Policy to require smart card authentication.

EXERCISE 6.7

Configuring Group Policy to Require Smart Card Logon

1. Open the Active Directory Users And Computers Utility.

2. Create a new top-level OU called Smart Card Test.

3.   Right-click the Smart Card Test OU and select Properties.

4.   In the Smart Card Test Properties dialog box, switch to the Group Policy tab and click Add. Press Enter to accept the default GPO name, and then click the Edit button.

5.   In the Group Policy Object Editor window, expand Computer Configuration ➢ Windows Settings ➢ Security Settings ➢ Local Policies ➢ Security Options.

6.   Double-click the Interactive Logon: Require Smart Card policy.

7.   In the Interactive Logon: Require Smart Card dialog box, select Enabled and click OK.

Using the Security Configuration And Analysis Utility

The power and flexibility of Windows-based operating systems are both a benefit and a liability. On the plus side, the many configuration options available allow users and systems administrators to modify and customize settings to their preference. On the negative side, however, the full level of functionality can cause problems. For example, novice users might attempt to delete critical system files or incorrectly uninstall programs to free up disk space.

So how can you prevent these types of problems? One method is to strictly enforce the types of actions that users can perform. Because most settings for the Windows Server 2003 interface can be configured in the Registry, you could edit the appropriate settings using the RegEdit command. However, this process can become quite tedious. Furthermore, manually modifying the Registry is a dangerous process and one that is bound to cause problems due to human error. In order to make the creation and application of security settings easier, Microsoft has included the Security Configuration And Analysis tool with Windows Server 2003.

The *Security Configuration And Analysis utility* can be used to create, modify, and apply security settings in the Registry through the use of security template files. *Security templates* allow systems administrators to define security settings once and then store this information in a file that can be applied to other computers.

These template files offer a user-friendly way of configuring common settings for Windows Server 2003 operating systems. For example, instead of searching through the Registry (which is largely undocumented) for specific keys, a systems administrator can choose from a list of common options. The template file provides a description of the settings, along with information about the Registry key(s) to which the modifications must be made. Templates can be stored and applied to users and computers. For example, we could create three configurations titled Level 1, Level 2, and Level 3. We may use the Level 3 template for high-level managers and engineers, whereas the Level 1 and Level 2 templates are used for all other users who require basic functionality.

The overall process for working with the Security Configuration And Analysis utility is as follows:

1. Open or create a security database file.
2. Import an existing template file.
3. Analyze the local computer.
4. Make any setting changes.
5. Save any template changes.
6. Export the new template (optional).
7. Apply the changes to the local computer (optional).

There is no default icon for the Security Configuration And Analysis utility. In order to access it, you must manually choose this snap-in from within the MMC.

Exercise 6.8 walks you through the steps you need to take to use the Security Configuration And Analysis utility. In this exercise, you will use this utility to create and modify security configurations.

EXERCISE 6.8

Using the Security Configuration And Analysis Utility

1. Click Start ➢ Run, type **mmc**, and press Enter. This opens a blank MMC.

2. In the File menu, select Add/Remove Snap-In. Click Add. In the Add Standalone Snap-In dialog box, select the Security Configuration And Analysis item, then click Add, then click Close.

3. You will see that the Security Configuration And Analysis snap-in has been added to the configuration. Click OK to continue.

EXERCISE 6.8 *(continued)*

4. Within the MMC, right-click Security Configuration And Analysis, and select Open Database. This displays a standard file selection (Open) dialog box. Change to a local directory on your computer, and create a new security database file named `SecurityTest.sdb`. Note the location of this file because you'll need it in later steps. Click OK.

5. You'll be prompted to open a Security Template file. By default, these files are stored within the Security\Templates directory of your Windows system root. On the Import Database dialog box, select `DC security.inf`, and place a check mark in the Clear This Database Before Importing box. Click Open to load the Security Template file.

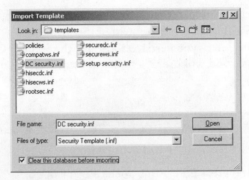

6. Now that you have created a security database file and opened a template, you can start performing useful security tasks. Within the Security Configuration And Analysis utility, you have access to several tasks.

   To analyze the security configuration of the local computer, right-click the Security Configuration And Analysis utility, and select Analyze Computer Now.

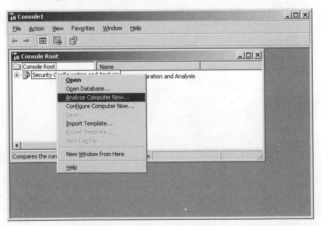

When prompted, enter the path to a local directory with the filename `securityTest.log`. Click OK to begin the analysis process.

EXERCISE 6.8 *(continued)*

7. You will now see the Security Configuration And Analysis utility begin to analyze your computer.

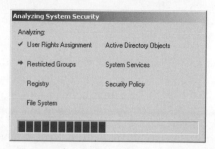

8. When the process has been completed, you can view the current security settings for the local computer. Navigate through the various items to view the current security configuration.

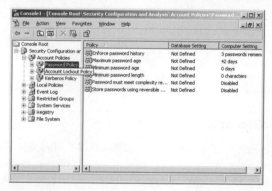

9. To make changes to this template, expand the Password Policy object under Account Policies. Double-click the Enforce Password History item. On the Enforce Password History Properties dialog box, place a check mark next to the Define This Policy In The Database option, and type **2** for Passwords Remembered.

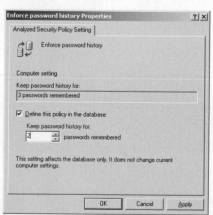

10. Click OK to make the setting change. Note that this change in setting was not enabled for the local computer—the change was implemented only within the security database file.

11. To save the changes to the Security Database file, right-click the Security And Configuration Analysis object, and select Save.

12. To export the current settings to a Template file, right-click the Security And Configuration Analysis object, and select Export Template. You are prompted for the location and filename to which these settings should be saved. Be sure to choose a meaningful name so that other systems administrators will understand the purpose of this template.

13. As of yet, the configuration change we made has not yet been applied to any machines. To apply the change to the local computer, right-click the Security And Configuration Analysis object, and select Configure Computer Now. You are prompted to enter the path for a Log file. Enter any path on the local computer, and specify SecurityTest2.log as the filename. Click OK. You should see the settings being applied to the local computer.

14. To quickly view the contents of the Log file for the most recent operation, right-click the Security And Configuration Analysis object, and select View Log.

15. When you are finished, exit the Security And Configuration Analysis tool by closing the MMC.

The *secedit.exe* Command

All of the functionality of the Security Configuration And Analysis utility has also been built into a command-line utility called secedit.exe. One advantage of using secedit.exe is that you can perform a batch analysis without having to use the graphical tools.

Just like the Security Configuration And Analysis utility, the command-line utility is database driven, meaning that you can use switches to access database and configuration files. The secedit.exe command performs the following high-level functions: analysis, configuration, export function, and validation. These are the same functions carried out by the Security Configuration And Analysis graphical utility (described in the previous section and exercise).

Table 6.3 lists the secedit.exe switches and their functions.

TABLE 6.3   *secedit.exe* Switches

Switch	Valid with Switch	Function
/analyze	Independent function	Analyzes system security.
/configure	Independent function	Configures system security by applying a stored template.

TABLE 6.3   *secedit.exe* Switches *(continued)*

Switch	Valid with Switch	Function
/refreshpolicy	Independent function	Reapplies security settings to the GPO.
/export	Independent function	Exports a template from the database to the template file.
/validate	Independent function	Validates the syntax of a security template.
[/DB *filename*]	/analyze, /configure, /export	Required with the /analyze and /configure commands. Optional with others. Specifies the path to the database file.
[/CFG *filename*]	/analyze, /configure, /export	Required if a new database file is specified. Specifies the path to a security template to import into the database.
[/log *logpath*]	/analyze, /configure, /export	Specifies the path to the log file generated during the operation.
[/verbose]	/analyze, /configure, /export	Specifies more detailed progress information.
[/quiet]	/analyze, /configure, /export	Suppresses screen output during the operation.
[/overwrite]	/configure	Optional only if [/CFG *filename*] is used. Completely overwrites the database rather than appending the database.
[/areas *area1 area2*]	/configure, /export	Specifies security areas to be applied to the system. Default is all areas. Options are SECURITYPOLICY, GROUP_MGMT, USER_RIGHTS, REGKEYS, FILESTORE, and SERVICES.
Machine_policy	/refreshpolicy	Refreshes security settings for the local computer.
User_policy	/refreshpolicy	Refreshes security settings for the current local user account.
/enforce	/refreshpolicy	Refreshes security settings even if no changes have been made to the GPO.

TABLE 6.3   *secedit.exe* Switches *(continued)*

Switch	Valid with Switch	Function
/MergedPolicy	/export	Merges local and domain policy in the export file.
Filename	/validate	Indicates the filename of the template to validate.

If any errors occur during the security configuration and analysis process, the results will be stored in the log file that is created. Be sure to examine this file for any errors that might be present in your configuration.

 Real World Scenario

Enforcing Consistent Security Policies

You are one of 50 systems administrators for a large, multinational organization. As is the case for most of these administrators, you're responsible for all operations related to a portion of an Active Directory domain. Specifically, your job is to manage all of the aspects of administration for objects contained within the Austin OU. The Austin office supports nearly 500 employees. Recently, security has become an important concern because the company is growing quickly and new employees are being added almost daily. In addition, the organization deals with customers' sensitive financial information, and the success of the business is based on this information remaining secure. You've been tasked with creating and implementing an Active Directory security policy for the Austin OU.

At first you start looking into the Group Policy settings that might be appropriate for attaining the desired level of security. You create different levels of security based on users' job functions. Specific policy options include restricting when users can access network resources and which resources they can access. You also begin to implement settings that "harden" your production servers, especially those that contain sensitive data.

A few days after you begin your analysis, you join the weekly company-wide IT conference call and learn that you're not alone in this task. It seems that systems administrators throughout the company have been given similar tasks. The only difference is that they're all asked to implement policies only for the specific Active Directory objects for which they're responsible. That gets you thinking about pooling resources: That is, although it might make sense to attack this task for just the Austin OU, wouldn't it be great if the entire organization could implement a consistent and uniform security policy? If every systems administrator decided to implement security policies in a different way, this would compromise consistency and ease of administration within the environment. And it's likely that many systems administrators will create useful security policies that the others overlooked. The idea of "think globally, act locally" may apply here.

The Security Configuration And Analysis tool that is included with Windows Server 2003 is designed to solve exactly this type of problem. You find that by using this tool, you can design a set of security configurations and then apply those policies to various computers within the environment. You decide to begin by creating security templates based on business needs. Because the environment has many different requirements (and some that are specific only to a few offices), your goal is to minimize the number of different security templates that you create while still meeting the needs of the entire organization. Perhaps the best way to proceed in this scenario is to pool resources: Many tech-heads are better than one! However, keep in mind that this will be more of a political task than a technical one, at least until the various administrators can come together. One of the results—and benefits—of Active Directory is that many of these decisions can be centralized so that the departmental administrators can spend their time helping users with specific issues rather than on duplication of effort. Regardless, creating the appropriate security policies is unlikely to be an easy task—you'll need to confer with systems administrators throughout the company and you'll need to talk to managers and business leaders as well. However, it will be worth the effort to ensure that the entire organization has implemented consistent security policies. Overall, a little extra work up front can save a lot of headaches in the long run.

Implementing an Audit Policy

One of the most important aspects of controlling security in networked environments is ensuring that only authorized users are able to access specific resources. Although systems administrators often spend much time managing security permissions, it is almost always possible for a security problem to occur.

Sometimes, the best way to find possible security breaches is to actually record the actions taken by specific users. Then, in the case of a security breach (the unauthorized shutdown of a server, for example), systems administrators can examine the log to find the cause of the problem.

The Windows Server 2003 operating system and Active Directory offer you the ability to audit a wide range of actions. In the following sections, you'll see how to implement auditing for Active Directory.

Overview of Auditing

The act of auditing relates to recording specific actions. From a security standpoint, auditing is used to detect any possible misuse of network resources. Although auditing does not necessarily prevent the misuse of resources, it does help determine when security violations occurred (or were attempted). Furthermore, just the fact that others know that you have implemented auditing may prevent them from attempting to circumvent security.

There are several steps that you need to complete in order to implement auditing using Windows Server 2003:

- Configure the size and storage settings for the audit logs.

- Enable categories of events to audit.

- Specify which objects and actions should be recorded in the audit log.

Note that there are trade-offs to implementing auditing. First and foremost, recording auditing information can consume system resources. This can decrease overall system performance and use up valuable disk space. Second, auditing many events can make the audit log impractical to view. If too much detail is provided, systems administrators are unlikely to scrutinize all of the recorded events. For these reasons, you should always be sure to find a balance between the level of auditing details provided and the performance-management implications of these settings.

Implementing Auditing

Auditing is not an all-or-none type of process. As is the case with security in general, systems administrators must choose specifically which objects and actions they want to audit.

The main categories for auditing include the following:

- Audit account logon events
- Audit account management
- Audit directory service access
- Audit logon events
- Audit object access
- Audit policy change
- Audit privilege use
- Audit process tracking
- Audit system events

In order to audit access to objects stored within Active Directory, you must enable the Audit Directory Service Access option. Then you must specify which objects and actions should be tracked.

Exercise 6.9 walks through the steps you must take to implement auditing of Active Directory objects on domain controllers. In order to complete the steps in this exercise, you must have already completed Exercise 6.1.

EXERCISE 6.9

Enabling Auditing of Active Directory Objects

1. Open the Domain Controller Security Policy tool (located in the Administrative tools program group).

EXERCISE 6.9 *(continued)*

2. Expand Computer Configuration, Windows Settings, Security Settings, Local Policies, Audit Policy.

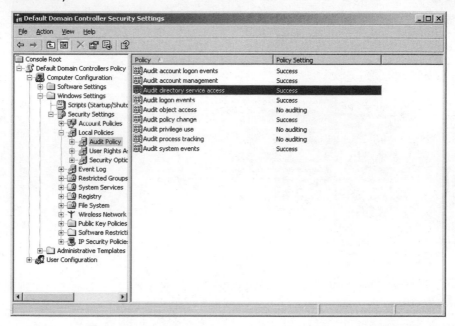

3. Double-click the setting for Audit Directory Service Access.

4. In the Audit Directory Service Access Properties dialog box, place a check mark next to the option for Define These Policy Settings, and check marks at Success and Failure. Click OK to save the settings.

5. Expand Computer Configuration, Windows Settings, Security Settings, Event Log to see the options associated with the event logs.

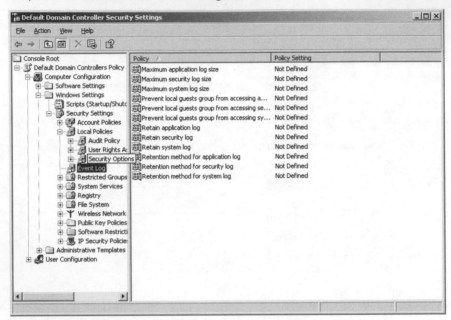

6. Double-click the Maximum Security Log Size item in the right pane of the Domain Controller Security Policy tool, and set the value to 2048KB in the Maximum Security Log Size dialog box. Click OK.

7. In the right pane of the Domain Controller Security utility, double-click the Retain Security Log item, and specify that events should be overwritten after seven days in the Retain Security Log dialog box. Click OK. You will be notified that the Retention Method For Security Log option will also be changed. Click OK to accept the changes.

8. When you are finished enabling auditing options, close the Domain Controller Security Policy tool.

Once you have enabled auditing of Active Directory objects, it's time to specify exactly which actions and objects should be audited. Exercise 6.10 walks through the steps required to enable auditing for a specific OU. In order to complete the steps in this exercise, you must have already completed Exercise 6.1 and Exercise 6.9.

EXERCISE 6.10

Enabling Auditing for a Specific OU

1. Open the Active Directory Users And Computers tool.

2. To enable auditing for a specific object, right-click the Engineering OU, and select Properties. Select the Group Policy tab on the Engineer Properties dialog box.

3. Highlight the Engineering Security Settings Group Policy object, if present, and select Properties. (You may need to create a new GPO. For more information, please see Chapter 8.)

4. Select the Security tab on the GPO Properties dialog box, and then click Advanced. Select the Auditing tab. You will see the current auditing settings for this Group Policy object.

5. Click the Edit button. Notice that you can view and change auditing settings based on the objects and/or properties. To retain the current settings, click OK.

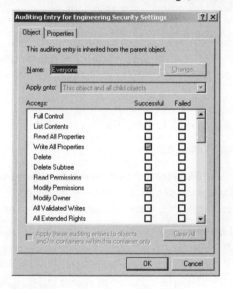

6. To exit the configuration for the Engineering object, click OK three more times.

7. When you are finished with the auditing settings, close the Active Directory Users And Computers tool.

For more complete details about all of the available auditing configuration options, see the Windows Server 2003 Help and Support Center.

Viewing Auditing Information

One of the most important aspects of auditing is regularly monitoring the audit logs. If this step is ignored, as it often is in poorly managed environments, the act of auditing is useless. Fortunately, Windows Server 2003 includes the *Event Viewer* tool, which allows systems administrators to quickly and easily view audited events. Using the filtering capabilities of Event Viewer, they can find specific events of interest.

Exercise 6.11 walks through the steps you must take to generate some auditing events and to examine the data collected for these actions. In this exercise, you will perform some actions that will be audited, and then you will view the information recorded within the audit logs. In order to complete this exercise, you must have already completed the steps in Exercise 6.1 and Exercise 6.10 .

EXERCISE 6.11

Generating and Viewing Audit Logs

1. Open the Active Directory Users And Computers tool.

2. Within the Engineering OU, right-click the Bob Engineer User account, and select Properties.

3. On the Bob Properties dialog box, add the middle initial A for this User account, and specify Software Developer in the Description box. Click OK to save the changes.

4. Within the Engineering OU, right-click the Robert Admin User account, and select Properties.

5. On the Bob Properties dialog box add a description of Engineering IT Admin, and click OK.

6. Close the Active Directory Users And Computers tool.

7. Open the Event Viewer tool from the Administrative Tools program group. Select the Security item. You will see a list of audited events categorized under Directory Service Access. Note that you can obtain more details about a specific item by double-clicking it.

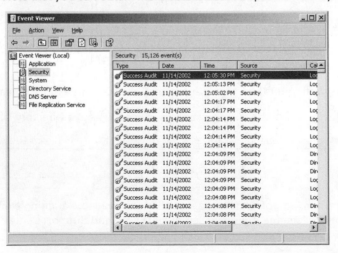

8. When you are finished viewing the security log, close the Event Viewer tool.

Real World Scenario

Real World Security Hacks for Your Windows Server 2003 Accounts

Always secure your domain controllers. In production environments, you could wind up very vulnerable to attack by not securing your accounts, which is not what you want. Once you have installed Windows Server 2003, you need to begin the lockdown process. Now more than ever, you need to analyze and address security issues for any default installation of any operating system or platform. With such an emphasis placed on security these days, each install you do needs to be addressed and it's no different with Windows Server 2003. After you complete a basic install, you should start a checklist of items that you want to lock down, remove, and audit or at least know about to keep yourself and your systems safe from threat.

After you install the system, you need to address a few issues pertaining to the installation. First, remember that most of the time, the new system has much in common with the old one as well as many other systems out there. The first common issues for Windows-based systems are the Guest and Administrator accounts. Not only can a hacker try to expose a weakness in this commonality, but also malware-based attacks have been known to use the built-in Administrator account as a potential starting point from which to gain entry to or compromise your system. This is very common these days; many of the virus attacks on most corporate networks have depended on this weakness.

When you keep default accounts in your server, you may be asking for trouble. Any password attack known to IT professionals today is based on the hacker knowing two things, the username and the password. If they have half the equation, as they do in the case of credentials (most of the time these are just a password tied to an account), then all they need is a good password cracking tool, a huge dictionary file, and some time.

Another option is to set those accounts up completely so that they function as an early alert system that lets you know someone is picking the lock on your door. If you get an account lockout (if you set it up and find it logged in your Event Viewer) on the default accounts, you can be pretty sure that you are under attack. You can't avoid this scenario when you leave default accounts in your design. Although you can't delete many of the default accounts, you will have the option of renaming them.

By default, the Guest account is not operational on either member servers or domain controllers. This is good news because it means that you don't really have to worry about it being exploited unless someone enables it. However, it is important that you check to make sure that it is not and does not become active.

The Administrator account, on the other hand, is a more powerful account that needs to be handled with care. This is because the server can be easily compromised if a hacker just compromises the administrative credentials of the system. Therefore, it is very important for you to know about this account and lock it down immediately after you finish installing the base NOS. To do so, you can rename the account with Group Policy or set it up as an account that is used only to log and audit attempts for use. If you decide to make a new Administrator account under a different name, make sure you don't give out the new name and, in addition, make sure you secure it. Normally, in smaller organizations, it's easier to just rename the account and then set it up as a trap, but doing so is up to you. Always try to create a backup Administrator account and use it instead, but if you do, you want to make sure you never lock yourself out of the system. To prevent this from happening, make sure you note what the new account will be called.

Summary

In this chapter, we talked about planning for and implementing security with Active Directory. Security cannot be overlooked; it's important to always consider how security may affect your deployment or lack of it—how it will ultimately affect your system if it is hacked. We also looked at the differences between security and distribution groups. Distribution groups are used for only one thing: email distribution lists. These groups are used with email applications (such as Microsoft Exchange Server 2003) to send email to the members of the group you create. They will not allow you to assign permissions, and you cannot use them to filter Group Policy settings. In the Windows Server 2003 operating system, security groups are used to manage user account and computer account access to shared resources and to filter Group Policy settings. We also explained other important items that pertain to security, such as what default groups are available after a base install of the operating system, and how to secure the most vulnerable accounts.

We then examined how permissions are managed. You can change permissions with Group Policy or simply by altering them right on the object. We also covered how delegation of control can be used to distribute administrative responsibilities. We wrapped up this chapter by discussed auditing—why it's important and how to get it done.

Thoroughly understanding each of these topics is important when you're implementing Active Directory in a business environment (and when you're preparing for the exam)! In the next chapter, we focus on Active Directory reliability and how to optimize it.

Exam Essentials

Understand the purpose of security principals.   Security principals are Active Directory objects that can be assigned permissions. Understanding how they work is vital to creating a secure Active Directory environment. Security principals include users, groups, and computers.

Understand group types and group scope.   The two major types of groups are security and distribution groups, and they have different purposes. Groups can be local, global, or universal. Domain local groups are used to assign permissions to local resources, such as files and printers. The scope of global groups is limited to a single domain. Universal groups can contain users from any domains within an Active Directory forest.

Understand the purpose and permissions of built-in groups.   The Active Directory environment includes several built-in local and global groups that are designed to simplify common systems administration tasks. For instance, members of the Administrators group are given full permissions to perform any functions within the Active Directory domain and on the local computer.

Understand how to use Group Policy to manage password and other security-related policies.
Through the use of Group Policy settings, you can configure password and account-related options. You can also specify to which users, groups, and OUs many of the settings apply.

Understand how to configure smart card authentication.   Smart card authentication requires a CA for issuing smart card certificates. To enroll a smart card certificate, you must first prepare a smart card enrollment station and then write certificate information to the smart cards using a smart card reader. Finally, to make smart cards useful, you should enable the Interactive Logon: Require Smart Card policy in the Group Policy Object Editor.

Understand how to use the Delegation of Control Wizard to allow distributed administration.
Delegation is the process by which a higher-level security administrator assigns permissions to other users. The Delegation of Control Wizard walks you through the steps of selecting for which object(s) you want to perform delegation, what permission you want to allow, and which users will have those permissions.

Learn how the Security Configuration And Analysis utility can simplify the implementation of security policies.   The Security Configuration And Analysis utility can be used to create, modify, and apply security settings in the Registry through the use of security template files. Security templates allow systems administrators to define security settings once and then store this information in a file that can be applied to other computers.

Understand the purpose and function of auditing.   Auditing helps determine the cause of security violations and helps troubleshoot permissions-related problems.

Review Questions

1. You are the systems administrator for a medium-sized Active Directory domain. Currently, the environment supports many different domain controllers, some of which are running Windows NT 4 and others that are running Windows 2000 and Server 2003. When running in this type of environment, which of the following types of groups cannot be used?

   A. Universal security groups

   B. Global groups

   C. Domain local groups

   D. Computer groups

2. Isabel is a systems administrator for an Active Directory environment that is running in native mode. Recently, several managers have reported suspicions about user activities and have asked her to increase security in the environment. Specifically, the requirements are as follows:

   - The accessing of certain sensitive files must be logged.

   - Modifications to certain sensitive files must be logged.

   - Systems administrators must be able to provide information about which users accessed sensitive files and when they were accessed.

   - All logon attempts for specific shared machines must be recorded.

   Which of the following steps should Isabel take to meet these requirements? (Choose all that apply.)

   A. Enable auditing with the Computer Management tool.

   B. Enable auditing with the Active Directory Users And Computers tool.

   C. Enable auditing with the Active Directory Domains And Trusts tool.

   D. Enable auditing with the Event Viewer tool.

   E. View the audit log using the Event Viewer tool.

   F. View auditing information using the Computer Management tool.

   G. Enable failure and success auditing settings for specific files stored on NTFS volumes.

   H. Enable failure and success auditing settings for logon events on specific computer accounts.

3. A systems administrator wants to allow another user the ability to change user account information for all users within a specific OU. Which of the following tools would allow them to do this most easily?

   A. Domain Security Policy

   B. Domain Controller Security Policy

   C. Computer Management

   D. Delegation of Control Wizard

4. Minh, an IT manager, has full permissions over several OUs within a small Active Directory domain. Recently, Minh has hired a junior systems administrator to take over some of the responsibilities of administering the objects within these OUs. She gives the new employee access to modify user accounts within two OUs. This process is known as what?

A. Inheritance

B. Transfer of control

C. Delegation

D. Transfer of ownership

5. A systems administrator wants to prevent users from starting or stopping a specific service on domain controllers. Which of the following tools can be used to prevent this from occurring?

A. Active Directory Users And Computers

B. Domain Controller Security Policy

C. Domain Security Policy

D. Local System Policy

6. As the network administrator of Wanton Accounting Services, you are just getting settled into a comfortable routine. The network was converted from Windows NT and is now deployed as a Windows Server 2003 network with two sites and one domain. Most of the problems that you have encountered have been from users who needed education on how to search the directory and other nuances of the new system. Recently, you were brought into a meeting with top management and you were told that a few employees who recently left the company joined a competitor. Management wanted to know if there were any attempts to obtain information about the company's accounts. They also wanted to know if anyone internal to the company was trying access the information improperly. When you informed them that you didn't know, the experience was not one that you would want to repeat. Because you are the network administrator, you do not have any control over the perimeter security of the network. What can you audit on the network to make sure that you can answer any future inquiries by management with confidence?

A. Logon/logoff—success

B. Logon/logoff—failure

C. File access and object access—success and failure

D. Write access for program files—success and failure

E. User rights—success and failure

7. You are almost finished helping with the migration of a Windows NT network to a Windows Server 2003 network. The current domain functional level is Windows 2000 Mixed mode. There are three locations, and the engineers are creating a single domain for now. There are many rumors that there will be a merger with one of your competitors, and the designers are considering adding a new domain to bring those users into the network. One of your jobs is to help come up with the administrative plans for the designers to manage the users. To outline your task, you are going to build a best-practices approach to giving permissions to resources on your mixed network. Which of the following approaches best suits your situation?

   A. Apply permissions to the domain local group and add the accounts to this group.

   B. Apply permissions to the domain local groups, add users to global groups, and add the global groups to the domain local groups.

   C. Apply permissions to global groups, add users to universal groups, and place these universal groups into global groups.

   D. Apply permissions to domain local groups, add the users to global groups, add the global groups into universal groups, and add the universal groups into the domain local groups.

8. Which of the following folders in the Active Directory Users And Computers tool is used when users from outside the forest are granted access to resources within a domain?

   A. Users

   B. Computers

   C. Domain Controllers

   D. Foreign Security Principals

9. Lance is a systems administrator for an Active Directory environment that contains four domains. Recently, several managers have reported suspicions about user activities and have asked him to increase security in the environment. Specifically, the requirements are as follows:

   - Audit changes to User objects that are contained within a specific OU.

   - Allow a special user account called Audit to view and modify all security-related information about objects in that OU.

   Which of the following steps should Lance take to meet these requirements? (Choose all that apply.)

   A. Convert all volumes on which Active Directory information resides to NTFS.

   B. Enable auditing with the Active Directory Users And Computers tool.

   C. Create a new Active Directory domain and create restrictive permissions for the suspected users within this domain.

   D. Reconfigure trust settings using the Active Directory Domains And Trusts tool.

   E. Specify auditing options for the OU using the Active Directory Users And Computers tool.

   F. Use the Delegation of Control Wizard to grant appropriate permissions to view and modify objects within the OU to the Audit user account.

10. You are installing a new software application on a Windows Server 2003 domain controller. After reading the manual and consulting with a security administrator, you find that you have the following requirements:

- The software must run under an account that has permissions to all files on the server on which it is installed.

- The software must be able to bypass file system security in order to work properly.

- The software must be able to read and write sensitive files stored on the local server.

- Users of the software must not be able to view sensitive data that is stored within the files on the server.

You decide to create a new User account for the software and then assign the account to a built-in local group. To which of the following groups should you assign the account?

A. Account Operators

B. Backup Operators

C. Guests

D. Domain Admins

11. Members of which of the following groups have permissions to perform actions in multiple domains?

A. Domain Admins

B. Domain Users

C. Administrators

D. Enterprise Admins

12. The Association of Pipe Builders has offices throughout the United States. It has a Windows Server 2003 network that is running in Windows 2000 Mixed domain functional level. The association has confidential information from several companies that needs to be kept that way. You created a shared folder named Confidential and published it in the directory to contain this confidential information. The manager of the department that manages this information has requested that you disable John's access to the share. When checking the properties of the share, you notice that a domain local group called Secret and another domain local group called Temporary have permissions to the Confidential share. You notice that John is the only member of the Temporary group, so instead of modifying John's account directly with a deny to the share, you simply delete the group. You immediately get a call from the manager that he has changed his mind and that John needs access to the resources. You re-create the Temporary group and add John back into the group. The next day you get a call from John telling you that he cannot access the resources. What is the best way for you to provide access for John to the resource?

A. Add John to the Secret group.

B. Grant John direct access to the share.

C. Grant access to the Confidential folder for the Temporary group.

D. Add the Temporary group into the Secret group.

13. Oscar, a systems administrator, has created a top-level OU called Engineering. Within the Engineering OU, he has created two OUs: Research and Development. Oscar wants to place security permissions on only the Engineering OU, so he blocks the inheritance of properties for the OUs. However, when he does so, he finds that the permissions settings for the child OUs are now unacceptable. Which of the following actions should he take to change the permissions for the child OUs?

   A. Open the ACL for each child OU and set permissions for each ACE.

   B. Rename the parent OU.

   C. Delete and re-create the child OUs.

   D. Delete and re-create the parent OU.

14. You are the systems administrator for a small Active Directory domain. Recently, you have hired an intern to assist you with managing user objects within the domain. You want to do the following:

   - Provide the intern with permissions to access Active Directory using the Active Directory Users And Computers tool.

   - Provide the intern with sufficient permissions to change the properties of user accounts and to create and delete user accounts.

   - Provide the intern with the ability to create groups and computers.

   - Prevent the intern from being able to make any other changes to the Active Directory environment.

   To which of the following groups should you add the user?

   A. Backup Operators

   B. Account Operators

   C. Enterprise Admins

   D. Domain Admins

   E. Guests

15. You want the security log to overwrite events that are more than nine days old. Looking at the following screen, what would you do next in order to accomplish this task?

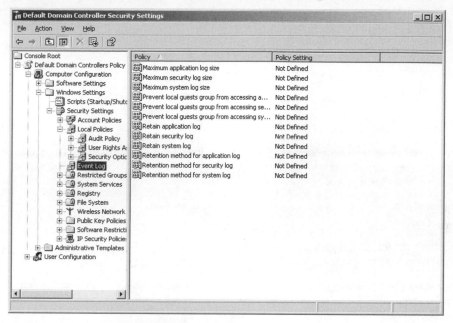

A. Double-click Maximum Security Log Size.

B. Double-click Retention Method For Security Log.

C. Double-click Retain Security Log.

D. Right-click Retention Method For Security Log.

16. As the network administrator for your company, you need to implement security on your Administrator account. Recently you have detected four attempts to access your server very late at night during business off hours. Which of the following is the best solution to this problem?

A. Delete the Administrator account.

B. Rename the Administrator account.

C. Activate the second Administrator account, the Guest account.

D. Active the second Administrator account, the Backup Operator account.

17. You are asked to implement security into your Active Directory deployment. You need to ensure that you have auditing set up properly. If you wanted to check and see if you had unauthorized access to your server, what would you consider checking?

A. Event Viewer logs ➤ application log

B. Event Viewer logs ➤ FRS log

C. Event Viewer logs ➤ system log

D. Event Viewer logs ➤ security log

18. You have just installed a Windows Server 2003 system into your current network. You are looking at the default accounts that are domain local. Which of the following accounts is not set up by default?

   A. Remote Administrators

   B. Administrators

   C. Backup Operators

   D. Print Operators

   E. Guests

   F. Users

19. After monitoring the Event Viewer logs on a Windows Server 2003 system, you see an entry in the log that claims that a database program recorded a file error. In what log would you most likely find this record?

   A. Event log

   B. Security log

   C. Application log

   D. System log

20. After monitoring the Event Viewer logs on your Windows Server 2003 systems, you find that a driver fails to load during startup. If the event is recorded, what log would you examine to find the entry?

   A. Event log

   B. Application log

   C. System log

   D. Security log

Answers to Review Questions

1. A. Because you are supporting Windows NT 4, Windows 2000, and Server 2003 domain controllers, you must run the environment in Windows 2000 Mixed domain functional level. Universal security groups are not available when you are running in Windows 2000 Mixed domain functional level.

2. B, E, G, H. The Active Directory Users And Computers tool allows systems administrators to change auditing options and to choose which actions are audited. At the file-system level, Isabel can specify exactly which actions are recorded in the audit log. She can then use Event Viewer to view the recorded information and provide it to the appropriate managers.

3. D. The Delegation of Control Wizard is designed to assist systems administrators in granting specific permissions to other users.

4. C. Delegation is the process of granting permissions to other users. Delegation is often used to distribute systems administration responsibilities. Inheritance is the transfer of permissions and other settings from parent OUs to child OUs. Transfer of control and transfer of ownership are not terms applicable to OUs.

5. B. The settings made in the Domain Controller Security Policy tool apply only to domain controllers.

6. C. Auditing for the success or failure of file access and object access tells you who is accessing any files that you want to watch. You can then create a report and notify management of who has accessed the files and who has tried and failed to access those files. However, because there may be collusion with someone inside the company, the success or failure of logon/logoff will not provide clear results in this situation. User rights refer to changing the authority of a user to system privileges and are not related to this problem. Auditing access for program files is usually associated with determining whether a virus is attempting to embed itself into your program files.

7. B. Because this is still a Windows 2000 Mixed domain functional-level network, universal groups are not available, so the best practice is to add users to global groups and apply permissions to the domain local groups where the resources reside. Even in a native-mode network, you do not want to place users into a universal group because the contents of universal groups are included in the Global Catalog and therefore will unnecessarily add to its size. When the migration is complete, the universal groups can be used to include global groups from multiple domains and then they can be placed in domain local groups that have permissions applied to them.

8. D. When resources are made available to users who reside in domains outside the forest, Foreign Security Principal objects are automatically created. These new objects are stored within the ForeignSecurityPrincipals folder.

9. Answers: B, E, F. The first step is to enable auditing. With auditing enabled, Lance can specify which actions are recorded. To give permissions to the Audit user account, he can use the Delegation of Control Wizard.

10. B. Members of the Backup Operators group are able to bypass file system security in order to back up and restore files. The requirements provided are similar to those for many popular backup software applications.

11. D. Members of the Enterprise Admins group are given full permissions to manage all domains within an Active Directory forest.

12. C. Once you delete a security principal such as a local domain group, it is lost forever, and any new one, even with the same name, needs to have the permissions reapplied to become effective. You could add John to the Secret group, but you don't know what other resources he would get access to by becoming a member of this group. Giving John direct access to the share would work, but it is not the best practice. You should always use groups to apply resources in order to maintain manageability of the network. Because the network is in Windows 2000 Mixed domain functional level, you cannot nest groups other than adding a global group into a domain local group.

13. A. When Oscar blocked inheritance, the child OUs did not retain the permissions of the parent OU. Therefore, he must use the ACL for each child and set specific permissions for each ACE in the list.

14. B. The user should be added to the Account Operators group. Although membership in the Enterprise Admins or Domain Admins group provides the user with the requisite permissions, these choices exceed the required functionality.

15. C. The Retain Security Log setting allows you to specify how long the security log should be retained before it gets overwritten.

16. B. When installing and using Windows Server 2003, always make sure you keep tabs on the use of the Administrator account. Often, this account can be manipulated and used for wrong-doing. You should rename the Administrator account if you have a problem with it or want to protect it because most hackers can easily find out half the credentials they need to get into the heart of your system. Malware also takes advantage of the Administrator account— if there is a blank password, for example. A dictionary file and a password-cracking tool can also be used to crack the Administrator account.

17. D. The Event Viewer is used to view logs. The security log records events such as valid and invalid logon attempts, as well as events related to resource use, such as the creating, opening, or deleting of files. For example, when logon auditing is enabled, an event is recorded in the security log each time a user attempts to log on to the computer. You must be logged on as Administrator or as a member of the Administrators group in order to turn on, use, and specify which events are recorded in the security log.

18. A. All domain local groups are correct except for Remote Administrators; this is not a default group created with the base OS install.

19. C. The Event Viewer is used to view logs. The application log contains events logged by programs. For example, a database program may record a file error in the application log. Events that are written to the application log are determined by the developers of the software program.

20. C. The Event Viewer is used to view logs. The system log contains events logged by Windows system components. For example, if a driver fails to load during startup, an event is recorded in the system log. Windows predetermines the events that are logged by system components.

Chapter
7

Active Directory Optimization and Reliability

MICROSOFT EXAM OBJECTIVES COVERED IN THIS CHAPTER:

✓ **Restore Active Directory directory services.**

- Perform an authoritative restore operation.
- Perform a nonauthoritative restore operation.

✓ **Troubleshoot Active Directory.**

- Diagnose and resolve issues related to the Active Directory database.

Keeping Active Directory running at its best is an important consideration for network environments of any size. The steps involved in optimizing performance include collecting and analyzing performance data and then applying this information to finding bottlenecks. The end result will be a better end user experience (reduced waiting for network resources) and improved performance of your resource investments.

Another important consideration when working with Active Directory is ensuring that your system information is safely backed up. Backups are useful when you lose data because of system failures, file corruptions, or accidental modifications of information.

When it comes to optimizing performance, a commonly used process is just plain trial and error. Although this can sometimes lead to better results, it depends on the validity of the performance measurements you have made. Does the server just *seem* to be operating faster? If that's your only guideline, it's probably time that you started collecting some hard statistics to back up that feeling.

Sometimes, performance optimization can feel like a luxury, especially if you can't get your domain controllers to the point where they are actually performing the services you intended for them, such as servicing printers or allowing users to share and work on files. The Windows Server 2003 operating system platform has been specifically designed to provide high availability services intended solely to keep your mission-critical applications and data accessible even in times of disaster. Occasionally, however, you might experience intermittent server crashes on one or more of the domain controllers or other computers in your environment. The most common cause of such problems is a hardware configuration issue. Poorly written device drivers and unsupported hardware can cause problems with system stability. Similarly, a failed hardware component (such as system memory) can cause problems. Sometimes memory chips come as part of a bad lot, or perhaps electrostatic discharge (ESD) has ruined them, or some other issue has occurred. No matter what, a problem with your memory chip only spells disaster for your server. Usually, third-party hardware vendors provide utility disks with their computers that can be used for performing hardware diagnostics on machines to help you find problems. These utilities are a good first step to resolving intermittent server crashes. When these utility disks are used in combination with the troubleshooting tips provided in this and other chapters of this book, you should be able to pinpoint most Active Directory–related problems that might occur on your network.

In this chapter, we'll cover tools and methods for measuring performance and troubleshooting failures in Windows Server 2003. Before you dive into the technical details, however, you should thoroughly understand what we're trying to accomplish and how we'll meet this goal.

> **Know How to Locate and Isolate Problems**
>
> It would be almost impossible to cover everything that could go wrong with your Windows Server 2003 system and/or Active Directory. This book covers many of the most likely and/or common issues you might come across, but anything is likely. Make sure you focus on the methodology used and how to locate and isolate a problem even if you are not 100-percent sure on what the problem may be. Use online resources to help you locate and troubleshoot the problem. And don't believe everything you read (something that is posted online can be wrong or misleading); test your changes in a lab environment and try to read multiple sources. Always use Microsoft Support (http://support.microsoft.com/) as one of your sources, because this site is most likely the right source of information because it's the product vendor. You won't be able to find and fix everything, but knowing where to find critical information that will aid you definitely won't hurt you either.

Overview of Windows Server 2003 Performance Monitoring

The first step in any performance optimization strategy is to be able to accurately and consistently measure performance. The insight that you'll gain from monitoring factors, such as network and system utilization, will be extremely useful when you go to measure the effects of any changes.

The overall process of performance monitoring usually involves the following steps:

1. Establish a baseline of current performance.
2. Identify the bottleneck(s).
3. Plan for and implement changes.
4. Measure the effects of the changes.
5. Repeat the process, based on business needs.

Note that the performance optimization process is never really finished because you can always try to gain more performance out of your system by modifying settings and applying other well-known tweaks. Before you get discouraged, realize that you'll reach some level of performance that you and your network and system users consider acceptable enough though it's not worth the additional effort it'll take to optimize performance further. Also note that as your network and system load increases (more users or users doing more), so will the need to reiterate this process. By continuing to monitor and measure, optimize, and make better, you will keep ahead of the pack and keep your end users happy.

Now that you have an idea of the overall process, let's focus on how changes should be made. Some important ideas to keep in mind when monitoring performance include the following:

Plan changes carefully. When you are working in an easy-to-use GUI-based operating system like the Windows Server 2003 platform, it's too easy to just remove a check mark here or there and then retest the performance. You should resist the urge to do this because some changes can cause large decreases in performance or can have an impact on functionality. Before you make haphazard changes (especially on production servers), take the time to learn about, plan for, and test your changes. Plan for outages and testing accordingly.

Utilize a test environment.   Test in a test lab that simulates a production environment. Do not make changes on production environments without first giving warning, or scheduling it for off-hours when fewer network and system users will be affected. Making haphazard changes in a production environment can cause serious problems. These problems will likely outweigh any benefits you could receive from making performance tweaks.

Make only one change at a time.   The golden rule of scientific experiments is that you should always keep track of as many variables as possible. When the topic is server optimization, this roughly translates into making only one change at a time.

One of the problems with making multiple system changes is that, although you may have improved performance overall, it's hard to determine exactly *which* change created the positive effects. It's also possible, for example, that changing one parameter increased performance greatly while changing another decreased it slightly. Although the overall result was an increase in performance, the second, performance-reducing option should be identified so the same mistake is not made again. To reduce the chance of obtaining misleading results, always try to make only one change at a time.

Remember, the main reason you want to make one change at a time is so that if you do make a mistake or quite possibly create another unexpected issue, you can still back out of the change. But if you make two or three changes at the same time and are not sure which one created the problem, you will have to undo all the changes and then make one alteration at a time to find the problem. If you make only one change at a time and follow that methodology every time, you won't find yourself in this situation.

> It's important to remember that some changes (especially when you're dealing with the Active Directory directory service and the schema) cannot be changed back, so plan accordingly.

Ensure consistency in measurements.   When you are monitoring performance, consistency is extremely important. You should strive toward having repeatable and accurate measurements. Controlling variables, such as system load at various times during the day, can help.

Assume, for instance, that you want to measure the number of transactions that you can simulate on the accounting database server within an hour. The results would be widely different if you ran the test during the month-end accounting close than if you ran the test on a Sunday morning. By running the same tests when the server is under a relatively static amount of load, you will be able to get more accurate measurements.

Maintain a performance history.   Earlier in this chapter, we mentioned that the performance optimization cycle is a continuous improvement process. Because many changes may be made over time, it is important to keep track of the changes that have been made and the results you experienced. Documenting this knowledge will help solve similar problems if they arise.

As you can see, you need to keep a lot of factors in mind when optimizing performance. Although this might seem like a lot to digest and remember, do not fear; as systems administrators you will learn some of the rules you need to know to keep your system running optimally. Fortunately, the tools included with Windows Server 2003 can help you organize the process and take measurements. Now that you have a good overview of the process, let's move on to look at the tools that can be used to set it in motion!

Using Windows Server 2003 Performance Tools

Because performance monitoring and optimization are vital functions in network environments of any size, Windows Server 2003 includes several performance-related tools. The first and most useful is the Windows Server 2003 *System Monitor*, which was designed to allow users and systems administrators to monitor performance statistics for various operating system parameters. Specifically, you can collect, store, and analyze information about CPU, memory, disk, and network resources using this tool, and this is only a handful of the things that can be monitored. By collecting and analyzing performance values, systems administrators can identify many potential problems. As you'll see later in this chapter, the System Monitor can also be used to monitor the performance of Active Directory and its various components.

The Windows Server 2003 System Monitor itself is an ActiveX control that can be placed within other applications. Examples of applications that can host the System Monitor control include web browsers and client programs like Microsoft Office's Word XP or Excel XP. This functionality can make it very easy for applications developers and systems administrators to incorporate the System Monitor into their own tools and applications.

For more common performance monitoring functions, you'll want to use the built-in Microsoft Management Console (MMC) version of the System Monitor called the Performance Console. You can easily access the System Monitor by opening the Performance icon in the Administrative Tools program group within your Start menu or the Control Panel. This launches the Performance MMC and loads and initializes the System Monitor with a handful of default counters.

You can choose from many different methods of monitoring performance when you are using the System Monitor. One method involves looking at a snapshot of current activity for a few of the most important counters; this allows you to find areas of potential bottlenecks and monitor the load on your servers at a certain point in time. You can also save the information to a log file for historical reporting and later analysis. This type of information is useful, for example, if you want to compare the load on your servers from three months ago to the current load. You'll get to take a closer look at this method and many others as you examine the System Monitor in more detail.

In the following sections, you'll learn about the basics of working with the Windows Server 2003 System Monitor and performance tools. Then, you'll apply these tools and techniques when you monitor the performance of Active Directory.

 Whenever you add services to Windows Server 2003 (such as installing Exchange Server 2003, for example), you also add to what it is that you can monitor. Your System Monitor grows as your system grows, so make sure that as you install services, you also take a look at what it is you can monitor.

Deciding What to Monitor

The first step in monitoring performance is to decide *what* you want to monitor. In Windows Server 2003, the operating system and related services include hundreds of performance statistics that you can track easily. All of these performance statistics fall into three main categories that you can choose to measure:

Performance objects   A performance object within the System Monitor is a collection of various performance statistics that you can monitor. Performance objects are based on various areas of system resources. For example, there are performance objects for the processor and memory, as well as for specific services such as web services. Later in this chapter, you'll see how you can use the Windows NT Directory Service (NTDS) performance object to monitor performance of Active Directory.

Counters   Counters are the actual parameters measured by the System Monitor. They are specific items that are grouped within performance objects. For example, within the Processor performance object, there is a counter for % Processor Time. This counter displays one type of detailed information about the Processor performance object (specifically, the amount of total CPU time all of the processes on the system are using).

Instances   Some counters will also have instances. An instance further identifies which performance parameter the counter is measuring. A simple example is a server with two CPUs. If you decide that you want to monitor processor usage (the Processor performance object) and, specifically, that you're interested in utilization (the %Total Utilization counter), you must still specify *which* CPU(s) you want to measure. In this example, you would have the choice of monitoring either of the two CPUs or a total value for both (using the Total instance).

You can specify which performance objects, counters, and instances you want to monitor by quickly and easily adding them to the System Monitor using the Add Counters dialog box. Figure 7.1 shows the various options that are available when you add new counters to monitor using the System Monitor.

FIGURE 7.1   Adding a new System Monitor counter

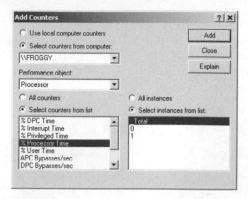

The exact items that you will be able to monitor will be based on your hardware and software configuration. For example, if you have not installed and configured the Internet Information Server (IIS) service, the options available within the Web Server performance object will not be available. Or, if you have multiple network adapters or CPUs in the server, you will have the option of viewing each instance separately or as part of the total value. The Windows Server 2003 version of System Monitor adds three counters by default when you start the utility: Memory: Pages/Sec; Physical Disk: Avg. Disk Queue Length; and Processor: % Processor Time. These counters provide a good starting point for monitoring overall system performance, but they are just that—the starting point to a long list of other things you can monitor closely with System Monitor.

You'll see the details of which counters are generally most useful later in this chapter.

Viewing Performance Information

The Windows Server 2003 System Monitor was designed to show information in a clear and easy-to-understand format. Based on the type of performance information you're viewing, however, you might want to change the display. You can use three main views to review statistics and information on performance:

Graph view   The Graph view is the default display that is presented when you first access the Windows Server 2003 System Monitor. The chart displays values using the vertical axis and time using the horizontal axis. It is useful for displaying values over a period of time and for visually seeing the changes in these values over that time period. Each point that is plotted on the graph is based on an average value calculated during the sample interval for the measurement being made. For example, you may notice overall CPU utilization starting at a low value at the beginning of the chart and then becoming much higher during later measurements. This indicates that the server has become busier (specifically, with CPU-intensive processes). Figure 7.2 provides an example of the Graph view.

FIGURE 7.2 Viewing information in the System Monitor Graph view

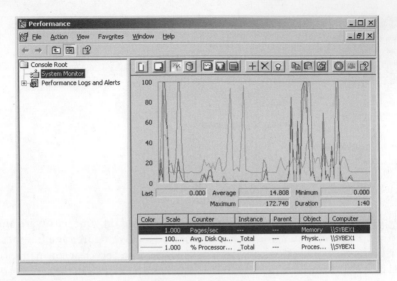

 A quick way to get to the Performance Console and view System Monitor is to go to Start ➤ Run and type **perfmon** in the Open box. After you press Enter, the Performance Console opens directly to System Monitor.

Histogram view The Histogram view shows performance statistics and information using a set of relative bar charts. This view is useful for viewing a snapshot of the latest value for a given counter. For example, if we were interested in viewing a snapshot of current system performance statistics during each refresh interval, the length of each of the bars in the display would give us a visual representation of each value. It would also allow us to visually compare each measurement relative to the others. You can also set the histogram to display an average measurement as well as minimum and maximum thresholds. Figure 7.3 shows a typical Histogram view.

Report view Like the Histogram view, the Report view shows performance statistics based on the latest measurement, or it displays an average measurement as well as minimum and maximum thresholds. This view is most useful for determining exact values because it provides information in numeric terms unlike the Chart and Histogram views, which provide information graphically. Figure 7.4 provides an example of the type of information you'll see in the Report view.

In the System Monitor, the same performance objects, counters, and instances may be displayed in each of the three views. This allows systems administrators to quickly and easily define the information they want to see once and then choose how it will be displayed based on specific needs. Most likely you will only use one view, but it's helpful to know what other views are available depending on what it is you are trying to assess.

FIGURE 7.3   Viewing information in the System Monitor Histogram view

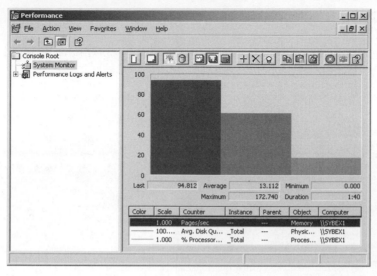

FIGURE 7.4   Viewing information in the System Monitor Report view

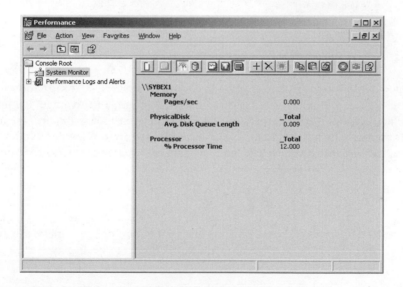

Managing System Monitor Properties

You can specify additional settings for viewing performance information within the properties of the System Monitor. You can access these options by clicking the Properties button in the taskbar or by right-clicking the System Monitor display and selecting Properties. These additional settings can be set using the following tabs:

General On the General tab (shown in Figure 7.5), you can specify several options that relate to the System Monitor view. First, you can choose from among the Graph, Histogram, and Report views. Next, you can enable or disable legends (which display information about the various counters), the value bar, and the toolbar.

FIGURE 7.5 General tab of the System Monitor Properties dialog box

For the Report and Histogram views, you can choose which type of information is displayed. Options include Default, Current, Minimum, Maximum, and Average. It's important to check these settings based on the type of information you're viewing because it will make a big difference in the type of data being collected. These options are not available for the Graph view, because the Graph view displays an average value over a period of time (the sample interval).

With the General tab, you can also choose the appearance (flat or 3D) and border options for the display. Another important setting is the update interval. By default, the display will be set to update every second. If you want the update frequency to decrease, you should increase the number of seconds between updates. The final option on the General tab allows you to specify whether or not you want to allow the same counter to be displayed twice in the same view.

Source On the Source tab (shown in Figure 7.6), you can specify the source for the performance information you would like to view. Options include current activity (the default setting) or data from a log file. If you choose to analyze information from a log file, you can also specify the time range for which you want to view statistics. We'll cover these selections in the next section.

FIGURE 7.6   Source tab of the System Monitor Properties dialog box

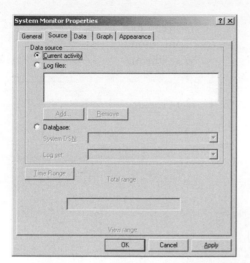

Data   The Data tab (shown in Figure 7.7) displays a list of the counters that have been added to the System Monitor display. These counters apply to the Chart, Histogram, and Report views. Using this interface, you can also add or remove any of the counters and change properties, such as the width, style, and color of the line, and the scale used for display.

Graph   On the Graph tab (shown in Figure 7.8), you can specify certain options that will allow you to customize the display of the System Monitor views. Specifically, you can add a title for the graph, specify a label for the vertical axis, choose to display grids, and specify the vertical scale range.

FIGURE 7.7   The Data tab of the System Monitor Properties dialog box

FIGURE 7.8   The Graph tab of the System Monitor Properties dialog box

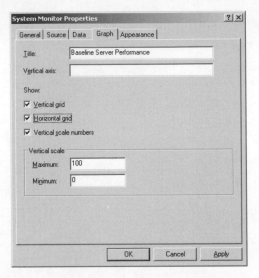

Appearance   Using the Appearance tab (see Figure 7.9), you can specify the colors for the areas of the display, such as the background and foreground. You can also specify the fonts that are used to display counter values in the System Monitor views. You can change settings to find a suitable balance between readability and the amount of information shown on one screen.

Now that you have an idea of the types of information System Monitor tracks and how this data is displayed, take a look at another feature—saving and analyzing performance data.

FIGURE 7.9   The Appearance tab of the System Monitor Properties dialog box

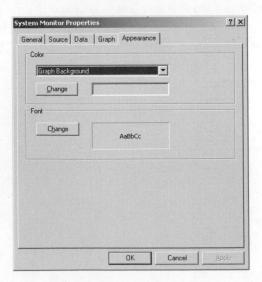

Saving and Analyzing Data with Performance Logs and Alerts

One of the most important aspects of monitoring performance is that it should be done over a given period of time. So far, we have discussed how you can use the System Monitor to view statistics in real time. We have, however, also alluded to using the System Monitor to save data for later analysis. Now let's take a look at how this is done.

When viewing information in the System Monitor, you have two main options with respect to the data on display:

View Current Activity   When you first open the Performance icon from the Administrative Tools folder, the default option is to view data obtained from current system information. This method of viewing measures and displays various real-time statistics on the system's performance.

View Log File Data   This option allows you to view information that was previously saved to a log file. Although the performance objects, counters, and instances may appear to be the same as those viewed using the View Current Activity option, the information itself was actually captured at a previous point in time and stored into a log file.

Log files for the View Log File Data option are created in the Performance Logs and Alerts section of the Windows Server 2003 Performance tool. Once there, you'll see three types of items available that allow you to customize how the data is collected in the log files. Let's take a look at each type of item in turn:

Counter logs   *Counter logs* record performance statistics based on the various performance objects, counters, and instances available in the System Monitor. The values are updated based on a time interval setting and are saved to a file for later analysis.

Trace logs   *Trace logs* record performance information to files based on system events. Some types of information are better monitored based on the occurrence of specific events instead of the passage of specified time intervals. There are several trace log types that can be included:

- ACPI Driver Trace Provider
- Active Directory: Core
- Active Directory: Netlogon
- Active Directory: SAM
- Active Directory: Kerberos
- DNS Trace
- Local Security Authority (LSA)
- NTLM Security Protocol
- Processor Trace Information
- Spooler Trace Control

Additionally, trace logs can be examined and analyzed through the use of third-party products. These third-party programs can include custom trace log providers for use with the Windows Server 2003 Performance Monitoring tools. Figure 7.10 shows the types of information that can be recorded using trace logs. To view the various trace logs, click the Provider Status button.

FIGURE 7.10   The available settings for trace logs

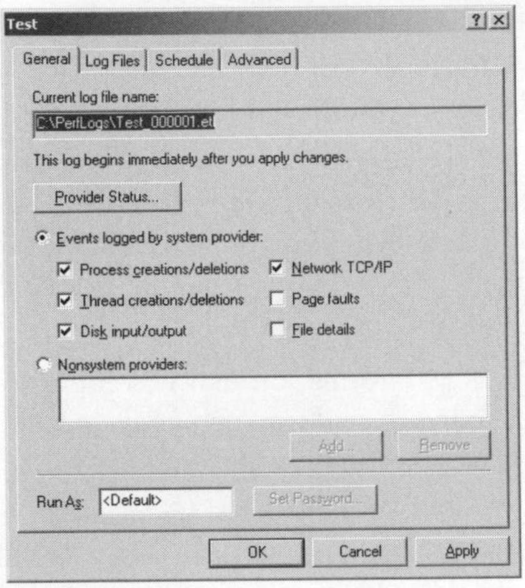

Alerts   *Alerts* monitor the standard performance objects, counters, and instances that are available with the Windows Server 2003 Performance Monitoring tools. However, they are designed to take specific actions when certain performance statistic thresholds are exceeded. For example, we could create an alert that gives a warning every time the CPU utilization on the local server exceeds 95 percent (as shown in Figure 7.11).

Systems administrators can configure various events to occur when an alert is to be fired off. Options include logging an entry in the application event log (which can be viewed using Event Viewer), sending a network message to a specific user or computer, starting a performance data log operation, or running a specific program (see Figure 7.12).

When you are saving performance information to files, you can use one of two main logging methods:

Circular logging   In circular logging, the data that is stored within a file is overwritten as new data is entered into the log. This is a useful method of logging if you only want to record information for a certain time frame (for example, the last four hours). Circular logging also conserves disk space by ensuring that the performance log file will not continue to grow over certain limits.

Linear logging   In linear logging, data is never deleted from the log files, and new information is added to the end of the log file. The result is a log file that continually grows, but the benefit is that historical information is retained.

FIGURE 7.11 Setting an alert on processor utilization

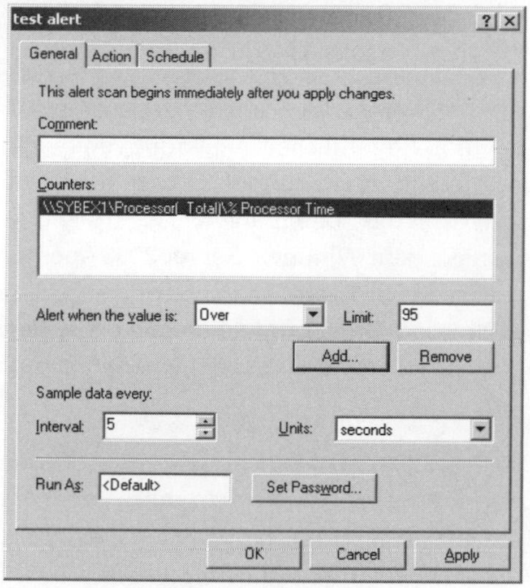

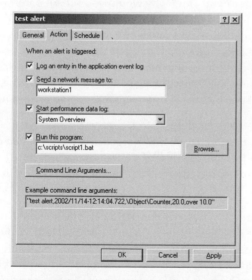

FIGURE 7.12 Setting alert actions

Now that we have an idea of the types of functions that are supported by the Windows Server 2003 Performance tool, let's move on to look at how this information can be applied to the task at hand—monitoring and troubleshooting Active Directory.

Real World Scenario

Real World Performance Monitoring

In our daily jobs as systems engineers and administrators, we come across systems that are in need of our help...and may even be asking for it. Beyond checking your Event Viewer, the System Monitor, and other tasks that are used to help troubleshoot, what is really the most common problem that occurs? Hard to say, but from the our experience, we'd say that many times you suffer performance problems if you have your Windows Server 2003 operating system installed on a sub-par system. Either the server hardware isn't enterprise class, or the minimum hardware requirements weren't addressed. Most production servers suffer from slow response times, lagging, and so on, because money wasn't spent where it should have been—on the server's hardware requirements.

Take a look at www.microsoft.com/windowsserver2003/evaluation/sysreqs/default.mspx to see the minimum Windows Server 2003 requirements. You have to make very sure that you follow these minimum requirements. That's not all though; as you will see by reading this chapter, most times the minimum requirements are just that—the bare minimum and not necessarily good enough, especially if you are running many services on your server or you have many network clients who will access the server.

Would you drive a truck over a glass bridge? No. Then why would you run an enterprise class server operating system hosting a mission-critical application such as Active Directory, email, and messaging on an antiquated desktop system? Most times this seems illogical when you read it, but in practice, it's common to find budgets squeezed to the point where your secondary domain controller is running on a high end-desktop. Just make sure that you consider this when you deploy a new system. Once you deploy it, open up the System Monitor and see if you are having issues by simply opening and running programs on the server itself.

It's also common to blame the network first, which is usually not the problem at all. Be careful of false positives and keep your mind focused on finding the root of the problem. If you come across other problems, document them, but continue to focus on finding (and fixing) the real issue.

If your enterprise-level servers aren't running with Redundant Array of Independent Disks (RAID) as an example, then you will most likely in need an upgrade on your system hardware. Most enterprise server class systems come with RAID as the minimum high availability you should have on any server of any size. RAID can help you in a pinch; when you lose a disk (and you will, based on the Mean Time Between Failure [MTBF]), you can quickly recover with minimal downtime and no loss of data.

Monitoring and Troubleshooting Active Directory Components

Active Directory utilizes many different types of server resources in order to function properly. For example, it uses memory to increase the speed of accessing data, CPU time to process information, and network resources to communicate with clients and Active Directory domain controllers. Additionally, it uses disk space for storing the Active Directory data store itself and the Global Catalog (GC).

The types and amount of system resources consumed by Active Directory are based on many factors. Some of the more obvious factors include the size of the Active Directory data store and how many users are supported in the environment. Other factors include the replication topology and the domain architecture. As you can see, all of the design issues you learned about in earlier chapters will play a role in the overall performance of domain controllers and Active Directory.

So how do all of these Active Directory requirements impact the server overall? Although the answer isn't always simple to determine, the System Monitor is usually the right tool for the job. In the following sections, we'll look at how you can use Windows Server 2003's Performance tool to monitor and optimize the performance of Active Directory.

Monitoring Domain Controller Performance

When it comes to performance, domain controllers have the same basic resource requirements as the other machines in your environment. The major areas to monitor for computers include the following:

- Processor (CPU) time
- Memory
- Disk I/O
- Disk space
- Network utilization

When you're deciding to monitor performance, you should carefully determine which statistics will be most useful. For example, if you're measuring the performance of a database server, CPU time and memory may be the most important. However, some applications may have high disk I/O and network requirements. Choosing what to monitor can be difficult because there are so many different options available. Many times it just takes experience and trial and error of using various performance objects to learn exactly how to monitor things. This chapter at least starts you on your journey if this is new to you, or it fills you in on how to monitor Active Directory if you are already a performance monitoring guru.

Table 7.1 provides an example of some common System Monitor counters and performance objects you might want to choose.

TABLE 7.1 Useful Counters for Monitoring Domain Controller Performance

Performance Object	Counter	Notes
Memory	Available MB	Displays the number of megabytes of physical memory (RAM) that is available for use by processes.
Memory	Pages/Sec	Indicates the number of pages of memory that must be read from or written to disk per second. A high number may indicate that more memory is needed.
Network Interface	Bytes Total/Sec	Measures the total number of bytes sent to or received by the specified network interface card.
Network Interface	Packets Received Errors	Specifies the number of received network packets that contained errors. A high number may indicate that there are problems with the network connection.
Network Segment	% Net Utilization	Specifies the percentage of total network resources being consumed. A high value may indicate network congestion.*
Paging File	% Usage	Indicates the amount of the Windows virtual memory file (paging file) that is in use. If this is a large number, the machine may benefit from a RAM upgrade.
Physical Disk	Disk Reads/Sec Disk Writes/Sec	Indicates the amount of disk activity on the server.
Physical Disk	Avg. Disk Queue Length	Indicates the number of disk read or write requests that are waiting in order to access the disk. If this value is high, disk I/O could potentially be a bottleneck.
Processor	% Processor Time	Indicates the overall CPU load on the server. High values generally indicate processor-intensive tasks. In machines with multiple processors, each processor can be monitored individually, or a total value can be viewed.
Server	Bytes Total/Sec	Specifies the number of bytes sent by the Server service on the local machine. A high value usually indicates that the server is responsible for fulfilling many outbound data requests (such as a file/print server).
Server	Server Sessions	Indicates the number of users who may be accessing the server.

TABLE 7.1 Useful Counters for Monitoring Domain Controller Performance *(continued)*

Performance Object	Counter	Notes
System	Processor Queue Length	Specifies the number of threads that are awaiting CPU time. A high number might indicate that a reduction in available CPU resources is creating a potential bottleneck.
System	Processes	Indicates the number of processes currently running on the system.
Web Service	Bytes Total/Sec	Indicates the number of bytes of data that has been transmitted to or from the local web service. This option is only available if IIS is installed and the web server is running.

*You must have the full version of Network Monitor installed on the local computer in order to view this counter.

Keep in mind that this list is not by any means a complete list of the items of interest—it's just a good guideline for some of the more common items that you may want to include. The key to determining what to monitor is to first understand the demands imposed by applications or services and then make appropriate choices. When monitored and interpreted properly, these performance values can be extremely useful in providing insight into overall system performance.

Monitoring Active Directory Performance with System Monitor

As you may have already guessed, the Windows Server 2003 operating system automatically tracks many performance statistics that are related to Active Directory. You can easily access these same statistics by using the System Monitor. The specific counters you'll want to monitor are part of the NTDS performance object and are based on several different functions of Active Directory, including those that follow:

- The Address Book (AB)
- The Directory Replication Agent (DRA)
- The Directory Service (DS)
- The Key Distribution Center (KDC)
- The Lightweight Directory Access Protocol (LDAP)
- The NT LAN Manager (NTLM) authentications
- The Security Accounts Manager (SAM)
- The Extended Directory Services (XDS)

Each of these performance objects can be useful when you are monitoring specific aspects of Active Directory. The specific counters you choose to monitor will depend on the aspects of Active Directory performance you're planning to examine. For example, if you want to measure performance statistics related to Active Directory replication (covered in Chapter 4, "Configuring Sites and Managing Replication"), you will probably want to monitor the DRA counters. Similarly, if you're interested in performance loads generated by Windows NT computers, you will want to monitor NTLM authentications and the SAM.

Perhaps the best way to learn about the various types of performance objects, counters, and instances that are related to Active Directory is by actually measuring these values and saving them for analysis. Exercise 7.1 walks you through the steps of working with various features of the Windows Server 2003 System Monitor. In this exercise, you will use various features of the Windows Server 2003 System Monitor to analyze performance information on a Windows Server 2003 domain controller.

EXERCISE 7.1

Monitoring Domain Controller and Active Directory Performance with Windows Server 2003 System Monitor

1. Open the Performance tool from the Administrative Tools program group.

2. In the left pane, right-click the System Monitor item and select Rename. Type **Domain Controller Performance**, and press Enter.

3. Click the Add Counter button (the button with the + sign), which will bring up the Add Counters dialog box.

4. In the Add Counters dialog box, select Use Local Computer Counters. Choose the Processor performance object from the Performance Object list, and then click Select Counters From List. Select the % Processor Time counter and the _Total instance. Note that you can click the Explain button to find more information about the various parameters that are available. Click the Add button to add the counter to the chart.

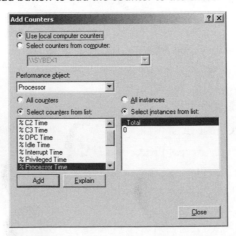

5. Add the following counters to the display by using the same process as in step 4.

Counter	Object	Instance
Total Query Received	DNS	N/A
Packets Sent in Bytes	FileReplicaConn	N/A
Page Faults/sec	Memory	N/A
DRA Inbound Properties Total/sec	NTDS	N/A
DRA Outbound Bytes Total/sec	NTDS	N/A
DS % Searches from LDAP	NTDS	N/A
DS Directory Reads/sec	NTDS	N/A
DS Directory Searches/sec	NTDS	N/A
LDAP Client Sessions	NTDS	N/A
NTLM Authentications	NTDS	N/A
% Usage	Paging File	_Total
% Disk Time	Physical Disk	_Total
Bytes Total/sec	Server	N/A
File Data Operations/sec	System	N/A
Bytes Total/sec	SMTP Server	_Total

6. When you are finished adding these counters, click the Close button to return to the main System Monitor window and view the counters that you selected.

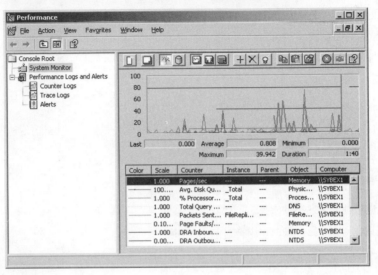

7. Click the View Histogram button to view information in the Histogram view. Click the various counters in the bottom pane of the display to view the actual statistical values for last, average, minimum, and maximum.

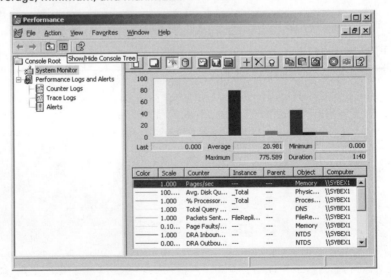

8. Click the View Report button to view information in the Report view. Note that you will be shown only the latest values for each of the counters that have been selected.

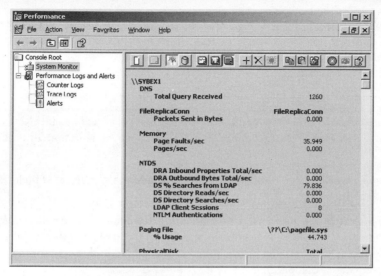

9. Click the View Chart button to return to the Graph view. Right-click the chart, and select Save As. Save the chart as a web page to a folder on the local computer and name it **Domain Controller Performance.htm**. You can open this file later if you want to record information for the same counters.

10. When finished, close the Windows Server 2003 System Monitor.

It is useful to have a set of performance monitor counters saved to files so that you can quickly and easily monitor the items of interest. For example, you may want to create a System Monitor file that includes statistics related to database services while another focuses on network utilization. In that way, whenever a performance problem occurs, you can quickly determine the cause of the problem (without having to create a System Monitor chart from scratch).

Monitoring Active Directory Performance Using Performance Logs and Alerts

In addition to using the System Monitor functionality of the Windows Server 2003 Performance tool, you can also monitor Active Directory performance statistics by using the *Performance Logs and Alerts* functionality included in the Performance Monitor.

Exercise 7.2 walks you through the steps for using these features to monitor Active Directory. Specifically, you create a counter log file, record performance statistics, and then later analyze this information using the System Monitor. In order to complete the steps in this exercise, you must have first completed the steps in Exercise 7.1.

EXERCISE 7.2

Using Performance Logs and Alerts to Monitor Active Directory Performance

1. Open the Performance tool from the Administrative Tools program group.

2. Under Performance Logs and Alerts, right-click Counter Logs and select New Log Settings From. Select the `Domain Controller Performance.htm` file that you created in Exercise 7.1.

3. You will see a warning that notifies you that some settings will be set at their defaults. Click OK to continue.

4. For the name of the new counter log, type **Domain Controller Log**, and click OK. When the counter Domain Controller Log dialog box appears, you will see that the default counters from the System Monitor settings are automatically added to this counter log. On the General tab, set the Sample Data interval to one second.

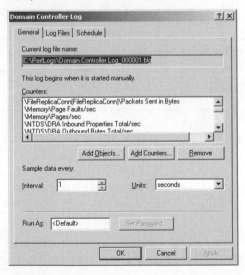

5. Click the Log Files tab. Verify that the log filename and location are appropriate. Also, note that you have an option to automatically generate log filenames. Leave the default setting at nnnnnn and the start number at 1. Change the log file type to Binary Circular File and click Configure to verify that the log file size is limited to 1MB.

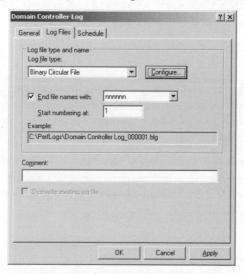

6. Click the Schedule tab and select Manually (Using The Shortcut Menu) for both the Start Log and Stop Log options. Leave all other settings at their defaults.

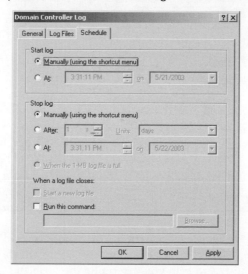

7. Click OK to create the counter log.

8. To start recording data for the counter log, right-click the Domain Controller Log item in the right windowpane and select Start. You will notice that the icon turns green. If your computer is not actively working (such as one in a test environment), you can simulate activity by running applications and searching Active Directory.

9. Wait at least two minutes for the data collection to occur, and then right-click the Domain Controller Log item and select Stop. The icon will turn red.

10. Click the System Monitor in the left pane, and click the View Log Data button. Select the Log Files radio button and click Add to add the file named `Domain_Controller_Log_000001.blg` from the directory in which you stored the counter data, and click OK. The Graph view will automatically be populated.

11. To filter the values displayed, right-click the chart and select Properties. On the Source tab, change the Time Range values to view only a specific amount of data. Note that you can only choose times that are within the sampling interval. Click OK to restrict the data.

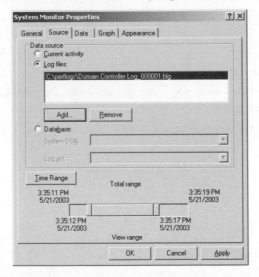

12. Examine the Chart, Histogram, and Report views. When finished, close the System Monitor.

By saving historical performance information, you can get a good idea of how your systems have performed over time. The next time your users complain about slow performance, you'll have some hard statistics to help you determine the problem!

Using Other Performance Monitoring Tools

The System Monitor allows you to monitor various different parameters of the Windows Server 2003 operating system and associated services and applications. However, there are three other tools that can be used for monitoring performance in Windows Server 2003. They are the *Network Monitor*, *Task Manager*, and *Event Viewer*. All three of these tools are useful for monitoring different areas of overall system performance and for examining details related to specific system events. In the following sections, we'll take a quick look at these tools and how they can best be used.

The Network Monitor

Although the System Monitor is a great tool for viewing overall network performance statistics, it isn't equipped for packet level analysis and doesn't give you much insight into what types of network traffic are traveling on the wire. That's where the Network Monitor tool comes in. There are two main components to the Network Monitor: the Network Monitor Agent and the Network Monitor tool itself.

The Network Monitor Agent is available for use with Windows 2000, XP, and Server 2003. You can install it by using the Add Or Remove Programs Control Panel applet. The agent allows for the tracking of network packets. When you install the Network Monitor Agent, you will also be able to access the Network Segment System Monitor counter.

On Windows Server 2003 computers, you'll see the Network Monitor icon appear in the Administrative Tools program group. You can use the Network Monitor tool to capture data as it travels on your network (see Figure 7.13).

FIGURE 7.13   Viewing network statistics using the Network Monitor

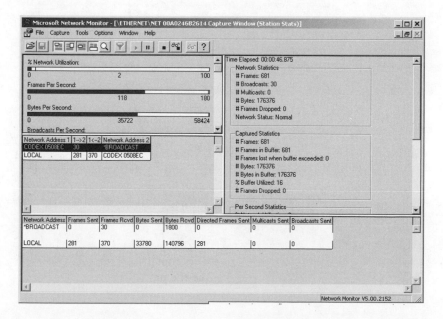

The version of Network Monitor that is available for free with Windows Server 2003 only allows the capture of information destined to or from the local computer. The full version of Network Monitor is available with Systems Management Server (SMS). This version places the network adapter in promiscuous mode and allows it to capture all data transferred on the network. For more information, see www.microsoft.com/management.

Once you have captured the data of interest, you can save it to a capture file or further analyze it using the Network Monitor. Figure 7.14 shows the level of detail that you can obtain by examining the captured packets. Experienced network and systems administrators can use this information to determine how applications are communicating and the types of data that are being passed via the network.

For the exam, you don't need to understand the detailed information that Network Monitor displays, but you should be aware of the type of information that you can view and when it would be appropriate to use Network Monitor.

FIGURE 7.14 Displaying the details of network packets using the Network Monitor

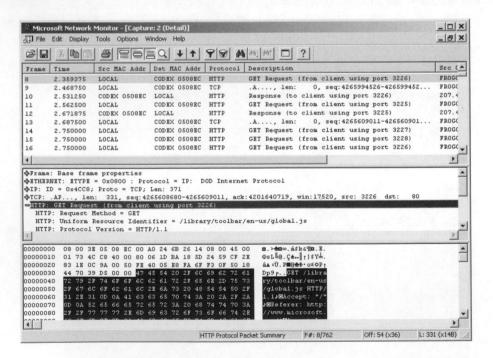

The Task Manager

The System Monitor is designed to allow you to monitor specific aspects of system performance over time. But what do you do if you want to get a quick snapshot of what the local system is doing? Clearly, creating a System Monitor chart, adding counters, and choosing a view is overkill. Fortunately, the Windows Server 2003 Task Manager has been designed to provide a quick overview of important system performance statistics without requiring any configuration. Better yet, it's always readily available.

The Task Manager can be easily accessed in several ways, including the following methods:

- Click Start ➢ Run and type **taskmgr**.
- Right-click the Windows taskbar, and then click Task Manager.
- Press Ctrl+Alt+Del, and then select Task Manager.
- Press Ctrl+Shift+Esc.

Each of these methods makes accessing a snapshot of the current system performance just a few short steps away.

Once you access the Task Manager, you will see the following five tabs:

Applications tab   The Applications tab (see Figure 7.15) shows you a list of the applications currently running on the local computer. This is a good place to check to determine which programs are running on the system. It is also useful for shutting down any applications that are marked as [Not Responding] (meaning that either the application has crashed or that it is performing operations and not responding to Windows Server 2003).

FIGURE 7.15   The Applications tab of the Task Manager

Processes tab   The Processes tab shows you all of the processes that are currently running on the local computer. By default, you'll be able to view how much CPU time and memory a particular process is using. By clicking any of the columns, you can quickly sort by the data values in that particular column. This is useful, for example, if you want to find out which processes are using the most memory on your server.

By accessing the performance objects in the View menu, you can add additional columns to the Processes tab. Figure 7.16 shows a list of the current processes running on a Windows Server 2003 computer.

FIGURE 7.16   Viewing process statistics and information using the Task Manager

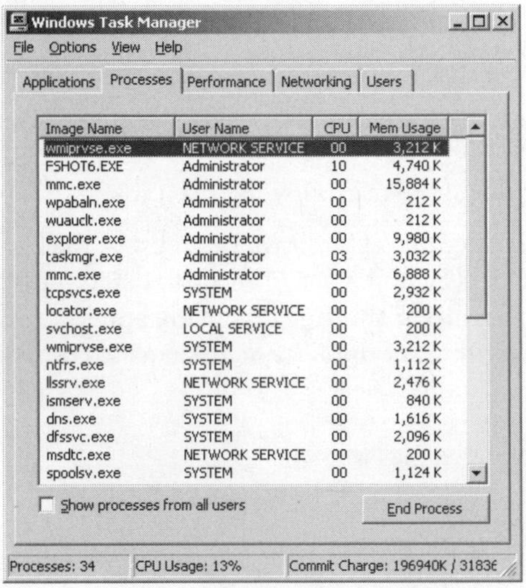

Performance tab   One of the problems with using the System Monitor to get a quick snapshot of system performance is that you have to add counters to a chart. Most systems administrators are too busy to take the time to do this when all they need is basic CPU and memory information. That's where the Performance tab of the Task Manager comes in. Using the Performance tab, you can view details about how memory is allocated on the computer and how much of the CPU is utilized (see Figure 7.17).

Networking tab   Similarly to the Performance tab, the Networking tab (see Figure 7.18) displays a graph of the current network utilization. The active connections are displayed at the bottom of the tab along with their connection speed, percentage of utilization, and status. The graph in the top part of the tab displays the percentage of utilization statistic in real time.

Users tab   The Users tab (see Figure 7.19) displays a list of the currently active user accounts. This is particularly useful for seeing who is online and quickly logging off or disconnecting any users. You can also send a console message to any remote user in the list by clicking the Send Message button (grayed out in Figure 7.19).

FIGURE 7.17 Viewing CPU and memory performance information using the Task Manager

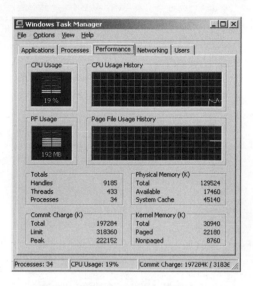

FIGURE 7.18 Viewing network information using the Task Manager

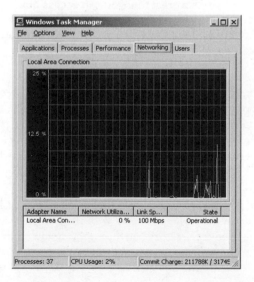

As you can see, the Task Manager is very useful for quickly providing important information about the system. Once you get used to using the Task Manager, you won't be able to get by without it!

FIGURE 7.19   Viewing user information using the Task Manager

 You can do a lot with the Task Manager, such as ending processes that have become intermittent, killing application that may hang the system, viewing NIC performance, and so on. Make sure you use Task Manager and familiarize yourself with all that it can do; it's a great tool you can access quickly to get an idea of what could be causing you problems. Event Viewer, Network Monitor, and System Monitor are all great tools for getting granular information on potential problems.

The Event Viewer

The Event Viewer is also useful for monitoring Active Directory information. Specifically, you can use the Directory Service log to view any information, warnings, or alerts related to the proper functioning of the directory services. You can access the Event Viewer by selecting Start ➤ Programs ➤ Administrative Tools ➤ Event Viewer. Clicking any of the items in the left pane displays the various events that have been logged for each item. The contents of Directory Services log are shown in Figure 7.20.

Notice in this example that each event is preceded by a blue "i" icon. That icon designates that these events are informational and do not indicate problems with the Directory Service. Rather, they record benign events such as Active Directory startup or a domain controller finding a Global Catalog server.

Problematic or potentially problematic events are indicated by a yellow Warning icon or a red Error icon, as shown in Figure 7.21. Warnings usually indicate a problem that wouldn't prevent a service from running but might cause undesired effects with the service in question. For example, I was configuring a site with some fictional domain controllers and IP addresses. As a result, my local domain controller's IP address wasn't associated with any of my sites, and the Event Viewer generated a Warning. In this case, the local domain controller could still function as a domain controller, but the site configuration could produce undesirable results.

Error events almost always indicate a failed service, application, or function. For instance, if the dynamic registration of a DNS client fails, the Event Viewer will generate an Error. As you can see, errors are more severe than warnings, because in this case, the DNS client cannot participate in DNS at all.

Double-clicking any event opens the event's Properties dialog box, as shown in Figure 7.22. The Event Properties dialog box displays a detailed description of the event.

FIGURE 7.20   The Directory Services log in Event Viewer

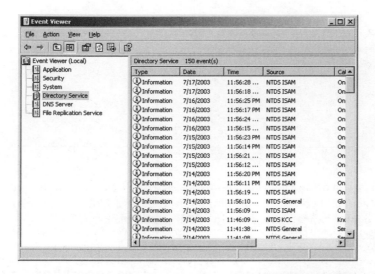

FIGURE 7.21   Information, Errors, and Warnings in Event Viewer

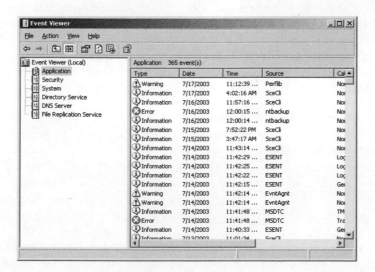

FIGURE 7.22 The Event Properties dialog box

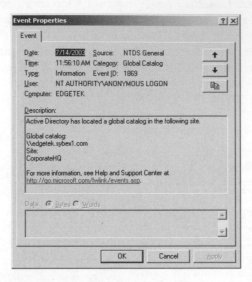

The Event Viewer can display literally thousands of different events, so it would be impossible to list them all here. The important point to be aware of is that information events are always benign, warnings indicate non-critical problems, and errors indicate show-stopping events.

Troubleshooting Active Directory Performance Monitoring

Monitoring performance is not always an easy process. As mentioned earlier, the act of performance monitoring can use up system resources. One of the problems that may then occur is that the System Monitor may not be able to obtain performance statistics and information quickly enough. If this occurs, you'll receive an error message similar to that shown in Figure 7.23. In this case, the suggestion is to increase the sample interval. This will reduce the number of statistics System Monitor has to record and display, and it may prevent the loss of any performance information.

FIGURE 7.23 A System Monitor error message

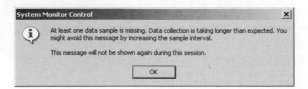

Sometimes, when you're viewing performance information in the Chart or Histogram view, the data is either too small (the bar or line is too close to the baseline) or too large (the bar or line is above the maximum value). In either case, you'll want to adjust the scale for the counter so that you can accurately see information in the display. For example, if the scale for the number of logons is 1 when it displays values from 0 to 100 and you frequently have more than 100 users per server, you might want to change the scale to a value less than 1. If you choose one-tenth, you will be able to accurately see up to 1000 user logons in the Chart and Histogram views. You can adjust the scale by right-clicking the System Monitor display, selecting Properties, and then accessing the Data tab.

Backup and Recovery of Active Directory

If you have deployed Active Directory in your network environment, your users now depend on it to function properly in order to do their jobs. From network authentications to file access to print and web services, Active Directory can be a mission-critical component of your business. Therefore, the importance of backing up the Active Directory data store should be evident. As we discussed in earlier chapters, it is important to have multiple domain controllers available to provide backup in case of a problem. The same goes for Active Directory itself—it too should be backed up by being saved. This way, if there is a massive disaster in which you need to restore your directory services, you will have that option available to you.

In addition to doing so because it is just good common sense, there are several reasons to back up data, including the following:

Protect against hardware failures.   Computer hardware devices have finite lifetimes, and all hardware eventually fails. We discussed this when we mentioned MTBF earlier. MTBF is the average time a device will function before it actually fails. There is also a rating derived from benchmark testing of hard disk devices that tells you when you may be at risk for an unavoidable disaster. Some types of failures, such as corrupted hard disk drives, can result in significant data loss.

Protect against accidental deletion or modification of data.   Although the threat of hardware failures is very real, in most environments, mistakes in modifying or deleting data are much more common. For example, suppose a systems administrator accidentally deletes all of the objects within a specific OU. Clearly, it's very important to be able to retrieve this information from a backup.

Keep historical information.   Users and systems administrators sometimes modify files but then later find that they require access to an older version of the file. Or a file is accidentally deleted, but a user does not discover that fact until much later. By keeping backups over time, you can recover information from these prior backups when necessary.

Protect against malicious deletion or modification of data.   Even in the most secure environments, it is conceivable that unauthorized users (or authorized ones with malicious intent!) could delete or modify information. In such cases, the loss of data might require valid backups from which to restore critical information.

Windows Server 2003 includes a Backup utility that is designed to back up operating system files and the Active Directory data store. It allows for basic backup functionality, such as scheduling backup jobs and selecting which files to back up. By default, the backup utility opens in Wizard mode and runs the Backup Or Restore Wizard automatically. If you want to run the Backup utility in the more traditional Advanced mode, you need to click the Advanced mode button on the opening screen of the wizard. Figure 7.24 shows the main screen for the Windows Server 2003 Backup utility in Advanced mode.

FIGURE 7.24   The main screen of the Windows Server 2003 Backup utility in Advanced mode

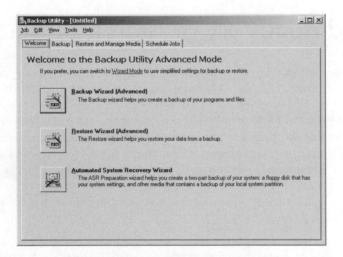

In the following sections, we'll look at the details of using the Windows Server 2003 Backup utility and how Active Directory can be restored when problems do occur.

Overview of the Windows Server 2003 Backup Utility

Although the general purpose behind performing backup operations—protecting information— is straightforward, there are many options that systems administrators must consider when determining the optimal backup and recovery scenario for their environment. Factors include what to back up, how often to back up, and when the backups should be performed.

In this section, you'll see how the Windows Server 2003 Backup utility makes it easy to implement a backup plan for many network environments.

Although the Windows Server 2003 Backup utility provides the basic functionality required to back up your files, you may want to investigate third-party products that provide additional functionality. These applications can provide options for specific types of backups (such as those for Exchange Server and SQL Server), as well as disaster recovery options, networking functionality, centralized management, and support for more advanced hardware.

Backup Types

One of the most important issues when dealing with backups is keeping track of which files have been backed up and which files need to be backed up. Whenever a backup of a file is made, the Archive bit for the file is set. You can view the attributes of system files by right-clicking them and selecting Properties. By clicking the Advanced button on the Properties dialog box, you will see the option File Is Ready For Archiving on the Advanced Attributes dialog box. Figure 7.25 shows an example of the attributes for a file.

FIGURE 7.25   Viewing the Archive attributes for a file

Although it is possible to back up all of the files in the file system during each backup operation, it's sometimes more convenient to back up only selected files (such as those that have changed since the last backup operation). There are several types of backups that can be performed:

Normal   *Normal backups* back up all of the selected files and then mark them as backed up. This option is usually used when a full system backup is made.

Copy   *Copy backups* back up all of the selected files, but do not mark them as backed up. This is useful when you want to make additional backups of files for moving files offsite or making multiple copies of the same data or for archival purposes.

Incremental   *Incremental backups* copy any selected files that are marked as ready for backup and then mark the files as backed up. When the next incremental backup is run, only the files that are not marked as having been backed up are stored. Incremental backups are used in conjunction with full (normal) backups. The general process is to make a full backup and then to make subsequent incremental backups. The benefit to this method is that only files that have changed since the last full or incremental backup will be stored. This can reduce backup times and disk or tape storage space requirements.

When recovering information from this type of backup method, a systems administrator will be required to first restore the full backup and then to restore each of the incremental backups.

Differential   *Differential backups* are similar in purpose to incremental backups with one important exception: Differential backups copy all files that are marked for backup but do not mark the files as backed up. When restoring files in a situation that uses normal and differential backups, you only need to restore the normal backup and the latest differential backup.

Figure 7.26 provides an example of the differences between the normal, incremental, and differential backup types.

FIGURE 7.26 Differences between the normal, incremental, and differential backup types

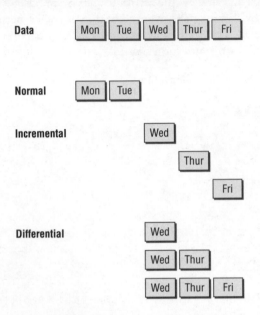

Daily   *Daily backups* back up all files that have changed during the current day. This operation uses the file time/date stamps to determine which files should be backed up and does not mark the files as having been backed up.

Note that systems administrators might choose to combine normal, daily, incremental, and differential backup types as part of the same backup plan. In general, however, it is sufficient to use only one or two of these methods (for example, normal backups with incremental backups). If you require a combination of multiple backup types, be sure that you fully understand which types of files are being backed up.

Backing Up System State Data

When planning to back up and restore Active Directory, the most important component is known as the *System State data*. System State data includes the components that the Windows Server 2003 operating system relies on for normal operations. The Windows Server 2003 Backup utility offers the ability to back up the System State data to another type of media (such as a hard disk, network share, or tape device). Specifically, it will back up the following components for a Windows Server 2003 domain controller (see Figure 7.27):

Active Directory   The Active Directory data store is at the heart of Active Directory. It contains all of the information necessary to create and manage network resources, such as users and computers. In most environments that use Active Directory, users and systems administrators rely on the proper functioning of these services in order to do their jobs.

Boot Files   Boot files are the files required for booting the Windows Server 2003 operating system and can be used in the case of boot file corruption.

COM+ Class Registration Database   The COM+ Class Registration database is a listing of all of the COM+ Class registrations stored on the computer. Applications that run on a Windows Server 2003 computer might require the registration of various share code components. As part of the System State backup process, Windows Server 2003 stores all of the information related to Component Object Model+ (COM+) components so that it can be quickly and easily restored.

Registry   The Windows Server 2003 Registry is a central repository of information related to the operating system configuration (such as desktop and network settings), user settings, and application settings. Therefore, the Registry is absolutely vital to the proper functioning of Windows Server 2003.

SYSVOL   The SYSVOL directory includes data and files that are shared between the domain controllers within an Active Directory domain. This information is relied upon by many operating system services for proper functioning.

Scheduling Backups

In addition to the ability to specify which files to back up, you can schedule backup jobs to occur at specific times. Planning *when* to perform backups is just as important as deciding what to back up. Performing backup operations can reduce overall system performance; therefore, you should plan to back up information during times of minimal activity on your servers. Figure 7.28 shows the Schedule functionality on the Schedule Jobs tab of the Window Server 2003 Backup utility.

FIGURE 7.27   Backing up the Windows Server 2003 System State data

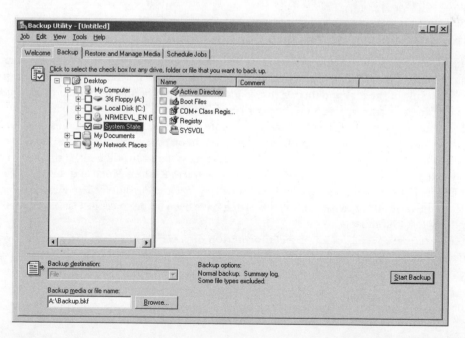

FIGURE 7.28 Scheduling jobs using the Windows Server 2003 Backup utility

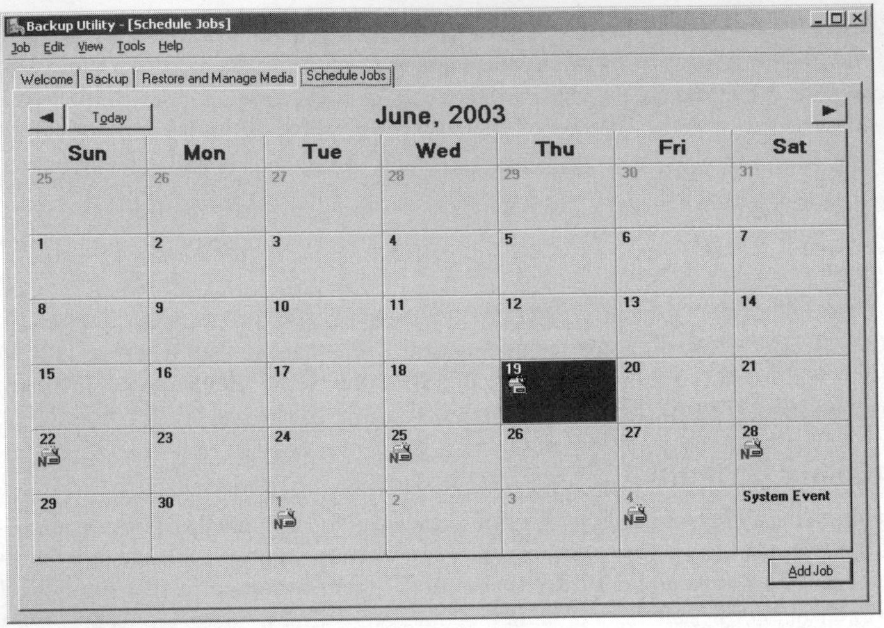

To add a backup operation to the schedule, you can simply click the Add Job button on the Schedule windows. This will start the Windows Server 2003 Backup Wizard (which we'll cover later in this chapter).

Restoring System State Data

In some cases, the Active Directory data store or other System State data may become corrupt or unavailable. This could be due to many different reasons. A hard disk failure might, for example, result in the loss of data. Or the accidental deletion of an OU and all of its objects might require a restore operation to be performed.

The actual steps involved in restoring System State data are based on the details of what has caused the data loss and what effect this data loss has had on the system. In the best case, the System State data is corrupt or inaccurate, but the operating system can still boot. If this is the case, all that you must do is boot into a special *Directory Services Restore Mode* and then restore the System State data from a backup. This process will replace the current System State data with that from the backup. Therefore, any changes that have been made since the last backup will be completely lost and must be redone.

In a worst-case scenario, all of the information on a server has been lost or a hardware failure is preventing the machine from properly booting. If this is the case, there are several steps that you must take in order to recover System State data. These steps include the following:

1. Fix any hardware problem that might prevent the computer from booting (for example, replace any failed hard disks).

2. Reinstall the Windows Server 2003 operating system. This should be performed like a regular installation on a new system.

3. Reinstall any device drivers that may be required by your backup device. If you backed up information to the file system, this will not apply.

4. Restore the System State data using the Windows Server 2003 Backup utility.

We'll cover the technical details of performing restores later in this section. For now, however, you should understand the importance of backing up information and, whenever possible, testing the validity of backups.

Backing Up Active Directory

The Windows Server 2003 Backup utility makes it easy to back up the System State data (including Active Directory) as part of a normal backup operation. We've already covered the ideas behind the different backup types and why and when they are used. Exercise 7.3 walks you through the process of backing up Active Directory. In order to complete this exercise, the local machine must be a domain controller, and you must have sufficient free space to back up the System State (usually at least 500MB).

EXERCISE 7.3

Backing Up Active Directory

1. Open the Backup utility by clicking Start ➢ All Programs ➢ Accessories ➢ System Tools ➢ Backup.

2. If the Backup tool is configured to start the Backup Or Restore Wizard at startup (the default), then the wizard appears automatically. Otherwise, click the Backup Wizard button in the Backup utility. Click Next to start the backup process.

3. If the Backup tool is configured to start automatically, choose Backup Files And Settings on the Backup Or Restore page and click Next to continue. If you clicked the Backup Wizard button in the Backup utility, then this page will not appear.

4. On the What To Backup page, select Let Me Choose What To Backup. Note that there are also options to back up all files on the computer and to back up only specific information. Click Next to continue.

5. On the Items To Back Up page, expand My Computer and place a check mark next to System State. Click Next.

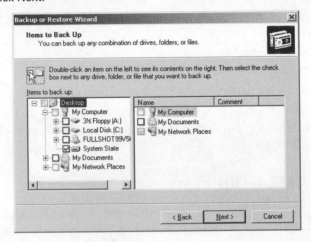

6. The Backup Type, Destination, And Name page will appear. You'll need to select where you want to back up this information. If you have a tape drive installed on the local computer, you'll have the option of backing up to tape. Otherwise, that option will be disabled. Select File for the backup media type, and then click Browse to find a suitable location for the backup file. The default file extension for a Windows Server 2003 Backup file is .bfk. You should ensure that the selected folder has sufficient space to store the System State data (which is usually more than 500MB). Click Next to continue.

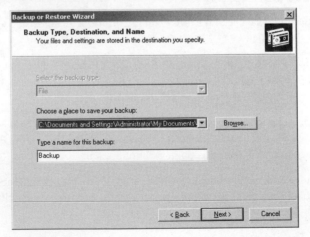

7. The Completing The Backup Or Restore Wizard page will now display a summary of the options you selected for backup. Verify that the files to be backed up and the location information are correct. Note that by clicking the Advanced button, you can select from among different backup types (such as copy, differential, and incremental) and can choose whether remote storage files will be backed up. Click Finish to begin the backup process.

8. The backup process will begin, and the approximate size of the backup will be calculated. On most systems, the backup operation will take at least several minutes. The exact amount of time required will be based on server load, server hardware configuration, and the size of the System State data. For example, backing up the System State on a busy domain controller for a large Active Directory domain will take much longer than a similar backup for a seldom-used domain controller in a small domain.

9. When the backup operation has completed, you will see information about the overall backup process. You can click the Report button to see information about the backup process (including any errors that might have occurred). Optionally, you can save this report as a text file to examine the information later.

10. When finished, click Close.

Restoring Active Directory

Active Directory has been designed with fault tolerance in mind. For example, it is highly recommended that each domain have at least two domain controllers. Each of these domain controllers contains a copy of the Active Directory data store. Should one of the domain controllers fail, the available one can take over the failed server's functionality. When the failed server is repaired, it can then be promoted to a domain controller in the existing environment. This process effectively restores the failed domain controller without incurring any downtime for end users because all of the Active Directory data is replicated to the repaired server in the next scheduled replication.

Real World Scenario

Managing Backups for Large, Active Servers

You are a systems administrator for a large organization. Your company has experienced dramatic growth in the last six months, and many new servers are being deployed. The existing servers in your environment have also been burdened with more users and data. For example, your most important servers are accessed from users around the world, and they're in use almost 24 hours a day. In order to accommodate the additional needs of users, you have been adding storage to current servers (most of which have plenty of room for expandability). Although this addresses the immediate concern—the need for more storage space—it raises other challenges. One of these is the important issue of performing backups.

Up until now, you have chosen to perform full backups of all of the data on your servers every night. However, the volume of data has grown greatly, and so, too, has the time required to perform the backups. It's clear that you cannot afford to perform full backups every night due to performance and storage considerations. Nevertheless, your business depends heavily on its IT resources, and any loss of data is unacceptable. You're tasked with coming up with a backup methodology. There's one catch, though: Due to budget limitations, you can't purchase larger, faster backup solutions (at least not in the short term). You've got to work with what you already have.

At first, this might seem like a problem: How can you back up a much larger amount of data in the same (or even less) time? There are two main constraints: First, the "backup window" is limited by the increased usage of the servers. The backup window includes the times during which your production servers can sustain the decrease in performance caused by backup operations. Second, your backup hardware can only store a limited amount of data per piece of media, and you're not always available to swap tapes in the middle of the night should the backup operation require more space.

Although this may seem like a difficult problem, you should be able to reduce backup times and storage requirements by using multiple backup types. An efficient design would take advantage of full, differential, and incremental backup types. You can use full backups as the basis of your strategy. Then, you can selectively choose to perform differential and/or incremental backups (instead of full backups) nightly. By examining your business requirements, you decide to implement the following weekly schedule:

- Full Backups (est. 8 hours): Sunday afternoons

- Differential backups: (est. 2 hours): Tuesday and Thursday nights

- Incremental backups: (est. 1/2–1 hour): Monday, Wednesday, Friday, and Saturday nights

By using these backup types, you can significantly reduce the amount of time backup operations will take. For example, during the week, you will only be backing up a relatively small subset of all of the data stored on your servers. Therefore, the backups will also use up less space on your backup media (read: fewer required media changes during the week!).

The use of multiple types of backup operations does come at a price, however. One potential issue is that, should you need to restore files, you may need to load data from multiple backup sets. This can be both time-consuming and risky (in the case of the loss or failure of a tape). Also, when you restore data, you must understand how to recover from failures at various times during the week. Overall, though, this solution gives you a good method for continuing to protect your organization's data. And it gives you an opportunity to use ingenuity to stay within budget!

In the real world, coming up with backup plans that meet real-world constraints can be a challenge. Fortunately, you're not alone in this type of problem, and there are many potential solutions. Before you think about investing in larger and faster storage solutions, consider using a combination of backup types to fit within your requirements (and budget). A little bit of planning can save costly upgrades and still provide the data protection your business requires.

For more information on promoting domain controllers, see Chapter 2, "Installing and Configuring Active Directory."

In some cases, you might need to restore Active Directory from backup media. For example, suppose a systems administrator accidentally deletes several hundred users from the domain and does not realize it until the change has been propagated to all of the other domain controllers. Manually re-creating the accounts is not an option because the objects' security identifiers will be different (and all permissions must be reset). Clearly, a method for restoring from backup is the best solution. You can elect to make the Active Directory restore authoritative or non-authoritative, as described in the following sections.

There are several features in Windows Server 2003 for solving boot-related problems and for reinstalling the operating system to fix corrupted files. These techniques are beyond the scope of this book (which focuses on restoring Active Directory). For more information on using the Recovery Console and the Installation Repair options, see *MCSA/MCSE: Windows Server 2003 Environment Management and Maintenance Study Guide* (70-290), by Lisa Donald with Suzan Sage London and James Chellis (Sybex, 2003).

Overview of Authoritative Restore

Restoring Active Directory and other System State data is an important process should system files or the Active Directory data store become corrupt or otherwise unavailable. Fortunately, the Windows Server 2003 Backup utility allows you to easily restore the System State data from a backup, should the need arise.

We mentioned earlier that in the case of the accidental deletion of information from Active Directory, you may need to restore the Active Directory data store from a recent backup. But what happens if there is more than one domain controller in the environment? Even if you did perform a restore, the information on this domain controller would be seen as outdated and it would be overwritten by the data from another domain controller (for more information on the replication process, see Chapter 4). And this data from the older domain controller is exactly the information you want to replace.

Fortunately, Windows Server 2003 and Active Directory allow you to perform what is called an *authoritative restore*. The authoritative restore process specifies a domain controller as having the authoritative (or master) copy of the Active Directory data store. When other domain controllers communicate with this domain controller, their information will be overwritten with Active Directory data stored on the local machine.

Now that we have an idea of how an authoritative restore is supposed to work, let's move on to looking at the details of performing the process.

Performing an Authoritative Restore

When restoring Active Directory information on a Windows Server 2003 domain controller, Active Directory services must not be running. This is because the restore of System State data requires full access to system files and the Active Directory data store. If you attempt to restore System State data while the domain controller is active, you will see the error message shown in Figure 7.29.

When recovering System State data using Windows Server 2003 Backup, you have the option of restoring data to an alternate location. However, this operation will only copy some components from the System State backup, and it will not restore Active Directory.

FIGURE 7.29   Attempting to restore System State while a domain controller is active

In general, restoring data and operating system files is a straightforward process. It is important to note that restoring a System State backup will replace the existing Registry, SYSVOL, and Active Directory files, so any changes you made since the last backup will be lost.

Exercise 7.4 walks you through the process of performing an authoritative restore on the System State and Active Directory information. This process uses the ntdsutil utility—which we first saw back in Chapter 2—to set the authoritative restore mode for a domain controller after the System State is restored but before the domain controller is rebooted. In order to complete this process, you must have first completed the steps in Exercise 7.3.

Any changes made to Active Directory since the backup performed in Exercise 7.3 will be lost after the completion of Exercise 7.4.

EXERCISE 7.4

Restoring the System State and Active Directory

1. Reboot the local machine. At the Operating System selection screen, select Windows Server 2003 and press the F8 key to enter the Windows Server 2003 boot options.

2. From the boot menu, choose Directory Services Restore Mode "Windows Server 2003 Domain Controllers Only" and press Enter. Verify that Windows Server 2003 is still selected and press Enter. The operating system will begin to boot in safe mode.

3. Log on to the computer as a member of the *local* Administrators group. Note that you cannot log on using any Active Directory accounts since network services and Active Directory have not been started.

4. You will see a message warning you that the machine is running in safe mode and that certain services will not be available. For example, a minimal set of drivers has been loaded, and you will not have access to the network. Click OK to continue.

5. When the operating system has finished booting, open the Backup utility by clicking Start ➢ All Programs ➢ Accessories ➢ System Tools ➢ Backup.

6. The Backup Or Restore Wizard should begin automatically if the Backup utility is still configured to do so. Click Next to begin the wizard.

7. On the Backup Or Restore page, select Restore Files And Settings and click Next to continue.

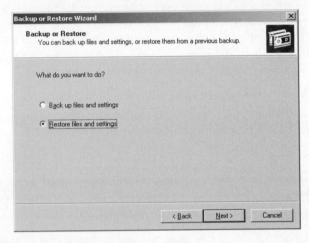

8. On the What To Restore page, expand the File item by clicking the plus (+) sign. Expand the Media item, and then click the check box next to the System State icon. Click Next to continue.

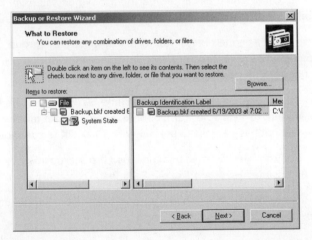

9. The Completing The Backup Or Restore Wizard page will display a summary of the recovery options that you selected. Click the Advanced button.

10. On the Where To Restore page, you can specify the location for the restored files. The options include the original location, an alternate location, or a single folder. For this exercise, verify that the Original Location option is selected, and then click Next.

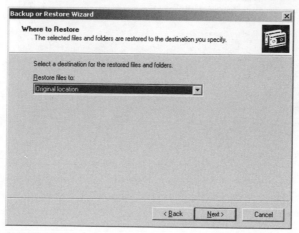

11. On the How To Restore page you will be prompted to specify how you want files to be restored. Select the Replace Existing Files option, and click Next.

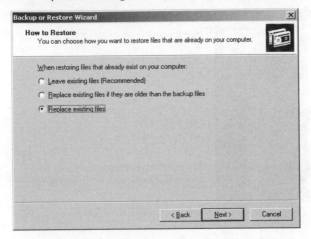

12. On the Advanced Restore Options page, use the default settings. Click Next.

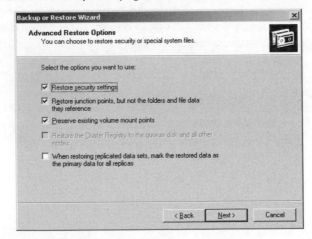

13. Click Finish on the Completing The Backup Or Restore Wizard page to begin the restore operation. The Windows Server 2003 Backup utility will begin to restore the System State files to the local computer.

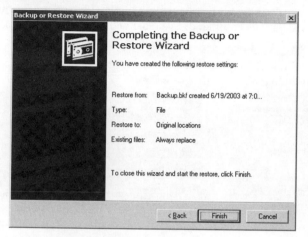

14. Once the System State data has been restored, you will see statistics related to the recovery operation on the Restore Progress dialog box. To view detailed information, click the Report button. When you are finished, click Close.

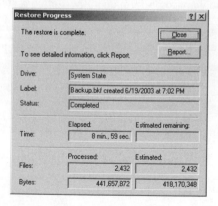

15. You will be prompted about whether or not you want to restart the computer. Select No.

16. Now, you will need to place the domain controller in authoritative restore mode. To do this, click Start ➤ Run and type **cmd**. At the command prompt, type **ntdsutil** and press Enter. Note that you can type the question mark symbol (**?**), and press Enter to view help information for the various commands available with the ntdsutil application.

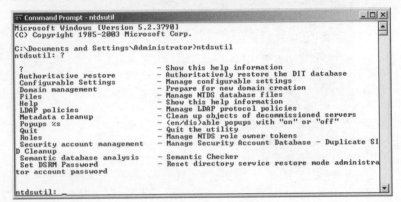

17. At the ntdsutil prompt, type **authoritative restore** and press Enter.

18. At the authoritative restore prompt, type **restore database** and press Enter. You will be asked whether or not you want to perform an authoritative restore. Click Yes.

19. The ntdsutil utility will begin the authoritative restore process. After the process has completed you will see a screen similar to the following graphic.

20. Type **quit** twice to exit ntdsutil. Then, close the command prompt by typing **exit**.

21. Finally, click Start ➤ Shut Down, and restart the computer. Following a reboot of the operating system, Active Directory and System State data will be current to the point of the last backup.

In addition to restoring the entire Active Directory database, you can also restore just specific subtrees within Active Directory using the `restore subtree` command in the ntdsutil utility. This allows you to restore specific information and is useful in the case of an accidental deletion of isolated material.

Following the authoritative restore process, Active Directory should be updated to the time of the last backup. Furthermore, all other domain controllers for this domain will have their Active Directory information overwritten by the results of the restore operation. The end result is an Active Directory environment that has been recovered from media.

Overview of Nonauthoritative Restore

Now that you understand why you would use an authoritative restore and how it is performed, it's an easy conceptual jump to understand what a nonauthoritative restore is. Remember that making a restore authoritative simply tells other domain controllers in the domain to recognize the restored machine as the newest copy of Active Directory for replication purposes. If you only have one domain controller, the authoritative restore process becomes moot; you can simply skip the steps required to make the restore authoritative and begin using the domain controller immediately after the normal restore is complete, as shown in steps 1 through 15 of Exercise 7.4.

If you have more than one domain controller in the domain and you need to perform a nonauthoritative restore, you can simply allow the domain controller to receive Active Directory database information from other domain controllers in the domain using normal replication methods.

Summary

Although tasks related to performance optimization and ensuring reliability of Active Directory domain controllers are only two among the seemingly endless tasks performed by systems administrators, they are very important factors in the overall health of a network environment. In this chapter, we covered many aspects of Active Directory optimization and reliability including using many tools that can help monitor and manage your systems and the basics of troubleshooting Active Directory in times of problem or disaster.

Monitoring performance on domain controllers is imperative to rooting out any issues that may affect your systems. If your systems are not running optimally, your end users may experience issues such as latency, or worse, you may experience corruption in your Active Directory database. Either way, it's important to know how to monitor the performance of domain controllers. In this chapter, we also looked at ways systems administrators can optimize the operations of domain controllers to ensure that end users receive adequate performance.

We also looked at how to use the various performance-related tools that are included with Windows Server 2003. Tools such as the Performance utility, Task Manager, Network Monitor, and Event Viewer can help you diagnose and troubleshoot system performance issues. The use of these tools is very common and they will definitely help you find typical problems related to memory, disk space, and any other hardware-related issues you may experience.

Knowing how to use tools to troubleshoot and test your systems is not only imperative to passing the exam, but also to performing your duties at work. In order to have a smoothly running network environment, it is vital that you understand the issues related to the reliability and performance of Active Directory and domain controllers.

Lastly, we covered the details of performing backups, the most commonly used form of reliability you can implement. We learned how to back up and restore System State data using the Windows Server 2003 Backup utility. Through the use of wizards and prompts, this backup tool can simplify an otherwise tedious process. Knowing how to restore System State data and the Active Directory database can really put you a cut above the rest, especially in times of disaster. By using the authoritative restore functionality, you can revert all or part of an Active Directory environment back to an earlier state. In our next chapter, we will continue our discussions on Group Policy and Active Directory.

Exam Essentials

Understand the methodology behind troubleshooting performance.   By following a set of steps that involves making measurements and finding bottlenecks, you can perform systematic troubleshooting of performance problems.

Be familiar with the features and capabilities of the Windows Server 2003 Performance tool for troubleshooting performance problems.   The Performance administrative tool is a very powerful method for collecting data about all areas of system performance. Through the use of performance objects, counters, and instances, you can choose to collect and record only the data of interest and use this information for pinpointing performance problems.

Know the importance of common performance counters.   There are several important performance-related counters that deal with general system performance. Know the importance of monitoring memory, CPU, and network usage on a busy server.

Understand the role of other troubleshooting tools.   The Windows Task Manager, Network Monitor, and Event Viewer can all be used to diagnose and troubleshoot configuration- and performance-related issues.

Understand how to troubleshoot common sources of server reliability problems.   Windows Server 2003 has been designed to be a stable, robust, and reliable operating system. Should you experience intermittent failures, you should know how to troubleshoot device drivers and buggy system-level software.

Understand the various backup types available with the Windows Server 2003 Backup utility.   The Windows Server 2003 Backup utility can perform full, differential, incremental, and daily backup operations. Each of these operations can be used as part of an efficient backup strategy.

Know how to back up Active Directory.   The data within the Active Directory database on a domain controller is part of the System State data. You can back up the System State to a file using the Windows Server 2003 Backup utility.

Know how to restore Active Directory.   Restoring the Active Directory database is considerably different from other restore operations. In order to restore some or all of the Active Directory database, you must first boot the machine into Directory Services Restore Mode.

Understand the importance of an authoritative restore process.   An authoritative restore is used when you want to restore earlier information from an Active Directory backup and you want the older information to be propagated to other domain controllers in the environment.

Review Questions

1. Susan is a systems administrator who is responsible for performing backups on several servers. Recently, she has been asked to take over operations of several new servers. Unfortunately, no information about the standard upkeep and maintenance of those servers is available. Susan wants to begin by making configuration changes to these servers, but she wants to first ensure that she has a full backup of all data on each of these servers.

   Susan decides to use the Windows Server 2003 Backup utility to perform the backups. She wants to choose a backup type that will back up all files on each of these servers, regardless of when they were last changed or if they have been previously backed up. Which of the following types of backup operations stores all of the selected files, without regard to the Archive bit setting? (Choose all that apply.)

   A. Normal

   B. Daily

   C. Copy

   D. Differential

   E. Incremental

2. A systems administrator wants to configure the operating system to generate an item in the Windows Server 2003 event log whenever the CPU utilization for the server exceeds 95 percent. Which of the following items within the Performance tool can they use to do this?

   A. System Monitor

   B. Trace logs

   C. Counter logs

   D. Alerts

3. A systems administrator boots the operating system using the Directory Services Repair Mode. He attempts to log in using a Domain Administrator account, but is unable to do so. What is the most likely reason for this?

   A. The account has been disabled by another domain administrator.

   B. The permissions on the domain controller do not allow users to log on locally.

   C. The Active Directory service is unavailable, and he must use the local Administrator password.

   D. Another domain controller for the domain is not available to authenticate the login.

4. Which of the following types of backup operations should be used to back up all of the files that have changed since the last full backup or incremental backup and marks these files as having been backed up?

   A. Differential

   B. Copy

   C. Incremental

   D. Normal

5. Following an authoritative restore of the entire Active Directory database, what will happen to the copy of Active Directory on other domain controllers for the same domain?

   A. The copies of Active Directory on other domain controllers will be overwritten.

   B. The information on all domain controllers will be merged.

   C. The other domain controllers will be automatically demoted.

   D. The copies of Active Directory on the restored domain controller will be overwritten.

6. Which of the following ntdsutil commands is used to perform an authoritative restore of the entire Active Directory database?

   A. `restore active directory`

   B. `restore database`

   C. `restore subtree`

   D. `restore all`

7. You are responsible for managing several Windows Server 2003 domain controller computers in your environment. Recently, a single hard disk on one of these machines failed, and the Active Directory database was lost. You want to perform the following:

   - Determine which partitions on the server are still accessible.

   - Restore as much of the system configuration (including the Active Directory database) as is possible.

   Which of the following could be used to help meet these requirements?

   A. Event Viewer

   B. System Monitor

   C. A hard disk from another server that is not configured as a domain controller

   D. A valid System State backup from the server

8. You have been hired as a consultant to research a network-related problem at a small organization. The environment supports many custom-developed applications that are not well documented. A manager suspects that one or more computers on the network is generating excessive traffic and is bogging down the network. You want to do the following:

   - Determine which computer(s) is/are causing the problems.

   - Record and examine network packets that are originating to/from specific machines.

   - View data related to only specific types of network packet.

   What tool should you use to accomplish all of the requirements?

   A. Task Manager

   B. System Monitor

   C. Event Viewer

   D. Network Monitor

9. Which of the following is not backed up as part of the Windows Server 2003 System State on a domain controller?

A. Registry

B. COM+ Registration information

C. Boot files

D. Active Directory database information

E. User profiles

10. Which of the following System Monitor performance objects can be used to measure performance statistics related to Active Directory? (Choose all that apply.)

A. Directory Services

B. LDAP

C. Network

D. Replication

E. NTDS

11. A systems administrator wants to measure performance related to Windows NT 4 logons. Which of the following counters of the NTDS performance object could provide this information?

A. Directory Replication Agent (DRA)

B. Directory Service (DS)

C. NTLM authentications

D. Lightweight Directory Access Protocols (LDAP)

12. Ron is a systems administrator who is responsible for performing backups on several servers. Recently, he has been asked to take over operations of several new servers, including backup operations. He has the following requirements:

- The backup must complete as quickly as possible.

- The backup must use the absolute minimum amount of storage space.

- He must perform backup operations at least daily with a full backup at least weekly.

Ron decides to use the Windows Server 2003 Backup utility to perform the backups. He wants to choose a set of backup types that will meet all of these requirements. He decides to back up all files on each of these servers every week. Then, he decides to store only the files that have changed since the last backup operation (regardless of type) during the weekdays. Which of the following types of backup operations should he use to implement this solution? (Choose two.)

A. Normal

B. Daily

C. Copy

D. Differential

E. Incremental

13. A systems administrator suspects that a domain controller is not operating properly. Another systems administrator has been monitoring the performance of the server and has found that this is not a likely cause of the problems. Where can the first systems administrator look for more information regarding details about any specific problems or errors that may be occurring?

   A. Task Manager

   B. Network Monitor

   C. System Monitor

   D. Event Viewer

14. Which of the following System Monitor views displays performance information over a period of time?

   A. Graph

   B. Histogram

   C. Report

   D. Current Activity

15. You are using the Backup Wizard to back up Active Directory. You want to ensure that the entire Active Directory is backed up while maintaining a minimum backup file size. In the following screen, where would you click in order to accomplish this task?

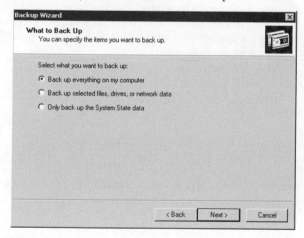

   A. Back Up Selected Files, Drives, Or Network Data

   B. Only Back Up The System State Data

   C. Back Up Everything On My Computer

   D. The Next button

16. In your current capacity as network administrator, you are looking to diagnose a problem with your current network infrastructure. You have 20 Windows Server 2003 servers and 1000 Windows XP Professional workstations spread out across 6 subnets. You need to test the connections between each server and determine how it connects to the network switches that are used to build the core of the network. Each server runs fine except for one. From the list below, what tools would you use to troubleshoot this server?

   A. Event Viewer, System Monitor, Network Monitor

   B. Task Manager, Network Monitor, Server Monitor

   C. Performance Monitor, System Monitor, Task Manager

   D. Event Viewer, Network Sniffer, NTBACKUP

17. You are the systems engineer responsible for 123 Ltd.'s new division. You need to deploy 5 new Windows Server 2003 systems. What do you need to create in order to make sure that you understand the normal load put on the systems under normal operations?

   A. Set up Task Manager.

   B. Initially baseline your systems.

   C. Deploy the Alerts in the Performance Console.

   D. Use Network Monitor to see current and future load.

18. As the IT Manager for your company's technology division, you are asked to deploy a method of finding problems on your connection to the network. You have three Windows Server 2003 systems and each is set up as a domain controller. What tools are incorporated with each server that will help you find problems on the network, more specifically on the network medium?

   A. Task Monitor

   B. Performance Monitor

   C. Network Monitor

   D. Event Monitor

19. You are the systems administrator for your company and responsible for the Active Directory infrastructure. After a disaster, you are asked to restore the Active Directory System State data information on a Windows Server 2003 domain controller. You try to run the restore and you get an error message. You are unable to perform the restore. From the list of possible choices, what may be causing this problem to occur?

   A. Active Directory services are running

   B. DNS services are still running

   C. The Backup service is not running

   D. The TCP/IP service is not running

20. You have been asked to deploy counters to monitor your CPU on a server that is performing poorly. What is the process of adding the % Processor Time counter and the _Total instance counters on a Windows Server 2003 system?

A. In the Add Counters dialog box, select Use Local Computer Counters. Choose the CPU performance object from the Performance Object list, and then click Select Counters From List. Select the % Processor Time counter and the _Total instance.

B. In the Add Counters dialog box, select Use Local Computer Counters. Choose the PROC performance object from the Performance Object list, and then click Select Counters From List. Select the % Processor Time counter and the _Total instance.

C. In the Add Counters dialog box, select Use Local Computer Counters. Choose the DISK performance object from the Performance Object list, and then click Select Counters From List. Select the % Processor Time counter and the _Total instance.

D. In the Add Counters dialog box, select Use Local Computer Counters. Choose the Processor performance object from the Performance Object list, and then click Select Counters From List. Select the % Processor Time counter and the _Total instance.

Answers to Review Questions

1. **A, B.** Normal and copy backup operations do not use the Archive bit to determine which files to back up, and they will include all files that are selected for backup on the server. The other backup types will store only a subset of files based on their dates or whether or not they have been previously backed up. For this reason, Susan should choose one of these operations to ensure that she performs a valid backup of all files on the servers before she makes any configuration changes.

2. **D.** Alerts fire in response to certain performance-related parameters, as defined by systems administrators. You can configure an alert to perform several different types of actions, including writing to the Windows Server 2003 event log.

3. **C.** When booting in Directory Services Repair Mode, Active Directory is not started, and network services are disabled. Therefore, the systems administrator must use a local account in order to log in.

4. **C.** Incremental backup operations copy files and mark them as having been backed up. Therefore, they are used when a systems administrator wants to back up only the files that have changed since the last full or incremental backup. Differential backups, although they will back up the same files, will not mark the files as having been backed up.

5. **A.** In an authoritative restore of the entire Active Directory database, the restored copy will override information stored on other domain controllers.

6. **B.** The `restore database` command instructs the ntdsutil application to perform an authoritative restore of the entire Active Directory database.

7. **D.** You can recover System State data from a backup, which always includes the Active Directory database. In this case, the Event Viewer and System Monitor wouldn't help you recover the database, but they might help you determine why the hard drive crashed in the first place.

8. **D.** Through the use of the Network Monitor application, you can view all of the network packets that are being sent to or from the local server. Based on this information, you can determine the source of certain types of traffic, such as pings. The other types of monitoring can provide useful information, but they do not allow you to drill down into the specific details of a network packet, nor do they allow you to filter the data that has been collected based on details about the packet.

9. **E.** The System State backup includes information that can be used to rebuild a server's basic configuration. All of the information listed, except for user profile data, is backed up as part of a System State backup operation.

10. **A, B, C, D, E.** The various counters that are part of the NTDS performance object provide information about the performance of various aspects of Active Directory. By collecting information for each of these performance objects, you can determine what areas of system performance might be having problems.

11. C. Windows NT 4 clients use the NTLM authentication method. By measuring this counter, you can determine how many authentication requests are being generated from pre–Windows 2000 computers.

12. Answers: A, E. In order to meet the requirements, Ron should use the normal backup type to create a full backup every week and the incremental backup type to back up only the data that has been modified since the last full or incremental backup operation.

13. D. The Event Viewer is the best tool for viewing information, warnings, and alerts related to Windows Server 2003 functions.

14. A. Using the Graph view, you can view performance information over a period of time (as defined by the sample interval). The Histogram and Report views are designed to show the latest performance statistics and average values.

15. B. Backing up the System State data will back up the entire Active Directory. Backing up everything on the computer will require a very large backup file.

16. A. Event Viewer is used to show you informational- and warning-based events tracked by the system. The logs are useful for finding problems in your system. System Monitor is used to monitor performance objects, set counters, and establish a baseline of your system. Network Monitor is used to look at the traffic (to the packet level) on your network. All tools are used to help find problems in your system.

17. B. Baseline your systems, get an idea of how they perform normally, and then you will know when they aren't performing as expected because the charts will be off. Make sure you document this procedure and consider setting up a linear rather than circular log.

18. C. Network Monitor is used to find network problems at the packet level. Make sure you are familiar with this tool for both the exam and in production environments where you can use it.

19. A. When restoring Active Directory System State data information on a Windows Server 2003 domain controller, Active Directory services must not be running. This is because the restore of System State data requires full access to system files and the Active Directory data store. If you attempt to restore System State data while the domain controller is active, you will see an error message. All other listed services will not interfere with the restore.

20. D. In the Add Counters dialog box, you first need to select Use Local Computer Counters. Then you need to choose the Processor performance object from the Performance Object list, and then click Select Counters From List. Finally, select the % Processor Time counter and the _Total instance.

Chapter 8

Planning, Implementing, and Managing Group Policy

MICROSOFT EXAM OBJECTIVES COVERED IN THIS CHAPTER:

✓ **Plan Group Policy strategy.**

- Plan a Group Policy strategy by using Resultant Set of Policy (RSoP) Planning mode.
- Plan a strategy for configuring the user environment by using Group Policy.
- Plan a strategy for configuring the computer environment by using Group Policy.

✓ **Configure the user environment by using Group Policy.**

- Automatically enroll user certificates by using Group Policy.
- Redirect folders by using Group Policy.

✓ **Deploy a computer environment by using Group Policy.**

- Automatically enroll computer certificates by using Group Policy.
- Configure computer security settings by using Group Policy.

✓ **Troubleshoot the application of Group Policy security settings. Tools might include RSoP and the gpresult command.**

One of the biggest challenges faced by systems administrators is the management of users, groups, and client computers. It's difficult enough to deploy and manage workstations throughout the environment. When you add in the fact that users are generally able to make system configuration changes, it can quickly become a management nightmare!

For example, imagine that a user notices that they do not have enough disk space to copy a large file. Instead of seeking help from the IT help desk, they may decide to do a little cleanup of their own. Unfortunately, this cleanup operation may involve deleting critical system files! Or, consider the case of users changing system settings "just to see what they do." Relatively minor changes, such as modifying TCP/IP bindings or Desktop settings, could cause hours of support headaches. Now, multiply these (or other common) problems by hundreds (or even thousands) of end users. Clearly, systems administrators need to have a way to limit the options available to users of client operating systems.

So how do you prevent problems like these from occurring in a Windows Server 2003 environment? Fortunately, there's a solution that's readily available and easy to implement that comes with the base operating system. One of the most important system administration features in Windows Server 2003 and Active Directory is the use of Group Policy. By using Group Policy objects (GPOs), administrators can quickly and easily define restrictions on common actions and then apply them at the site, domain, or organizational unit (OU) level. In this chapter, you will see how group policies work and then look at how they can be implemented within an Active Directory environment.

An Introduction to Group Policy

One of the strengths of Windows-based operating systems is their flexibility. End users and systems administrators can configure many different options to suit the network environment and their personal tastes. However, this flexibility comes at a price—generally, many of these options should not be changed by end users. For example, TCP/IP configuration and security policies should remain consistent for all client computers. In addition, an end user really doesn't need to be able to change these types of settings in the first place.

In previous versions of Windows, system administrators could use system policies (`config.pol` or `ntconfig.pol` files) to restrict some functionality at the Desktop level. They could make settings for users or computers; however, these settings focused primarily on preventing the user from performing such actions as changing their Desktop settings. The system administrators managed these changes by modifying Registry keys. This method made it fairly difficult for them to create and distribute policy settings. Furthermore, the types of configuration options available in the default templates were not always sufficient, and systems administrators often had to dive through cryptic and poorly documented Registry settings to make the changes they required.

Windows Server 2003's *group policies* are designed to allow systems administrators the ability to customize end user settings and to place restrictions on the types of actions that users can perform. Group policies can be easily created by systems administrators and then later applied to one or more users or computers within the environment. Although they ultimately do affect Registry settings, it is much easier to configure and apply settings through the use of Group Policy than it is to manually make changes to the Registry. For ease of management, Group Policy settings can be managed from within the Active Directory environment, utilizing the structure of users, groups, and OUs.

There are several different potential uses for group policies. We covered one of them, managing security settings, in Chapter 6, "Planning Security for Active Directory," and we'll cover the use of group policies for software deployment in Chapter 9, "Software Deployment through Group Policy." The focus of this chapter is on the technical background of group policies and how they apply to general configuration management.

Let's begin by looking at how group policies function.

Group Policy Settings

Group Policy settings are based on Group Policy *administrative templates*. These templates provide a list of user-friendly configuration options and specify the system settings to which they apply. For example, an option for a user or computer that reads "Require a Specific Desktop Wallpaper Setting" would map to a key in the Registry that maintains this value. When the option is set, the appropriate change is made in the Registry of the affected user(s) and computer(s).

By default, Windows Server 2003 comes with several administrative template files that you can use to manage common settings. Additionally, systems administrators and application developers can create their own administrative template files to set options for specific functionality.

Most Group Policy items have three different settings options:

Enabled   Specifies that a setting for this Group Policy object has been configured. Some settings require values or options to be set.

Disabled   Specifies that this option is disabled for client computers. Note that disabling an option *is* a setting. That is, it specifies that the systems administrator wants to disallow certain functionality.

Not Configured   Specifies that these settings have been neither enabled nor disabled. Not Configured is the default option for most settings. It simply states that this Group Policy will not specify an option and that settings from other policy settings may take precedence.

The specific options available (and their effects) will depend on the setting. Often, you will need additional information. For example, when setting the Account Lockout policy, you must specify how many bad login attempts may be made before the account is locked out. With this in mind, let's look at the types of user and computer settings that can be managed.

Group Policy settings can apply to two types of Active Directory objects: Users and Computers. Because both Users and Computers can be placed into groups and organized within OUs, this type of configuration simplifies the management of hundreds, or even thousands, of computers.

The main types of setting options you can configure within User and Computer Group Policies are as follows:

Software Settings   Software Settings options apply to specific applications and software that might be installed on the computer. Systems administrators can use these settings to make new applications available to end users and to control the default configuration for these applications.

For more information on configuring software settings using Group Policy and the (Group Policy Management Console) GPMC, see Chapter 9.

Windows Settings   Windows Settings options allow systems administrators to customize the behavior of the Windows operating system. The specific options that are available here differ for differ from those of users and computers. For example, the user-specific settings let you configure Internet Explorer (including the default home page and other settings), whereas the computer settings include security options, such as account policy and event log options.

Administrative Templates   Administrative Templates options are used to further configure user and computer settings. In addition to the default options available, systems administrators can create their own administrative templates with custom options.

Figure 8.1 provides an example of the types of options that can be configured with Group Policy.

FIGURE 8.1   Group Policy configuration options

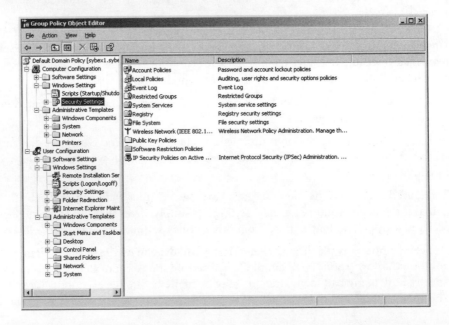

Later in this chapter, we'll look into the various options available in more detail.

Group Policy settings do not take effect immediately. You must run the gpupdate command at the command prompt or wait for the regular update cycle (30 minutes by default) in order for the policy changes to take effect.

Group Policy Objects

So far, we have been talking about what group policies are designed to do. Now, it's time to drill down into determining exactly how they can be set up and configured.

For ease of management, group policies may be contained in items called *Group Policy objects (GPOs)*. GPOs act as containers for the settings made within Group Policy files; this simplifies the management of settings. For example, as a systems administrator, you might have different policies for users and computers in different departments. Based on these requirements, you could create a GPO for members of the Sales department and another for members of the Engineering department. Then you could apply the GPOs to the OU for each department.

Another important concept is that Group Policy settings are hierarchical—that is, Group Policy settings can be applied at three different levels:

Sites   At the highest level, GPOs can be configured to apply to entire sites within an Active Directory environment. These settings apply to all of the domains and servers that are part of a site. Group Policy settings that are managed at the site level may apply to more than one domain. Therefore, they are useful when you want to make settings that apply to all of the domains within an Active Directory tree or forest.

For more information on sites, see Chapter 4, "Configuring Sites and Managing Replication."

Domains   Domains are the second level to which GPOs can be assigned. GPO settings that are placed at the domain level will apply to all of the User and Computer objects within the domain. Usually, systems administrators will make master settings at the domain level.

Organizational units   The most granular level of settings for GPOs is at the OU level. By configuring Group Policy options for OUs, systems administrators can take advantage of the hierarchical structure of Active Directory. If the OU structure is planned well, it will be easy to make logical GPO assignments for various business units at the OU level.

Based on the business need and the organization of the Active Directory environment, systems administrators might decide to set up Group Policy settings at any of these three levels. Because the settings are cumulative by default, a User object might receive policy settings from the site level, from the domain level, and from the OUs in which it is contained.

 Group Policy settings can also be applied to the local computer (in which case Active Directory is not used at all), but this limits the manageability of the Group Policy settings.

Group Policy Inheritance

In most cases, Group Policy settings will be cumulative. For example, a GPO at the domain level might specify that all users within the domain must change their passwords every 60 days, and a GPO at the OU level might specify the default Desktop background for all users and computers within that OU. In this case, both settings will apply, and users within the OU will be forced to change their password every 60 days and have the default Desktop setting.

So what happens if there's a conflict in the settings? For example, suppose we could create a scenario where a GPO at the site level specifies that users are to change passwords every 60 days whereas one at the OU level specifies that they must change passwords every 90 days. Since Password policies for GPOs, though available, are not applied at the OU or site level. Only Password policies at the domain level are applied. Although hypothetical, this raises an important point about *inheritance*. By default, the settings at the most specific level (in this case, the OU that contains the User object) will override those at more general levels.

Although the default behavior is for settings to be cumulative and inherited, systems administrators can modify this behavior. Two main options can be set at the various levels to which GPOs might apply:

Block Policy Inheritance   The Block Policy Inheritance option specifies that Group Policy settings for an object are not inherited from its parents. This might be used, for example, when a child OU requires completely different settings from a parent OU. Note, however, that blocking policy inheritance should be managed carefully because this option allows other systems administrators to override the settings made at higher levels.

Force Policy Inheritance   The Force Policy Inheritance option can be placed on a parent object and ensures that all lower-level objects inherit these settings. In some cases, systems administrators want to ensure that Group Policy inheritance is not blocked at other levels. For example, suppose it is corporate policy that all Network accounts are locked out after five incorrect password attempts. In this case, you would not want lower-level systems administrators to override the option with other settings.

This option is generally used when systems administrators want to globally enforce a specific setting. For example, if a password expiration policy should apply to all users and computers within a domain, a GPO with the Force Policy Inheritance option enabled could be created at the domain level.

One final case must be considered: if there is a conflict between the computer and user settings, the user settings will take effect. If, for instance, a default Desktop setting is applied for the Computer policy, and a different default Desktop setting is applied for the User policy, the one specified in the User policy will take effect. This is because the user settings are more specific, and they allow systems administrators to make changes for individual users, regardless of the computer they're using.

Planning a Group Policy Strategy

Through the use of Group Policy settings, systems administrators can control many different aspects of their network environment. As you'll see throughout this chapter, there are ways in which user settings and computer configurations can be configured using GPOs. Windows Server 2003 includes many different administrative tools for performing these tasks. However, it's important to keep in mind that, as with many aspects of using Active Directory, a successful Group Policy strategy involves planning.

Because there are hundreds of possible GPO settings and many different ways in which they can be implemented, you should start by determining the business and technical needs of your organization. You might start by grouping your users based on their work functions. You might find, for example, that users in remote branch offices require particular network configuration options. In that case, Group Policy settings might be best implemented at the site level. Or, you might find that certain departments have varying requirements for disk quota settings. In this case, it would probably make the most sense to apply GPOs to the appropriate department OUs within the domain.

The overall goal should be to reduce complexity (for example, by reducing the overall number of GPOs and GPO links), while still meeting the needs of your users. By taking into account the various needs of your users and the parts of your organization, you can often determine a logical and efficient method of creating and applying GPOs. Although it's rare that you'll come across a right or wrong method of implementing Group Policy settings, you will usually encounter some that are either better or worse than others.

By implementing a logical and consistent set of policies, you'll also be well prepared to troubleshoot any problems that might come up, or to adapt to your organization's changing requirements. Later in this chapter you'll see some specific methods for determining effective Group Policy settings before you apply them.

Implementing Group Policy

Now that we've covered the basic layout and structure of Group Policies and how they work, let's look at how you can implement them in an Active Directory environment. In this section, you'll start by creating GPOs. Then, you'll apply these GPOs to specific Active Directory objects and take a look at how to use administrative templates.

Creating GPOs

Although there is only one Group Policy editing application included with Windows Server 2003, you can access it in several ways. This is because systems administrators may choose to apply the Group Policy settings at different levels within Active Directory. In order to create or link GPOs at different levels, you can use the following tools:

Local Security Policy   This administrative tool allows you to quickly access the Group Policy settings that are available for the local computer. These options will apply to the local machine and to users that access it. You must be a member of the local administrators group to access and make changes to these settings.

Domain Security Policy   Often, you will want to set Group Policy options that apply to the entire domain. This tool, which is available on Windows Server 2003 computers that are functioning as domain controllers, allows you to quickly make those changes.

Domain Controller Security Policy   In many environments, you will want to provide additional or customized security settings for your domain controllers. Using this administrative tool, you can easily customize Group Policy settings for the domain controller.

Active Directory Sites And Services   Used for linking GPOs at the site level. This method is commonly used by systems administrators who want to apply certain Group Policy settings based on the physical implementation of their Active Directory environment. For example, you might want to have users in remote branch offices have one collection of settings, while users in the Corporate office may require other settings.

Active Directory Users And Computers   Used for linking GPOs at the domain or OU level. This is the main method by which you will create and link GPOs for the objects (including Users, Groups, and Computers) within an Active Directory domain. As you'll see later in this chapter, by combining security settings, you can achieve very granular control regarding to which objects GPO settings apply.

Group Policy Management Console (GPMC)   You can use the Group Policy Management Console (GPMC) to manage Group Policy deployment from one single console. The GPMC provides a single solution for managing all Group Policy–related tasks and is also best suited to handle enterprise-level tasks such as forest-related work. The GPMC is available in Windows Server 2003 R2 installation, or directly from Microsoft's website at www.microsoft.com/windowsserver2003/gpmc/default.mspx.

The GPMC allow administrators to manage the Group Policy and GPOs whether their enterprise solution spans multiple domains and sites within one or more forests, or whether it is local to one site all from one easy-to-use console. The GPMC adds flexibility, manageability, and functionality. Using this console, you can perform other functions such as backup and restore, importing, copying, and so on.

We will learn how to use the GPMC in Chapter 9.

MMC Group Policy snap-in   By directly configuring the Microsoft Management Console (MMC) Group Policy snap-in, you can access and edit GPOs at any level of the hierarchy. This is also a useful option because it allows you to modify the local Group Policy settings and create a custom console that is saved to the Administrative Tools program group.

Exercise 8.1 walks you through the process of creating a custom MMC snap-in for editing Group Policy settings.

 WARNING   You should be careful when making Group Policy settings because certain options might prevent the proper use of systems on your network. Always test Group Policy settings on a small group of users before you deploy GPOs throughout your organization. You'll probably find that some settings need to be changed in order for them to be effective.

EXERCISE 8.1

Creating a Group Policy Object Using MMC

1. Click Start ➢ Run, type **mmc**, and press Enter.

2. On the File menu, click Add/Remove Snap-In.

3. Click the Add button. In The Add Standalone Snap-In dialog box, select Group Policy Object Editor from the list, and click Add.

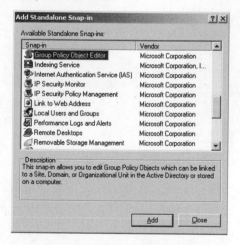

4. In the Select Group Policy Object Wizard, click Browse (note that you can set the scope to Domains/OUs, Sites, or Computers).

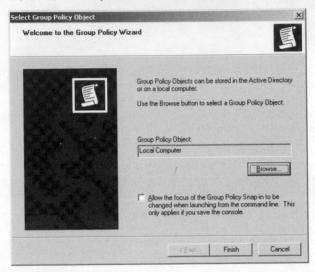

5. On the Domains/OUs tab, click the New Policy button (located to the right of the Look In drop-down list).

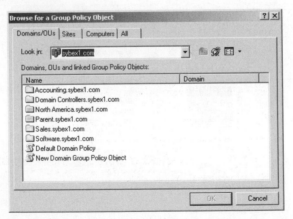

EXERCISE 8.1 *(continued)*

6. To name the new object, type **Test Domain Policy**. Click OK to select the Policy object.

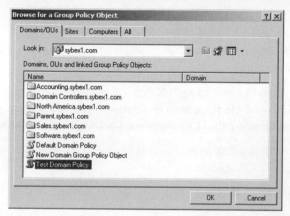

7. Place a check mark next to the Allow The Focus Of The Group Policy Snap-In To Be Changed When Launching From The Command Line option. This will allow the context of the snap-in to be changed when you launch the MMC item.

8. Click Finish to create the Group Policy object. Click Close in the Add Standalone Snap-In dialog box. Finally, click OK in the Add/Remove Snap-In dialog box to add the new snap-in.

9. Next, we'll make some changes to the default settings for this new GPO. Open the following items: Test Domain Policy, Computer Configuration, Windows Settings, Security Settings, Local Policies, Security Options.

10. Double-click the Interactive Logon: Do Not Display Last User Name option.

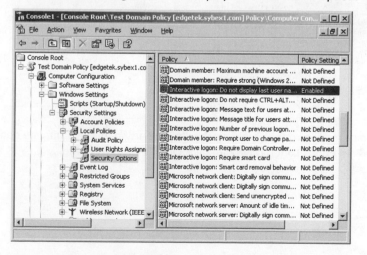

EXERCISE 8.1 *(continued)*

11. On the Template Security Policy Setting dialog box, place a check mark next to the Define This Policy Setting In The Template option, and then select Enabled. Click OK to save the setting.

12. In the Group Policy Object Editor, double-click the Interactive Logon: Message Text For Users Attempting to Log On option.

13. Place a check mark next to the Define This Policy Setting In The Template option, and then type the following: **By logging onto this domain, you specify that you agree to the usage policies as defined by the IT department**. Click OK to save the setting.

14. In the Group Policy Object Editor, double-click the Interactive Logon: Message Title For Users Attempting To Log On option.

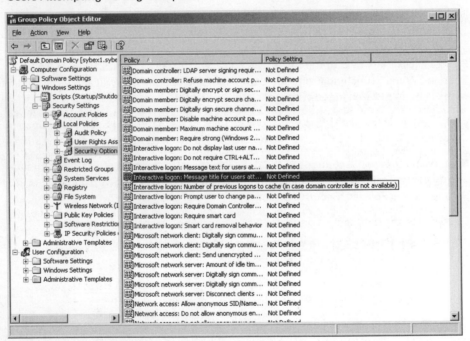

15. Place a check mark next to the Define This Policy Setting In The Template option, and then type **Test Policy Logon Message**. Click OK to save the setting.

EXERCISE 8.1 *(continued)*

16. To make changes to the user settings, expand the following objects in the Group Policy Object Editor: Test Domain Policy, User Configuration, Administrative Templates, Start Menu & Task Bar.

17. Double-click the Add Logoff To The Start Menu option. Note that you can get a description of the purpose of this setting by clicking the Explain tab. You can also see this description in the right pane of the MMC when the policy is selected. Select Enabled, and then click OK.

18. On the Group Policy Object Editor, expand the following objects: Test Domain Policy, User Configuration, Administrative Templates, System.

19. Double-click the Don't Run Specified Windows Applications option.

20. In the Don't Run Specified Windows Applications Properties dialog box, select Enabled, and then click the Show button. To add to the list of disallowed applications, click the Add button. When prompted to enter the item, type **wordpad.exe**. To save the setting, click OK three times.

21. To change network configuration settings, click Test Domain Policy, User Configuration, Administrative Templates, Network, Offline Files. Note that you can change the default file locations for several different network folders.

22. To change script settings (covered later in this chapter), click Test Domain Policy ➤ Computer Configuration ➤ Windows Settings ➤ Scripts (Startup/Shutdown). Note that you can add script settings by double-clicking either the Startup and/or the Shutdown item.

23. The changes you have made for this GPO are automatically saved. You can optionally save this customized MMC console by selecting Save As from the Console menu. Then provide a name for the new MMC snap-in (such as **Group Policy Test**). You will now see this item in the Administrative Tools program group.

24. When you are finished modifying the Group Policy settings, close the MMC tool.

Note that Group Policy changes do not take effect until the next user logs in. That is, users who are currently working on the system will not see the effects of the changes until they log off and log in again. GPO's are reapplied every 90 minutes with a 30 minute offset. In other words, users that are logged on will have there policies reapplied every 60–120 minutes. Not all settings are reapplied (i.e., software settings or Password policies)

Linking GPOs to Active Directory

Creating a GPO is the first step in assigning group policies. The second step is to link the GPO to a specific Active Directory object. As mentioned earlier in this chapter, GPOs can be linked to sites, domains, and OUs.

Exercise 8.2 walks through the steps you must take to assign a GPO to an OU within the local domain. In this exercise, you will link the Test Domain Policy GPO to an OU. In order to complete the steps in this exercise, you must have first completed Exercise 8.1.

EXERCISE 8.2

Linking GPOs to Active Directory

1. Open Active Directory Users and Computers tool.

2. Create a new top-level OU called **Group Policy Test**.

3. Right-click the Group Policy Test OU, and click Properties.

4. On the Group Policy Test Properties dialog box, select the Group Policy tab. To add a new policy at the OU level, click Add.

5. Enter a descriptive name for the GPO such as Group Policy Test GPO. Note that you can also add additional GPOs to this OU. When multiple GPOs are assigned, you can also control the order in which they apply by using the Up and Down buttons. Finally, you can edit the GPO by clicking the Edit button, and you can remove the link (or, optionally, delete the GPO entirely) by clicking the Delete button.

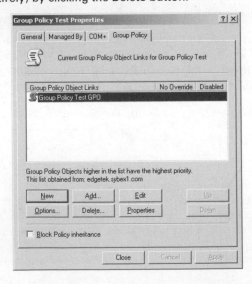

6. To save the GPO link, click OK in the OU Properties dialog box.

7. When finished, close the Active Directory Users And Computers tool.

Note that the Active Directory Users And Computers tool offers a lot of flexibility in assigning GPOs. You could create new GPOs, add multiple GPOs, edit them directly, change priority settings, remove links, and delete GPOs all from within this interface. In general, creating new GPOs using the Active Directory Sites And Services or the Active Directory Users And Computers tool is the quickest and easiest way to create the settings you need.

To test the Group Policy settings, you can simply create a User or Computer account within the Group Policy Test OU that you created in Exercise 8.2. Then, using another computer that is a member of the same domain, you can log on as the newly created user. First, you should see the pre-logon message that you set in Exercise 8.1. After logging on, you'll also notice that the other changes have taken effect. For example, you will not be able to run the WordPad.exe program.

 When testing Group Policy settings, it is very convenient to use the Terminal Services functionality of Windows Server 2003. Although it is beyond the scope of this book, this feature allows you to have multiple simultaneous logon sessions to the same computer. With respect to Group Policy, it is useful when you want to modify Group Policy settings and then quickly log on under another user account to test them. For more information on using Terminal Services, see *MCSA/MCSE: Windows Server 2003 Environment Management and Maintenance Study Guide (70-290), Section Edition* by Lisa Donald with James Chellis (Sybex, 2006).

Using Administrative Templates

There are many different options that Group Policy settings can modify. Microsoft has included some of the most common and useful items by default, and they're made available when you create new GPOs or when you edit existing ones. You can, however, create your own templates and include them in the list of settings.

By default, several templates are included with Windows Server 2003. These are as follows:

Common.adm   This template contains the policy options that are common to both Windows 95/98/Me and Windows NT 4 computers.

Conf.adm   This template contains the policy options for configuring NetMeeting options on Windows 2000, XP Professional, and Server 2003 client computers. This template cannot be used with 64-bit versions of Windows.

Inetcorp.adm   This template contains Dial-Up, Language, and Temporary Internet Files settings.

Inetres.adm   This template contains the policy options for configuring Internet Explorer options on Windows 2000 and XP client computers.

Inetset.adm   This template contains additional Internet settings such as Autocomplete and display settings.

System.adm This template contains common configuration options and settings for Windows 2000 and XP client computers.

Windows.adm This template contains policy options for Windows 95/98/Me computers.

Winnt.adm This template contains policy options that are specific to the use of Windows NT 4.

Wmplayer.adm This template contains the policy options for configuring Windows Media Player options on Windows 2000, XP, and Server 2003 client computers. This template cannot be used with 64-bit versions of Windows.

Wuau.adm This template contains the policy options for configuring Windows Update and Automatic Update.

These Administrative Template files are stored within the inf subdirectory of the system root directory. It is important to note that the use of the Windows.adm, Winnt.adm, and Common.adm files is not supported in Windows Server 2003. These files are primarily provided for backward compatibility with previous versions of Windows.

The *.adm files are simple text files that follow a specific format that is recognized by the Group Policy Object Editor. Following is an excerpt from the system.adm file:

```
CATEGORY !!WindowsComponents
  CATEGORY !!WindowsExplorer
  KEYNAME "Software\Microsoft\Windows\CurrentVersion
          \Policies\Explorer"

  POLICY !!ClassicShell
    EXPLAIN !!ClassicShell_Help
    VALUENAME "ClassicShell"
  END POLICY

  POLICY !!NoFolderOptions
    EXPLAIN !!NoFolderOptions_Help
    VALUENAME "NoFolderOptions"
  END POLICY

  POLICY !!NoFileMenu
        EXPLAIN !!NoFileMenu_Help
    VALUENAME "NoFileMenu"
    END POLICY

  POLICY !!NoNetConnectDisconnect
          EXPLAIN !!NoNetConnectDisconnect_Help
    VALUENAME "NoNetConnectDisconnect"
  END POLICY
```

```
POLICY !!NoShellSearchButton
    EXPLAIN !!NoShellSearchButton_Help
    VALUENAME "NoShellSearchButton"
    END POLICY

POLICY !!NoViewContextMenu
        EXPLAIN !!NoViewContextMenu_Help
    VALUENAME "NoViewContextMenu"
    END POLICY
```

Notice that the various options that are available for modification are specified within the Administrative Template file. If necessary, systems administrators can create custom Administrative Template files that include more options for configuration.

To add new administrative templates when modifying GPOs, simply right-click the Administrative Templates object in the Group Policy Object Editor and select Add/Remove Templates, which brings up the Add/Remove Templates dialog box (see Figure 8.2).

FIGURE 8.2   Adding administrative templates when creating GPOs

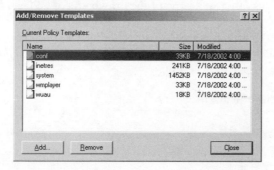

Managing Group Policy

Once you have implemented GPOs and applied them to sites, domains, and OUs within Active Directory, it's time to look at some ways to manage them. In the following sections, you'll look at how multiple GPOs can interact with one another and ways you can provide security for GPO management. These are very important features of working with Active Directory, and if you properly plan Group Policy, you can greatly reduce the time the help desk spends troubleshooting common problems.

Real World Scenario

Replication and FRS

To provide a policy across a forest (as an example), you need a policy that you can replicate to other systems. How do you get this? As we learned in the first half of this book, replication is handled by Active Directory and the File Replication Service (FRS). In the SYSVOL folder of each domain controller, each domain GPO maintains a single folder named the Group Policy Template (GPT). The GPT stores *.adm files. GPO replication is handled by the FRS. As you learned earlier this text, the FRS handles replication not only for Active Directory, but also for the GPTs for GPOs throughout your domain. There is also an adm subfolder in the GPT of which you should take note. This subfolder is replicated to each domain's domain controllers. Replication may also be affected if your *.adm files are too large.

Managing GPOs

One of the benefits of GPOs is that they're modular and can apply to many different objects and levels within Active Directory. This can also be one of the drawbacks of GPOs if they're not managed properly. A common administrative function related to using GPOs is finding all of the Active Directory links for each of these objects. You can do this when you are viewing the Links tab of the GPO Properties dialog box. As shown in Figure 8.3, clicking the Find Now button shows which objects are using a particular GPO.

FIGURE 8.3 Viewing GPO links to Active Directory

In addition to the common function of delegating permissions on OUs, you can also set permissions regarding the modification of GPOs. The best way to accomplish this is to add users to the Group Policy Creator/Owners built-in security group. The members of this group are able to modify security policy. You saw how to add users to groups back in Chapter 6.

Filtering Group Policy

Another method of securing access to GPOs is to set permissions on the GPOs themselves. You can do this by opening an object's Properties dialog box, switching to the Group Policy tab, selecting a GPO, and clicking the Properties button to open the GPO Properties dialog box. From the Security tab of the GPO Properties dialog box you can view the specific permissions that are set on the GPO itself (see Figure 8.4).

FIGURE 8.4   GPO security settings

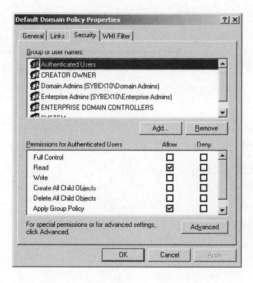

The permissions options include the following:

- Full Control
- Read
- Write
- Create All Child Objects
- Delete All Child Objects
- Apply Group Policy

Of these, the Apply Group Policy setting is particularly important because you use it to filter the scope of the GPO. *Filtering* is the process by which selected security groups are included or excluded from the effects of the GPOs. To specify that the settings should apply to a GPO, you should select Allow for both the Apply Group Policy and Read settings. These settings will be applied only if the security group is also contained within a site, domain, or OU to which the GPO is linked. In order to disable GPO access for a group, choose Deny for both of these settings. Finally, if you do not want to specify either Allow or Deny effects, leave both boxes blank. This is effectively the same as having no setting.

In Exercise 8.3, you will filter Group Policy using security groups. In order to complete the steps in this exercise, you must have first completed Exercises 8.1 and 8.2.

EXERCISE 8.3

Filtering Group Policy Using Security Groups

1. Open the Active Directory Users And Computers administrative tool.

2. Create two new Global Security groups within the Group Policy Test OU and name them **PolicyEnabled** and **PolicyDisabled**.

3. Right-click the Group Policy Test OU, and select Properties. Select the Group Policy tab.

4. Highlight Test Domain Policy, and click the Properties button.

5. On the Security tab of the GPO Properties dialog box, click Add, and enter the PolicyEnabled and the PolicyDisabled groups. Click OK.

6. Highlight the PolicyDisabled group, and select Deny for the Read and Apply Group Policy permissions. This prevents users in the PolicyDisabled group from being affected by this policy.

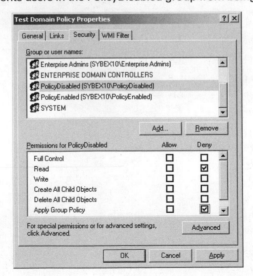

7. Highlight the PolicyEnabled group, and select Allow for the Read and Apply Group Policy permissions. This ensures that users in the PolicyEnabled group will be affected by this policy.

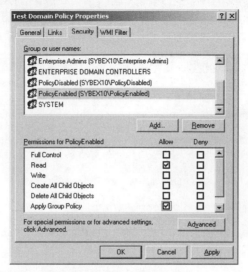

8. Click OK to save the Group Policy settings. You will be warned that Deny takes precedence over any other security settings. Select Yes to continue.

9. Click OK to save the change to the properties of the OU.

10. When finished, close the Active Directory Users And Computers administrative tool.

By using these settings, you can ensure that only the appropriate individuals will be able to modify GPO settings.

Delegating Administrative Control of GPOs

So far, you have learned about how you can use Group Policy to manage user and computer settings. What you haven't done is determine who can modify GPOs. It's very important to establish the appropriate security on GPOs themselves for two main reasons. First, if the security settings aren't set properly, users and systems administrators can easily override them. This defeats the purpose of having the GPOs in the first place. Second, having many different systems administrators creating and modifying GPOs can become extremely difficult to manage. When problems arise, the hierarchical nature of GPO inheritance can make it difficult to pinpoint the problem.

Fortunately, through the use of the Delegation of Control Wizard, determining security permissions for GPOs is a simple task. You saw the usefulness of the Delegation of Control

Wizard in Chapter 5, "Administering Active Directory" and in Chapter 6, "Planning Security for Active Directory."

Exercise 8.4 walks you through the steps you must take to grant the appropriate permissions to a User account. Specifically, the process involves delegating the ability to manage Group Policy links on an Active Directory object (such as an OU). In order to complete this exercise, you must have first completed Exercises 8.1 and 8.2.

EXERCISE 8.4

Delegating Administrative Control of Group Policy

1. Open the Active Directory Users And Computers tool.

2. Expand the local domain, and create a user named **Policy Admin** within the Group Policy Test OU.

3. Right-click the Group Policy Test OU, and select Delegate Control.

4. Click Next to start the Delegation of Control Wizard.

5. On the Users Or Groups page, click Add. Enter the Policy Admin account, and click OK. Click Next to continue.

6. On the Tasks To Delegate page, select Delegate The Following Common Tasks, and place a check mark next to the Manage Group Policy Links item. Click Next to continue.

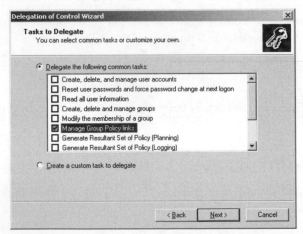

7. Finally, click Finish on the final page of the wizard to complete the Delegation of Control Wizard and assign the appropriate permissions. Specifically, this will allow the Policy Admin user to create GPO links to this OU (and, by default, any child OUs).

8. When you are finished, close the Active Directory Users And Computers tool.

Real World Scenario

Understanding Delegation

Although we have talked about delegation throughout the text, it's important to rediscuss it here when talking about OUs, Group Policy, and Active Directory. Once configured, Active Directory administrative delegation allows an administrator to delegate tasks (usually admin related) to specific user accounts of groups. What this means is that if you don't manage it all, the user accounts (or groups) you choose will be able to manage their portion of the tree. It's very important to consider the benefits of Active Directory Delegation (AD Delegation). AD Delegation will help you manage the assigning of administrative control over objects in Active Directory, such as users, groups, computers, printers, domains, sites, and so on. AD Delegation is used to create more administrators, which essentially saves time. A great example would be if you have a company whose IT department is small and located in the central location that connects up three other smaller remote sites. Those three sites do not warrant a full time IT person to work there, so the manager on staff (as an example) can become an administrator for that portion of the tree; the user accounts for the staff at the remote site are managed by that manager. What this does is keep the burden of having to do trivial administrative work, such as unlocking user accounts or changing passwords, and thus it reduces costs.

Controlling Inheritance and Filtering Group Policy

Controlling inheritance is an important function when you are managing GPOs. Earlier in this chapter, you learned that, by default, GPO settings flow from higher-level Active Directory objects to lower-level ones. For example, the effective set of Group Policy settings for a user might be based on GPOs assigned at the site level, the domain level, and in the OU hierarchy. In general, this is probably the behavior you would want.

In some cases, however, you might want to block Group Policy inheritance. You can accomplish this easily by selecting the properties for the object to which a GPO has been linked. On the Group Policy tab, you will be able to set several useful options regarding inheritance. The first (and most obvious) option is the Block Policy Inheritance check box located at the bottom of the Group Policy tab of the Group Policy Object Properties dialog box (see Figure 8.5). By enabling this option, you are effectively specifying that this object starts with a clean slate—that is, no other Group Policy settings will apply to the contents of this Active Directory site, domain, or OU.

There is, however, a way that systems administrators can force inheritance. They do this by setting the No Override option to prevent other systems administrators from making changes to default policies. You can set the No Override option by clicking the Options button on the Group Policy tab for the object to which the GPO applies. Doing so brings up the GPO's Option dialog box (see Figure 8.6). Notice that you can also choose to temporarily disable a GPO. This is useful during troubleshooting and when you are attempting to determine which GPOs are causing certain behavior.

FIGURE 8.5   Blocking GPO inheritance

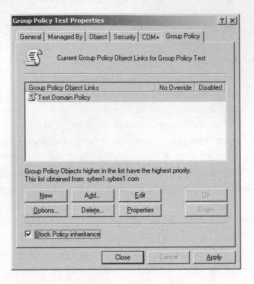

FIGURE 8.6   Setting the No Override GPO option

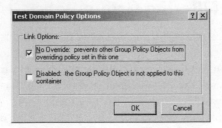

Exercise 8.5 walks you through the steps you need to take to manage inheritance and filtering of GPOs.

EXERCISE 8.5

Managing Inheritance and Filtering of GPOs

1. Open the Active Directory Users And Computers administrative tool.

2. Create a top-level OU called **Parent**.

3. Right-click the Parent OU, and select Properties. Select the Group Policy tab and click the New button to create a new GPO. Name the new object **Master GPO**.

4. Click the Options button on the Group Policy tab.

5. On the Master GPO Options dialog box, place a check mark next to the No Override option. This ensures that administrators of OUs contained within the Parent OU will not be able to override the settings defined in this GPO. To save the settings, click OK. Notice that a check mark appears next to the Master GPO in the No Override column in the list of Group Policy object links.

6. On the Group Policy tab of the Parent OU Properties dialog box, create another GPO and name it **Optional GPO**. Click the OK button to save the changes.

7. Within the Parent OU, create another OU called **Child**.

8. Right-click the Child OU, and select Properties.

9. Select the Group Policy tab, and place a check mark in the Block Policy Inheritance check box. This option prevents the inheritance of GPO settings from the Parent OU for the Optional GPO settings. Note that because the No Override setting for the Master GPO was enabled on the Parent OU, the settings in the Master GPO will take effect on the Child OU regardless of the setting of the Block Policy Inheritance box. Click OK to save the changes.

10. When you are finished, close the Active Directory Users And Computers tool.

Assigning Script Policies

Systems administrators might want to make several changes and settings that would apply during the computer startup or user logon. Perhaps the most common operation logon scripts perform is mapping network drives. Although users can manually map network drives, providing this functionality within login scripts ensures that mappings stay consistent and that users need only remember the drive letters for their resources.

Script policies are specific options that are part of Group Policy settings for users and computers. These settings direct the operating system to the specific files that should be processed during the startup/shutdown or logon/logoff processes. You can create the scripts themselves by using the *Windows Script Host (WSH)* or by using standard batch file commands. WSH is a utility included with the Windows Server 2003 operating system. It allows developers and systems administrators to quickly and easily create scripts using the familiar Visual Basic Scripting Edition (VBScript) or JScript (Microsoft's implementation of JavaScript). Additionally, WSH can be expanded to accommodate other common scripting languages.

To set script policy options, you simply edit the Group Policy settings. As shown in Figure 8.7, there are two main areas for setting script policy settings:

Startup/Shutdown Scripts These settings are located within the Computer Configuration ➢ Windows Settings ➢ Scripts (Startup/Shutdown) object.

Logon/Logoff Scripts   These settings are located within the User Configuration ➢ Windows Settings ➢ Scripts (Logon/Logoff) object.

FIGURE 8.7   Viewing Startup/Shutdown script policy settings

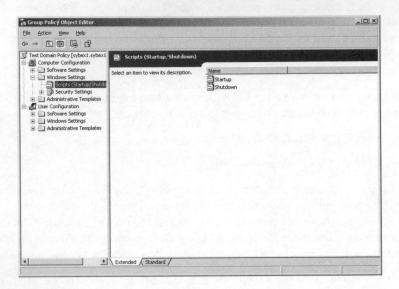

To assign scripts, simply double-click the setting, at which time its Properties dialog box will appear. For instance, if you double-click the Startup setting, the Startup Properties dialog box appears, as shown in Figure 8.8. To add a script filename, click the Add button. When you do, you will be asked to provide the name of the script file (such as `MapNetworkDrives.vbs` or `ResetEnvironment.bat`).

FIGURE 8.8   Setting scripting options

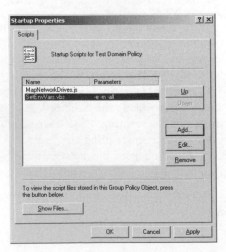

Note that you can change the order in which the scripts are run by using the Up and Down buttons. The Show Files button opens the directory folder in which you should store the Logon script files. In order to ensure that the files are replicated to all domain controllers, you should be sure that you place the files within the SYSVOL share.

Managing Network Configuration

Group policies are also useful in network configuration. Although many different methods handle network settings at the protocol level—such as Dynamic Host Configuration Protocol (DHCP)—Group Policy allows administrators to set which functions and operations are available to users and computers.

Figure 8.9 shows some of the features that are available for managing Group Policy settings. The paths to these settings are as follows:

Computer Network Options   These settings are located within the Computer Configuration, Administrative Templates, Network Connections folder.

User Network Options   These settings are located within the User Configuration, Administrative Templates, Network folder.

FIGURE 8.9   Viewing Group Policy User network configuration options

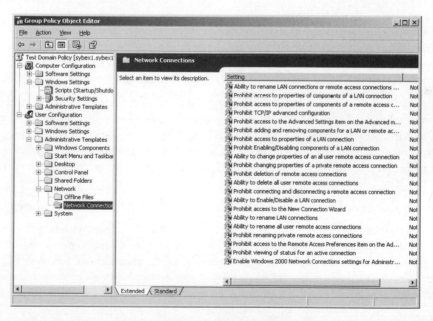

Some examples of the types of settings available include the following:

- The ability to allow or disallow the modification of network settings. In many environments, the improper changing of network configurations and protocol settings is a common cause of help desk calls.

- The ability to allow or disallow the creation of Remote Access Service (RAS) connections. This option is very useful, especially in larger networked environments, because the use of modems and other wide area network (WAN) devices can pose a security threat to the network.

- Setting of offline files and folders options. This is especially useful for keeping files synchronized for traveling users and is commonly configured for laptops.

Each setting includes detailed instructions in the description area of the GPO Editor window. By using these configuration options, systems administrators can maintain consistency for users and computers and can avoid many of the most common troubleshooting calls.

Automatically Enrolling User and Computer Certificates in Group Policy

Group Policy can also be used to automatically enroll user and computer certificates, making the entire certificate process transparent to your end users. Before you go on, you should understand what certificates are and why they are an important part of network security.

Think of a digital certificate as a carrying case for a public key. A certificate contains the public key and a set of attributes, like the key holder's name and e-mail address. These attributes specify something about the holder: their identity, what they're allowed to do with the certificate, and so on. The attributes and the public key are bound together because the certificate is digitally signed by the entity that issued it. Anyone who wants to verify the certificate's contents can verify the issuer's signature.

Certificates are one part of what security experts call a *public-key infrastructure (PKI)*. A PKI has several different components that you can mix and match to achieve the desired results. Microsoft's PKI implementation offers the following functions:

Certificate authorities (CAs)   Issue certificates, revoke certificates they've issued, and publish certificates for their clients. Big CAs like Thawte and VeriSign may do this for millions of users; you can also set up your own CA for each department or workgroup in your organization if you want. Each CA is responsible for choosing what attributes it will include in a certificate and what mechanism it will use to verify those attributes before it issues the certificate.

Certificate publishers   Make certificates publicly available, inside or outside an organization. This allows widespread availability of the critical material needed to support the entire PKI.

PKI-savvy applications   Allow you and your users to do useful things with certificates, like encrypt email or network connections. Ideally, the user shouldn't have to know (or even necessarily be aware) of what the application is doing—everything should work seamlessly and automatically. The best-known examples of PKI-savvy applications are web browsers like Internet Explorer and Netscape Navigator and email applications like Outlook and Outlook Express.

Certificate templates   Act like rubber stamps: by specifying a particular template as the model you want to use for a newly issued certificate, you're actually telling the CA which optional attributes to add to the certificate, as well as implicitly telling it how to fill some of the mandatory attributes. Templates greatly simplify the process of issuing certificates because they keep you from having to memorize the names of all the attributes you might potentially want to put in a certificate.

Learn More about PKI

Because the exam doesn't go deeply into PKI, it's recommended that you do some extra research on your own because it is a very important technology and shouldn't be overlooked. When discussing certificates, it's important to also mention PKI and its definition. PKI is actually a simple concept with a lot of moving parts. When broken down to its bare essentials, PKI is nothing more than a server and workstations utilizing a software service to add security to your infrastructure. When you use PKI, you are adding a layer of protection. To learn more, visit the following URLs on Microsoft's website.

Windows Server 2003 PKI Information: www.microsoft.com/windowsserver2003/technologies/pki/default.mspx

PKI Operations Guide: www.microsoft.com/technet/prodtechnol/windowsserver2003/technologies/security/ws03pkog.mspx

---

 Installing and configuring a CA goes beyond the scope of this book. For more information, see the *MCSE: Windows Server 2003 Network Infrastructure Planning and Maintenance Study Guide (70-293), Second Edition* by Mark Foust with James Chellis (Sybex, 2006).

The Autoenrollment Settings policy determines whether or not users and/or computers are automatically enrolled for the appropriate certificates when necessary. By default, this policy is turned on, but you can make changes to the settings as shown in Exercise 8.6.

In Exercise 8.6, you will learn how to configure automatic certificate enrollment in Group Policy. You must have completed the other exercises in this chapter in order to proceed with this exercise.

EXERCISE 8.6

Configuring Automatic Certificate Enrollment in Group Policy

1. Open the Active Directory Users And Computers administrative tool.

2. Open the Parent OU you created in the previous exercise and open the Master GPO.

3. Open Computer Configuration, Windows Settings, Security Settings, Public Key Policies.

4. Double-click Autoenrollment Settings in the right pane.

EXERCISE 8.6 *(continued)*

5. The Autoenrollment Settings Properties dialog box will appear. Notice that the Enroll Certificates Automatically setting is enabled by default. Check the Renew Expired Certificates, Update Pending Certificates, And Remove Revoked Certificates and the Update Certificates That User Certificate Templates check boxes.

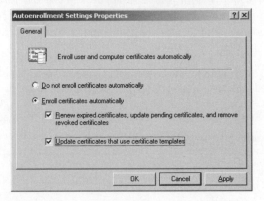

6. Click OK to close the Autoenrollment Settings Properties dialog box.

Redirecting Folders Using Group Policy

The last specific set of Group Policy settings that you will learn about are the *folder redirection* settings. Group Policy provides a means of redirecting the My Documents, Desktop, and Start menu folders, as well as cached application data, to network locations. Folder redirection is particularly useful for the following reasons:

- When using roaming user profiles, a user's My Documents folder is copied to the local machine each time he logs on. This often requires high bandwidth consumption and time if the My Documents folder is large. If you redirect the My Documents folder, it stays in the redirected location, and the user opens and saves files directly from there.

- Documents are always available no matter where the user logs on.

- Data in the shared location can be backed up during the normal backup cycle without user intervention.

- Data can be redirected to a more robust server-side administered disk that is less prone to physical and user errors.

When you decide to redirect folders, you have two options: basic and advanced. Basic redirection redirects everyone's folders to the same location (but each user gets their own folder within that location). Advanced redirection redirects folders to different locations based on group membership. For instance, you could configure the Engineers group to redirect their folders to // Engineering1/My_Documents/ and the Marketing group to //Marketing1/My_Documents/. Again, each individual user still gets their own folder within the redirected location.

To configure folder redirection, follow the steps in Exercise 8.7. You must have completed the other exercises in this chapter in order to proceed with this exercise.

EXERCISE 8.7

Configuring Folder Redirection in Group Policy

1. Open the Active Directory Users And Computers administrative tool.

2. Open the Parent OU that you created in the previous exercises and open the Master GPO.

3. Open User Configuration, Windows Settings, Folder Redirection, My Documents.

4. Right-click My Documents and select Properties.

5. On the Target tab of the My Documents Properties dialog box, choose the Basic - Redirect Everyone's Folder To The Same Location selection from the Setting drop-down menu.

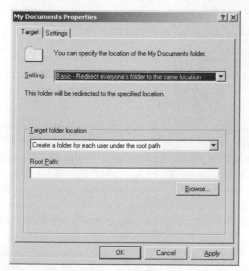

EXERCISE 8.7 *(continued)*

6. Leave the default option for the Target Folder Location drop-down menu and specify a network path in the Root Path field.

7. Click the Settings tab. All of the default settings are self-explanatory and should typically be left on the default. Click OK when you are done.

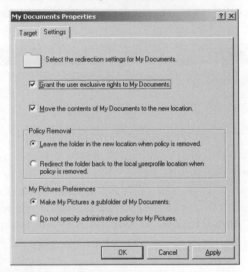

 Real World Scenario

Folder Redirection Facts

Try not to mix up the concepts of *folder redirection* and *offline folders*, especially in a world of ever increasing mobile users. Folder redirection and offline folders are different features. The way that Windows Server 2003 folder redirection works is that the system uses a pointer that moves the folders you want to a location you specify. Users do not see any of this because it is transparent to them. One problem with folder redirection is that it does not work for mobile users, users who will be offline and who will not have access to files that they may need. Offline folders, however, are copies of folders that were local to you. Files are now available locally to you on the system you have with you. They are also located back on the server where they are stored. Next time you log in, the folders are synchronized so that the copies of the data stay the same, which is a perfect feature for mobile users, whereas folder redirection provides no benefit for the mobile user.

Troubleshooting Group Policy

Due to the wide variety of configurations that are possible when you are establishing Group Policy, you should be aware of some common troubleshooting methods. These methods will help isolate problems in policy settings or GPO links.

One possible problem with GPO configuration is that logons and system startups may take a long time. This occurs especially in large environments when the Group Policy settings must be transmitted over the network and, in many cases, slow WAN links. In general, the number of GPOs should be limited because of the processing overhead and network requirements during logon. By default, GPOs are processed in a synchronous manner. This means that the processing of one GPO must be completed before another one is applied (as opposed to asynchronous processing, where they can all execute at the same time).

The most common issue associated with Group Policy is the unexpected setting of Group Policy options. In Windows 2000 Server, administrators spent countless hours analyzing inheritance hierarchy and individual settings to determine why a particular user or computer was having policy problems. For instance, say a user named jchellis complains that the Run option is missing from his Start menu. The jchellis user account is stored in the San Jose OU, and you've applied group policies at the OU, domain, and site level. To determine the source of the problem, you would have to manually sift through each GPO to find the Start menu policy as well as figure out the applicable inheritance settings.

Luckily, Windows Server 2003 adds a handy new feature called *Resultant Set of Policy (RSoP)* that displays the exact settings that actually apply to individual users, computers, OUs, domains, and sites after inheritance and filtering have taken effect. In the example just described, you could run RSoP on the jchellis account and view a single set of Group Policy settings that represent the settings that actually apply to the jchellis account. In addition, each setting's Properties dialog box displays the GPO that the setting is derived from, as well as the order of priority, the filter status, and other useful information, as you will see a bit later.

RSoP actually runs in two modes:

Logging Mode   *Logging mode* displays the actual settings that apply to users and computers like in the example in the preceding paragraph.

Planning Mode   *Planning mode* can be applied to users, computers, OUs, domains, and sites, and it is used before any settings have actually been applied. Like its name implies, planning mode is used to plan GPOs.

Additionally, you can run the command-line utility `gpresult.exe` to quickly get a snapshot of the Group Policy settings that apply to a user and/or computer. Let's take a closer look at the two modes and the `gpresult.exe` command.

RSoP in Logging Mode

RSoP in Logging mode can only query policy settings for users and computers. The easiest way to access RSoP in Logging mode is through the Active Directory Users And Computers tool, although you can run it as a standalone MMC snap-in if you want to.

To analyze the policy settings for jchellis from the earlier example, right-click the user icon in Active Directory Users And Computers and select All Tasks ➢ Resultant Set of Policy (Logging). The Resultant Set of Policy Wizard appears. The wizard walks you through the steps necessary to view the RSoP for jchellis.

The Computer Selection page, shown in Figure 8.10, requires you to select a computer for which to display settings. Remember that a GPO contains both user and computer settings, so you must choose a computer that the user has logged on to in order to continue with the wizard. If the user has never logged on to a computer, then you must run RSoP in planning mode, because there is no logged policy information for that user yet.

FIGURE 8.10   The Computer Selection page of the Resultant Set of Policy Wizard

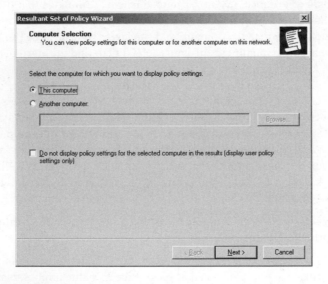

The User Selection page, shown in Figure 8.11, requires you to select a user account to analyze. Because we selected a user from Active Directory Users And Computers tool, you should notice that the username is filled in automatically. This screen is most useful if you are running RSoP in MMC mode and don't have the luxury of selecting a user contextually.

FIGURE 8.11   The User Selection page of the Resultant Set of Policy Wizard

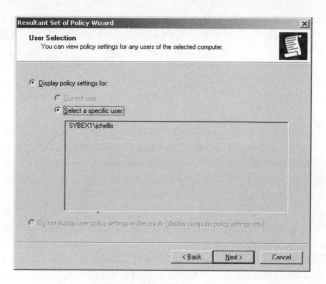

The Summary Of Selections page, shown in Figure 8.12, displays a summary of your choices and provides an option for gathering extended error information. If you need to make any changes before you begin to analyze the policy settings, you should click the Back button on the Summary screen. Otherwise, click Next.

FIGURE 8.12   The Summary of Selections page of the Resultant Set of Policy Wizard

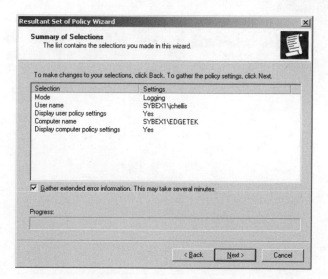

After the wizard is complete, you will see the Resultant Set of Policy window shown in Figure 8.13. This window looks very much like the Group Policy Object Editor window, but it only displays the policy settings that apply to the user and computer that you selected in the Resultant Set of Policy Wizard. You can see these user and computers at the topmost level of the tree.

Any warnings or errors display as a yellow triangle or red X over the applicable icon at the level where the warning or error occurred. To view more information about the warning or error, right-click the icon, select Properties, and select the Error Information tab, as shown in Figure 8.14.

You cannot make changes to any of the individual settings, because RSoP is a diagnostic tool and not an editor, but you can get more information about settings by clicking a setting and selecting Properties from the pop-up menu.

The Setting tab of the setting's Properties dialog box, shown in Figure 8.15, displays the actual setting that applies to the user in question based on GPO inheritance. The Explain tab simply offers an expanded description of the individual policy, which can usually be inferred from the policy name. The Precedence tab, shown in Figure 8.16, is probably the most interesting tab in the dialog box because it shows you all of the GPOs, in order of priority, that apply to the user. You can see in the figure that the San Jose GPO takes precedence, which would explain why the user doesn't see the Run option in their Start menu. From here, you could take the necessary steps to fix the user's problem or inform the user that their policy doesn't allow them to use the Run option on the Start menu.

FIGURE 8.13   The Resultant Set of Policy window for user jchellis on computer EDGETEK

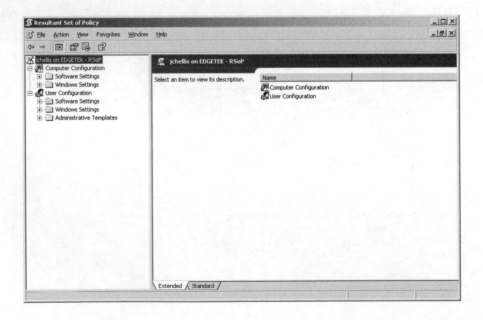

FIGURE 8.14   The Error Information tab of the Computer Configuration Properties dialog box

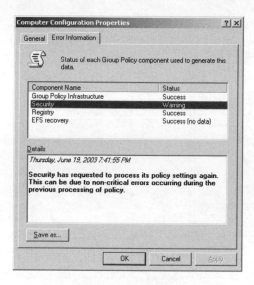

FIGURE 8.15   The Setting tab of the Setting Properties dialog box

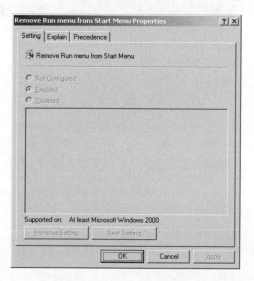

FIGURE 8.16 The Precedence tab of the Setting Properties dialog box

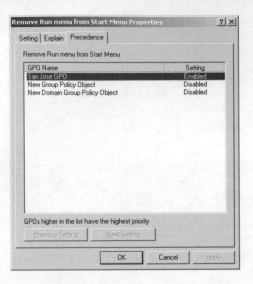

In Exercise 8.8, you'll learn how to run RSoP in Logging mode. Note that you must have completed the previous exercises in this chapter to complete this exercise.

EXERCISE 8.8

Running RSoP in Logging Mode

1. Open the Active Directory Users And Computers administrative tool.

2. Open the Parent OU you created in the previous exercises. Make several changes to the Desktop policies in the Optional GPO and the Master GPO. Be sure to refresh the GPO settings with the gpupdate command.

3. Open the Child OU and add a user named **TestUser1**.

4. Log on to the network as TestUser1 to establish an RSoP log, then log off and log on as an administrator.

5. Open the Active Directory Users And Computers administrative tool.

6. Right-click the TestUser1 account and select All Tasks ➢ Resultant Set of Policy (Logging) to open the Resultant Set of Policy Wizard.

7. On the Computer Selection page, select the computer that TestUser1 used to log on to the network in step 4. Click Next.

8. TestUser1 should already be selected on the User Selection page, so click Next to continue.

EXERCISE 8.8 *(continued)*

9. Verify that the information on the Summary Of Selections page is correct and click Next.

10. Click the Finish button on the Completing The Resultant Set of Policy Wizard page to open the Resultant Set of Policy window.

11. Check some of the Desktop settings that you changed in step 2. Right-click a setting and select Properties from the pop-up menu. You should see the resultant policy on the Setting tab and the order of precedence on the Precedence tab.

EXERCISE 8.9

Running RSoP in Planning Mode

1. Open the Active Directory Users And Computers administrative tool.

2. Open the Parent OU you created in the previous exercise.

3. Right-click the Parent OU and select All Tasks ➢ Resultant Set of Policy (Planning) to open the Resultant Set of Policy Wizard.

4. On the User And Computer Selection page, the Parent OU information should be filled in for you for both the user and computer. You could make changes to this screen if desired—for example, if you want to view the RSoP for users in one OU who log on to computers in another OU. Click Next to continue.

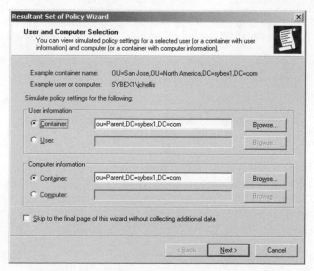

EXERCISE 8.9 *(continued)*

5. On the Advanced Simulation Options page don't make any changes at this time. This screen is used to simulate special network conditions such as slow network connections or loopback processing. Click Next to continue.

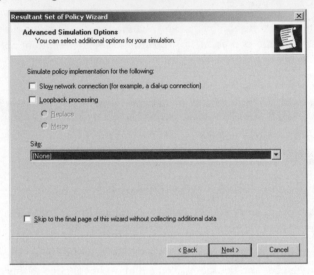

6. On the User Security Groups page, select hypothetical security groups that you would place users and computers into under the planned scenario. Click Next to continue.

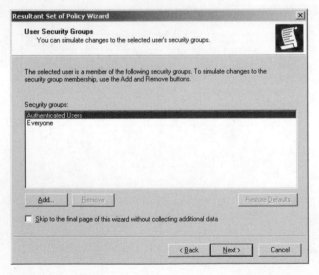

7. On the WMI Filters For Users page, you can specify any Windows Management Instrumentation (WMI) filters that you may have applied to GPOs. WMI filters go beyond the scope of this book, so just click Next and leave the default settings.

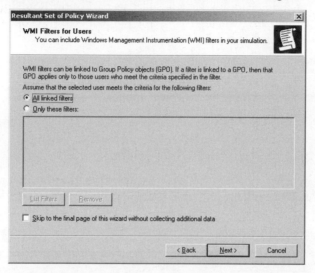

8. The Summary Of Selections page appears. This displays a summary of the selections you made in the wizard. You can elect to gather extended error information, and you can choose a domain controller on which to run the simulated RSoP. Click Next when you are ready to run the simulation.

9. Click Finish on the Completing The Resultant Set Of Policy Wizard page to open the Resultant Set Of Policy window.

10. Click through the various policy settings in the Resultant Set Of Policy window to see the GPO settings for a user and computer stored in the Parent OU.

RSoP in Planning Mode

Running RSoP in Planning mode isn't much different from running RSoP in Logging mode, but the RSoP Wizard asks for a bit more information than you saw earlier.

In the earlier example, you saw that jchellis couldn't see the Run option in the Start menu because his user account is affected by the San Jose GPO in the San Jose OU. As an administrator, you could plan to move his user account to the North America OU. Before doing so, you could verify his new policy settings by running RSoP in Planning mode on user jchellis under the scenario that you've already moved him from the San Jose OU to the North America OU. At this point, you haven't actually moved the user, but you can see what his settings would be if you did.

Exercise 8.9 shows you how to run RSoP in Planning mode. Note that you must have completed the previous exercises in this chapter to continue.

Using the *gpresult.exe* Command

gpresult.exe is a command-line utility that's included as part of the RSoP tool. Running the command by itself without any switches returns the following Group Policy information about the local user and computer:

- The name of the domain controller from which the local machine retrieved the policy information

- The date and time in which the policies were applied

- Which policies were applied

- Which policies were filtered out

- Group membership

You can use the switches shown in Table 8.1 to get information for remote users and computers and to enable other options.

TABLE 8.1   gpresult Switches

Switch	Description
/S *systemname*	Generates RSoP information for a remote computer name
/USER *username*	Generates RSoP information for a remote username
/V	Specifies verbose mode, which displays more verbose information such as user rights information
/Z	Specifies an even greater level of verbose information
/SCOPE MACHINE	Displays maximum information about the computer policies applied to this system
/SCOPE USER	Displays maximum information about the user policies applied to this system
>*textfile.txt*	Writes the output to a text file

For example, to obtain information about user jchellis in a system called EDGETEK, you would use the command gpresult /S EDGETEK /USER jchellis.

Through the use of these techniques, you should be able to track down even the most elusive Group Policy problems. Remember, however, that good troubleshooting skills do not replace the need for adequate planning and maintenance of GPO settings!

Real World Scenario

Troubleshooting Logon Performance Problems

You are a systems administrator for a medium-sized Active Directory environment. Several weeks ago, you were asked to design and implement the organization's Group Policy security settings. You spent several days designing a working strategy that was easy to maintain. In order to best suit the needs of your users, you also decided to create nine different Group Policy objects. You designed each GPO to contain information about a specific set of permissions. You also had to take into account that the established OU structure within your single Active Directory domain environment consists of a fairly deep hierarchy (for example, many OUs are nested to four levels). In order to work with this system, you linked the nine GPOs you created to these OUs at various levels, which resulted in dozens of links. Before you deployed your solution, you performed several tests to ensure that the resulting policies were what you intended. The settings seemed to work well, and they met the business needs.

Recently, however, you have received several complaints from users throughout the environment; they are complaining about slow performance during login. Based on their reports, the system seems to hang on the Applying Security Settings dialog box, during which time they cannot access their systems. To determine the cause, you examine the network and find no performance problems. Furthermore, the issue seems to have arisen just after you implemented the GPO links. You determine that the problem must be due to the large number of GPO links. After consulting several resources for more information, your opinion seems to be validated—the issue is likely caused by having so many GPO links. You also find out that the GPOs themselves must be processed synchronously (that is, one after the other). You know that this will add significantly to the logon time, regardless of network and other issues.

You can solve this problem by reducing the number of GPO links. For example, if users that are contained in OUs that are four levels deep within the OU structure have many different GPOs that must be applied during login, perhaps you can consolidate the GPOs into a few, more complicated ones. Or, you can take the settings that you have in some GPOs and repeat them in others (so fewer would have to be applied). Overall, you might sacrifice some of the ease with which you could administer features, but your users could save significant time during logon attempts.

Although the initial GPO policy you established above met some of your business requirements (for example, maintaining a good level of security), it failed to meet others (for instance, acceptable performance during logon operations). As is always the case, remember that your technical solutions must meet business goals, and performance issues with GPO links are no exception. Be sure to adequately test logon performance before you begin your GPO rollout.

Summary

In this chapter, we examined Active Directory's solution to a common headache for many systems administrators: policy settings. Specifically, we discussed topics that covered Group Policy.

We covered the fundamentals of Group Policy including its fundamental purpose. Group Policy is used to enforce granular permissions for users in an Active Directory environment. Group policies can restrict and modify the actions that are allowed for users and computers within the Active Directory environment.

Also group policies can restrict and modify the actions that are allowed for users and computers within the Active Directory environment. Certain Group Policy settings may apply to users, computers, or both. Computer settings affect all users that access the machines to which the policy applies. User settings affect users, regardless of which machines they log on to.

Group Policy objects (GPOs) can be linked to Active Directory objects. This link determines to which objects the policies apply. GPO links can interact through inheritance and filtering to result in an effective set of policies.

We also learned that administrative templates can be used to simplify the creation of GPOs. We covered the basic default templates that come with Windows Server 2003.

As well, administrators can delegate control over GPOs in order to distribute administrative responsibilities. Delegation is an important concept because it allows for distributed administration.

The final portion of the chapter covered the Resultant Set of Policy (RSoP) tool, which can be used in Logging mode or Planning mode to determine exactly which set of policies apply to users, computers, OUs, domains, and sites.

In the next chapter, we will close out our discussion on Group Policy.

Exam Essentials

Understand the purpose of Group Policy.   Group Policy is used to enforce granular permissions for users in an Active Directory environment.

Understand user and computer settings.   Certain Group Policy settings may apply to users, computers, or both. Computer settings affect all users that access the machines to which the policy applies. User settings affect users, regardless of which machines they log on to.

Know the interactions between Group Policy objects and Active Directory.   GPOs can be linked to Active Directory objects. This link determines to which objects the policies apply.

Understand filtering and inheritance interactions between GPOs.   For ease of administration, Group Policy objects can interact via inheritance and filtering. It is important to understand these interactions when implementing and troubleshooting Group Policy.

Know how Group Policy settings can affect script policies and network settings.   Special sets of Group Policy objects can be used to manage network configuration settings.

Understand how delegation of administration can be used in an Active Directory environment. Delegation is an important concept because it allows for distributed administration.

Know how to use the Resultant Set of Policy (RSoP) tool to troubleshoot and plan Group Policy. Windows Server 2003 introduces the new RSoP tool, which can be run in Logging mode or Planning mode to determine exactly which set of policies apply to users, computers, OUs, domains, and sites.

Review Questions

1. A systems administrator is planning to implement GPOs in a new Windows Server 2003 Active Directory environment. In order to meet the needs of the organization, he decides to implement a hierarchical system of Group Policy settings. At which of the following levels is he able to assign Group Policy settings? Choose all that apply.

   A. Sites

   B. Domains

   C. Organizational units (OUs)

   D. Local system

2. Ann is a systems administrator for a medium-sized Active Directory environment. She has determined that several new applications that will be deployed throughout the organization use Registry-based settings. She would like to do the following:

   - Control these Registry settings using Group Policy.
   - Create a standard set of options for these applications and allow other systems administrators to modify them using the standard Active Directory tools.

   Which of the following options can she use to meet these requirements? (Choose all that apply.)

   A. Implement the Inheritance functionality of GPOs.

   B. Implement delegation of specific objects within Active Directory.

   C. Implement the No Override functionality of GPOs.

   D. Create administrative templates.

   E. Provide administrative templates to the systems administrators that are responsible for creating Group Policy for the applications.

3. Script policies can be set for which of the following events? Choose all that apply.

   A. Logon

   B. Logoff

   C. Startup

   D. Shutdown

4. John is developing a standards document for settings that are allowed by systems administrators in an Active Directory environment. He wants to maintain as much flexibility as possible in the area of Group Policy settings. In which of the following languages can script policies be written? (Choose all that apply.)

   A. Visual Basic Scripting Edition (VBScript)

   B. JScript

   C. Other Windows Script Host (WSH) languages

   D. Batch files

5. The process of assigning permissions to set Group Policy for objects within an OU is known as

    A. Promotion

    B. Inheritance

    C. Delegation

    D. Filtering

6. You are a systems administrator for a medium-sized Active Directory environment. Specifically, you are in charge of administering all objects that are located within the North America OU. The North America OU contains the Corporate OU. You want to do the following:

    ▪ Create a GPO that applies to all users within the North America OU except for those located within the Corporate OU.

    ▪ Be able to easily apply all Group Policy settings to users within the Corporate OU, should the need arise in the future.

    ▪ Accomplish this task with the least amount of administrative effort.

Which two of the following options meets these requirements?

    A. Enable the Inheritance functionality of GPOs for all OUs within the North America OU.

    B. Implement delegation of all objects within the North America OU to one administrator and then remove permissions for the Corporate OU. Have this administrator link the GPO to the North America OU.

    C. Create a GPO link for the new policy at level of the North America OU.

    D. Create special administrative templates for the Corporate OU.

    E. Enable the Block Inheritance option on the Corporate OU.

7. The process by which lower-level Active Directory objects inherit Group Policy settings from higher-level ones is known as

    A. Delegation

    B. Inheritance

    C. Cascading permissions

    D. Overriding

8. To disable GPO settings for a specific security group, which of the following permissions should be applied?

    A. Deny Write

    B. Allow Write

    C. Enable Apply Group Policy

    D. Disable Apply Group Policy

9. Trent is a systems administrator in a medium-sized Active Directory environment. He is responsible for creating and maintaining Group Policy settings. For a specific group of settings, he has the following requirements:

   ▪ The settings in the Basic Users GPO should remain defined.

   ▪ The settings in the Basic Users GPO should not apply to any users within the Active Directory environment.

   ▪ The amount of administrative effort to apply the Basic Users settings to an OU in the future should be minimal.

   Which of the following options can Trent use to meet these requirements?

   A. Enable the No Override option at the domain level.

   B. Enable the Block Policy Inheritance option at the domain level.

   C. Remove the link to the Basic Users GPO from all Active Directory objects.

   D. Delete the Basic Users GPO.

   E. Rename the Basic Users GPO to break its link with any existing Active Directory objects.

10. A systems administrator wants to ensure that certain GPOs applied at the domain level are not overridden at lower levels. Which option can they use to do this?

    A. The No Override option

    B. The Block Policy Inheritance option

    C. The Disable option

    D. The Deny permission

11. GPOs assigned at which of the following level(s) will override GPO settings at the domain level?

    A. OU

    B. Site

    C. Domain

    D. Both OU and site

12. A systems administrator wants to ensure that only the GPOs set at the OU level affect the Group Policy settings for objects within the OU. Which option can they use to do this (assuming that all other GPO settings are the defaults)?

    A. The No Override option

    B. The Block Policy Inheritance option

    C. The Disable option

    D. The Deny permission

13. In order to be accessible to other domain controllers, logon/logoff and startup/shutdown scripts should be placed in which of the following shares?

    A. Winnt

    B. System

    C. C$

    D. SYSVOL

14. Matt, a systems administrator, has recently created a new Active Directory domain. The domain forms a tree with the three other domains in the environment, and all of the domains are configured in a single site. He is planning to implement Group Policy, and has the following requirements:

- Several GPOs must be created to accommodate five different levels of user settings.

- The GPOs may be assigned at any level within the Active Directory environment.

- All users within the Engineering domain must receive specific GPO assignments.

At which of the following levels can Matt create a single GPO link in order for it to affect all four domains in the environment?

A. Sites

B. OUs

C. Domains

D. Local computer

E. Domain controllers

15. You want to link a GPO to the Group Policy Test OU. You right-click the OU and the following menu appears. In order to accomplish this task, what would you click next?

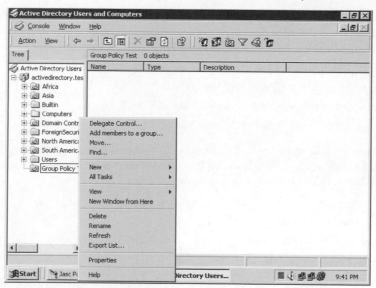

A. Properties

B. Delegate Control

C. All Tasks

D. Add Members To A Group

16. You are the systems administrator for 123 Corp. You have been tasked with helping your mobile users find a way to access stored company files. You need to set up a solution that allows your mobile users the flexibility they need to use data stored on local servers within your organizations network. Which of the following is the best way to do this?

    A. Offline folders

    B. Folder redirection

    C. SYSVOL replication

    D. Folder replication

17. As the administrator responsible for your company's Active Directory deployment, you are asked to provide a solution for Group Policy management. You need to use a tool that allows you to manage Group Policy forest-wide. Which tool allows you to manage Group Policy across the enterprise, is downloadable from Microsoft, and adds features such as services for backing up Group Policy?

    A. Active Directory Sites And Services tool

    B. Active Directory Users And Computers tool

    C. Group Policy Management Console (GPMC)

    D. The Resultant Set of Policy (RSoP) tool

18. Your CIO asks you, the lead designer for your company, to use a tool that will help you plan for the use of Group Policy in your organization. From the following list of available tools, which tool will allow you to help design Group Policy for your organization?

    A. Resultant Set of Policy (RSoP) Reservation Mode

    B. Resultant Set of Policy (RSoP) Preparing Mode

    C. Resultant Set of Policy (RSoP) Return Mode

    D. Resultant Set of Policy (RSoP) Planning Mode

19. You are attempting to add a layer of security in your current domain of about 5 Windows Server 2003 systems and 40 Windows XP Professional workstations. You are asked about using certificates. What system is this technology part of?

    A. TKI—temporary key infrastructure

    B. PKI—public key infrastructure

    C. DCS—digital certificate system

    D. OTP—one time passwords

20. You are the lead network administrator for your company. You have been tasked with the responsibility of creating GPOs and linking specific settings to targeted computers. You'll be using the GPOs to store the settings. You need to link specific settings to specific OUs and you may need to link them elsewhere. What are the other two levels in which you can link settings within Active Directory? (Choose all that apply.)

    A. Sites

    B. Groups

    C. Computers

    D. Domains

Answers to Review Questions

1. Answers: A, B, C, D. GPOs can be set at all of the levels listed. You cannot set GPOs on security principals such as users or groups.

2. Answers: D, E. Administrative templates are used to specify the options available for setting Group Policy. By creating new administrative templates, Ann can specify which options are available for the new applications. She can then distribute these templates to other systems administrators in the environment.

3. Answers: A, B, C, D. Script policies can be set for any of the events listed.

4. Answers: A, B, C, D. The Windows Script Host (WSH) can be used with any of the above languages. Additionally, standard batch files can also be used.

5. C. The Delegation of Control Wizard can be used to allow other systems administrators permission to add GPO links to an Active Directory object.

6. Answers: C, E. The easiest way to accomplish this task is to create GPO links at the level of the parent OU (North America) and block inheritance at the level of the child OU (Corporate).

7. B. Inheritance is the process by which lower-level Active Directory objects inherit GPO settings from higher-level ones. You should always be aware of how inheritance will apply to your Active Directory hierarchy when configuring GPOs.

8. D. To disable the application of Group Policy on a security group, the Apply Group Policy option should be disabled. This is particularly useful when you don't want GPO settings to apply to a specific group, even though that group may be in an OU that includes the GPO settings.

9. C. Systems administrators can disable a GPO without removing its link to Active Directory objects. This prevents the GPO from having any effects on Group Policy but leaves the GPO definition intact so that it can be enabled at a later date.

10. A. The No Override option ensures that the Group Policy settings cannot be changed by the settings of lower-level Active Directory objects. This is particularly useful when you want settings to apply to all users at lower levels within the hierarchy, even if their OU's GPO settings are different.

11. A. GPOs at the OU level take precedence over GPOs at the domain level. GPOs at the domain level, in turn, take precedence over GPOs at the site level.

12. B. The Block Policy Inheritance option prevents group policies of higher-level Active Directory objects from applying to lower-level objects as long as the No Override option is not set.

13. D. By default, the contents of the SYSVOL share are made available to all domain controllers. Therefore, scripts should be placed in these directories.

14. A. GPO links at the site level affect all of the domains that are part of a site. Therefore, Matt can create a single GPO link at the Site level.

15. A. In order to link a GPO to an OU, you would use the Group Policy tab of the OU Properties dialog box. From there, you can create new GPOs, add GPOs to the OU, and configure each GPO.

16. A. Folder redirection and offline folders are different features. The way that Windows Server 2003 folder redirection works is that the system uses a pointer that moves the folders you want to a location you specify. When data is needed, it's available, but once the user is mobile (not local), the data is no longer not accessible. A way to fix this is to use the Offline Folders feature, which allows you to keep folders with information synchronized—thus you'd have a local copy on your local system that you'd take with you while you were on the move and you'd be able to synchronize it with a copy on the server when you returned. Copies of the data stay the same, which is a perfect feature for mobile users, whereas folder redirection provides no benefit for the mobile user.

17. C. The Group Policy Management Console (GPMC) is a Microsoft-based downloadable tool that allows you full control and flexibility when you're deploying and managing Group Policy; it also provides add-on features and backup services.

18. D. Resultant Set of Policy (RSoP) Planning Mode is the mode used when designing Group Policy; this tool will help you design and plan your Group Policy deployment before you execute it.

19. B. PKI stands for public key infrastructure. Certificates are part of PKI, which is used to add a layer of security into your client/server infrastructure. The rest of the answers are incorrect distracters.

20. Answers: A, D. Group Policy settings are kept in GPOs. GPOs can be linked to sites, domains, and OUs.

Chapter

9

Software Deployment through Group Policy

MICROSOFT EXAM OBJECTIVES COVERED IN THIS CHAPTER:

✓ **Configure the user environment by using Group Policy.**

- Distribute software by using Group Policy.

✓ **Deploy a computer environment by using Group Policy.**

- Distribute software by using Group Policy.

✓ **Maintain installed software by using Group Policy.**

- Distribute updates to software distributed by Group Policy.

- Configure automatic updates for network clients by using Group Policy.

Throughout this book, you have been learning about the importance of implementing and administering a network environment based on the Windows Server 2003 operating system. Although the proper configuration of Active Directory and client/server operating systems is very important, the real power of the computer for end users is in the applications they use. From simple word processors to spreadsheets and client/server applications, applications are what all types of users within a typical business need to help them complete their jobs.

From an end user's viewpoint, it's very easy to take software for granted. For example, many have come to expect computers to run messaging applications, productivity applications, and games. However, from the view of a systems administrator and the help desk staff, deploying and maintaining software can be a troublesome and time-consuming job. Regardless of how much time is spent installing, updating, reinstalling, and removing applications based on users' needs, there seems to be no end to the process. New applications come out that need to be tested and quite possibly used, and you also need to update, upgrade, and service the current software applications you use.

The real reason for deploying and managing networks in the first place is to make the applications that they support available. Why would you deploy a client/server-based system if you weren't serving anything? End users are often much more interested in being able to do their jobs using the tools they require than in worrying about network infrastructure and directory services. In the past, software deployment and management have been troublesome and time-consuming tasks, mostly due to poorly written code that hampered the system on which it was installed, software that made the base OS unstable, or the lack of a way to easily distribute it.

Fortunately, Windows Server 2003 and Active Directory provide many improvements to the process of deploying and managing software. Through the use of Group Policy objects (GPOs) and the Microsoft Installer (MSI), software deployment options can be easily configured, deployed, and managed. The applications themselves can be made available to any users who are part of the Active Directory environment. Furthermore, systems administrators can automatically assign applications to users and computers and allow programs to be installed automatically when they are needed.

In this chapter, we'll look at how Windows Server 2003 and Active Directory can be used to deploy and manage software throughout the network, and you'll see how to troubleshoot problems should they arise.

Overview of Software Deployment

It's difficult enough to manage applications on a standalone computer. It seems that the process of installing, configuring, and uninstalling applications is never finished. Add in the hassle of computer reboots and reinstalling corrupted applications, and the reduction in productivity can be very real.

When they manage software in network environments, software administrators have even more concerns. First and foremost, they must determine which applications specific users require. Then, IT departments must purchase the appropriate licenses for the software and acquire any necessary media. Next, they need to actually install the applications on users' machines. This process generally involves help desk staff visiting computers or it requires end users to install the software themselves. Both processes entail several potential problems, including installation inconsistency and lost productivity from downtime experienced when applications were installed. As if this wasn't enough, the system administrators still need to manage software updates and remove unused software.

One of the key design goals for Active Directory was to reduce some of the headaches involved in managing software and configurations in a networked environment. To that end, Windows Server 2003 offers several features that can make the task of deploying software easier and less error prone. Before you dive into the technical details, though, you need to examine the issues related to software deployment.

The Software Management Life Cycle

Although it may seem that the use of a new application requires only the installation of the necessary software, the overall process of managing applications involves many more steps. When managing software applications, there are three main phases to the life cycle of applications:

Deploying software   The first step in using applications is to install them on the appropriate client computers. Generally, some applications are deployed during the initial configuration of a PC, and others are deployed when they are requested. In the latter case, this often used to mean that systems administrators and help desk staff would have to visit client computers and manually walk through the installation process. With Windows Server 2003 and Active Directory, the entire process can be automated.

It is very important to understand that the ability to easily deploy software does not necessarily mean that you have the right to do so. Before you install software on client computers, you must make sure that you have the appropriate licenses for the software. Furthermore, it's very important to take the time to track application installations. As many systems administrators have discovered, it's much more difficult to inventory software installations after they've been performed. Another issue you may encounter is lacking available resources (such as not meeting the minimum hardware requirements) and facing problems such as limited hard disk space or memory that may not be able to handle the applications you want to load and use. You may also find that your user account does not have the permission to install software. It's important to consider not only how you will install software, but if you can.

Maintaining software Once an application is installed and in use on client computers, you need to ensure that the software is maintained. You must apply changes due to bug fixes, enhancements, and other types of updates in order to ensure that programs are kept up to date. This is normally done with service packs, hot fixes, and updates. As with the initial software deployment, software maintenance can be a tedious process. Some programs require that older versions be uninstalled before updates are added. Others allow for automatically upgrading over existing installations. Managing and deploying software updates can consume a significant amount of the IT staff's time.

Using Windows Update

Make sure you learn about Windows Update, a service that allows you to connect to Microsoft's website and download what your system may need to bring it up to compliance. This tool is very helpful if you are running a standalone system, but if you want to deploy software across your enterprise, the best way to accomplish this is to first test the updates you are downloading and make sure you can use them and that they are not buggy and then use a tool such as the Windows Server Update Service (WSUS), formally called the Software Update Services (SUS).

You can check for updates at Microsoft's website (http://update.microsoft.com). You can also visit : www.microsoft.com/windowsserversystem/updateservices/downloads/WSUS.mspx and get WSUS.

Removing software At the end of the life cycle for many software products is the actual removal of unused programs. Removing software is necessary when applications become outdated or when users no longer require their functionality. One of the traditional problems with uninstalling applications is that many of the installed files may not be removed. Furthermore, the removal of shared components can sometimes cause other programs to stop functioning properly. Also, users often forget to uninstall applications that they no longer need, and these programs continue to occupy disk space and consume valuable system resources.

Each of these three phases of the software maintenance life cycle is managed by the MSI. Now that you have an overview of the process, let's move on to look at the actual steps involved in deploying software using Group Policy.

 The Microsoft Windows Installer (sometimes referred to as Microsoft Installer or Windows Installer) is an application installation and configuration service. An instruction file (Microsoft Installer package) contains information about what needs to be done to install a product. It's common to confuse the two.

The Windows Installer

If you've installed newer application programs (such as Microsoft Office XP), you probably noticed the updated setup and installation routines. Applications that comply with the updated standard use the *Windows Installer* specification and MSI software packages for deployment. Each package contains information about various setup options and the files required for installation. Although the benefits may not seem dramatic on the surface, there's a lot of new functionality under the hood.

The Windows Installer was created to solve many of the problems associated with traditional application development. It has several components, including the Installer service (which runs on Windows 2000, XP, and Server 2003 computers), the Installer program (`msiexec.exe`) that is responsible for executing the instructions in a *Windows Installer package*, and the specifications for third-party developers to use to create their own packages. Within each installation package file is a relational structure (similar to the structure of tables in databases) that records information about the programs contained within the package.

In order to appreciate the true value of the Windows Installer, you'll need to look at some of the problems with traditional software deployment mechanisms, and then at how the Windows Installer addresses many of these.

Application Installation Issues

Before the Windows Installer, applications were installed using a setup program that managed the various operations required for a program to operate. These operations included copying files, changing Registry settings, and managing any other operating system changes that might be required (such as starting or stopping services). However, this method included several problems:

- The setup process was not robust, and aborting the operation often left many unnecessary files in the file system.

- The process included uninstalling an application (this also often left many unnecessary files in the file system) and remnants in the Windows Registry and operating system folders. Over time, these remnants would result in reduced overall system performance and wasted disk space.

- There was no standard method for applying upgrades to applications, and installing a new version often required users to uninstall the old application, reboot, and then install the new program.

- Conflicts between different versions of dynamic link libraries (DLLs)—shared program code used across different applications—could cause the installation or removal of one application to break the functionality of another.

Benefits of the Windows Installer

Because of the many problems associated with traditional software installation, Microsoft created the Windows Installer. This system provides for better manageability of the software installation process and, as we'll see later in this chapter, allows systems administrators more control over the deployment process. Specifically, benefits of the Windows Installer include the following:

Improved software removal   The process of removing software is an important one since remnants left behind during the uninstall process can eventually clutter up the Registry and file system. During the installation process, the Windows Installer keeps track of all of the changes made by a setup package. When it comes time to remove an application, all of these changes can then be rolled back.

More robust installation routines   If a typical setup program is aborted during the software installation process, the results are unpredictable. If the actual installation hasn't yet begun, then the Installer generally removes any temporary files that may have been created. If, however, the file copy routine starts before the system encounters an error, it is likely that the files will not be automatically removed from the operating system. In contrast, the Windows Installer allows you to roll back any changes when the application setup process is aborted.

Ability to use elevated privileges   Installing applications usually requires the user to have Administrator permissions on the local computer because file system and Registry changes are required. When installing software for network users, systems administrators thus have two options. The first is to log off of the computer before installing the software, then log back on as a user who has Administrator permissions on the local computer. This method is tedious and time-consuming. The second is to temporarily give users Administrator permissions on their own machines. This method could cause security problems and requires the attention of a systems administrator.

Through the use of the Installer service, the Windows Installer is able to use temporarily elevated privileges to install applications. This allows users, regardless of their security settings, to execute the installation of authorized applications. The end result is that this saves time and preserves security.

Support for repairing corrupted applications   Regardless of how well a network environment is managed, critical files are sometimes lost or corrupted. Such problems can prevent applications from running properly and cause crashes. Windows Installer packages provide you with the ability to verify the installation of an application and, if necessary, replace any missing or corrupted files. This support saves time and lessens the end-user headaches associated with removing and reinstalling an entire application to replace just a few files.

Prevention of file conflicts   Generally, different versions of the same files should be compatible with each other. In the real world, however, this isn't always the case. A classic problem in the Windows world is the case of one program replacing DLLs that are used by several other programs. Windows Installer accurately tracks which files are used by certain programs and ensures that any shared files are not improperly deleted or overwritten.

Automated installations   A typical application setup process requires end users or systems administrators to respond to several prompts. For example, a user may be able to choose the program group in which icons will be created and the file system location to which the program will be installed. Additionally, they may be required to choose which options are installed. Although this type of flexibility is useful, it can be tedious when rolling out multiple applications. By using features of the Windows Installer, however, users are able to specify setup options before the process begins. This allows systems administrators to ensure consistency in installations and saves time for users.

Advertising and on-demand installations   One of the most powerful features of the Windows Installer is its ability to perform on-demand software installations. Prior to Windows Installer, application installation options were quite basic—either a program was installed or it was not. When setting up a computer, systems administrators would be required to guess which applications the user might need and install all of them.

The Windows Installer supports a function known as advertising. Advertising makes applications appear to be available via the Start menu. However, the programs themselves may not actually be installed on the system. When a user attempts to access an advertised application, the Windows Installer automatically downloads the necessary files from a server and installs the program. The end result is that applications are installed only when needed, and the process requires no intervention from the end user. We'll cover the details of this process later in this chapter.

To anyone who has managed many software applications in a network environment, all of these features of the Windows Installer are likely welcome ones. They also make life easier for end users and application developers who can focus on the "real work" their jobs demand.

Windows Installer File Types

When performing software deployment with the Windows Installer in Windows Server 2003, you may encounter several different file types. These are as follows:

Microsoft Windows Installer (MSI) packages   In order to take full advantage of Windows Installer functionality, applications must include Microsoft Windows Installer packages. These packages are normally created by third-party application vendors and software developers and include the information required to install and configure the application and any supporting files.

Microsoft Transformation (MST) files   *Microsoft Transformation (MST) files* are useful when customizing the details of how applications are installed. When a systems administrator chooses to assign or publish an application, they may want to specify additional options for the package. If, for instance, a systems administrator wants to allow users to install only the Microsoft Word and Microsoft PowerPoint components of Office XP, they could specify these options within a transformation file. Then, when users install the application, they will be provided with only the options related to these components.

Microsoft patches (MSP)   In order to maintain software, *patches* are often required. Patches may make Registry and/or file system changes. Patch files are used for minor system changes and are subject to certain limitations. Specifically, a patch file cannot remove any installed program components and cannot delete or modify any shortcuts created by the user.

Initialization files   In order to provide support for publishing non–Windows Installer applications, *initialization files* can be used. These files provide links to a standard executable file that is used to install an application. An example might be \\server1\software\program1\

`setup.exe`. These files can then be published and advertised, and users can access the *Add or Remove Programs* icon to install them over the network.

Application assignment scripts (AAS)   *Application assignment scripts* store information regarding assigning programs and any settings that the systems administrator makes. These files are created when Group Policy is used to create software package assignments for users and computers.

Each of these types of files provides functionality that allows the system administrator to customize software deployment. Windows Installer packages have special properties that can be viewed by right-clicking the file in Windows Explorer and choosing Properties (see Figure 9.1).

FIGURE 9.1   Viewing the properties of an MSI package file

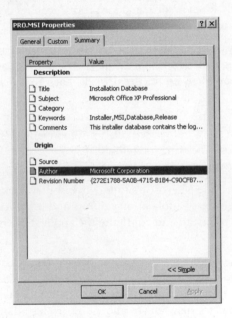

Deploying Applications

The functionality provided by Windows Installer offers many advantages to end users who install their own software. That, however, is just the beginning in a networked environment. As you'll see later in this chapter, the various features of Windows Installer and compatible packages allow systems administrators to centrally determine applications that users will be able to install.

There are two main methods of making programs available to end users using Active Directory: *assigning* and *publishing*. Both publishing and assigning applications greatly ease the process of deploying and managing applications in a network environment.

In the following sections, you'll look at how the processes of assigning and publishing applications can make life easier for IT staff and users alike. The various settings for assigned and published applications are managed through the use of GPOs.

Assigning Applications

Software applications can be assigned to users and computers. Assigning a software package makes the program available for automatic installation. The applications advertise their availability to the affected users or computers by placing icons within the Programs folder of the Start menu.

When applications are assigned to a user, programs will be advertised to the user, regardless of which computer they are using. That is, icons for the advertised program will appear within the Start menu, regardless of whether the program is installed on that computer or not. If the user clicks an icon for a program that has not yet been installed on the local computer, the application will automatically be accessed from a server and will be installed on the computer.

When an application is assigned to a computer, the program is made available to any users of the computer. For example, all users who log on to a computer that has been assigned Microsoft Office XP will have access to the components of the application. If the user did not previously install Microsoft Office, they will be prompted for any required setup information when the program first runs.

Generally, applications that are required by the vast majority of users should be assigned to computers. This reduces the amount of network bandwidth required to install applications on demand and improves the end user experience by preventing the delay involved when installing an application the first time it is accessed. Any applications that may be used by only a few users (or those with specific job tasks) should be assigned to users.

Publishing Applications

When applications are published, they are advertised, but no icons are automatically created. Instead, the applications are made available for installation using the Add Or Remove Programs icon in the Control Panel. Software can be published only to users (not computers). The list of available applications is stored within Active Directory, and client computers can query this list when they need to install programs. For ease of organization, applications can be grouped into categories.

NOTE   One of the most important things to remember about implementing and deploying software with Active Directory and Group Policy is that you can publish the installation to a User account but not to a Computer account. Because the user needs to authorize the installation, you cannot use Computer accounts.

Implementing Software Deployment

So far, you have become familiar with the issues related to software deployment and management from a theoretical level. Now it's time to drill down into the actual steps required to deploy software using the features of Active Directory. In the following sections, you will walk through the steps required to create an application distribution share point, to publish and assign applications, to update previously installed applications, to verify the installation of applications, and to update Windows operating systems.

Preparing for Software Deployment

Before you can install applications on client computers, you must make sure that the necessary files are available to end users. In many network environments, systems administrators create shares on file servers that include the installation files for many applications. Based on security permissions, either end users or systems administrators can then connect to these shares from a client computer and install the needed software. The efficient organization of these shares can save the help desk from having to carry around a library of CD-ROMs and can allow you to install applications easily on many computers at once.

 One of the problems in network environments is that users frequently install applications whether or not they really require them. They may stumble upon applications that are stored on common file servers and install them out of curiosity. These actions can often decrease productivity and may violate software licensing agreements. You can help avoid this by placing all of your application installation files in hidden shares (for example, "software$").

Exercise 9.1 walks you through the process of creating a software distribution share point. In this exercise, you will prepare for software deployment by creating a directory share and placing certain types of files in this directory. In order to complete the steps in this exercise, you must have access to the Microsoft Office XP installation files (via CD-ROM or through a network share) and have 600MB of free disk space.

EXERCISE 9.1

Creating a Software Deployment Share

1. Using Windows Explorer, create a folder called **Software** that you can use with application sharing. Be sure that the volume on which you create this folder has at least 600MB of available disk space.

2. Within the Software folder, create a folder called **Office XP**.

3.   Copy all of the installation files for Microsoft Office XP from the CD-ROM or network share containing the files to the Office XP folder that you created in step 2.

4.   Right-click the Software folder (created in step 1), and select Sharing And Security. In the folder properties dialog box, choose Share This Folder, and type **Software** in the Share Name text box and **Software Distribution Share Point** in the Description text box. Leave all other options as the default, and click OK to create the share.

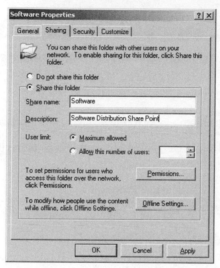

Once you have created an application distribution share, it's time to actually publish and assign the applications. This topic is covered next.

Publishing and Assigning Applications

As we mentioned earlier in this chapter, software packages can be made available to users through the use of publishing and assigning. Both of these operations allow systems administrators to leverage the power of Active Directory and, specifically, GPOs to determine which applications are available to users. Additionally, the organization provided by organizational units (OUs) can help group users based on their job functions and software requirements.

The general process involves creating a GPO that includes software deployment settings for users and computers and then linking this GPO to Active Directory objects.

If you're unfamiliar with creating and linking GPOs, see Chapter 8, "Planning, Implementing, and Managing Group Policy."

Exercise 9.2 walks you through the steps you need to take to publish and assign applications. In this exercise, you will create and assign applications to specific Active Directory objects using Group Policy objects. In order to complete the steps in this exercise, you must have first completed Exercise 9.1.

EXERCISE 9.2

Publishing and Assigning Applications Using Group Policy

1. Open the Active Directory Users And Computers tool from the Administrative Tools program group.

2. Expand the domain, and create a new top-level OU called **Software**.

3. Within the Software OU, create a user named **Jane User** with a login name of **juser** (choose the defaults for all other options).

4. Right-click the Software OU and select Properties.

5. On the Software Properties dialog box, select the Group Policy tab, and click New.

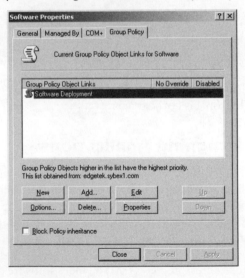

6. For the name of the new GPO, type **Software Deployment**.

EXERCISE 9.2 *(continued)*

7. To edit the Software Deployment GPO, click Edit. Expand the Computer Configuration ➢ Software Settings object.

8. Right-click the Software Installation item, and select New ➢ Package.

9. Navigate to the Software share that you created in Exercise 9.1.

10. Within the Software share, double-click the Office XP folder and select the appropriate MSI file depending on the version of Office XP that you have. Office XP Professional is being used in this example, so you'll see that the PRO.MSI file is chosen. Click Open.

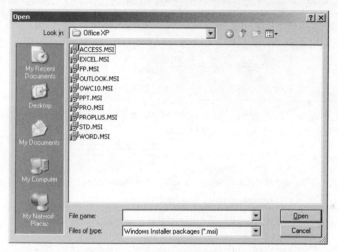

11. In the Deploy Software dialog box, choose Advanced. Note that the Published option is unavailable because applications cannot be published to computers. Click OK to return to the Deploy Software dialog box.

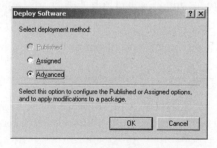

EXERCISE 9.2 *(continued)*

12. To examine the deployment options of this package, click the Deployment tab. Accept the default settings by clicking OK.

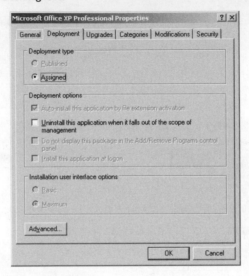

13. Within the Group Policy Object Editor, expand the User Configuration ➢ Software Settings object.

14. Right-click the Software Installation item, and select New ➢ Package.

15. Navigate to the Software share that you created in Exercise 9.1.

16. Within the Software share, double-click the Office XP folder, and select the appropriate MSI file. Click Open.

17. For the Software Deployment option, select Published in the Deploy Software dialog box and click OK.

18. Close the Group Policy Object Editor, and then click Close to close the Properties of the Software OU.

The overall process involved with deploying software using Active Directory is quite simple. However, you shouldn't let the intuitive graphical interface fool you—there's a lot of power under the hood of these software deployment features! Once you've properly assigned and published applications, it's time to see the effects of your work.

Applying Software Updates

The steps described in the previous section work only when you are installing a brand-new application. However, software companies often release updates that need to be installed on top of existing applications. These updates could consist of bug fixes or other changes that are required to keep the software up to date. You can apply software updates in Active Directory by using the Upgrades tab of the software package Properties dialog box found in the Group Policy Object Editor.

In Exercise 9.3, you will apply a software update to an existing application. You should add the upgrade package to the GPO in the same way that you added the original application in steps 8 through 12 of Exercise 9.2. You should also have completed Exercise 9.2 before attempting this exercise.

EXERCISE 9.3

Applying Software Updates

1. Open the Active Directory Users And Computers tool from the Administrative Tools program group.

2. Right-click the Software OU, and select Properties.

3. To edit the Software Deployment GPO, click Edit. Expand the Computer Configuration ➢ Software Settings object.

4. Right-click the upgrade package (not the original package) and select Properties from the context menu to bring up the Properties dialog box.

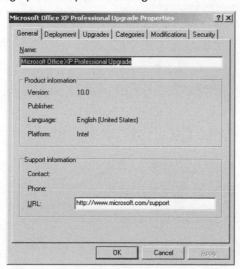

EXERCISE 9.3 *(continued)*

5. Select the Upgrades tab and click the Add button.

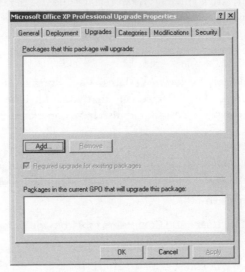

6. Click the Current Group Policy Object radio button in the Add Upgrade Package dialog box. Select the package to which you want to apply the upgrade. Consult your application's documentation to see if you should choose the Uninstall The Existing Package radio button or the Package Can Upgrade Over The Existing Package radio button.

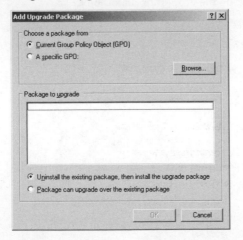

7. Click OK to close the Add Upgrade Package dialog box.

8. Click OK to save the changes and close the Package Properties dialog box.

You should understand that not all upgrades make sense in all situations. For instance, if MegaSoft 6 files are incompatible with the MegaSoft 10 application, then your MegaSoft 6 users might not want you to perform the upgrade without taking additional steps to ensure that they can continue to use their files. In addition, users might have some choice about what version they use when it doesn't affect the support of the network.

Regardless of the underlying reason for allowing this flexibility, you should be aware that there are two basic types of upgrades that are available for administrators to provide to the users:

Mandatory upgrade   Forces everyone who currently has an existing version of the program to upgrade according to the GPO. Users who have never installed the program for whatever reason will be able to install only the new upgraded version.

Nonmandatory upgrade   Allows users to choose whether they would like to upgrade. This upgrade type also allows users who do not have their application installed to choose which version they would like to use.

Verifying Software Installation

In order to ensure that the software installation settings you make in a GPO have taken place, you can log in to the domain from a Windows XP Professional computer that is within the OU to which the software settings apply. When you log in, you will notice two changes. First, the application is installed on the computer (if it was not installed already). In order to access the application, all a user needs to do is click one of the icons within the Program group of the Start menu. Note also that applications are available to any of the users who log on to this machine. Also, the settings apply to any computers that are contained within the OU and to any users who log on to these computers.

If you publish an application to users, the change may not be as evident, but it is equally useful. When you log on to a Windows XP Professional computer that is a member of the domain and use a user account from the OU where you published the application, you will be able to automatically install any of the published applications. You can do this by accessing the Add Or Remove Programs icon in the Control Panel. By clicking Add New Programs, you access a display of the applications available for installation.

By clicking the Add button in the Add New Programs section of the Add Or Remove Programs dialog box, you will automatically begin the installation of the published application.

Configuring Automatic Updates in Group Policy

So far you've seen the advantages of deploying application software in Group Policy. Group Policy also provides a way to install operating system updates across the network for Windows 2000, XP, and Server 2003 machines using Windows Update in conjunction with SUS and/or WSUS). WSUS is the newer version of SUS and is used on a Windows Server 2003 system to update systems. As you might remember from earlier, WSUS and SUS are patch management tools that help you deploy updates to your systems in a controlled manner.

Windows Update is available through the Microsoft website and is used to provide the most current files for the Windows operating systems. Examples of updates include security fixes, critical updates, updated help files, and updated drivers. You can access Windows Updates by clicking the Windows Updates icon in the system tray.

 Learn more about WSUS at www.microsoft.com/windowsserversystem/ updateservices/default.mspx.

SUS is used to leverage the features of Windows Update within a corporate environment by downloading Windows updates to a corporate server, which in turn provides the updates to the internal corporate clients. This allows administrators to test and have full control over what updates are deployed within the corporate environment.

Within an enterprise network that is using Active Directory, you would typically see automatic updates configured through Group Policy. Group policies are used to manage configuration and security settings via Active Directory. Group Policy is also used to specify what server a client will use for automatic updates.

If the SUS client is a part of an enterprise network that is using Active Directory, you would configure the client via Group Policy.

In Exercise 9.4, you learn how to configure Group Policy on a Windows Server 2003 domain controller.

EXERCISE 9.4

Configuring Software Update Services in Group Policy

1. Open Active Directory Users And Computers from the Administrative Tools program group.

2. Right-click the domain and select Properties.

3. Click the Group Policy tab on the domain Properties dialog box and select the Default Domain Policy. Click the Edit button.

4. Expand Default Domain Policy, Computer Configuration, Administrative Templates, Windows Components, Windows Update to access the Windows Update settings.

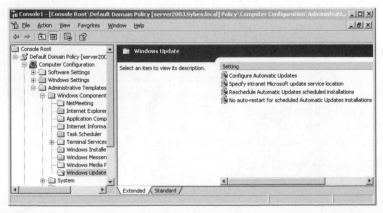

5. Click the Configure Automatic Updates option.

6. The Configure Automatic Updates Properties dialog box appears. On the Setting tab, you can configure whether automatic updates are configured, enabled, or disabled. If automatic updates are enabled, you can select Notify For Download And Notify For Install, Auto Download And Notify For Install, or Auto Download And Schedule The Install. You can also specify the schedule that will be applied for the install day and the install time.

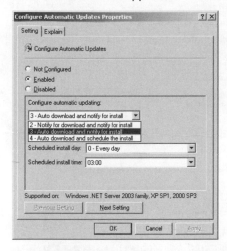

7. To configure which server will provide automatic updates, click the Next Setting button in the Configure Automatic Updates Properties dialog box. This brings up the Specify Intranet Microsoft Update Service Location Properties dialog box. You can configure the status of the intranet Microsoft update service location as Not Configured, Enabled, or Disabled; you can also configure the HTTP name of the server that will provide intranet service updates and the HTTP name of the server that will act as the intranet SUS statistics server.

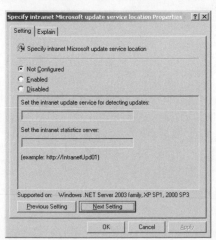

EXERCISE 9.4 *(continued)*

8. To configure rescheduling of automatic updates, click the Next Setting button in the Specify Intranet Microsoft Update Service Location Properties dialog box. This brings up the Reschedule Automatic Updates Scheduled Installations Properties dialog box. You can enable and schedule the amount of time that automatic updates waits after system startup before it attempts to proceed with a scheduled installation that was previously missed.

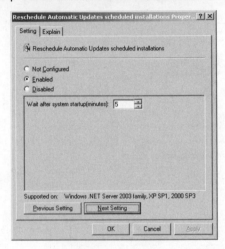

9. To configure auto-restart for scheduled automatic updates installations, click the Next Setting button in the Reschedule Automatic Updates Scheduled Installations Properties dialog box. This brings up the No Auto-Restart For Scheduled Automatic Updates Installations dialog box. You use this option if the computer needs to restart after an update. You can choose to wait until the next time the computer is restarted or to restart the computer automatically as a part of the update.

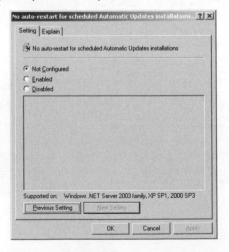

10. When you are done making setting changes, click the OK button.

You should be familiar with two security templates: Wuau.adm (for Windows 2000 Server), which is available through the Software Update Services installation; and System.adm (for Windows Server 2003), which automatically applies the group policy settings that are used by SUS.

Configuring Software Deployment Settings

In addition to the basic operations of assigning and publishing applications, you can use several other options to specify the details of how software is deployed. You can access these options from within a GPO by right-clicking the Software Installation item (located within Software Settings in User Configuration or Computer Configuration).

In the following sections, you will examine the various options that are available and their effects on the software installation process.

The Software Installation Properties Dialog Box

The most important software deployment settings are contained in the Software Installation Properties dialog box, which you can access by right-clicking the Software Installation item and selecting Properties from the pop-up menu. The following sections describe the features contained on the various tabs of the dialog box.

Managing Package Defaults

On the General tab of the Software Installation Properties dialog box, you'll be able to specify some defaults for any packages that you create within this GPO. Figure 9.2 shows the General options for managing software installation settings.

The various options available include the following:

Default Package Location This setting specifies the default file system or network location for software installation packages. This is useful if you are already using a specific share on a file server for hosting the necessary installation files.

New Packages options These settings specify the default type of package assignment that will be used when you add a new package to either the user or computer settings. If you'll be assigning or publishing multiple packages, you may find it useful to set a default here. Selecting the Advanced option enables Group Policy to display the package Properties dialog box each time a new package is added.

FIGURE 9.2 General settings for software settings

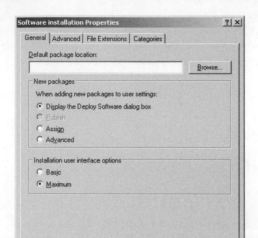

Installation User Interface Options When they are installing an application, systems administrators may or may not want end users to see all of the advanced installation options. If Basic is chosen, the user will only be able to configure the minimal settings (such as the installation location). If Maximum is chosen, all of the available installation options will be displayed. The specific installation options available will depend on the package itself.

The Advanced Tab

The Advanced tab includes several options for configuring advanced software installation properties. The only option you need to be concerned with is the following:

Uninstall The Applications When They Fall Out Of The Scope Of Management So far, you have seen how applications can be assigned and published to users or computers. But what happens when effective GPOs change? For example, suppose that User A is currently located within the Sales OU. A GPO that assigns the Microsoft Office XP suite of applications is linked to the Sales OU. Now, I decide to move User A to the Engineering OU, which has no software deployment settings. Should the application be uninstalled, or should it remain?

If the Uninstall The Applications When They Fall Out Of The Scope Of Management option is checked, applications will be removed if they are not specifically assigned or published within GPOs. In our earlier example, this means that Office XP would be uninstalled for User A. If, however, this box is left unchecked, the application would remain installed.

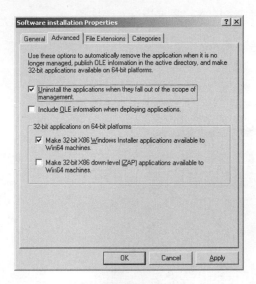

Managing File Extension Mappings

One of the potential problems associated with using many different file types is that it's difficult to keep track of which applications work with which files. For example, if you received a file with the extension .abc, you would have no idea which application you would need to view it. And Windows would not be of much help, either.

Fortunately, through software deployment settings, systems administrators can specify mappings for specific *file extensions*. For example, you could specify that whenever users attempt to access a file with the extension .vsd, the operating system should attempt to open the file using the Visio diagramming software. If Visio is not installed on the user's machine, the computer could automatically download and install it (assuming that the application has been properly advertised).

This method allows users to have applications automatically installed when they are needed. The following is an example of the sequence of events that might occur:

1. A user receives an email message that contains an Adobe Acrobat file attachment.

2. The computer realizes that Adobe Acrobat, the appropriate viewing application for this type of file, is not installed. However, it also realizes that a file extension mapping is available within the Active Directory software deployment settings.

3. The client computer automatically requests the Adobe Acrobat software package from the server and uses the Microsoft Windows Installer to automatically install the application.

4. The computer opens the attachment for the user.

Notice that all of these steps were carried out without any further interaction with the user.

You can manage file extension mappings by right-clicking the Software Installation item, selecting Properties, and then clicking the File Extensions tab. Figure 9.3 shows how file extension settings can be managed. By default, the list of file extensions that you'll see is based on the specific software packages you have added to the current GPO.

FIGURE 9.3 Managing file extensions

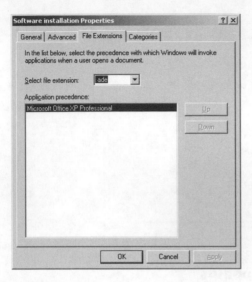

Creating Application Categories

In many network environments, the list of supported applications can include hundreds of items. For users who are looking for only one specific program, searching through a list of all of these programs can be difficult and time-consuming.

Fortunately, there are methods for categorizing the applications that are available on your network. You can easily manage the application categories for users and computers by right-clicking the Software Installation item, selecting Properties, and then clicking the Categories tab.

Figure 9.4 shows you how application categories can be created. It is a good idea to use category names that are meaningful to users because it will make it easier for them to find the programs they're looking for.

Once the software installation categories have been created, you can view them by opening the Add Or Remove Programs item in the Control Panel. When you click Add New Programs, you'll see that there are several options in the Category drop-down list. Now, when you select the properties for a package, you will be able to assign the application to one or more of the categories.

Removing Programs

As we discussed in the beginning of the chapter, an important phase in the software management life cycle is the removal of applications. Fortunately, using Active Directory and Windows Installer packages, the process is simple. To remove an application, you can right-click the package within the Group Policy settings and select All Tasks ➢ Remove (see Figure 9.5).

FIGURE 9.4 Creating application categories

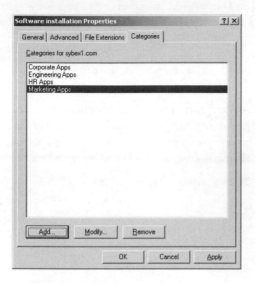

FIGURE 9.5 Removing a software package

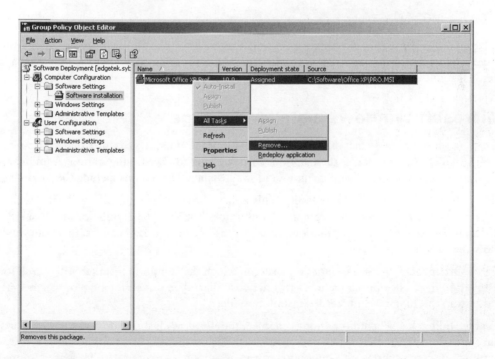

When choosing to remove a software package from a GPO, you have two options:

Immediately Uninstall The Software From Users And Computers   Systems administrators can choose this option to ensure that an application is no longer available to users who are affected by the GPO. When this option is selected, the program will be automatically uninstalled from users and/or computers that have the package. This option might be useful, for example, if the licensing for a certain application has expired or if a program is no longer on the approved applications list.

Allow Users To Continue To Use The Software, But Prevent New Installations   This option prevents users from making new installations of a package, but it does not remove the software if it has already been installed for users. This is a good option if the company has run out of additional licenses for the software, but the existing licenses are still valid.

Figure 9.6 shows the two removal options that are available.

FIGURE 9.6   Software removal options

If you no longer require the ability to install or repair an application, you can delete it from your software distribution share point by deleting the appropriate Windows Installer package files. This will free up additional disk space for newer applications.

Microsoft Windows Installer Settings

There are several options that influence the behavior of the Windows Installer that you can set within a GPO. You can access these options by navigating to User Configuration, Administrative Templates, Windows Components, Windows Installer. The options include the following:

Always Install With Elevated Privileges   This policy allows users to install applications that require elevated privileges. For example, if a user does not have the permissions necessary to modify the Registry but the installation program must make Registry changes, this policy will allow the process to succeed.

Search Order   This setting specifies the order in which the Windows Installer will search for installation files. The options include n (for network shares), m (for searching removal media), and u (for searching the Internet for installation files).

Disable Rollback   When this option is enabled, the Windows Installer does not store the system state information that is required to roll back the installation of an application. Systems administrators may choose this option to reduce the amount of temporary disk space required during installation and to increase the performance of the installation operation. However, the drawback is that the system cannot roll back to its original state if the installation fails and the application needs to be removed.

Disable Media Source For Any Install   This option disallows the installation of software using removable media (such as CD-ROM, DVD-ROM, or floppy disks). It is useful for ensuring that users install only approved applications.

With these options, systems administrators can control how the Windows Installer operates for specific users who are affected by the GPO.

Optimizing and Troubleshooting Software Deployment

Although the features in Windows Server 2003 and Active Directory make software deployment a relatively simple task, there are still many factors that systems administrators should consider when making applications available on the network. In this section, you will learn about some common methods for troubleshooting problems with software deployment in Windows Server 2003 and optimizing the performance of software deployment.

Specific optimization and troubleshooting methods include the following:

Test packages before deployment.   The use of Active Directory and GPOs makes publishing and assigning applications so easy that systems administrators may be tempted to make many applications available to users immediately. However, the success of using the Windows Installer is at least partially based on the quality of the programming of developers and third-party software vendors.

Before unleashing an application on the unsuspecting user population, you should always test the programs within a test environment using a few volunteer users and computers. The information gathered during these tests can be invaluable in helping the help desk, systems administrators, and end users during a large-scale deployment.

Manage Group Policy scope and links.   One of the most flexible aspects of deploying software with Active Directory is the ability to assign Group Policy settings to users and computers. Because it is so easy to set up GPOs and link them to Active Directory objects, it might be tempting to modify all of your existing GPOs to meet the current software needs of your users. Note, however, that this can become difficult to manage.

An easier way to manage multiple sets of applications may be to create separate GPOs for specific groups of applications. For example, one GPO could provide all end-user productivity applications (such as Microsoft Office XP and Adobe Acrobat Reader), whereas another GPO could provide tools for users in the Engineering department. Now, whenever the software requirements for a group changes, systems administrators can just enable or disable specific GPOs for the OU that contains these users.

Roll out software in stages.   Installing software packages over the network can involve high bandwidth requirements and reduce the performance of production servers. If you're planning to roll out a new application to several users or computers, it's a good idea to deploy the software in stages. This process involves publishing or assigning applications to a few users at a time, through the use of GPOs and OUs.

Verify connectivity with the software distribution share.   If clients are unable to communicate with the server that contains the software installation files, the Windows Installer will be unable to automatically copy the required information to the client computer, and installation will fail. You should always ensure that clients are able to communicate with the server and verify the permissions on the software installation share.

Organize categories.   The list of applications that are available in a typical network environment can quickly grow very large. From standard commercial Desktop applications and utilities to custom client/server applications, it's important to organize programs based on functionality. Be sure to group software packages into categories that end users will clearly recognize and understand when searching for applications.

Create an installation log file.   By using the msiexec.exe command, you can create an installation log file that records the actions attempted during the installation process and any errors that may have been generated.

Reduce redundancy.   In general, it is better to ensure that applications are not assigned or published to users through multiple GPOs. For example, if a user almost always logs on to the same workstation and requires specific applications to be available, you may consider assigning the applications to both the user and the computer. Although this scenario will work properly, it can increase the amount of time spent during logon and the processing of the GPOs. A better solution would be to assign the applications to only the computer (or, alternatively, to only the user).

Manage software distribution points.   When users require applications, they will depend on the availability of installation shares. To ensure greater performance and availability of these shares, you can use the Windows Server 2003 Distributed File System (DFS). The features of DFS allow for fault tolerance and the ability to use multiple servers to share commonly used files from a single logical share point. The end result is increased uptime, better performance, and easier access for end users. Additionally, the underlying complexity of where certain applications are stored is isolated from the end user.

Encourage developers and vendors to create Microsoft Windows Installer packages.   Many of the benefits of the software deployment features in Windows Server 2003 rely on the use of MSI packages. To ease the deployment and management of applications, ensure that in-house application developers and third-party independent software vendors use MSI packages that were created properly. The use of MSI packages will greatly assist systems administrators and end users in assigning and managing applications throughout the life cycle of the product.

Enforce consistency using MSI options.   One of the problems with applications and application suites (such as Microsoft Office XP) is that end users can choose to specify which options are available during installation. Although this might be useful for some users, it can cause compatibility and management problems. For example, suppose a manager sends a spreadsheet containing Excel pivot tables to several employees. Some employees are able to access the pivot tables (because they chose the default installation options), but others cannot (because they chose not to install this feature). The users who cannot properly read the spreadsheet will likely generate help desk calls and require assistance to add in the appropriate components.

One way to avoid problems such as these is to enforce standard configurations for applications. For example, we may choose to create a basic and an advanced package for Microsoft Office XP. The Basic package would include the most-used applications, such as Microsoft Word, Microsoft Outlook, and Microsoft Excel. The advanced package would include these applications plus Microsoft PowerPoint and Microsoft Access.

Create Windows Installer files for older applications.   Although there is no tool included with Windows Server 2003 to automatically perform this task, it will generally be worth the time to create Windows Installer files for older applications. This is done through the use of third-party applications that are designed to monitor the Registry, file system, and other changes that an application makes during the setup process. These changes can then be combined into a single MSI package for use in software deployment.

By carefully planning for software deployment and using some of the advanced features of Windows Server 2003, you can make software deployment a smooth and simple process for systems administrators and end users alike.

 Real World Scenario

Understanding Application Architecture and Managing Software Rollouts

The world of computing has moved through various stages and methodologies throughout the past several decades. Real-world business computing began with large, centralized machines called mainframes. In this model, all processing occurred on a central machine and "clients" were little more than keyboards and monitors connected with long extension cords. A potential disadvantage of this setup was that clients relied solely on these central machines for their functionality, and the mainframe tended to be less flexible.

Then, with the dramatic drop in the cost of personal computers, the computing industry moved more to a client-based model. In this model, the majority of processing occurred on individual computers. The drawback, however, was that is was difficult to share information (even with networking capabilities), and such critical tasks as data management, backup, and security were challenges.

Since then, various technologies have appeared to try to give us good features from both worlds. A new and promising method of delivering application has been through the Application Service Provider (ASP) model. In this method, clients are relatively "thin" (that is, they do not perform much processing, nor do they store data); however, users still have access to the tools they need to do their jobs. The software provider is responsible for maintaining the software (including upgrades, backups, security, performance monitoring, etc.), and your company might engage an ASP through a monthly-fee arrangement.

In some respects, during the past several years, we've moved back toward housing business-critical functionality on relatively large, central servers. However, we've retained powerful client machines that are capable of performing processing for certain types of applications. In a lot of cases, that makes sense. For example, users of Microsoft Office applications have several advantages if they run their applications on their own machines. It might make sense to place other applications, such as a centralized sales-tracking and management tool, on a server. However, the fact remains that modern computers are only marginally useful without software applications that make practical use of their power and features.

As an IT professional, it's important that you understand the business reasons when evaluating application architecture. Traditionally, the deployment of standard Windows applications was a tedious, error-prone, and inexact process. For example, if a user deleted a critical file, the entire application may have had to be removed and reinstalled. Or, if an application replaced a shared file with one that was incompatible with other applications, you could end up in a situation affectionately referred to as "DLL Hell." Microsoft has attempted to address the sore spot of application deployment and management with the use of Active Directory and Windows Installer technology. However, it's up to developers and system administrators to take full advantage of these new methods.

As an IT professional, you should urge developers to create installation packages using the Windows Installer architecture. In many ways, it's much simpler to create an Installer package than it is to create the old-style setup programs. On the IT side, be sure that you take advantage of Active Directory's ability to assign and publish applications. And, when it comes time to update a client-side application, be sure to make use of the Windows Installer's ability to generate patch files that can quickly and easily update an installation with minimal effort. This method can roll out application updates to thousands of computers in just a few days!

All of these features can cut down on a large amount of support effort that's required when, for example, a user needs to install a file viewer for a file that they received via email. And, for applications that just don't make sense on the Desktop, consider using ASPs. Outsourced applications can allow you to avoid a lot of these headaches altogether. There's a huge array of options, and it's up to you to make the best choice for your applications!

Summary

In this chapter, we covered software deployment through Group Policy. Software is a very important (and often overlooked) component of deploying Windows Server 2003 and Active Directory. What good does all this infrastructure do you when what it basically all boils down to is end-user productivity and the applications that they use to do their jobs? When dealing with client applications, you have to consider the software life cycle. IT professionals face many challenges with client applications, including development, deployment, maintenance, and troubleshooting.

While learning about Group Policy, we also covered and learned about the Windows Installer. There are many benefits to using the Windows Installer. For instance, using the Windows Installer is a new way to install applications on Windows-based machines. It offers a more robust method for making the system changes required by applications, and it allows for a cleaner uninstall. Windows Installer–based applications can also take advantage of new Active Directory features. Make sure that you are comfortable with using the Windows Installer.

In this chapter, we also learned about publishing applications via Active Directory and the difference between publishing and assigning applications. Some applications can be assigned to users and computers so that they are always available. They can be published to users so that they may be installed with a minimal amount of effort when a user requires them.

We also learned how to prepare for software deployment. Before your users can take advantage of automated software installation, you must set up an installation share and provide the appropriate permissions.

If you know how to configure application settings when using Active Directory and Group Policy, you can configure application settings to be set across the enterprise. Using standard Windows Server 2003 administrative tools, you can create an application policy that meets your requirements. One of the many features is the automatic, on-demand installation of applications when needed.

Last, we tied up the chapter with common problems and basic troubleshooting steps you should take when trying to fix problems using Group Policy. Being able to troubleshoot problems with software deployment will save you a lot of time and help you pass your examination. In sum, Group Policy is a tool that allows you to control the desktops within your organization and it's a worthwhile tool to learn and master.

Exam Essentials

Identify common problems with the software life cycle. IT professionals face many challenges with client applications, including development, deployment, maintenance, and troubleshooting.

Understand the benefits of the Windows Installer. Using the Windows Installer is an updated way to install applications on Windows-based machines. It offers a more robust method for making the system changes required by applications, and it allows for a cleaner uninstall. Windows Installer–based applications can also take advantage of new Active Directory features.

Understand the difference between publishing and assigning applications. Some applications can be assigned to users and computers so that they are always available. They can be published to users so that they may be installed with a minimal amount of effort when a user requires them.

Know how to prepare for software deployment. Before your users can take advantage of automated software installation, you must set up an installation share and provide the appropriate permissions.

Know how to configure application settings using Active Directory and Group Policy. Using standard Windows Server 2003 administrative tools, you can create an application policy that meets the needs of your requirements. Features include automatic, on-demand installation of applications as well as many other features.

Create application categories to simplify the list of published applications. It's important to group applications by functionality or the users to whom they apply, especially in organizations that support a large number of programs.

Be able to troubleshoot problems with software deployment. There are several methods for deploying applications and for testing to make sure that they are working properly. Should you find a problem with a particular installation of software, you can use these methods to repair and/or remove the specific product.

Review Questions

1. Alicia is a systems administrator for a large organization. Recently, the company has moved most of its workstations and servers to the Windows Server 2003 platform and Alicia wants to take advantage of the new software deployment features of Active Directory. Specifically, she wants to do the following:

   - Make applications available to users through the Add Or Remove Programs item in the Control Panel.

   - Group applications based on functionality or the types of users who might require them.

   - Avoid the automatic installation of applications for users and computers.

   Which of the following steps should Alicia take to meet these requirements? (Choose all that apply.)

   A. Create application categories.

   B. Set up a software installation share and assign the appropriate security permissions.

   C. Assign applications to users.

   D. Assign applications to computers.

   E. Create new file extension mappings.

   F. Create application definitions using Active Directory and Group Policy administration tools.

2. A systems administrator has created a Software Deployment GPO. Which tool can they use to link this GPO to an existing OU?

   A. Active Directory Users And Computers tool

   B. Active Directory Domains And Trusts tool

   C. Add Or Remove Programs item from the Control Panel

   D. Computer Management

3. Emma wants to make a specific application available on the network. She finds that using Group Policy for software deployment will be the easiest way. She has the following requirements:

   - All users of designated workstations should have access to Microsoft Office XP.

   - If a user moves to other computers on which Microsoft Office XP is not installed, they should not have access to this program.

   Which of the following options should Emma choose to meet these requirements?

   A. Assign the application to computers.

   B. Assign the application to users.

   C. Publish the application to computers.

   D. Publish the application to users.

4. A systems administrator wants to ensure that a particular user will have access to Microsoft Office XP regardless of the computer to which they log on. Which of the following should they do?

    A. Assign the application to all computers within the environment and specify that only this user should have access to it.

    B. Assign the application to the user.

    C. Publish the application to all computers within the environment and specify that only this user should have access to it.

    D. Publish the application to the user.

5. A systems administrator wants to ensure that a particular group of users will be able to install Microsoft Office XP by using the Add Or Remove Programs item in the Control Panel. They do not want the applications to be automatically installed. Which of the following should they do?

    A. Assign the application to their computers.

    B. Assign the application to the users.

    C. Publish the application to their computers.

    D. Publish the application to the users.

6. The files required to install published and assigned applications are stored where?

    A. The Active Directory data store

    B. File shares

    C. The Global Catalog

    D. The System32 directory on all domain controllers

    E. The System32 directory on specific domain controllers

7. In order to install assigned or published applications, a user must have which of the following permissions?

    A. Ability to modify the Registry

    B. Local Administrator permissions

    C. Ability to create directories

    D. No special permissions

8. You are responsible for applications management in your medium-sized network environment. Recently, your organization began deploying a new custom-developed application to your users. On slow client machines, the installation process can take a long time. In some cases, users have chosen to abort the installation process so that they can perform it at a later time. You are now receiving complaints from several users who say that they attempted to cancel the installation process, but the system changes that the application made were not rolled back.

    Which of the following Windows Installer settings may be responsible for this?

    A. Always Install With Elevated Privileges

    B. Disable Rollback

    C. Disable Search Order

    D. Disallow Uninstall

9. Which of the following statements is true regarding the actions that occur when a software package is removed from a GPO that is linked to an OU?

A. The application will be automatically uninstalled for all users with the OU.

B. Current application installations will be unaffected by the change.

C. The systems administrator may determine the effect.

D. The current user may determine the effect.

10. You have recently created a new software deployment package for installing a new line of business application on many users' systems. You have the following requirements:

- You want to use the features of Active Directory and Group Policy to automatically deploy the software.

- The software should be installed on specific machines within the environment only.

- The application must be made available with minimal user intervention.

Which of the following steps must be performed in order to meet these requirements? (Choose all that apply.)

A. Refresh Active Directory.

B. Synchronize all domain controllers.

C. Rebuild the Global Catalog.

D. Manually copy the required files to an appropriate file share and set the appropriate permissions on the share.

E. Assign the application to the appropriate computers.

F. Publish the application to the appropriate computers.

11. Andrew is a help desk operator for a large organization. Recently, he has been receiving a large number of calls from users who are attempting to open files for which they do not have viewers. For example, one user wants to open a file named MarketingInfo.ppt, but they do not have the Microsoft PowerPoint viewer installed. Andrew has the following requirements:

- The appropriate application should automatically be installed when a user clicks specific file types.

- Applications should not be automatically installed in other circumstances.

- The installation of applications, when they are needed, should require minimal user intervention.

Which of the following Group Policy software deployment features should Andrew use? (Choose all that apply.)

A. Categories

B. Publishing options

C. Assignment options

D. File extensions

E. None of the above

12. An applications developer wants to create a patch for an existing application. Which of the following types of files should they create?

A. MSI

B. MSP

C. ZAP

D. AAS

E. None of the above

13. How can a systems administrator get more information about a specific Windows Installer setup file?

A. By right-clicking the file and selecting Properties in Windows Explorer

B. By issuing a search within Active Directory

C. By querying the Global Catalog

D. None of the above

14. Jenny is responsible for application deployment in a medium-sized company that is using Active Directory. She has already configured her Windows Server 2003 computers to deploy new applications (that are packaged using the Windows Installer) automatically. However, she has recently been tasked with the automatic deployment of some applications that use a legacy installation routine.

How can Jenny create a Windows Installer package from a legacy setup program?

A. By right-clicking the `Setup.exe` file for the application and choosing Migrate

B. By right-clicking the `Setup.exe` file for the application and choosing Upgrade To Windows Installer

C. By adding the application to Active Directory

D. By placing the application within a Shared Folder object and then assigning the application to the appropriate client computers

E. None of the above

15. You want to publish an application by using a GPO. In the following GPO, what would you do next in order to publish an application?

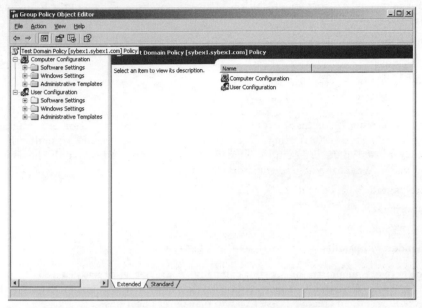

A. Right-click Software Settings under Computer Configuration and select New ➤ Package.

B. Expand Software Settings under Computer Configuration, right-click Software Installation, and select New ➤ Package.

C. Expand Software Settings under User Configuration, right-click Software Installation, and select New ➤ Package.

D. Right-click Software Settings under User Configuration and select New ➤ Package.

16. You are the Systems Administrator for 123 Inc. You are asked by your management team to provide a solution for deploying Microsoft Office XP. This application, when deployed, needs to have standard configurations, meaning all settings need to be the same. How can this be done?

A. Use MSI options to enforce the settings.

B. Use the System Console to make the changes.

C. Use the Sites And Services MMC.

D. Use Registry settings in a new key to change the settings.

17. As the lead network administrator for your company, you need to make sure that you have installation shares available to your end users when you deploy software via Group Policy. You need to have fault tolerance implemented in the file sharing solution that is in place. Which of the following provides the solution you require?

A. Using the Distributed File System (DFS)

B. Using the Encrypted File System (EFS)

C. Using the New Technology File System (NTFS)

D. Using the Microsoft File System (MFS)

18. You are the network administrator responsible for deploying software in your organization. You need to implement a patch management solution on Windows Server 2003 that allows you to manage the updates that you install via Microsoft's website. Which of the following can you use?

A. SUS only

B. SUS and WSUS

C. TUS and SUS

D. SUS v2 and WSUS

19. You want to deploy a solution that forces everyone who has an existing version of a program to upgrade according to a GPO's settings. You also want to make sure that it's set so that those who have never installed the program for whatever reason are able to install only the new, upgraded version. What can you implement to make this the case?

A. In Band upgrade

B. In Place upgrade

C. Mandatory upgrade

D. Nonmandatory upgrade

20. You are the network administrator for your company. Your supervisor has just asked you to create an easy way to deploy and manage applications in a network environment. Which of the following could you do to create an easier way to manage applications?

A. Set alarms.

B. Set performance counters.

C. Assign permissions.

D. Assign and publish programs.

Answers to Review Questions

1. Answers: A, B, F. Alicia should first create an application share from which programs can be installed. Then, she can define which applications are available on the network. The purpose of application categories is to logically group applications in the Add Or Remove Programs item in the Control Panel. The other options can result in the automatic installation of applications for users and computers (something that she wants to avoid).

2. A. Group Policy links can be created within the Active Directory Users And Computers tool. Because GPOs apply to domains, OUs, and sites, none of the other options would work.

3. A. Assigning the application to the computer will ensure that all users who access the workstation will have access to Microsoft Office XP. You cannot publish to computers, and assigning or publishing the application to users would mean that only those users could use the application and they would be able to access it from any machine on the network.

4. B. Assigning the application to the user ensures that the user will have access to Microsoft Office XP, regardless of the computer they use. The other options would mean that the user either wouldn't have access to the application at all, or would need to log on to a specific computer.

5. D. When applications are published to users, they can easily install the programs using the Add Or Remove Programs item in the Control Panel. Applications cannot be published to computers, and assigning the application would mean that it is automatically installed when the user tries to access it on the Start menu.

6. B. Published and assigned applications must be stored within a share on a file server and must be accessible to client computers. Files cannot be stored in the Active Directory data store or in the Global Catalog, and the other options simply wouldn't work properly.

7. D. The Windows Installer is able to use the Installer service to bypass user permissions for installing software. Therefore, the user performing the installation is not required to have any special permission.

8. B. Disabling rollback can improve performance and reduce disk space requirements, but this option prevents rolling back from a failed installation.

9. C. The systems administrator can specify whether the application will be uninstalled or if future installations will be prevented.

10. Answers: D, E. It is the responsibility of the systems administrator to copy installation files to a software deployment share point and ensure that users can access these files. Once this is done, the applications can be assigned to various computers within the environment.

11. Answers: B, D. Publishing makes the applications available for automatic installation. File extension settings can be used to specify the applications that are installed when specific file types are accessed. This method requires minimal user intervention because it occurs automatically in the background.

12. B. Microsoft patch (MSP) files are used to update existing applications.

13. A. Details about MSI files can be viewed by right-clicking the file and selecting Properties. The other options may be available, but only if software deployment is configured within Active Directory.

14. E. In order to create a Windows Installer package from a legacy setup program, the application must be repackaged, or you must use a third-party utility. These applications and utilities must be obtained from third-party software vendors and are not included as a supported part of the Windows Server 2003 operating system.

15. C. Software can only be published to users, not computers. You can assign software to users or computers.

16. A. One way to avoid problems such as these is to enforce standard configurations for applications. For example, we may choose to create a basic and an advanced package for Microsoft Office XP. The Basic package would include the most-used applications, such as Microsoft Word, Outlook, and Excel. The advanced package would include these applications plus PowerPoint and Access.

17. A. When users require applications, they will depend on the availability of installation shares. To ensure greater performance and availability of these shares, you can use the Windows Server 2003 DFS. The features of DFS allow for fault tolerance and the ability to use multiple servers to share commonly used files from a single logical share point. The end result is increased uptime, better performance, and easier access for end users. Additionally, the underlying complexity of where certain applications are stored is isolated from the end user.

18. B. You can use SUS or WSUS to provide a patch management solution.

19. C. There are two basic types of upgrades that are available for administrators to provide to users: the mandatory upgrade and the nonmandatory upgrade. mandatory upgrade forces everyone who has an existing version of the program to upgrade according to the GPO. Users who have never installed the program for whatever reason are able to install only the new, upgraded version. The nonmandatory upgrade allows users to choose whether they would like to upgrade or not. This upgrade type also allows users who do not have their application installed to choose which version they would like to use.

20. D. You can make programs available to end users using Active Directory using two methods: assigning and publishing. Doing both greatly eases the process of deploying and managing applications in a network environment. You can make software packages available to users in this way. Both of these operations allow systems administrators to use the power of Active Directory and, specifically, GPOs to determine which applications are available to users. Additionally, the organization provided by OUs can help group users based on their job functions and software requirements.

Glossary

A

Active Directory Installation Wizard (DCPROMO)   The tool that is used for promoting a Windows Server 2003 or 2000 Server computer to a domain controller. Using the Active Directory Installation Wizard, systems administrators can create trees and forests. See also *promotion*.

Active Directory replication   A method by which Active Directory domain controllers synchronize information. See also *intersite replication and intrasite replication*.

Add or Remove Programs   Control Panel applet that allows for installing and uninstalling software applications and components of the Windows Server 2003 operating system.

administrative templates   Templates that specify additional options that can be set using the Group Policy Editor tool.

alerts   A system-monitoring feature that is generated when a specific counter exceeds or falls below a specified value. Through the Performance Logs And Alerts utility, administrators can configure alerts so that a message is sent, a program is run, or a more detailed log file is generated.

application assignment scripts   Script files that specify which applications are assigned to users of the Active Directory.

application data partitions   Portion of the Active Directory that is dedicated to application data and replicated along with the rest of the Active Directory database.

assigning   The process by which applications are made available to computers and/or users.

auditing   The act of recording specific actions that are taken within a secure network operating system. Auditing is often used as a security measure to provide for accountability. Typical audited events include logon and logoff events, as well as accessing files and objects.

authoritative restore   Specifies that the contents of a certain portion of the Active Directory on a domain controller should override any changes on other domain controllers, regardless of their sequence numbers. An authoritative restore is used to restore the contents of the Active Directory to a previous point in time.

B

bi-directional trust   See *two-way trust*.

bridgehead servers   Used in Windows Server 2003 replication to coordinate the transfer of replicated information between Active Directory sites.

C

caching-only DNS server   A DNS server that is not the authority for any specific zone but can resolve DNS queries. Caching-only DNS servers are used to improve performance.

categories   A grouping of applications that is available for installation by users through the Add Or Remove Programs item in the Control Panel. Categories are useful for managing large lists of available applications.

child domain   A relative term that describes a subdomain of another domain.

Computer object   An Active Directory object that is a security principal and that identifies a computer that is part of a domain.

Connection object   An object that can be defined as part of the Active Directory's replication topology using the Active Directory Sites And Services tool. Connection objects are automatically created to manage Active Directory replication, and administrators can use them to manually control details about how and when replication operations occur.

Contact object   Active Directory object that defines the contact information for a single entity such as an individual or company. Primarily used for reference or automatic mailing lists.

copy backup   A backup type that backs up selected folders and files but does not set the archive bit.

counter logs   Files that contain information collected by the Windows Performance tool. Counter logs can be used to track and analyze performance-related statistics over time.

cross-forest trusts   A new Windows Server 2003 feature that lets you implement trusts between all domains in one forest and all domains in another forest.

D

daily backups   A backup type that backs up all of the files that have been modified on the day that the daily backup is performed. The Archive attribute is not set on the files that have been backed up.

DC   See *domain controller (DC)*.

delegation   The process by which a user who has higher-level security permissions grants certain permissions over Active Directory objects to users who are lower-level security authorities. Delegation is often used to distribute administrative responsibilities in a network environment.

Delegation of Control Wizard   A Windows Server 2003 tool used for delegating permissions over Active Directory objects. See also *delegation*.

differential backups   A backup type that copies only the files that have been changed since the last normal backup (full backup) or incremental backup. A differential backup backs up only those files that have changed since the last full backup, but it does not reset the archive bit.

Directory Services Restore mode   A special boot mode for Windows Server 2003 domain controllers. The Directory Services Restore mode is used to boot a domain controller without starting Active Directory services. This enables systems administrators to log on locally to restore or to troubleshoot any problems with the Active Directory.

distinguished name   The fully qualified name of an object within a hierarchical system. Distinguished names are used for all Active Directory objects and in the Domain Name System (DNS). No two objects in these systems should have the same distinguished name.

distribution groups   A collection of Active Directory users that are used primarily for email distribution.

DNS   See *Domain Name System (DNS)*.

DNS namespace   A hierarchical network naming structure designed to resolve host names to IP addresses. Typical DNS names within a namespace are hierarchical, ranging from most specific on the left to least specific on the right (e.g., `server1.mycompany.com`).

domain   In Microsoft networks, an arrangement of client and server computers referenced by a specific name that shares a single security permissions database. On the Internet, a domain is a named collection of hosts and subdomains, registered with a unique name by the InterNIC.

domain controller (DC)   A Windows Server 2003 computer that includes a copy of the Active Directory data store. Domain controllers contain the security information required to perform services related to the Active Directory.

domain functional levels   Similar to modes in Windows 2000. Windows Server 2003 domain functional level includes all of the new features included in Windows Server 2003, but requires that all domain controllers run Windows Server 2003. The Windows 2000 Native domain functional level offers all of the functionality of Native mode in Windows 2000, but all of the domain controllers must run either Windows Server 2003 or Windows 2000 Server. The Windows 2000 Mixed domain functional level offers the least amount of functionality but supports domain controllers running Windows Server 2003, Windows 2000 Server, and Windows NT4 Server.

domain local group   An Active Directory security or distribution group that can contain Universal groups, Global groups, or accounts from anywhere within an Active Directory forest.

Domain Name System (DNS)   The TCP/IP network service that translates textual Internet network addresses into numerical Internet network addresses.

Domain Naming Master   The Active Directory domain controller that is responsible for handling the addition and removal of domains within the Active Directory environment.

domain trees   A set of Active Directory domains that share a common namespace and are connected by a transitive two-way trust. Resources can be shared between the domains in an Active Directory tree.

E

Event Viewer   A Windows Server 2003 utility that tracks information about the computer's hardware and software, as well as security events. This information is stored in three log files: the Application log, the Security log, and the System log.

external trusts   Provide access to resources on a Windows NT 4 domain or forest that cannot use a forest trust.

F

FAT   See *File Allocation Table (FAT)*.

File Allocation Table (FAT)   The file system used by MS-DOS and available to other operating systems, such as Windows (all versions), OS/2, and Macintosh. FAT (now known as FAT16) has become something of a standard for mass-storage compatibility because of its simplicity and wide availability. FAT has fewer fault-tolerance features than the NTFS file system and can become corrupted through normal use over time.

file extension   The three-letter suffix that follows the name of a standard file system file. Using Group Policy and software management functionality, systems administration can specify which applications are associated with which file extensions.

filtering   The process by which permissions on security groups are used to identify which Active Directory objects are affected by Group Policy settings. Through the use of filtering, systems administrators can maintain a fine level of control over Group Policy settings.

folder redirection   A Group Policy setting that automatically redirects special folders (such as My Documents) to an alternate location.

foreign security principals   Active Directory objects used to give permissions to other security principals that do not exist within an Active Directory domain. Generally, foreign security principals are automatically created by the services of the Active Directory.

forest   A collection of Windows 2000 domains that does not necessarily share a common namespace. All of the domains within a forest share a common schema and Global Catalog, and resources can be shared between the domains in a forest.

forwarding   The process by which a DNS server sends a request for name resolution to another DNS server. Forwarding is often used to improve performance and to restrict network traffic over slow connections.

functional levels   See *domain functional levels*.

G

GC See *Global Catalog (GC)*.

Global Catalog (GC) A portion of the Active Directory that contains a subset of information about all of the objects within all domains of the Active Directory data store. The Global Catalog is used to improve performance of authentications and for sharing information between domains.

Global Catalog (GC) server A Windows Server 2003 Active Directory domain controller that hosts a copy of the Global Catalog. See also *Global Catalog (GC)*.

global group An Active Directory security group that contains accounts only from its own domain.

gpresult.exe A command-line interface for RSoP. See also *Resultant Set of Policy (RSoP)*.

Group Policy Settings that can affect the behavior of, and the functionality available to, users and computers.

Group Policy object (GPO) link A link between a Group Policy object and the Active Directory objects to which it applies. Group Policy objects can be linked to sites, domains, organizational units, and other Active Directory objects.

Group Policy objects (GPOs) A collection of settings that control the behavior of users and computers.

groups Security entities to which users can be assigned membership for the purpose of applying the broad set of group permissions to the user. By managing permissions for groups and assigning users to groups, rather than assigning permissions to users, administrators can more easily manage security.

I

incremental backups A backup type that backs up only the files that have changed since the last normal or incremental backup. It sets the archive attribute on the files that are backed up.

Infrastructure Master The Windows Server 2003 domain controller that is responsible for managing group memberships and transferring this information to other domain controllers within the Active Directory environment.

inheritance The process by which settings and properties defined on a parent object implicitly apply to a child object.

initialization files Files used to specify parameters that are used by an application or a utility. Initialization files are often used by setup programs to determine application installation information.

Internet Protocol (IP)   The Network layer protocol upon which the Internet is based. IP provides a simple connectionless packet exchange. Other protocols such as TCP use IP to perform their connection-oriented (or guaranteed delivery) services.

intersite replication   The transfer of information between domain controllers that reside in different Active Directory sites.

intrasite replication   The transfer of information between domain controllers that reside within the same Active Directory site.

IP   See *Internet Protocol (IP)*.

iteration   The incremental process by which DNS names are resolved to IP addresses.

L

LAN   See *local area network (LAN)*.

LDAP   See *Lightweight Directory Access Protocol (LDAP)*.

licensing server   A Windows Server 2003 computer that is responsible for managing software licenses. Licensing server properties can be set using the Active Directory Sites And Services tool.

Lightweight Directory Access Protocol (LDAP)   A protocol used for querying and modifying information stored within directory services. The Active Directory can be queried and modified through the use of LDAP-compatible tools.

linked value replication   A new Windows Server 2003 feature that only replicates the part of the Active Directory that changed since the last replication cycle.

local area network (LAN)   A network of well-connected computers that usually reside within a single geographic location (such as an office building). An organization typically owns all of the hardware that makes up its LAN.

Logging mode   An RSoP mode that pulls policy information from a log based on actual logon activity. See also *Resultant Set of Policy (RSoP)*.

M

Master DNS server   A DNS server that is responsible as an authority for name resolutions within a DNS zone. Each DNS zone can have only one master DNS server.

member server   A server that participates in the security of Active Directory domains but does not contain a copy of the Active Directory data store.

N

Network Monitor   A Windows Server 2003 utility that can be used for monitoring and decoding packets that are transferred to and from the local server.

normal backup   A backup type that backs up all selected folders and files and then marks each file that has been backed up as archived.

NTFS   See *Windows New Technology File System (NTFS)*.

O

operations masters   Special domain controllers that are solely responsible for specific parts of the Active Directory, such as the schema, domain naming, and relative ID (RID).

organizational unit (OU)   Used to logically organize the Active Directory objects within a domain.

OU   See organizational unit (OU).

P

parent   A relative term that describes a domain that is a parent of another domain. Parent domains may contain child domains (also called subdomains).

patch   A Windows Installer file that updates application code. Patches can be used to make sure that new features are installed after an application has already completed installation.

PDC   See *Primary Domain Controller (PDC)*.

Performance Logs And Alerts   A Windows Server 2003 utility used to log performance-related data and generate alerts based on this data.

permissions   Security constructs used to regulate access to resources by username or group affiliation. Permissions can be assigned by administrators to allow any level of access (such as read-only, read/write, or delete) by controlling the ability of users to initiate object services. Security is implemented by checking the user's security identifier (SID) against each object's access control list (ACL).

Planning mode   An RSoP mode that is used to plan Group Policy changes before putting them into effect. See also *Resultant Set of Policy (RSoP)*.

primary DNS server   A DNS server that is authoritative for a zone and that is able to receive updates of DNS information.

Primary Domain Controller (PDC)   Used in Windows NT 4 domains to hold the master copy of the domain information.

Primary Domain Controller (PDC) Emulator Master   Responsible for maintaining backward compatibility with Windows NT domain controllers.

Printer object   An Active Directory object that identifies printers that are published within domains.

promotion   The act of converting a Windows Server 2003 or 2000 Server computer to a domain controller. See also *Active Directory Installation Wizard (DCPROMO)*.

publishing   Making applications available for use by users through Group Policy and Software Installation settings. Published applications can be installed on demand or when required by end users through the use of the Add Or Remove Programs item in the Control Panel.

R

realm trusts   Used to connect to a non-Windows domain that uses Kerberos authentication. Realm trusts can be transitive or nontransitive, one-way or two-way.

recursion   The process by which DNS servers or clients use other DNS servers to resolve DNS names to TCP/IP address queries.

relative ID (RID) Master   The domain controller that is responsible for generating unique identifiers for each of the domains within an Active Directory environment.

Remote Procedure Call (RPC) protocol   A protocol used to allow communications between system processes on remote computers. The RPC protocol is used by the Active Directory for intrasite replication. See also *intrasite replication*.

replication   The transfer of information between domain controllers.

resource record (RR)   A DNS entry that specifies the availability of specific DNS services. For example, an MX record specifies the IP address of a mail server, and Host (A) records specify the IP addresses of workstations on the network.

Resultant Set of Policy (RSoP)   A new Windows Server 2003 tool that automatically calculates the actual policy for a user or group based on site, domain, and OU placement, as well as inheritance settings.

reverse lookup zone   A DNS zone that is used to resolve a TCP/IP address to a DNS name.

RID   See *Relative ID (RID) Master*.

root domain   In DNS, the name of the top of the Internet domain hierarchy. Although the root domain does not have a name, it is often referred to as ".".

RPC   See *Remote Procedure Call (RPC) protocol*.

RR   See *resource record (RR)*.

S

schema   A database structure for all of the types of objects that are supported within the Active Directory, along with the attributes for each of these objects.

Schema Master   A Windows Server 2003 domain controller that is responsible for maintaining the master copy of the Active Directory schema. There is only one Schema Master per Active Directory forest. See also *schema*.

script policy   A setting within Group Policy objects that specifies login, logoff, startup, and shutdown script settings.

secondary DNS server   A DNS server that is used to resolve DNS names to TCP/IP addresses. Secondary servers contain a read-only copy of the DNS database.

Security Configuration And Analysis utility   A Windows Server 2003 utility used for creating security profiles and managing security settings across multiple machines.

security groups   Active Directory objects that can contain users or other groups and that are used for the management and assignment of permissions. Users are placed into security groups, and then permissions are granted to these groups. Security groups are considered to be security principals. See also *security principal*.

security principal   An Active Directory object that is used to assign and maintain security settings. The primary security principals are Users, Groups, and Computers.

security templates   Files used by the Security Configuration And Analysis tool for defining and enforcing security settings across multiple computers.

Shared Folder object   An Active Directory object that specifies the name and location of specific shared resources that are available to users of the Active Directory.

shortcut trust   A direct trust between two domains that implicitly trust each other.

Simple Mail Transfer Protocol (SMTP)   A TCP/IP-based protocol that is primarily used for the exchange of Internet email. SMTP can also be used by the Active Directory to manage intersite replication between domain controllers. See also *intersite replication*.

single master operations   Specific functions that must be managed within an Active Directory environment but are only handled by specific domain controllers. Some single master operations are unique to each domain, and some are unique to the entire Active Directory forest.

site   A collection of well-connected TCP/IP subnets. Sites are used for defining the topology of Active Directory replication.

site link   A link between two or more Active Directory sites. See also *site*.

site link bridges   A connection between two or more Active Directory site links. A site link bridge can be used to create a transitive relationship for replication between sites. See also *site and site link*.

SMTP   See *Simple Mail Transfer Protocol (SMTP)*.

subnet   A collection of TCP/IP addresses that define a particular network location. All of the computers within a subnet share the same group of TCP/IP addresses and have the same subnet mask.

System Monitor   A Windows Server 2003 tool used for monitoring performance. The System Monitor includes chart, histogram, and report views.

System State data   Information used to manage the configuration of a Windows Server 2003 operating system. For Windows Server 2003 domain controllers, the System State data includes a copy of the Active Directory data store. The Windows Server 2003 Backup utility can be used to back up and restore the System State data.

T

Task Manager   A Windows Server 2003 utility that can be used to quickly and easily obtain a snapshot of current system performance.

TCP/IP   See *Transmission Control Protocol/Internet Protocol (TCP/IP)*.

trace log   A log file that can be created through the use of the Windows Server 2003 Performance tool. Trace logs record specific events and can be analyzed through the use of compatible utilities.

transformation files   A type of file used by the Windows Installer to modify the behavior of the application-installation process.

transitive trusts   A trust relationship that allows for implicit trusts between domains. For example, if Domain A trusts Domain B and Domain B trusts Domain C, then Domain A implicitly trusts Domain C. See also *trust* and *two-way trust*.

Transmission Control Protocol/Internet Protocol (TCP/IP)   A suite of Internet protocols upon which the global Internet is based. TCP/IP is a general term that can refer either to the TCP and IP protocols used together or to the complete set of Internet protocols. TCP/IP is the default protocol for Windows Server 2003.

trees   A set of Active Directory domains that share a common namespace and are connected by a transitive two-way trust. Resources can be shared between the domains in an Active Directory tree.

trust   A relationship between domains that allows for the sharing of resources.

two-way trust   Occurs when two domains trust each other equally.

U

Universal group   An Active Directory security or distribution group that can contain members from, and be accessed from, any domain within an Active Directory forest. A domain must be running in native mode to use Universal groups.

User object   An Active Directory object that is a security principal and that identifies individuals that can log on to a domain.

W

WAN   See *wide area network (WAN)*.

wide area network (WAN)   A distributed network, typically connected through slow, and sometimes unreliable, links. The various sites that make up a WAN are typically connected through leased lines.

Windows Installer   A Windows service that provides for the automatic installation of applications through the use of compatible installation scripts.

Windows Installer package   Special files that include the information necessary to install Windows-based applications.

Windows New Technology File System (NTFS)   A secure, transaction-oriented file system developed for Windows NT, Windows 2000, and Window Server 2003. NTFS offers features such as local security on files and folders, data compression, disk quotas, and data encryption.

Windows Script Host (WSH)   A utility for running scripts on Windows-based computers. By default, WSH includes support for the VBScript and JScript languages. Through the use of third-party extensions, scripts can be written in other languages.

Windows Server 2003 domain functional level   Offers all of the features of Windows Server 2003 but requires that all domain controllers in the domain run Windows Server 2003.

Windows Server 2003 R2   Interim update to the Windows server operating system. R2 allows Service Pack 1 and other feature packs to be included with Windows Server 2003 without waiting for the next release of the Windows Server operating system.

WSH   See *Windows Script Host (WSH)*.

Z

zone   A portion of the DNS namespace that is managed by a specific group of DNS servers.

zone transfer   The synchronization of information between DNS servers that are responsible for servicing the same DNS zone.

Index

Note to the reader: Throughout this index **boldfaced** page numbers indicate primary discussions of a topic. *Italicized* page numbers indicate illustrations.